Being There and the Evolution of a Screenplay

Being There and the Evolution of a Screenplay

3 Draft Scripts with Commentary

Aaron Hunter

BLOOMSBURY ACADEMIC
NEW YORK · LONDON · OXFORD · NEW DELHI · SYDNEY

BLOOMSBURY ACADEMIC
Bloomsbury Publishing Inc
50 Bedford Square, London, WC1B 3DP, UK
1385 Broadway, New York, NY 10018, USA
29 Earlsfort Terrace, Dublin 2, Ireland

BLOOMSBURY, BLOOMSBURY ACADEMIC and the Diana logo are trademarks
of Bloomsbury Publishing Plc

First published in the United States of America 2021
This paperback edition published in 2022
Copyright © Aaron Hunter, 2021

For legal purposes the Acknowledgments on p. xv constitute an extension of this copyright page.

Cover design by Eleanor Rose
Film still © ArenaPAL; Film stock © Getty Images; Edited scripts courtesy
of Spertus Institute for Jewish Learning and Leadership

All rights reserved. No part of this publication may be reproduced
or transmitted in any form or by any means, electronic or mechanical,
including photocopying, recording, or any information storage or retrieval
system, without prior permission in writing from the publishers.

Bloomsbury Publishing Inc does not have any control over, or responsibility for, any
third-party websites referred to or in this book. All internet addresses given in this book
were correct at the time of going to press. The author and publisher regret any
inconvenience caused if addresses have changed or sites have ceased to exist, but
can accept no responsibility for any such changes.

Library of Congress Cataloging-in-Publication Data
Names: Hunter, Aaron, author.
Title: Being there and the evolution of a screenplay : 3 draft scripts with
commentary / Aaron Hunter.
Other titles: Being there (Motion picture)
Description: New York : Bloomsbury Academic, 2020. |
Includes bibliographical references and index.
Identifiers: LCCN 2020031035 (print) | LCCN 2020031036 (ebook) |
ISBN 9781501348358 (hardback) | ISBN 9781501372377 (paperback) |
ISBN 9781501348365 (epub) | ISBN 9781501348372 (ePDF)
Classification: LCC PN1997 .B315 H86 2020 (print) |
LCC PN1997.B315 (ebook) | DDC 791.43/7–dc23
LC record available at https://lccn.loc.gov/2020031035
LC ebook record available at https://lccn.loc.gov/2020031036

ISBN:	HB:	978-1-5013-4835-8
	PB:	978-1-5013-7237-7
	ePDF:	978-1-5013-4837-2
	eBook:	978-1-5013-4836-5

Typeset by Newgen KnowledgeWorks Pvt. Ltd., Chennai, India

To find out more about our authors visit www.bloomsbury.com and sign up for our newsletters.

In the spirit in which it was conceived, I dedicate this project to screenwriting students everywhere. May it help you in some small way find your style and your voice.

Contents

Preface ix
Acknowledgments xv
Note on the Text xvi

Introduction: The Evolution of a Screenplay 1

1   Jerzy Kosinski: January 1978 37
    Introduction 37
    Script 39

2   Robert C. Jones: December 1978 183
    Introduction 183
    Script 188

3   Robert C. Jones: January 1979 333
    Introduction 333
    Script 338

Appendix: Getting a Guy to Walk on Water 453
Bibliography 463
Index 465

Preface

What Is This Book and Whom Is It For?

This book's genesis has its roots in two seemingly separate strands of professional interest. As so often happens in academia, areas of inquiry cross-pollinate and, on occasion, bear strange fruit. In the case of this book, the cross-pollination occurred between one of my primary areas of scholarly research and teaching that I have been doing for the last several years. The result is a book that should appeal to a variety of different audiences based on why one might wish to own a copy of the script for the film *Being There* (Lorimar/United Artists 1979).[1]

My primary area of research concerns 1970s Hollywood, particularly the ways in which the auteur paradigm has limited scholarly and popular conceptions of the so-called New Hollywood era. Often framed as a decade of directors, the Hollywood of the '70s was in fact highly collaborative, with dramatically creative approaches to filmmaking flowering across all areas of production. The number of talented innovators is too vast to mention here, but even a cursory list of names shows how the era's production personnel brimmed with imagination and ingenuity: names like Gordon Willis and John A. Alonzo (cinematography), Dede Allen and Verna Fields (editing), Polly Platt and Richard Sylbert (production design), Walter Murch and Alan Splet (sound design), not to mention the scores of fantastic screenwriters.[2] In *Authoring Hal Ashby: The Myth of the New Hollywood Auteur* (Bloomsbury 2016), I argued that, rather than an era solely of single authorship dominated by genius directors, 1970s Hollywood was better conceived as a cinema of multiple authorship, in whose films the traces of their many potential authors could be detected with careful reading. That text included a detailed analysis of the production of *Being There* as a case study of not only how director Hal Ashby incorporated collaborative authorship into his filmmaking but also how the creative marks of his collaborators on the film could be read in other films they worked on, both with Ashby and with other directors.

Independently of that research, in my teaching career I began convening screenwriting modules in 2015 and have kept steadily at it, at the BA and MA levels. I love teaching these courses. Often daunted at first, students generally come to a deep appreciation of the creative outlet the modules afford and the insight into film production they provide. The courses typically combine screenwriting practice with explorations of narrative theory, and the process of working through some of the issues this raises with students tends to benefit my own research, particularly those components of it that rely on textual and formal analysis. Furthermore, students tend to be game for workshopping and creative exercises, which helps provide a creatively stimulating classroom environment. However, the one area of screenwriting they often struggle with is rewriting, and all that it entails. While the courses are meant, in part, to prepare students for roles in the creative industries, they are often uncomfortable giving constructive feedback to their peers. At the same time, once wedded to their own ideas for character and narrative, it can be difficult for them to see why they should change those ideas. This is not isolated to the creative writing classroom, of course. Romantic notions about creativity—Wordsworth's "spontaneous overflow of powerful feeling"—permeate a variety of artistic discourses, at least on some level. The truth that revising, reworking, and rewriting are not only necessary components of polishing written work but also a fundamental part of the creative process itself runs counter to those romantic ideals of spontaneous genius.

To counter this in class, I often ask students to work through sections of a script that underwent dramatic changes across several drafts, particularly if there were different writers involved. If they see the work of an award-winning or well-known writer dramatically rewritten—especially by another writer—they can begin to see how integral the revision process is, regardless of one's talent, reputation, or "genius." The ending of *Being There* is one text I have found some success with. From Jerzy Kosinski's novel through his original draft of the script in 1971, to later iterations by Kosinski and then Robert C. (Bob) Jones, and finally to alterations made to the script during the film's production, the ending underwent several major changes of location, narrative development, and character involvement. These changes radically affect not only the tone of the narrative, or the sense of dramatic resolution, but also the meaning of the entire text. Working through such changes with students—analyzing how each change works, what it brings to the script, what it loses—has been a tremendous help in conveying to them the fundamental importance that rewriting has to the creative process.

Thus, this book was born. Why not publish three different versions of the script in its entirety—some with major changes between drafts, some with subtle but still substantial changes? As the script was written by Jerzy Kosinski and Robert C. Jones, with input by director Hal Ashby, such an endeavor builds on previous work I have done on multiple authorship and *Being There*. More importantly, though, if students and other burgeoning scriptwriters could investigate and analyze the dramatic revision process of an award-winning screenplay,[3] perhaps they could better understand the importance of that process to their own work.

Throughout the process of putting this book together, a question that I grappled with was whether *Being There* was the right text for this kind of project. It is a film beloved by those who have seen it, based on a novel that is equally beloved. Among its high-caliber cast are stars of Classical Hollywood (Melvyn Douglas), New Hollywood (Jack Warden), and performers who were part of the transition between these eras during the late 1950s and '60s (Shirley MacLaine and Peter Sellers, in his final great role). Released in December of 1979, it could be deemed one of the last great New Hollywood films. More importantly for this project, its script has been recognized by the Writers Guild of America as one of the top 101 in screen history (81st). Yet, it does not have the same cachet as some of Hollywood's better-loved scripts, anything from *Sunset Blvd.* (Paramount 1950) to *Chinatown* (Paramount 1974) to more recently praised scripts like *Lost in Translation* (American Zoetrope/Focus Features 2003), *Eternal Sunshine of the Spotless Mind* (Anonymous Content/Focus Features 2004), or *The Social Network* (Columbia 2010). Even the script for a film like *Die Hard* (20th Century Fox 1988) would seem to have more clout in screenwriting circles than *Being There*. So why choose it?

First, for practical reasons. The main being that, as a scholar who has researched Hal Ashby for over a decade, I had access not only to materials, including the scripts themselves, but also to figures associated with the film, in particular Bob Jones. I also had contacts with other Ashby researchers (including biographer Nick Dawson and documentary filmmaker Amy Scott) who kindly provided me with further material and put me in contact with other individuals associated not only with the film but also with some of the estates involved. A second, but equally important, practical reason was that, as mentioned, I have been using drafts of *Being There* scripts as material in screenwriting courses for several years and was intimately familiar with its efficacy as text for teaching screenwriting and revision.

Such practical reasons, however, are hardly justification on their own for choosing this film as the backbone of such a project. When I teach screenwriting, I not only focus on the process of revision but also highlight the importance—the necessity, even—of what I call "collaborative revision." This term can entail a variety of creative relationships. Generally, collaboration in terms of screenwriting is framed as the relationship between a team of two or more writers working in tandem on a project, like Wes Anderson and Owen Wilson, or the Coen brothers. Such creative partnerships have deep roots in Hollywood history, whether as one-offs (Mankiewicz and Welles) or long-term partnerships over multiple projects (the abovementioned Anderson and Wilson). There is much to be gained by studying the scripts that result from such partnerships, not only in terms of better understanding how collaboration works but also for gaining insight into the deeper mechanisms of film authorship more generally. However, collaborative revision wears other guises. Workshopping scripts in a writers' group, soliciting feedback from trusted creative friends and colleagues, and responding to notes from production partners (producers, directors, cast) are all forms of collaborative relationships, which do not require sitting down at a table face-to-face. Furthermore, scripts are often written by more than one individual or team, not as partners, per se, but rather as one writer being brought into the production to modify an existing screenplay in some way, by adding scenes, trimming scenes, polishing dialogue, strengthening B-stories, or doing a complete overhaul.[4] This is also a form of collaboration, even if long-distance in nature, because the new writer(s) must respond to the earlier draft(s) in considering elements of narrative arc, character development, and themes, among other aspects. Thus the new writer's work will necessarily be informed by the work of the previous writer(s). This is true even in the case of a total rewrite (which is rare in Hollywood).

In this regard, *Being There* works as an ideal case study. The first draft was written by novelist Jerzy Kosinski (probably in collaboration with his graduate student, Larry Eilenberg),[5] based on his own novel of the same title.[6] Kosinski then reworked the script into two additional drafts based on feedback from the film's director, Hal Ashby, and producer, Andrew Braunsberg. Bob Jones was brought in for significant rewrites, which he performed on his own, and then again in close consultation with Ashby. Through each of these drafts, remnants of preceding versions can be discerned as can recommendations, or notes, from nonwriting collaborators. For example, after submitting a draft in January of 1978, Kosinski was informed the film's setting would be moved from Manhattan to Washington, DC, so in his draft of July 1978, he sets the film in DC. The new setting leads to some of the finished film's striking imagery and allows for thematic developments that deepen preexisting themes from Kosinski's work that he might not have added on his own, such as the juxtaposition of elaborate wealth and power in Washington, with the poverty of some of its slums. Such examples abound across the drafts. *Being There* is by no means the only such Hollywood script to incorporate such various forms of collaboration, but its development by one writer from his own novel, then by an independent second writer, who then works closely with the film's director, exhibits a confluence of various types of collaborative revision that should prove useful for students and scholars of screenwriting.

The development of *Being There* exemplifies how revision can transform a literary script into a more cinematic one. I write more about the concept of the "cinematic" in relation to Hollywood screenplays in the Introduction, but for now it is enough to highlight that Kosinski was a novelist with little screenwriting experience. His understanding of character, his ability to construct set pieces that develop with increasing complexity, and his eye for social absurdities in American life are present in all his drafts. However, he also incorporates a variety of literary mechanisms that are typical of burgeoning screenwriters: interior thoughts and feelings, long stretches of exposition, and intricately detailed description. Modern Hollywood screenwriting generally eschews these conventions, and has done for decades. Jones, on the other hand, had years of experience in Hollywood, as both an editor and writer, and was intimately familiar with industry standards of describing on the page only what can be seen on screen. Comparing drafts of the two writers is immensely instructive in seeing how a screenplay's cinematic qualities can be developed and refined without sacrificing elements of character or narrative.

Finally, *Being There* is an intriguing script for such a project because of the way it resists categorization as a typical Hollywood script or a more thoroughly "indie" script. To be sure, it was packaged, financed, produced, and distributed as a joint production (Lorimar and United Artists), like most of its indie-minded siblings of the New Hollywood era. It features big stars. On a narrative level, it could be said to include such standard features of the typical Hollywood script as a three-act structure, an inciting incident, subplots and B-stories, and noticeable elements of narrative and character resolution. On the other hand, though, it shares with indie cinema such elements as an ambiguous, even opaque, protagonist, murky character objectives, and an open ending that has few discernable roots in earlier moments of the script. My point with this book, as I discuss more later, is not to prescribe a specific approach to screenwriting character and narrative—more Hollywood or more indie—but rather to illustrate how the revision process can benefit screenplays of all stripes. *Being There*, with one foot in the indie world and one in the more typically

Hollywood world, is well suited to serve as an example to screenwriters regardless of how mainstream or offbeat their aspirations.

With these justifications in mind, I settled on *Being There* as an appropriate text for the project. As I developed the idea into a proposal, it occurred to me that the book might have wider appeal than to students of screenwriting only. Below, then, are a few thoughts on who might appreciate or benefit from this book's structure and purpose.

Film enthusiasts: *Being There* is one of the great American film scripts. Adapted by Kosinski and Jones from Kosinski's novel of the same name, the film has maintained a relevance to these times that far belies its 1970s origins—particularly in recent years when its tale of a simple-minded gardener ascending to the highest echelons of American corporate and political power has appeared almost predictive. Yet the film's screenplay has never been published.[7] For fans of the film, or film in general, or collectors of screenplays, this book provides the completed shooting script of *Being There*, in its entirety. A reader who feels inclined to forgo the scholarly inquiry of the introduction, or to read only the final version of the script, can simply turn to page 338 and there it is.

Screenwriting students: As discussed above, one of the primary audiences for the book is those learning how to write for the screen or those honing that craft. This is not limited to students in film school or other scriptwriting courses or seminars. Anybody who is interested in developing their screenwriting skills should find this text's illustration of the rewriting process instructive. To that end, I want to leave room for exploration and discovery. My introduction to the book and the shorter introductions to each draft of the script include some discussion of specific changes and other close comparisons. However, the intention of this book is *not* to be a detailed comparative analysis of all three scripts in full. The work highlights some of the key changes that were made during preproduction (and in one significant instance during production), and it analyzes the significance of those changes on narrative and character development and on the scripts' overall tone. At the same time, though, one of the intentions of the book is to encourage students to explore the texts themselves, whether on their own or within the classroom with peers and an instructor. It is my hope that doing so will help students develop their critical approach to reading scripts as well as strengthen their own process of writing and rewriting.

Film scholars: A broad category, obviously, but I hope this book might be of interest to other Ashby or Kosinski scholars, to those researching 1970s Hollywood, and to the many scholars doing exciting work in the still expanding field of screenplay analysis. Scholars of the film are likely already familiar with *Being There*'s scripting process, having been detailed in several other texts. The ability to compare these three scripts, however, should shine a light on questions such as how committed to the project Kosinski was, how substantial Jones's contributions were, and how similar Ashby's role in the scripting process on this film was compared to his contributions to other scripts he directed. For scholars of '70s Hollywood, I hope the book will help foreground and support important work being done on screenwriting of the era. New Hollywood screenwriters have been one of the tragic casualties of the directors' cinema trope that has for so long been the scaffolding of New Hollywood, as if all the persistent narrative and thematic developments of the era's films came only from the minds of the men who directed them. Finally, for scholars of screenwriting—who have been cultivating a fertile mix of film theory, philosophy, and narrative analysis—I am not sure how much new this book will add to that discourse. I do hope, however, that it will effectively deploy some of key arguments that such scholarship has developed in recent years. In which case, it might be a useful example of theory in action.

Notes

1. In keeping with previous practice, film titles throughout this book are followed by parentheticals that include, in addition to the year of release, the name of production and distribution companies rather than the conventional practice of naming the film's director. This is in keeping with the book's support of a multiple-authorship reading of Hollywood film production.
2. For a careful, close study of how the rise of the auteur paradigm impacted Hollywood screenwriting, in particular the career of Waldo Salt, see Oliver Grunner, "Hippie Superannuated Leprechaun: Waldo Salt, Screenwriting, and the Hollywood Renaissance," *Historic Journal of Film, Radio and Television*, 39, no. 2 (2019), 251–70.
3. The script for *Being There* won an award for Best Comedy Adapted from Another Medium from Writers Guild of America (WGA) (1980) and a British Academy for Film and Television Arts (BAFTA) award for Best Screenplay (1981). In 2005 it was voted by the WGA as one of the best 101 scripts of all time.
4. According to the WGA *Screen Credits Manual* (2018): "When writers perform services as a team, even if just for a single project, writing credit to the team must be designated with an ampersand ('&') between the names of the team members. Use of the word 'and' between writers' names in a credit indicates that the writers did their work separately, one usually rewriting the other."
5. James Park Sloan, *Jerzy Kosinski: A Biography* (New York: Plume, 1997), 298.
6. While this book includes little on the topic of novel-to-film adaptation, one of my hopes is that scholars working in that field might find its presentation of these three drafts useful, especially if looked at in conjunction with the original novel.
7. There are various versions of the script available on the internet, but nearly all of them are poorly formatted and riddled with misspellings and other typographical errors.

Acknowledgments

Massive thanks first to Katie Gallof at Bloomsbury. When I approached Katie with the idea for a book about screenplay revision that would include three full drafts of a script, I still had not decided if the idea was sound or a bit crazy. Katie responded right away that if she could get it published she would, and she has been incredibly supportive throughout the process, including in helping me think of novel ways to package and promote the book. Her staff at Bloomsbury, particularly Erin Duffy, have also been incredibly helpful.

Perhaps the most difficult part of the process was acquiring the rights to publish these scripts. Jerzy Kosinski's literary estate is held in several institutions. Eventually I tracked down the copyright holders for *Being There*—both the novel and the script—to the Spertus Institute for Jewish Learning and Leadership in Chicago. Their attorney, Daniel G. M. Marre, of Perkins Coie LLP was instrumental in helping me acquire the rights. Spertus librarian Kathleen Bloch was incredibly helpful in getting me drafts of the script, including those with Kosinski's handwritten notes and changes. Additionally, while Bob Jones holds no legal copyright to the script, he kindly gave his blessing and best wishes for his work to be published in this format, for which I am deeply grateful.

Thanks to the Margaret Herrick Library in Los Angeles, particularly Louise Hilton, for helping me acquire various copies of the *Being There* script. My colleagues at Maynooth University were supportive throughout the process, and my thanks especially go to Maria Pramaggiore, mentor extraordinaire. Likewise, I thank my screenwriting students at Maynooth for their continued and creative openness to my various and sometimes unorthodox approaches to teaching—and for reading through *lots* of pages of different *Being There* scripts with me. Hal Ashby biographer Nick Dawson is a font of wisdom on all things Ashby and was incredibly kind in sharing *Being There* materials with me. Once again, Jennie Carlsten provided wonderfully keen, insightful feedback on various iterations of my writing.

Finally, I thank Betti and Otis, for everything.

Note on the Text

To my knowledge there are six extant major drafts of the screenplay to *Being There*: Jerzy Kosinski's 1971 draft, written soon after the release of the novel; his January 1978 draft, which was the first he submitted once the film had entered preproduction; his final draft, of July 1978, submitted with major changes based on notes from Ashby and his production team; Robert C. Jones's original draft from December of 1978; the shooting script from January of 1979, written by Jones after several weeks' script conferencing with Ashby; and finally, an "as produced" transcript version based on the completed film. There may be other drafts as well—tucked away in old file cabinets or dusty shoe boxes—but these six constitute the major body of *Being There* scripts.

Due to constraints of space, this book produces only three of those scripts in their entirety—Kosinski's January '78 draft, Jones's first draft of December '78, and the shooting script of January '79. The Introduction to this book will discuss the genesis of these three drafts in more detail and outline more specifically why they were chosen over the others. However, it is worth noting here that these three drafts represent, I believe, the purest distillation of each contributor's intentions for the film, and so the most focused snapshot of how the writing and revision of the script was approached by each of the writers. As I offer some analysis of the scripts throughout this work, I include examples from and discussions of the other drafts as well, particularly Kosinki's two other versions.

In terms of reproducing the text of the scripts, my and Katie's aim has been to present them as closely to the original as possible. Again, constraints of space make it difficult to simply offer photographic reproductions of all the pages (the type would be too small, there would be too many pages, etc.), so pagination will differ from the original scripts. Also, while maintaining Courier font, which best resembles the original typed pages, modern software programs will affect such aspects as character size and word spacing.

All three scripts feature typographical issues specific to their writer(s) and draft. I have attempted to maintain all the quirks of each script (e.g., Kosinski's draft is inconsistent in its use of ellipses marks, and all the drafts are inconsistent in their use of compound nouns). For the most part, all quirks and errors in the scripts are left unremarked upon. The one exception is actual misspellings, including hyphenation, for which I have resorted to the old [*sic*] standby, as inelegant as it may be. I have strived to maintain the scripts' errors for reasons of historical accuracy, but also to be clear that I was not—intentionally or unintentionally—defacing the original work of these writers. Thus, any misspellings followed by [*sic*] are in the original documents; any misspellings not followed by [*sic*] are the fault of my transcription.

Finally, Kosinski's draft includes scene numbers. While the standard today is not to include scene numbers for spec scripts and drafts, I have retained his numbering here not only because they are a part of the document but also because he often refers to earlier scenes by number. Jones's first draft does not include scene numbers, standard practice for a revision. However, his final draft, as a likely shooting script, does include them, and I have retained those as well.

Introduction: The Evolution of a Screenplay

Being There is the story of Chance, a simpleminded gardener. Through a series of coincidences and increasingly unlikely events, Chance moves through the corridors of American corporate, media, and political power, unintentionally convincing those around him that he is a deep-thinking, semiretired, wealthy industrialist. As the narrative begins, Chance has spent his entire life in the home of the "Old Man," a moneyed recluse. Chance is the Old Man's gardener, and he spends his free time watching TV, mimicking the behavior he sees there. Early in the narrative, the Old Man dies, and Chance, who is not mentioned in his will or any of his legal papers, is forced to leave the only home he has known. While simpleminded (his condition is never specified), Chance has grown up around wealth and he displays the speech and mannerisms of the upper class. He has also grown accustomed to wearing the Old Man's many expensively tailored suits. Thus, when he inadvertently meets Eve Rand, socialite and wife of the wealthy industrialist Benjamin Rand, it makes some sense that Eve, and later her husband as well, would mistake Chance for the kind of fellow traveler signified by his appearance and demeanor. The Rands suppose him to be Chauncey Gardiner (a possible relative of Basil and Perdita Gardiner, on whose island the Rands occasionally summer), a sagacious businessman who is currently down on his luck due to overly burdensome governmental regulation and taxation. Once the Rands accept him, however, Chance soon finds himself befriending the US president and Soviet ambassador, being interviewed for television and print, and being vetted for high positions in politics and business. It is satire with touches of farce, taking a seemingly gentle but probing stab at American media culture and its fascination with surface over substance, as well as the insidious ways that American political, business, and media elites intermingle.

Being There was published as a short novel by Jerzy Kosinski in 1970. Kosinski was a Polish émigré who had survived the Holocaust and arrived in the United States in 1957, at the age of 25, where he strived to make a career as a writer. By 1970, he had achieved one major publishing success with *The Painted Bird* (1965), and was the recipient of several grants and awards, including a Guggenheim Fellowship and a Ford Foundation grant.[1] These successes were notable, and Kosinski was well on his way to becoming a celebrity author in a fashion that would become oddly prominent in the United States of the 1970s—including evenings spent at Studio 54.[2] In the early 1970s, however, he still was not able to live on the earnings of his writing alone, and had taken guest teaching positions at several prestigious US universities, including Yale. With the publication of *Being There* and the novel's unmitigated success—"Along with glowing reviews and brisk sales came interviews that began to treat Kosinski not merely as a writer but as a literary star"[3]—Kosinski moved into the literary stratosphere, a position he would occupy for much of the next decade, with regular appearances on *The Tonight Show* and *The Dick Cavett Show* as well as on magazine covers and in films.

In 1979, a film version of *Being There* was released by Lorimar Pictures and United Artists. The film stars Peter Sellers in what many consider his last great—indeed one of his greatest—roles. Sellers plays Chance's simplemindedness as kind naiveté, upon which is fashioned both his allure to those he meets and the plot's believability to viewers. Sellers's decision to play Chance this way stems in part from the film's version of the character as a much older figure. Whereas the novel offers a younger, more virile version of the gardener, a man whose attractiveness is a vital component of how others perceive him, Sellers's film version must deploy subtler forms of charm. The film also stars Shirley MacLaine as Eve Rand, Melvyn Douglas as Benjamin Rand (a role for which he won an Academy Award), Richard Dysart as Dr. Allenby, and Jack Warden as the US president. It was directed by Hal Ashby, who had been in sporadic talks with Sellers about making the film for several years. After the success of his 1978 film *Coming Home* (United Artists 1978), Ashby had signed a three-film deal with Lorimar, and was—for a very brief period in his career—in a position to make nearly any film he wanted. He had garnered enough reputational capital as a director to insist that Sellers play Chance, against the initial wishes of Kosinski and his producers, who would have preferred a younger, more conventionally attractive actor like Ryan O'Neal. Like the novel, the film was a financial and critical success, garnering over $30 million in the United States alone (on a $7 million budget), and ecstatic reviews from most major film critics.[4]

The script-to-screen process for *Being There* took seven and a half years. That is, if we count from Kosinski's first attempt to adapt his 1970 novel into a screenplay, which he made in August 1971.[5] At the time, Kosinski was a visiting professor and fellow with the Davenport/Calhoun College Seminar at Yale University,[6] and his motivation for writing the draft was twofold. First, Kosinski constructed an exercise for class around the script (the script's cover page indicates twenty-five copies were made and directs the reader to "Return to the Instructor").[7] Kosinski's biographer describes some of the ingenious teaching methods Kosinski employed while at Yale, and working on a script of his own successful novel just a year after its publication fits these descriptions.[8] Second, despite public protestations otherwise at the time, Kosinski was keen to see a film version of *Being There* produced, so he had begun working on this draft of the screenplay with one of his graduate students, Larry Eilenberg, in the hopes of moving it into production.[9]

Over the next two years, Kosinski availed of every connection known to him in trying to get the film made. Detailed extensively elsewhere,[10] his efforts saw several deals almost come to fruition between 1971 and 1973; these featured Gore Vidal as scriptwriter and, variously, Sidney Lumet, Hal Ashby, or Kosinski's friend and fellow Polish émigré Roman Polanski as director. Famously, Peter Sellers became infatuated with the book soon after reading it in 1971 and was attached to most of these early iterations. However, as is often the case with spec scripts, these endeavors ultimately proved fruitless. Despite Kosinski's growing reputation as a novelist, and the rampant critical and commercial success of *Being There* the novel—contemporary critics compared Kosinski to both Beckett and Borges[11]—he was as yet unable to parlay that success into substantial Hollywood clout. As a result, Kosinski's fervor for the project subsided as he went to work on future novels. He was also kept busy serving two terms as president of PEN from 1973 to 1975.

The project remained in limbo for the next several years until late 1977 when Andrew Braunsberg, a friend of Kosinski's who had produced films for Polanski, approached the novelist about potential film projects.[12] Kosinski, his passion for a *Being There* film revived, told Braunsberg about the previous attempts to produce it. Braunsberg approached Ashby, unaware of his earlier interest in the project. Ashby agreed to direct as long as Sellers could still play Chance. While this casting choice was a brief sticking point, Ashby eventually got his way, and, with the pieces in place, *Being There* went into preproduction in early 1978.

Kosinski was commissioned to adapt his own script and he completed a new draft in January of 1978. This draft (reproduced in its entirety in Chapter 1) is different from the 1971 draft in significant ways. Still set in Manhattan, as was the novel, the January '78 draft goes into more detail about Chance's background and his relationship to the Old Man. It includes descriptions of political unrest at many of Benjamin Rand's corporate enterprises—mainly labor unrest, which Kosinski seems to be tying to the various real-world economic crises of the late 1970s. He makes more explicit narrative and visual connections between the Old Man and Benjamin Rand, particularly in their respective deathbed scenes. Ashby, Braunsberg, and Lorimar provided notes (including Ashby's insistence that the setting be moved to Washington, DC),[13] and Kosinski went to work on a third draft, which he submitted in July of 1978. By now, Kosinski's script had ballooned from an already lengthy 136 pages to an unwieldy 154.

After receiving the July '78 draft, Ashby was still dissatisfied. He believed that Kosinski was fighting too hard to correct issues he might have had with the book, and that he was "a little afraid of the character he had drawn in Chance."[14] Ashby called his friend and long-time colleague, Robert C. (Bob) Jones, and asked him to take a crack at the script. Jones had begun his career in Hollywood as an editor, working on several films in the late 1960s and early 1970s, including *Guess Who's Coming to Dinner* with Stanley Kramer (Columbia 1967) and *Love Story* with Arthur Hiller (Paramount 1970). With Ashby, he had edited *The Last Detail* (Columbia 1973), *Shampoo* (Columbia 1975), and *Bound for Glory* (United Artists 1976). Wanting to move into writing, he had done uncredited script work on *Bound for Glory* and then served as the final writer (after Nancy Dowd and Waldo Salt) on *Coming Home*, for which he had won an Academy Award. Jones, with his background in editing and screenwriting, possessed what Ashby described as a "cinematic" awareness that he believed Kosinski lacked.[15] Jones submitted his first draft (Chapter 2 of this book) in December of 1978, at which point Ashby said he knew he "was into the script." Over the next several weeks, Ashby and Jones worked closely together to assemble what would become the final draft of the script (Chapter 3 of this book), which they completed in January of 1979.[16]

Thus, in a little under seven and a half years, the script for *Being There* went through at least five drafts, with two separate writers and significant input from Ashby. While the final script hews closely to Kosinski's original novel in terms of narrative, character, and pacing, it differs from the novel and earlier drafts in significant ways—most notably in its heightened ambiguity and scripted ending—ways that will be discussed in detail later in this introduction.

This book presents three of those drafts in full; there are several reasons for this. First and foremost, *Being There* is one of the great scripts of American cinema. Unlike most boilerplate Hollywood screenplays, it features an elusive, ambiguous protagonist who possesses little in the way of recognizable goals or motivations. His one desire, to find a garden to work in after he is evicted from his lifelong residence, is so restrained throughout the film that Chance can hardly be described as working toward it. Furthermore, he exhibits minimal character development in the sense that most Hollywood narratives demand, remaining blithely unaware of the events that occur around him or of their ramifications, even when they result from his own behavior. Yet Chance's performance as a cipher rather than a traditional protagonist gives the film much of its punch. Viewers, at once in on the joke and also acutely aware that there might be something deeper going on, watch to see what kind of shenanigans Chance's simplemindedness will lead him toward, and to anticipate the reactions of those around him. Despite the unconventional nature of the central character, the narrative still comprises a three-act structure with building tension, a recognizable climax, and an emotionally rich, albeit unconventional, conclusion. The result is a script that, much like its protagonist, replicates recognizable screenwriting conventions while also skewing them in unexpected, often delightful fashion. Little wonder, then, that the Writers Guild of America (WGA) has included it in their list of the top 101 screenplays of all time (81st). Thus, one motivation behind this book is to make such a valuable script available to academics, screenwriters, and film fans alike.

A second reason to include three full scripts is to promote consideration of what a screenplay is—how its ideas are conveyed on the page, the role it plays in production, how it comes to life on screen—what makes it, as Ashby would say, "cinematic." Films are often spoken and written about in terms of their scripts, but films are not scripts. Rather, they are a realization of an idea that is given its primary textual structure in the script. Character and narrative development, action, and oftentimes visual and sonic information are all contained within a script, but none of them are fully realized until performers, cameras, sets, and other practical elements are involved and captured on film or digitally. So, what is a script? An idea? A foundation? A blueprint? Furthermore, what makes one draft better, or at least more suitable for filming, than another? Is it simply that the act of filming endows the shooting script with a primacy that might equally have been endowed upon another draft had it been the one chosen for production? Or is there something to Ashby's implication that some scripts are more cinematic in nature than others? These are questions that film scholars have grappled with for decades. While this introduction cannot hope to do justice to the nuances of these many arguments, examining these three scripts in dialogue with each other can provide some insight into the processes of how an idea becomes a script, and how a specific script becomes the "blueprint."

Finally, these three scripts can shed light on the complicated but necessary work of revision. In my teaching practice, I find it challenging to impart to students the importance of screenplay revision and its potential for creative reward. Some take to it, to be sure, but in my experience students and early-career writers often conflate revision with proofreading: spelling correction, proper formatting, and the like. The notions that a story might benefit from and be strengthened by the input of others, that cutting or moving scenes, changing or removing characters, shortening dialogue, or drastically reducing literary description can dramatically improve the cinematic quality of a script, are difficult to take on board when one has a personal stake in the script's genesis and ideas, especially within the confines of a twelve- to fifteen-week semester. This is understandable—the creative process is often highly personal, and romanticized ideals of individual creativity dominate popular discourses. In fact, it is not only students for whom the process can be difficult. While Hollywood history is rife with stories of meddlesome producers or overbearing directors ruining scripts, there are also numerous examples of writers who were adamant their scripts not be changed, but where the subsequent changes are generally accepted as having improved the film—Robert Towne and the ending of *Chinatown* (Paramount 1974), for example. The genesis of this project derived from in-class efforts to examine script revision "in action" by looking at various drafts of scripts and designing exercises around comparative analysis of draft-to-draft changes of specific scenes. The goal of such exercises is to encourage students to look for the cinematic in a script and to come to conclusions on their own (or in groups) about which changes work, and why.

In this introduction, I will elaborate on these three reasons—the publication of the script of *Being There*, an interrogation of what a script is and what makes one work, and a discussion of the vital importance of revision to the screenwriting process. While this will include some script analysis, my intention here is not to examine all the changes—major or minor—that occur from one draft to the next. Rather, I hope to facilitate reader interaction with the texts. Students of screenwriting—whether within an institution or on their own—should find much to consider about the revision process in closely examining these scripts and their changes and development.

To that end, I will begin by considering what scripts are and how they work. As mentioned, a growing body of scholarship has been devoted to questions around the ontology of the screenplay—not only in its relation to the finished film but also in the relationships between different drafts. For example, Noël Carrol describes screenplays as "ontologically ingredients in the motion pictures with which they are associated rather than being independent works."[17] Ted Nannicelli, on the other hand, argues that "at least some screenplays can be autonomous art insofar as they are … special kinds of literary works."[18] Disputes such as these derive, at least in part, from the screenplay's dual nature as both the presentation of fully formed narrative and character and also the blueprint for a completely separate, filmed consideration of narrative and character. Certainly, one of the primary goals of the screenwriter is to produce a script that reads well to the producers, actors, and agents with the reputational capital and financial power to move the film into production, but also cinematic in scope and vision to those who will film it, such as the director, cinematographer, designers, and, again, actors. Understanding the process of getting the script into such a shape is one of the primary considerations of this book.

Thus, I next consider revision—its aims, how it works, and what the relationship is between one draft, subsequent drafts, and the final film. The question of a script's cinematic quality or traits often determines what gets trimmed and what gets cut completely, but also what stays in. However, the notion of the cinematic can be highly elusive: is it related to a script's potential for visual storytelling? For example, with *Being There*, the decision to move the setting from Manhattan to Washington allowed the filmmakers to contrast imagery of DC slums with the capitol's more famous architectural projections of power and wealth. On the other hand, "cinematic" could just as aptly describe the narrative conventions that have come to be associated with Hollywood screenplay structure—three acts, recognizable character motivation, narrative closure, and the like. For example, and as I discuss in more detail below, all of Kosinski's drafts end with Chance leaving the Rand mansion to pay a visit to Rand's secretive friends, the shady financiers who will determine who becomes the next president. Eve Rand and the rest of the household characters drop out of the film completely. Jones, on the other hand, sets the film's conclusion at Rand's funeral on his private grounds, allowing for several instances of narrative closure (e.g., Rand's death mirrors the death of the Old Man, which started Chance's journey; Chance will stay at the house, which ends his search for a garden to call his own; and in Jones's written drafts, Chance and Eve embrace to end the film, which also provides closure to Eve's search for companionship after her husband passes). At the same time, however, Jones redrafts the financiers as Rand's pallbearers at the funeral, which allows him to replicate much of the dialogue that ended Kosinski's drafts. Jones's changes bear discernable remnants of Kosinski's original, creating a palimpsestuous[19] relationship between the various iterations—a relationship that is not uncommon in screenwriting revision, but can be difficult to elucidate. Why a writer chooses to keep certain elements and discard others—whether their own or those of a previous writer on the project—is a complicated process affected by the writer's own sense of story needs, as well as larger film demands, which may be articulated by a director, producer, or studio.[20] In this section, I touch on some of the guiding principles of screenplay revision that might help in understanding that process.

Finally, I move on to analyze some of the key differences between the three drafts presented here—in terms of both how the changes came about and what they mean for the final film. This section will also include some material from the other, unpublished drafts, as well as from the original novel. The authorship of *Being There* is a complicated and contentious question. There is no doubt that the produced film is a direct descendent of Kosinski's original 1970 novel: the main characters and situations are derived directly from the novel (with some changes); the vital subplot of Chance's addiction to TV remains; the frustration of the press and government at not being able to uncover Chance's roots provides comic relief and makes implicit connections between the two bodies in both novel and film. All of Kosinski's drafts include these elements. This is probably why WGA arbitration ruled in Kosinski's favor when he requested Jones's name be removed from the script in the spring of 1979—it would be difficult to argue that Jones wrote one-third of the final script, as the WGA's rules require for authorial recognition. Yet the changes that Jones did make (some in conference with Ashby) are so significant and changed the film so dramatically that not to recognize him as one of the film's primary screenwriters is not only unjust but also overlooks how collaboration informs the creative process. In analyzing particular sequences from the different drafts, I demonstrate how, through the creative process, Jones refined and cinematized Kosinski's foundational ideas and structure.

Cinematic Screenwriting

Before moving on to these discussions, however, I want to outline briefly what I mean by the term "cinematic," which I use throughout this introduction. As applied to screenwriting, "cinematic" has a variety of potential meanings. For the writers of screenwriting manuals, it might refer to narrative structure, particularly the prescriptive approaches developed by writers like Syd Field (the "paradigm") or Blake Snyder (the "beat sheet"). Throughout his work, Field describes a screenplay as beholden to the "context of structure,"[21] and his well-known paradigm is an effort to codify that structure to fit a highly specific blueprint: three acts, each with a specific task; readily identifiable plot points that redirect narrative and character; clear resolution. For Snyder, the "magic of storytelling on film" depends on a writer's ability to "execute and realize structure,"[22] and he takes Field's paradigm and codifies it even further by breaking it into fifteen detailed narrative beats. He even goes so far as to assign page numbers to each beat, based on a 110-page script.[23]

These and similar approaches to screenwriting purport to ground themselves in centuries of narrative theory—Field regularly references Aristotle in his work, especially when discussing narrative structure and elements of narrative and character unity. Acquiring an understanding of traditional narrative structure will be of benefit to any burgeoning screenwriter, and I regularly discuss and analyze variations on traditional structure with my students. However, that is not the understanding of "cinematic" that I use in this book. First of all, while Field, Snyder, and others tailor their approach to narrative to the feature film, particularly in terms of page count and run time, their conception of structure is firmly grounded in literature and theater. Introduce the world, deploy well-rounded characters with identifiable goals, create conflict by putting obstacles in their way, let the characters develop as they respond to those obstacles and attempt to overcome the conflicts, and resolve the various character and narrative strands via a climax during which those strands are woven together. These are the roots of traditional narrative whether in ancient epics, nineteenth-century novels, modern pop songs, or even good jokes. While they can be integral components of a good script, they are not inherently cinematic in their own right. Second, not all scripts or films are grounded in traditional narrative. There are minor variations—multiple protagonists, directionless plots, ambiguous endings—and there are the more ambitious deviations of avant-garde cinema and surrealism. These films and their scripts, however, can be just as cinematic as the more traditionally narrative driven. In his analysis of the American independent screenplay, *Me and You and Memento and Fargo*, J. J. Murphy describes how screenplays remain the foundation of "cinematic storytelling" even as independent films deviate, sometimes wildly, from the classical Hollywood notions of narrative development and continuity.²⁴ Attempting to map Field's paradigm or Snyder's beat sheet onto the scripts of art cinema can be an exercise in frustration,²⁵ or even pointlessness, and Murphy spends ample time in his introduction articulating how the prescriptions of screenwriting manuals are unsuited for understanding the cinematic quality of American indie cinema.

A second conceptualization of the "cinematic" in terms of screenwriting has less to do with narrative or character development (although they are linked) and more to do with understanding the screenplay's role in articulating how those elements will appear in the film medium. This is true of mainstream films, indie films, or the avant-garde. In the modern screenplay, elements like exposition, emotion, motivation, or character traits must be described in ways that can be seen or heard on screen. This is the nub of cinematic writing, and scripts that practice it will convey to readers that, regardless of the type of film, the script is ready for production. Field describes such writing as "a story told in pictures."²⁶ In Murphy's discussion of Hal Hartley's script for the film *Trust*, he discusses a particularly effective scene as being pared down "to its most basic cinematic elements,"²⁷ which consists of terse descriptions of action and Hartley's characteristically minimalist dialogue. Little in the way of detailed description or interior thought or emotion.

This cinematic approach is the opposite of a more literary style of writing, which allows for descriptions of emotional and psychological interiority, character motivations, as well as detailed exposition and backstory. Film scripts, even more so than narrative fiction, must adhere to the old maxim, show, don't tell. Scripts that are ready for production will eschew descriptions of character emotion—when a student includes a description like, "he is sad," the first question is always, "how do we know?" The script must display his sadness, via dialogue, action, or even elements of mise-en-scéne, in a way that communicates the emotion to the eventual viewer—he stares down into his coffee cup as he repeatedly stirs it with a spoon, he gazes out onto a rainy afternoon as raindrops stream down the window, or, simply, he cries. Likewise, scripts will avoid detailed description of character backstory or personality, and refrain from explaining motivation.

One of the difficulties in teaching screenwriting is that for many students such literary conventions *are* good writing—they will have learned them not only from creative writing classes but also from ceaseless exposure to written fiction, whereas few screenwriting students will have read more than a handful of scripts. In a sense, to become adept at the screenplay form, a writer must unlearn many of the conventions they have come to believe are necessary to telling a story. This is where the revision process becomes so vital. When working out a character's personality, backstory, or motivations, it may be useful or even necessary for a writer to engage in literary description. The same is true for writers trying to convey geographic space, which might require detailed description in a first draft, or writers drafting complicated intercut sequences. As the writer becomes more confident and sure about those various aspects of the script, the revision process, especially when done collaboratively, is where the literary components will be pared down and excised. These three drafts of *Being There* exemplify how that process works, with subsequent drafts becoming increasingly cinematic and ready for production. Before moving on to an analysis of some of the key changes that occurred between drafts, it will be helpful to take a brief look at how the modern Hollywood script developed into its present form.

What Is a Screenplay?

As various scholars have demonstrated, the screenplay, at least conceptually speaking, is nearly as old as film itself. Often consisting of little more than notes or a brief memo,[28] the earliest proto-scripts bear little resemblance to the modern screenplay with its prescribed, recognizable conventions and formatting. In her influential essay, "Blueprints for Feature Films: Hollywood's Continuity Scripts," and elsewhere,[29] Janet Staiger outlines in great detail how the continuity script began to develop during Hollywood's first major growth spurt from 1908 to 1917. During this period, films lengthened (in terms of both shooting days and duration), and narrative complexity grew to incorporate multiple locations, events, and instances of time. Filmmakers needed a fuller command of what to shoot on which days and in which locations. They were also developing the storytelling strategies and techniques that would come to constitute standard Hollywood style: coverage, medium shots and close-ups, match cuts, crosscutting, and so on. As Staiger writes, "These techniques continued to intensify the need for a written, preproduction layout, a blueprint of the film, in order to ensure that the standard would not be violated."[30] Additionally, these advances not only added to organizational demands but also required a growing number of crewmembers to take responsibility for discrete production and postproduction tasks. This would eventually lead to the departmental structure so integral to Hollywood's classical era. Thus, as Hollywood filmmaking increased in complexity, eschewing the stationary camera and evolving the language and form that today is generally recognized as cinematic, screenplay form followed suit.

It is important to note, as Staiger does, that these developments were as intimately tied to industrial changes as they were to artistic necessity. When a cameraman was shooting his own idea in natural light on one reel of film with a small troupe of performers, a few notes or a brief outline would suffice. But as the industry changed—due to a plethora of conditions including audience expectation, technological progress, studio organization, and the growing creativity and ambition of filmmaking crews—so, too, did the screenplay in its early forms. Building upon and expanding Staiger's work, Steven Price outlines a century of changes and development in the Hollywood screenplay. Generally, as films became more complex and crews more regimented, the requirements for the screenplay developed as well; for several years, this also meant a gradual change in name to match the changes in conception of what a script should be (the term "screenplay" would not come into regular use until the 1930s). Both Staiger and Price make clear that none of these changes—in style or name or otherwise—can be pegged to a specific film production or moment in time. Rather, like so many artistic and technological developments, they came along in fits and starts, with plenty of overlap between eras, approaches, and naming conventions.

Staiger breaks these changes down into six broad periods, which Price builds upon, and it is instructive to consider them, not least because they demonstrate how the cinematic concerns of a given era drove what filmmakers saw as fundamental to a functioning screenplay. These six periods and their approximation of a screenplay are as follows:

1. 1896–1907: the "cameraman system," in which little more than memos were necessary;
2. 1907–9: the "director system," in which the director was assisted by one or more crewmembers and so a functional outline of some sort was required;
3. 1909–1914: the "director-unit system," which roughly coincides with the period of growing complexity articulated by Staiger and discussed above, in which the increasing number of crew and intricacy of productions required a more detailed blueprint, often called a "scenario";
4. 1914–late 1920s: the "central producer system," or the consolidation of studio power, which led to the emergence of sound cinema. During this time the "continuity" script developed (both Price and Staiger discuss this era as the transition from the short succinct outlines of the early years to the screenplays of the modern era that we are familiar with today);
5. 1930s–1950s: the "producer-unity system," during which the demands of sound and dialogue, along with the increased industrialization of Hollywood filmmaking, led to the first "master scene" screenplays, very like those still in use today, in which each scene is succinctly described in terms of location, time, and cast involved, with specific dialogue;
6. 1950s–present: the "package-unit system," which saw the breakdown of the studio system and its rigid hierarchies, allowing for more individualistic and idiosyncratic approaches to scriptwriting as well as a greater reliance on collaboration.[31]

These periods, particularly the latter two, can be broken down further based on stylistic changes that did not dramatically affect the overall construction of screenplay formatting, but did inform its formal elements. For example, Price outlines a very gradual shift that began in the final era of studio dominance that saw screenplays drop the inclusion of such directing techniques as specific camera movements, framing decisions, or editing transitions because "most directors justifiably see the handling of the camera as in their province."[32] Price also details the effects of the rise of the screenwriting manual in the wake of Syd Field's 1979 *Screenplay*. That influential text and its descendants have bequeathed upon us a period within the "package-unit system" in which the mainstream Hollywood screenplay's form has become highly standardized: a rigid master-scene structure based around the notions that films consist of three acts and that one page of screenplay equates to one minute of screen time.[33]

In whatever its form—rudimentary and loose or modern and tightly prescribed—what all these historical variations share is how they serve as an intermediary between the mental conception of a potential film (whether by camera operator, writer, producer or other filmmaker) and that conception's realization in its final utterance as a film. Regardless of the specific form it has taken throughout history, the screenplay is always a dialogic text; it remains grounded in its initial conception while also subject to change or flux throughout the production process. Price describes it as a "modular text,"[34] by which he means neither fully a blueprint—a fixed form—as is often conceptualized, nor a text completely in flux, subject to the vagaries and whims of production. What the work of Staiger and Price[35] demonstrates is how integral the concept of the cinematic is to the development of the screenplay. As the scope of filmmaking changed, as the desires of filmmakers and studios to challenge and expand the possibilities of Hollywood filmmaking grew, so too did the ability of the screenplay to act as a foundational, organizational text,[36] intimately tied to a given era's ability to produce screen narratives, and its understanding of how those narratives should be structured.

Screenwriting as Rewriting

In a well-known interview with *The Paris Review* in 1958, George Plimpton asks Ernest Hemingway about his rewriting process, and he confesses to having rewritten the ending to *A Farewell to Arms* "39 times." Plimpton then asks him, "What was it that had stumped you?" Hemingway replies, "Getting the words right."[37] It is a pithy reply, typical of Hemingway at his most withholding and disgruntled. But it also manages to convey the deeper truths for which the best of Hemingway's terse writing is admired. Getting the words right does not mean simply choosing the appropriate words, or even arranging them correctly on the page. Nor is it merely a question of the order in which events are relayed, how characters are described, or the surprise that comes with the deployment of key plot points. Rather, getting the words right encompasses all those elements and more. It requires an understanding of issues such as tone, voice, irony, and mood. It demands a familiarity with genre and concepts of unity and ambiguity. This is only one of the many reasons that revision is such a vital part of the writing process. To balance all these issues in a first draft is a near impossibility, even for the most seasoned of writers. Characters change in the process of writing; plot points that seemed vital in the initial conception become redundant or sometimes even ludicrous; and small tonal shifts can lead to dramatic changes in genre. Imagine if, when first scripting *Dr. Strangelove* (Columbia Pictures 1964), Stanley Kubrick and Peter George had decided to stick with their concept of a tense political thriller, if they had not detected the narrative's dark comedy and brought in Terry Southern to work on the script. *Dr. Strangelove* would have become a very different film. It was only in the process of writing and revisiting the first draft that Kubrick saw that forcing the film into a thriller template was removing the humor that he deemed necessary to conveying the plot's dark, twisted absurdity.

Without a doubt, writing and revising a screenplay is very different from writing works of literary fiction. Getting the words right is a different task, driven by the need to convey ideas and concepts to an entirely different type of reader. Screenplays, at least in their professional context, are meant to be read by producers, directors, studio heads, and actors, and to convey with a high degree of immediacy how the action and dialogue described on the page will translate to the screen. This generally requires a reader with a specific skill set: the mental ability to transpose the formatting of a modern screenplay into its potential for visual and aural representation. This makes screenplays, in some ways, anti-literary in their construction. In the introduction to his 2008 edited collection, *Authorship in Film Adaptation*, Jack Boozer describes the screenplay format as "intrusive" to the reader. He writes, "Its written style is less intimate and rich than fiction. It points to the potential specificity and power of fully realized, framed, and mobile iconic imagery ready for editing."[38] This contrasts heavily with the kind of interior mental and emotional imagery that literary fiction regularly aims for.

This is why the literary aspects of screenplays may not be the best measure of their artistry. A good deal of scholarship in recent years has been dedicated to the status of the screenplay as art, and that scholarship often revolves around two primary issues: the literary merit of the screenplay and the screenplay's "incomplete" nature. For example, in his 2011 article, "Why Can't Screenplays Be Artworks," Ted Nannicelli works to refute Noël Carroll's argument that screenplays are not art.[39] Nannicelli takes pains to be clear that he is not arguing that screenplays *are* art, only that they cannot be categorically denied status as art—in other words, they *could be* art.[40] In doing so, he accepts an argumentative framework (an appealing one, no doubt) that if we can deem scripts *literary*, then we can deem them *art*. In another essay, "The Ontology and Literary Status of the Screenplay: The Case of 'Scriptfic,'" Nannicelli makes a more concerted argument in favor of the screenplay as art, or at least some screenplays as art.[41] In this article, Nannicelli is particularly concerned with "scriptfic," a form of fan fiction consisting of scripts of various sorts (one-off features, virtual series based on preexisting series, or original virtual series) that are designed to be written for, posted to, and read by web-based fan communities that have developed around this practice.[42] In Nanniclli's view, because the majority of these scripts are designed solely to be read by an interested, engaged readership—a readership markedly different from the professional class noted above—and also not to be produced for the screen, they can be considered "complete, autonomous works" that their readership communities appreciate as literature.[43] Thus, it is their "completeness," at least in part, which endows them with artistry. Vitally, for this audience, the scriptfic form is not "intrusive" in the way that Boozer argues.

Although there is not space here to explore them in full, there are further arguments along these lines with variations—for example, arguments that compare the screenplay to a theater play or musical composition (is the composed score itself art, even if its written form precludes most from reading it, or is it each performed interpretation of the composition that makes it art?) or, interestingly, arguments comparing the screenplay to a piece of dance choreography, which may or may not be written at all, and when so, sometimes only in sketch or outline form (thus, in a way, reminiscent of the proto-screenplays of early cinema). It is not my intention to diminish or disregard these debates—there is a rich vein of film scholarship concerning questions not only of artistry (and not only of the screenplay) but also of who is or can be deemed a film artist (including a growing body of work interrogating standard framings of film authorship). However, I bring them up here because questions about a screenplay's artistic quality or merit tie directly into how best to understand the process of script revision. Certainly, revision alone does not imply art—plenty of written texts, from business reports to political speeches to real estate advertisements, undergo revision processes without being deemed art (correspondingly, we do often recognize the artistic elements of some of these texts); conversely, there are numerous improvisational practices that are deemed artistic precisely because they eschew processes of revision. With screenplays, however, it is the effort to create something cinematic, rather than strictly literary, that imbues the process with artistry. Furthermore, the cinematic nature of the script is, by default, tied to the produced film (or, at the least, the potentially produced film), notwithstanding Nannicelli's compelling arguments about scriptfics. I would argue, then, that the artistry of the screenplay lies outside strict conceptions of the literary and is inherent in its being part of a larger artistic endeavor. This conception helps clarify the aims of the screenplay revision process.

In his 2016 screenwriting manual, *Screenwriting Is Rewriting: The Art and Craft of Professional Revision*, veteran Hollywood screenwriter Jack Epps Jr. titles his first chapter "Notes" and begins, "You've finished your first draft."[44] While much of the text goes on to give advice familiar to anybody who has even cursory knowledge of the screenwriting manual trade (with sections on character development, themes, obstacles and conflict, dialogue, etc.), it is telling that Epps begins his text with an assumption that the first draft has been written, and that he does so in a chapter with the subtitle, "Receiving and Organizing Notes." Epps's assumption—or, at the very least, his contextual framing—is that the vital work of screenwriting comes *after* the first draft has been written. Furthermore, opening with a chapter on receiving notes conveys the importance that Epps places on collaboration. Throughout the chapter, Epps advises both that screenplays will "undergo a great deal of change over the course of your rewrite"[45] and that a serious screenwriter should "try to get notes from at least three different people."[46] This emphasis on both the potential for dramatic change and the necessity for strong collaborators has been a component of Hollywood screenwriting at least since the shift to the package-unit system, discussed above, when, as Price recognizes, a greater reliance on collaboration became the norm.[47] This is worth reiterating for any burgeoning screenwriters who might be reading this book—your script will change, and those changes are likely to be more effective when strong collaborators are involved. This is not a sign that an initial idea is weak or that somebody is not a good writer. Rather, it is a sign that the initial idea has great potential, particularly if producers, directors, writers, or other trusted collaborators are willing to take the time to read the work, give detailed feedback, and even take a pass at the next draft. Boozer describes how this process is often overlooked in popular conceptions of filmmaking: "The closed fixation only on literary source and finished film both in journalistic reviews and scholarly study has often shown an indifference to the evolving intentions of producers, writers, and directors and their shifting levels of input and authority."[48] While Boozer is specifically describing the process of adapting literary texts to film (which, in the case of *Being There*, actually applies and has likewise affected popular and scholarly conceptions of its scriptwriting process[49]), the observation pertains to scriptwriting in general. Conceptions of redrafting rarely figure into popular, or even critical, understandings of screenwriting except in cases of "too many cooks," when the presence of a great number of screenwriters is often taken to indicate a troubled production.

Accepting the importance of collaborative revision, the question becomes what precisely improves a good idea or a solid first draft. Cutting material, adding dialogue, or shifting narrative beats toward the cinematic may make sense conceptually, but what does it mean in practice? One step actually entails the removal of traditionally literary components: detailed, sometimes florid description; interior thoughts and monologues; descriptions of character feelings and reactions. As obvious as this can seem to film scholars and practitioners, in my teaching experience, students find this one of the most challenging aspects of screenwriting. We are generally raised to encounter written fiction in literary texts and when students take their first tentative steps as writers in their teens and early twenties, it is natural for them to want to replicate the styles of their favorite writers or genres, particularly when describing a character and her thoughts, feelings, and motivations. However, the old maxim "show, don't tell" has much stricter application to film writing and students can struggle with it. Describing a character as "angry" or "sad" is easy, and in a certain regard, gets straight to the point. But, as every teacher of screenwriting has asked numerous times, how do we "see" angry? Novice instincts are often to describe, habitually in great detail, why a character is feeling a certain way or what they are thinking about a certain situation. This is the influence of literary fiction, and it is not necessarily "bad" writing. In early drafts, describing a character's thoughts and feelings can be an effective step toward defining that character, for both the writer and any potential early readers. It can be beneficial to the writing process not to worry overly much about the presence of such literary devices in first drafts, and removing them through workshopping and collaboration can serve as a great entry into the importance and effectiveness of the redrafting process. But in the end, excising those literary maneuvers is a necessary step in pushing the script toward the cinematic.

While cutting the overtly descriptive internal components is key to producing a cinematic screenplay, there are other types of description that go into a script as well. Epps describes how "description should produce *images* in the mind of your reader. The reader should see the movie" (emphasis in original).[50] In that vein, Epps, like many another screenwriting guru, gives such advice as cutting descriptive words, trimming the "heads and tails" of scenes, and cutting dialogue while maintaining its "flow."[51] These skills come with practice, from the process of responding to notes, and from being open to shaping a script that is cinematic, despite what that might mean about cutting or changing the original idea. For example, and as I discuss in more depth below, every iteration of *Being There*—from Kosinski's novel to the finished film—begins in the day or two leading up to the Old Man's death, which is the incident that leads to Chance's expulsion from the house. However, every written text apart from the final script opens with Chance in the garden, where he spends much of the day (and multiple pages of text) going about his duties. Jones's final script, on the other hand, begins with Chance waking up in bed, turning on the television in his room, and getting dressed before heading out to the garden. Jones keeps him in the garden for only a few moments before cutting to some of his other household duties, and then to his lunch. In Kosinski's three drafts and Jones's first, the opening two or three pages are spent describing Chance in his garden. In the Kosinski draft presented here, the Old Man does not die until the bottom of page eighteen. In Jones's first draft, we discover the

Old Man's death at the bottom of page four. In the final draft, we still see Chance in the garden and still get a sense of the grandeur of his living situation. Vitally, Chance's position in the household remains ambiguous—at first glance, he could be the master of the house. However, in the final draft we discover the Old Man is dead halfway through page two. As the Old Man's death is the catalyst for Chance's journey, getting to his death this early allows Jones to have Chance exit the house on page fourteen, as opposed to nineteen in his first draft or twenty-seven in Kosinski's. These gradual trimmings maintain the visual components of Chance in his garden while dramatically increasing the script's cinematic flow. Furthermore, by allowing the film to arrive at Chance's meeting with Eve Rand much earlier, the final draft also allows more time for Chance to interact with, and confound, the various bigwigs he encounters—the foundation upon which so many of the film's themes are built. Thus, by trimming the opening, the film can have a more leisurely, and thereby more effective, middle section.

Changes such as these, which include cutting whole scenes, paring back dialogue, and reworking characters, exemplify the effectiveness of thoughtful revision. In this case, in addition to moving more quickly to place Chance with the Rands, the changes also allow the film to introduce a tone of ambiguity around the protagonist that the film will flirt with until its closing scene, and to set up early conflicts and key character interactions that reverberate throughout the film. Below, I compare three sections of the film, based on the three drafts included in this collection as well as other drafts and the original novel. The point is not so much to show that one approach or another is "better," or to lionize one draft over all the others. Rather, what I hope to show with this analysis is how the process of revision, including from one writer to the next, when done effectively can push a script—no matter how brimming with ideas it may be originally—toward a more cinematic, but still malleable, blueprint.

Comparing Three Scripts

The script for *Being There* underwent vast changes during the scattered, seven-year process of preparing it for production. Many of those changes are nearly invisible—Kosinski drafted and redrafted the script on different occasions for different reasons. In doing so, he added and cut elements of both the novel and his original draft that Jones in turn either cut or restored in his drafts. Examining how closely Jones's final version hews to the novel can be deceptive because, in addition to adapting the novel, his process included responding to Kosinski's drafts and to what Ashby found trepidatious and uncinematic about them. Other changes, while often subtle, are indicative of the passage of time over those seven years. 1971 and 1978 were different worlds in many ways—Watergate had been uncovered, the Vietnam War had ended, the "dream" of the counterculture was on life support, and many of its movements, including civil rights and the women's movement, had stalled, at least as compared to their energy and effectiveness earlier in the decade. When the novel and first draft were written, the counterculture was still thriving and while it was decidedly anti-Nixon in scope, even Nixon's administration was passing affirmative action laws, expanding the rights of women and minorities by, for example, passing Title IX, and protecting the environment with the Clean Air and Water amendments. By the time the film was produced, Nixon had been felled by Watergate, and the country had ushered in and was about to reject a short era of liberal federal governance and was on the cusp of the Reagan years.[52] These social and political changes were highly relevant to and reshaped a narrative about the incestuous relationship between government and corporations, about government agencies invading individual privacy, and about a populace deadened to much of it through their addiction to watching television.

It is also worth noting that Kosinski was not a scriptwriter by trade, but a novelist. His drafts rely heavily on the aforementioned literary devices of the novelist—long, detailed passages of description, the relaying of interior thoughts and feelings—that a seasoned screenwriter would have avoided, at least by the second draft. And, particularly in his earlier drafts, he incorporates much of the in-script directing that, as Price notes, had long been disappearing from professional scripts. For example, his first script is rife with camera framing and movement directions, and all his scripts use parentheticals extensively to direct actors. The presence of these elements does not necessarily make Kosinski's drafts "bad," but they do indicate his lack of familiarity with standard screenplay conventions. Jones, on the other hand, had worked in the industry for over a decade and had recently garnered an Academy Award for screenwriting. This does not necessarily mean Jones's scripts are "better" than Kosinski's, but it suggests he was better prepared, professionally speaking at least, to craft the sort of cinematic script Ashby and the production were seeking.

These differences are plain in each of the drafts' opening sequences. As stated above, the novel opens with Chance in the garden—the first two sentences read: "It was Sunday. Chance was in the garden."[53] It quickly moves on to Chance in the house, and Chance watching TV. In four pages of deft prose, Kosinski sketches Chance's daily routine, gives the reader insight into some of Chance's thoughts about the world, and has the Old Man die. Here is how he opens his first draft of the script from 1971 (for the opening of Kosinski's second draft, and Jones's two drafts, see pages 39, 188, and 338, respectively):

```
EXT: STREET—DAY

Early Spring

ELS: An exquisite Manhattan street, somewhere in the
East 70's

CAMERA TRACKS along the street and stops across the street
in front of an old, imposing looking TOWNHOUSE.

MSQ.S—THE TOWNHOUSE -- the view is from across the street.
THE TOWNHOUSE was built around 1910 in a style reminiscent
of English and French domestic architecture of the 18th
century. Its façade, its window-sills and its immense main
```

door are of the same period. The exterior of THE TOWNHOUSE has clearly not been cleaned since it was built. There are curtains visible in the windows, and the brass fixtures of the main door are brightly polished.

CAMERA TILTS AND MOVES UPWARD IN A CRANE SHOT. A multi-directional TV antenna is protruding from the roof of THE TOWNHOUSE; it looks almost out of proportion to the roof.

The CAMERA passes the third floor of THE TOWNHOUSE and, as if going through the TV antenna, moves over the roof and passes two small chimneys -- a faint smoke is drifting from one of them.

CAMERA CROSSES the roof and tilts down.
ELS—A typical medium-size townhouse garden still so common to Manhattan's best residential areas, at the rear of THE TOWNHOUSE. It is early spring. There are trees, a lot of bushes, but as yet no flowers in the garden. The trees seem to be at least thirty years old.

CREDITS BEGIN

LS—CAMERA still looking down at garden.

ELS—A MAN -- strolling without apparent direction down the walkways of the garden.

CREDITS CONTINUE

THE MAN stops now and then as if attracted by something we can't see in the trees or in the bushes.

LS CAMERA PANS following THE MAN as he heads toward a thick reddish brick wall, about eleven feet high, which separates the garden from the street and from the neighboring townhouses. The color and architecture of the wall indicate that it too is around thirty years old, and was built as an addition to the House.

CAMERA CRANES DOWN VERY SLOWLY toward THE MAN strolling through the garden.

CREDITS CONTINUE

LMS—Three modern, brightly painted sprinklers are splashing water in various parts of the garden.

MS—of THE MAN—This is CHANCE: He is tall, at least five feet eleven inches, approximately thirty-five to forty years old, fair, and masculine. CHANCE's pure looks are of those few blessed by good health, balanced and peaceful disposition and trust in what comes next in life. In terms of his appearance and manner, CHANCE is an incarnation of the corporate man's ideal, and is a man the largest corporations would like to have sit on their boards.

ATTENTION: The actor portraying CHANCE cannot display any scars, or artificial teeth, or anything which would indicate that he ever needed medical assistance. CHANCE always walks very erect, yet is not rigid. He is conventionally handsome but only in the most ordinary, not effeminate, way. He wears dark sunglasses and is dressed in a very well-tailored suit of plain dark cloth, over his white shirt he wears a tie and vest. His wardrobe is of the 1920's, which means that it is once more fashionable today. CHANCE is also wearing gardening gloves and a gardener's apron over his suit. He smiles easily, very often, and his smile is extremely natural, open-faced and ENGAGING. This ENGAGING facet of his smile appears whenever he is confronted by a situation beyond his comprehension.

Whenever CHANCE watches TV -- and as often as he does, whether alone, or in front of others who talk to him while he is watching, he watches the TV set casually, his face never shows any sign of interest in what he sees or an emotion of being absorbed. And so, it seems, that CHANCE is not really watching TV but merely acknowledges its presence. Hence, when he watches TV while at the same time talking to or being addressed by others, CHANCE never projects an image of being rude or inattentive to them; if anything, he seems to be rather pensive, reflecting on what others just said to him, and pondering his answer.

MCU—CHANCE's hands in gloves gently touching some of the newly emerged leaves as if testing their rigidity. He does the same with a new sprout of a branch. Now and then he carefully removes an old piece of bark or dead leaf.

LMS—THE CAMERA FOLLOWS CHANCE: CHANCE looks toward the sky as if checking the time, then turns around and walks toward the rear of THE TOWNHOUSE. On the way CHANCE turns off all the sprinklers. (The rear of THE TOWNHOUSE is of the same

```
quality as the front: there is only one door leading to
the garden and a single large window on the ground floor next
to the door. The is where CHANCE's quarters are.)

CREDITS END

MS—CHANCE opens the door and enters.⁵⁴
```

The first thing to notice is the amount of description compared with how little actually occurs here. In three pages, the script conveys only about thirty seconds of screen time to depict a somewhat rundown city townhouse, its garden, and its well-dressed gardener. It lingers over certain locales or items, when much briefer description would do ("three modern, brightly painted sprinklers"). Extensive descriptions of the state of the garden, the age of different additions to the house, and Chance himself are certainly evocative. They might work effectively as literary fiction (although, as pointed out above, Chance's introduction in the novel is much succincter). However, they are too detailed, too precise for a Hollywood screenplay. The director, the production designer, the cinematographer, and the actor are going to make most of the decisions about how this scene looks, how it is shot, and how the actor performs within in it (not to mention framing and camera movements, which, here, are described with a variety of industry acronyms like "ELS" for "extreme long shot").

This is precisely the type of "literary" writing that does not work in a script, but that novice screenwriters often feel comfortable with. In the early 1970s, Kosinski was an accomplished writer of fiction, but his inexperience in the field of filmmaking shows. It is on further display with his depiction of Chance, particularly his note about "the actor portraying" him and in the description of Chance's TV watching habits. Both of these passages exemplify a combination of telling over showing and directing within the script. Both passages describe Chance not as he appears in the first scene in the garden (as a viewing audience would encounter him), but rather in an idealized manner as he appears in the writer's head. For example, we simply cannot know what Chance's full wardrobe is like, how often he smiles, or how he always walks simply by seeing him in the garden for half a minute. A viewer might infer some of these things about the character based on those thirty seconds, but it is for only those thirty seconds that the character is able to make such an impression, so that is all that the writer should describe. As far as his television-viewing habits go, as of yet there is no TV in the garden and no description yet of Chance watching TV (this will change), so, once again, there is no way to know what Chance's viewing habits are like or even, aside from the hint given by the large TV antenna on the roof, that he is a regular TV viewer.

Kosinski is clearly enamored of the idea of writing for film, and this introduction displays some imaginative approaches that are alive to the possibility of film narrative. It displays a sense of Hollywood grammar in its use of long establishing shots that cut to medium shots and medium close-ups, and the long take that passes over the front of the house's exterior, "through" the TV antenna, and down into the back garden is laden with potential for fluid visual storytelling. Solid scriptwriting does not necessarily have to preclude such vision, but when it comes to actual production, it will be the director and the department heads who make such decisions, so unless a certain shot, camera move, or editing transition is absolutely necessary, avoiding their inclusion is generally best practice. However, I do advise students that if they deem the inclusion of a particular shot necessary, they should describe precisely what occurs in the shot and the film crew will understand how to frame it. From the excerpt above, for example, when Chance enters, rather than specify an extreme long shot and then a pan, a writer could briefly describe the garden, and then Chance first within it and then walking across it. The eleven-foot hedges alone will inform the director how much space needs to be framed, and Chance's movement will imply the pan.

Much of the first draft's literary bent can be ascribed to Kosinski's inexperience with the format; however, where it becomes especially valuable is in how it informs his draft of January 1978. This version, submitted early in the production process, appears to be an updating of the '71 script rather than a full-on rewrite with the new production in mind. Gone are the directorial acronyms—in the intervening years Kosinski must have learned how outdated and unnecessary their inclusion was—but inserted into this draft are a raft of new scenes and characters. The plotting is both more sweeping and more complicated. For example, beginning on the script's second page (see page 40) and sprinkled throughout, Kosinski adds scenes of domestic political and labor strife, usually directed at Benjamin Rand or one of his corporations. These scenes seem intended to counterbalance the narrative's depiction of Rand as a kindly old man, near death and eager to make sure Eve and Chance are both taken care of after he departs, a reminder that Rand's form of rapacious capitalism has consequences for the world outside the upper echelons of society depicted in *Being There*. In one sense, these scenes could be considered cinematic in that they lend the film an epic grandeur; they contextualize the worlds of wealth and power that the film and its protagonist move through so casually. However, they also serve to interrupt the film's early flow, and they continually redirect the film's attention away from Chance and its other main characters.

Further complications come in this draft's development of back stories for such characters as Franklin, the lawyer who evicts Chance from the Old Man's house, or in its various side plots, usually of a bumbling nature, such as scenes with the president's handlers, the journalists attempting to cover Chance's story, or the Soviet apparatchiks under pressure to determine Chance's true identity. All these characters appear in the novel and the final film, although to lesser degrees than they do here. The effort to expand on their stories in order to provide a broader view of Chance's world, as well as some comic relief, represents an admirable attempt to make the film more broadly cinematic. However, it is also these inclusions—both the scenes of unrest and the expanded subplots—that must have led Ashby to perceive a reticence on Kosinski's part to engage fully with his own protagonist.

A return to the opening sequence exemplifies the effect of this reticence on the second draft's narrative flow. Even with all the camera directions of the first draft removed, it takes longer here for Chance to be introduced and then reenter the house from the garden because of the inclusion of the first two scenes of unrest. An examination of this draft's full introduction of Chance displays the intrusive effect of these intercuts even further: due to the scenes of protest and the introduction of the first back stories, it takes thirteen pages before Chance gets a line of dialogue. This trend continues throughout this draft of script. Just as events in Chance's life are building in dramatic fashion, the script cuts away from him to secondary characters or to more social scenes that, in the end, are never fully explained or resolved.

A further examination of this January '78 draft shows how informed it is by the '71 draft. While the shot descriptions are gone for the most part (e.g., the direction "shown from above" is included to describe the TV antenna), the draft retains the note concerning the actor who plays Chance and, notably, still describes Chance as being between 35 and 40 years old—despite Sellers having been cast. Descriptions of the Manhattan townhouse and its garden remain literary and ornate, and the script persists in telling the reader about Chance's television-viewing habits long before it shows us Chance engaged in any actual watching. Kosinski certainly displays cinematic instincts in terms of what he wanted to see on screen, but his efforts to convey those instincts in the format of a Hollywood screenplay remain decidedly literary rather than cinematic. What is more, while some of this has been pared back in Kosinski's final draft from July of 1978, there is more that remains. Based on notes from Ashby and producer Andrew Braunsberg, Kosinski changes the setting to Washington, DC.[55] He also reduces the description of the house and garden. However, much of the direction regarding Chance's appearance remains, albeit not in the form of a note to crew:

```
The MAN is CHANCE. He is of average height, powerfully
built, with jaws that suggest raw strength, approximately
forty-five years old. CHANCE is a charismatic figure. His
looks are of the few blessed by good health, with a peaceful
disposition and a trust in what comes next in life.

CHANCE does not have any scars, or artificial teeth, or any
sign indicating that he ever needed medical assistance. He
always walks erect, yet is not rigid. He personifies health,
both physical and mental. He has all his hair, doesn't wear
eyeglasses; he speaks contemporary American English, with no
trace of any regional accent or idiom.

Whatever CHANCE does, whether alone or with others, he does
it effortlessly, almost casually; his face never shows any
sign of profound interest in what he is engaged in at the
moment, no emotion being absorbed.

When CHANCE watches TV, and as often as he does, he appears
to merely acknowledge its presence. CHANCE never projects an
image of being rude or inattentive; he is pensive, perhaps
reflecting on what has taken place, perhaps pondering his
reactions. He smiles easily, very often, and his smile is
extremely natural, open faced and engaging.

From the moment we see him, it is obvious that CHANCE is
a man of a different wisdom.
```

> In terms of his appearance and manner, CHANCE is an incarnation of the U.S. corporate man's visual ideal.
>
> From time to time CHANCE looks toward the sky as if to verify what he expects and knows about capricious nature which, on its own, doles out snow and sunshine as he does his gardening. Then he turns around and walks toward the rear of the TOWNHOUSE.

It is understandable that Ashby might have been frustrated on receiving this draft. While he had worked with a variety of screenwriters in the past, each with their own approach, these drafts by Kosinski remain persistently noncinematic, and also persistently forceful in their insistence on certain key points that had already been decided otherwise by the production. For example, he has increased Chance's seeming age to "45" here, still ludicrously young compared not only to Sellers's 55 at the time but also to Sellers's even older appearance in the film. It is easy to comprehend why, at this point, with production slated to begin in less than six months, Ashby might have turned to a writer like Jones with whom he had worked on several occasions and whom he trusted.

Looking at Jones's first draft (December 1978), one is struck almost immediately not only by how much more streamlined the writing is but also by the script's awareness of how screen-based storytelling works. In Jones's introduction (see page 189), the initial description of the house, the garden, and Chance is one paragraph. In Kosinski's drafts, this takes three to four pages. Jones then deftly establishes his draft's cinematic quality (and his experience as an editor) by intercutting a series of short sequences inside and outside of the Old Man's home as Chance goes about his daily routine, attending to vintage cars, working in the potting shed, and watching television in his bedroom. In fact, Jones subtly introduces the television in the very first short scene: as Chance works in the garden, "CLASSICAL MUSIC is heard in the distance," and in the third scene, still on page one, it is revealed that this classical music is, in fact, a Boston Pops concert being broadcast on television. By the end of page two, Chance has spent an entire day going about his life at a leisurely pace—because of his attire ("a well-tailored suit of the 1920's," as in Kosinski), he could quite easily be the man of the house. The crucial point here is that everything about Chance, everything the audience can discern about him up to this point, is described as occurring on screen.

As Chance's day comes to an end, a key moment of screenwriting palimpsest occurs with the appearance of Louise, the Old Man's black maid. Kosinski was equivocal about the character of Louise in his various iterations of the text. In the novel and in the January '78 draft, Louise has left the house at some point prior to the start of the narrative, and has been replaced by a maid "from abroad" with a "strange accent"[56] in the novel, or Gertrude, who seems to be from Germany, in the January '78 draft. In the '71 and July '78 drafts, however, Kosinski alters this so that Louise is still the maid of the house. Thus, Louise has been a presence, whether physically or historically, in all of Kosinski's versions and Jones cements her as the contemporary maid (played memorably by Ruth Attaway). His drafts will take advantage of Louise's presence to allow the character a few very pointed comments about racial disparity and hypocrisy in America. For example, late in the film (see Chapter 2, page 281) when Chance is making his first appearance on TV, Louise watches the broadcast from her new group home, and comments:

```
                    LOUISE
          An' it's for sure a White man's world in
          America, hell, I raised that boy since he was
          the size of a pissant an' I'll say right now he
          never learned to read an' write - no sir! Had
          no brains at all, was stuffed with rice puddin'
          between the ears! Shortchanged by the Lord
          and dumb as a jackass an' look at him now!
          Yes, sir - all you gotta be is white in America
          an' you get whatever you want! Just listen
          to that boy - gobbledegook!
```

This and a few other observations about race in America could also be read as palimpsestuous in the sense that Kosinski's January '78 draft had attempted to cast the events of the film against a backdrop of civil and racial discord. Here, however, they are grounded in natural, organic developments of place and character rather than forced asides with nameless protesters who otherwise have little to do with the narrative.

Ashby said, after reading this draft, that he felt like he was "into" the film, but it remains necessary to examine the opening sequence of the final draft to fully understand how collaborative revision can work when writers engage with their peers in the redrafting process. After Jones submitted his first draft in December of '78, he and Ashby spent several weeks into the new year redrafting the script for the final, January 1979 draft, which was used for shooting. In that version, the opening achieves even greater succinctness by jettisoning a whole day in the life of Chance. Jones's first draft describes two successive days of Chance's life in the Old Man's home, over the course of which he takes part in most of the same activities: gardening, attending to saplings in the potting shed, maintaining the old car, visiting his own bedroom, and eating meals. There is something to be said about filmic representations of repetition—deftly shot and edited, they can quickly convey a diverse array of repetitive activities and a character's attitude toward them, from the soul-crushing mundanity of a housewife's daily routine in *Jeanne Dielman* (Paradise Films 1975) to the hypnotic hyperactivity of drug abuse in *Requiem for a Dream* (Thousand Words 2000).

In the case of Chance, however, especially as he is presented in the final film, such repetition would likely rend the shroud of ambiguity so vital for the film's success. Much of what makes *Being There* work is that from the very beginning the viewing audience is as likely as the other characters in the film to accept Chance, albeit briefly, as an upper-class man of refinement and grace, thanks in part to his attire, composure, and accent. It is easier for us to believe that Eve and Benjamin Rand, or the president of the United States, could mistake Chance for such a man if we have believed so ourselves. Seeing him putter about the garden briefly and attend to his classic cars, makes it easy to read Chance as the kind of retired gentleman of leisure who takes loving care of his possessions. Repeating Chance's daily routine over two days would remove some of this vital ambiguity by endowing his living situation and his role within the household with more specific clarity. Thus, it was cut. So, too, the first conversation with Louise. In the December '78 draft (191), after Chance's first full day of work, he has dinner prepared for him by Louise, at which she informs him that the Old Man is getting weaker. She also describes Chance's conversational non sequiturs as "gobbledegook." With the information that there's an Old Man upstairs, that he's sick and Louise is taking care of him (as well as serving Chance), and that she considers Chance silly at best, Chance is quickly defined as an "other" in the house, before the Old Man dies. And then we see Chance spend another day at work.

Consider, then, the final draft (339). The script conveys much of the same information—Chance's working day and demeanor, Louise's presence, the existence of the Old Man—but contextually it comes across differently because of the acceleration that comes with cutting the first day. There is no conversation about the Old Man's illness. Louise's first words, after being greeted by Chance, are "He's dead, Chance! The Old Man's dead." As a result, before the viewer even has a chance to determine who Chance is, or what his living situation or role in the house are, somebody called the Old Man dies and the narrative begins, and this starts near the top of the second page. This is a fantastic example of narrative efficiency and concision that, rather than harming characters, themes, or narrative, enhances them by providing the viewer with all the necessary information while maintaining the ambiguity essential to the film's plot and thematic development.

It is not clear who made the decision to cut the opening day and Chance's first conversation with Louise. Ashby was known to have cut opening scenes in order to pare back exposition and maintain a certain amount of opacity around film protagonists. For example, the original drafts of *Shampoo* (Columbia 1975) began with Jackie (Julie Christie) and Jill (Goldie Hawn) having a discussion, over lunch, about George (Warren Beatty): what kind of lover he was and his difficulties with commitment. Ashby preferred to open the film with a scene of George making love with Felicia (Lee Grant) in the dark and then running off to the house of Jill, his other girlfriend—again "showing" us George's sexual proclivities rather than telling us via conversation.[57] On the other hand, Jones by this point was a practiced screenwriter whose past as an editor had provided him with a keen sense of timing. And the two had seven years' experience of intense collaboration together—Jones once described not being able to recall precisely whether the idea for the long dissolves in *The Last Detail* (Columbia 1973) had come from him or Ashby because they were working so closely together.[58] Whose idea it was, however, is less important than that the cut came about through the process of collaborative script revision. Building on Kosinski's very solid foundation, Jones, and then Jones and Ashby, construct an opening to the film that stays true to Kosinski's setting, true to his central protagonist, and true to the themes that pervade his novel, while at the same time crafting a more cinematic opening that trusts the audience to make their own discoveries about Chance and his life.

Such instances, both small and large, abound throughout the scripts, with Kosinski redrafting his own work (sometimes extensively, sometimes subtly), Jones reworking it further, and Jones-with-Ashby giving it additional tightening. A fascinating example of how these various iterations interact is found in the scene when Chance, now a guest at Rand's mansion under the mistaken name Chauncey Gardiner, meets the president of the

United States and gives him some "sage" advice. This scene is vital to the plot of the film as it is the president's quoting of Chance's advice on television later that day that thrusts Chance into the media spotlight and onto the world stage. One of the larger changes to occur between drafts is the description of the president. There is a show-don't-tell element to these changes, as well as a sense that "the president of the United States," the movie version, does not need a lot of description; films have taught us that anybody who can evince a stately demeanor can play the president on screen (although Jack Warden, perhaps channeling Gerald Ford, plays him more bumbling than commanding). Here are Kosinski's descriptions, first from the '71 draft:

> THE PRESIDENT, in his late fifties, is of medium height and wears a dark suit similar to the one presently worn by RAND. He seems to be a man of exceptionally rugged constitution. His head is square and his features well-molded. His voice is low, his eyes scrutinizing. He is courteous, though a bit impatient, and he expects those he talks to, to reach their point quickly and briefly.[59]

Here Kosinski engages in the sort of extended literary description that is common to his scripts. In the January '78 rewrite (see 92), he builds on that:

> THE PRESIDENT of The United States is in his late fifties, of medium height and wears a suit similar to the one RAND's wearing. A mid westerner [sic], he seems to be a man of exceptionally rugged constitution. His head is square and his features well-molded. His voice is low, his eyes scrutinizing. He is courteous, though a bit impatient, and he expects those he talks to to reach their point quickly and briefly.

These two passages are roughly the same, although in the second version, the president has become a Midwesterner. After the producers read this second draft, they sent Kosinski extensive notes (he reportedly did not like this process very much), and he reworked parts of the third draft more significantly than he had the second. Here is the July '78 entrance of the president:

> The door is being held open. THE PRESIDENT enters.[60]

That is the extent of it—no descriptions of the president's clothing, demeanor, or background and no mention of personal traits or behaviors that have not yet occurred on screen, such as expecting people with whom he speaks "to reach their point quickly." Jones takes Kosinski's final description and tweaks it slightly. In all of Kosinski's versions, including the novel, the president is brought into the room at Rand's mansion where Rand and Chance are waiting. Building on a line of dialogue in which Rand tells Chance he likes to make people wait for him, Jones has Rand and Chance go to the waiting president rather than vice versa. Here is the December '78 version (see 251):

> Rand and Chance come into the Library and the President goes
> to Rand with both hands outstretched.

And here is January '79 (see 388):

> A somewhat nervous PRESIDENT waits for Rand and Chance. When
> they enter, he goes to Rand with both hands out-stretched.

These versions do not differ significantly from Kosinski's final effort, but the subtle changes do convey differences of tone and meaning that can affect one's reaction to the scene. The president is nervous about meeting Rand—the country's economy is in difficult straits and Rand was meant to give a calming speech at a financial institute but cannot due to ill health, so the president is taking his place. He has come to Rand for economic advice, but the two do not always see eye-to-eye on such issues, so the president is at once trying to make a good impression while also gleaning from Rand some keen insights that he can include in his speech to pacify a nervous financial industry. Rand, though, is also nervous. His illness has made him weak and he does not want to appear feeble in front of the president. In Kosinski's drafts, Rand waits at his desk and rises briefly when the president enters. By having Rand enter instead, and by showing the president pacing nervously, Jones shifts the balance of power slightly in Rand's favor. One could argue that this accounts for the president's willingness to accept Chance for the man Rand takes him to be.

This willingness of the president is aided by a further subtle change that Jones makes. For much of the scene, the president and Rand discuss the state of the economy. This dialogue constantly changes from one draft to the next, with Kosinski's earlier versions relying heavily on financial and economic jargon, which gets partially edited out of each subsequent draft. Near the end of their conversation, the president asks Chance for his thoughts about the current economic situation. Kosinski changes the dialogue slightly from one draft to the next, but Chance basically says the same thing in each. For example, in January '78 (see 96):

> CHANCE stares pensively at the PRESIDENT, but his stare is
> blank. After a pause
>
>   CHANCE
>   (a thought dawns on him)
>   Yes, there's a lot of uprooting--
>   but we all know in nature
>   everything has its season: there
>   are spring and summer, but there
>   are also fall and winter.
>   (he pauses)
>   ... And then spring and summer
>   again. As long as the roots are not
>   severed and we are strong, the plants
>   survive the winter.
>
> RAND looks at CHANCE and nods his head approvingly. The
> PRESIDENT also looks at CHANCE. An engaging smile lights
> CHANCE's face.

                    PRESIDENT
             (seizes the chance to avoid
             clashing with RAND)
        I must admit, Chauncey, that what you've
        just said is one of the most refreshing
        thoughts I've heard in a very long
        time!

He rises and stands erect, his back to the fireplace, facing RAND and CHANCE:

                    PRESIDENT
             (reflecting on what CHANCE has
             just said)
        Given our understanding of its mechanics,
        our economic system remains--like
        nature, in the long run--stable and
        rational.
             (he pauses for a moment
             then turns to RAND)
        We welcome the inevitable seasons
        of nature, yet even you, the
        mighty Republicans, are so quickly
        upset by the seasons of the economy.
        The country must realize that a
        President can't cause an economic
        miracle. ...

This is the only time Chance speaks in the scene, and it is on these words of "wisdom" that the president will build his speech later in the day, which leads to Chance's fame. Jones tweaks this scene in two ways. First, he adds a silly running gag in which, every time the president or Rand says the word "chance," Chance perks up and says "yes?" Second, and more importantly, Jones splits Chance's dialogue into two segments, so it becomes a conversation with the president. Here is the version from the January '79 draft, which is virtually identical to December '78:

                    PRESIDENT
        Do you agree with Ben, Mr. Gardiner? Or
        do you think we can stimulate growth
        through temporary incentives?
                    CHANCE
             (a beat)
        As long as the roots are not severed, all is well
        and all will be well in the garden.

```
                        PRESIDENT
            (a pause)
      ... In the garden?

                        CHANCE
      That is correct. In a garden, growth has its
      season. There is spring and summer, but there
      is also fall and winter. And then spring and
      summer again ...

                        PRESIDENT
            (staring at Chance)
      ... Spring and summer ...
            (confused)
      Yes, I see ... Fall and winter.
            (smiles at Chance)
      Yes, indeed.

                        RAND
            (interrupts)
      I think what my most insightful friend is
      building up to, Mr. President, is that we
      welcome the inevitable seasons of nature, yet
      we are upset by the seasons of our economy.

                        CHANCE
      Yes. That is correct. There will be growth in
      the spring.

                        PRESIDENT
            (pleased)
      ... Well, Mr. Gardiner, I must admit, that is
      one of the most refreshing and optimistic
      statements I've heard in a very, very long
      time.
            (he rises)
      ... I envy your good, solid sense, Mr.
      Gardiner – that is precisely what we lack on
      Capitol Hill.
            (glances at watch)
      I must be going.
            (holds out hand to Chance)
      ... This visit has been most enlightening ...
```

At first glance, these changes might not seem to improve or even change the scene dramatically. In terms of information presented to us, we do not learn anything new. However, the changes represent a fine example of just how elusive the term "cinematic" can be when describing a screenplay, and also just how effectively its deployment can alter a scene in vital ways. When Chance perks up every time he hears his name (remember, the president and Rand think of him as Chauncey Gardiner), he disrupts the flow of the president's dialogue, keeping him off-balance throughout. It is silly, but it also reminds the viewer that Chance is there, in a scene where for a long stretch he has nothing else to do. More importantly though, by breaking Chance's dialogue into smaller bits, it turns what could have been a slightly daffy non sequitur into a dialogue, which allows the president to convincingly come around to accepting Chance's words as wisdom.

There are numerous scenes and sequences like this throughout all the drafts, and a student of scriptwriting would do well to examine the three drafts presented here closely. Kosinski's literary description, internal landscapes, and extensive backstories are all excised from Jones's drafts, and yet Jones displays an extensive knowledge of them and something close to reverence in the way he works incidents cut from Kosinski's descriptions into moments of dialogue or action. For example, early in the novel Kosinski describes Chance visiting the Old Man's bedroom: "Chance began walking the three flights upstairs. He did not trust the elevator since the time black Louise had been trapped in it for hours."[61] Jones takes this and reformulates it into a running gag about the elevator in Rand's mansion. Chance, never having been in one, thinks of it as a very small room. He is baffled by its lack of a television and unsure why he is meant to enter the small room, stand for a minute, then exit. Rand's butler thinks Chance is joking, and finds his seemingly put-on bafflement terribly amusing.

Scholars comparing these three drafts would benefit as much from analyzing short scenes such as this as they do the film's bigger, more obvious set pieces. The refinement of such scenes, via changes large and small, illustrates how a script can be transformed through the processes of revision and collaboration. Other scenes to analyze might include: Chance's interaction with Franklin, the lawyer who evicts him from the Old Man's house, and his assistant Ms. Hayes (as well as Franklin's treatment throughout the scripts); Chance's exit from the Old Man's house; Chance's first encounter with Eve Rand when he is struck by her limousine; Chance's first encounters with Rand; Chance's appearance on the television talk show; and Eve's several attempts to seduce Chance leading up to the scene in which he watches her masturbate. Each of these scenes has roots in the novel, thus conceived of by Kosinski. Yet all go through processes of such refinement that their deployment on screen often becomes very different than originally envisioned. An important question that can guide analysis of these changes might be whether the changes make the sequences more cinematic. The answer might not necessarily be "yes." But if it is, what makes them more cinematic—which elements, developed by Kosinski himself or by Jones, mold the sequences in such a way that Ashby (and Braunsberg) would decide that now it was ready for filming? To return to Epps's statement, "The reader should see the movie."[62] If this is the case, then the root question to ask is whether Kosinski's and Jones's changes make "seeing" the movie possible, and if so, how.

No discussion of *Being There* can be complete without an examination of the many iterations of its ending. The film, famously, ends with Chance walking across a pond of water on Rand's grounds, umbrella in hand, while the president's voice can be heard delivering Rand's eulogy from elsewhere on the grounds. But this ending was not scripted; rather, it was devised near the end of principal production and filmed after the scripted ending had already been shot.[63] I will look briefly at how the walking-on-water scene came about in an appendix to this book, but for now, I would like to keep the focus of discussion on the many revisions to the written, scripted ending.

Kosinski's three endings are very similar, with only minor revisions from the '71 draft through the July '78 draft. Most of these changes have to do with minor descriptions of characters and cutting or refining dialogue, and I will examine some of that shortly. It is worth noting first, though, that these scripted endings are quite different from the novel's. A significant difference results from a major change between the novel and Kosinski's scripts: in the novel, Benjamin Rand is a minor character. His presence looms throughout—he is, after all, the benefactor whose largess will assure Chance continues to live a protected life of leisure and gardening—but once he introduces Chance to the president and then orchestrates Chance's first "date" with Eve, his illness incapacitates him and he practically drops out of the latter third of the book. The novel ends with Chance and Eve at a formal ball. Chance is at once connected to Eve, but also distanced from her—he sees her "embraced by a tall, heavily decorated general," which does not seem to bother him.[64] He leaves the ballroom for the garden outside, takes a breath of fresh air, and feels at peace. Much like the scripts and film to come, there is an ambiguity about Chance's future, but he seems to have secured a place within whatever will become of Rand's household once the man passes, resulting in his peace of mind.

In Kosinski's scripts, Benjamin Rand is transformed into a central character throughout the film. Even as his health worsens, he continues to meet with Chance and discuss his future as a potential replacement for Rand in the world of business, and also as a possible partner for Eve. In Rand's final appearance in all three drafts, he explains his intention for Chance to meet some of his "friends and business associates." This penultimate scene gets progressively longer from draft to draft as Rand explains his plans for Chance's future. There are, however, two vital differences that develop through Kosinski's drafts. In the '71 version, as Rand and Chance speak, Eve remains in the room. In both drafts from '78, after the conversation begins, Rand asks Eve to leave the room before he goes into detail about his plans for Chance. In these versions, Eve's exit from this scene marks her final appearance in the film, which results in the feeling that her storyline is sloughed off completely. The second significant change concerns Rand's state of health at the end of the scene, which worsens each time Kosinski redrafts. In '71, after Chance has agreed to meet with Rand's associates, Rand simply asks his assistant to get a car ready, and the scene ends. His health, while still poor, seems steady. In January '78, as the conversation ends, "Rand's shoulders slump down and his chest seems to collapse," and the scene ends on a note of ambiguity about Rand's health that will only be resolved in the next scene when we find out he has passed away. The July '78 draft is more definitive, and a vital step toward what Jones would do with the script. As the conversation with Chance comes to an end, Rand stops speaking mid-sentence, and then: "Unable to muster more strength, he slumps down, dead." Thus, by the July '78 draft, both Benjamin and Eve Rand have been effectively excised from the film's conclusion.

While these changes are significant, the scripts also share a major narrative development with the novel. In the book, just before the action moves to Chance and Eve at the ball, there is a scene in which several new characters are introduced. A small group of important, but potentially shady, men have gathered to discuss the future of the country. They seem to be discussing a political campaign, perhaps for the presidency. One of them claims, "Duncan has decided not to run with me. That leaves us, at present, without a candidate."[65] They proceed to discuss who might be a qualified candidate for the position in question, and eventually come to the idea of Chance. They believe he would make an ideal candidate because "he has no background. And so he's not and cannot be objectionable to anyone!"[66] This leads them to the conclusion that, pun intended, "Gardiner is our one chance." That line, or a variation of it, will remain in every draft of the script as well as the finished film.

When it comes to scripting this moment, Kosinski moves it to a final scene, intercut with Chance's limousine journey to meet with the men. Dialogue and key details of this scene are tweaked by Kosinski from one draft to the next. For example, in '71, the meeting is presided over by "the president," thus making one of the novel's main secondary characters a part of the conspiracy. In January '78, this same man is described as the "Republican Candidate for president" (thus implying that the current president is a Democrat, which corresponds with his friendly but antagonistic relationship with Rand). In July '78, the man's role is not described specifically. The two '78 drafts add extensive detail. For example, the men have a lengthy discussion about the reasons for Duncan's ineligibility. They also discuss Rand's will (confirming his death), and reveal that he left half of his estate to Chance, thus removing any ambiguity about Chance's position post-film.

These men are the group of friends and business associates that Rand arranged for Chance to meet in his last act in the film, and presumably the scene is taking place in anticipation of Chance's visit. The first script cuts to Chance three times, while both '78 drafts cut to him four times. He is driven in one of Rand's limos, arrives at the grounds, and walks among greenery outside the house—a garden in the first two drafts, and inside a conservatory in the final draft. Each draft ends with a close-up of Chance smiling enigmatically directly into the camera. This ending, with the shady businessmen discussing Chance's future, and, indeed, the future of the United States, provides key narrative and thematic closure to the film. Chance, in his inadvertent disguise, has now duped everybody—even the oligarchy, the power behind the power, has fallen for the ruse and is willing to place Chance in a central position of American political and financial power. That Chance has little experience seems not to matter to them at all, and if they were to find out about his cognitive difficulties, one can assume that probably would not matter either; if the president or vice president is their puppet, mental deficiency might even be regarded as a desirable quality, making him easier to manipulate (as long, of course, as enough of the American populace can remained convinced of his brilliance). Thus, by the end of these drafts, some of Kosinski's key thematic ideas have come to fruition: the pervasiveness of television, the manipulation of the people, and derision about the decline of serious thinking in the United States.

However, these drafts lack cinematic and narrative resolution. First, by introducing several new characters with very little context, the scripts blunt the dramatic force of Chance's resolution with Rand in the previous scene. The intercutting with Chance's arrival at the house shows an awareness of cinematic possibility, but Chance has so little to do in his scenes that they are rendered visually staid and the narrative thrust rapidly dissipates (one could argue the same happens in the novel). By abandoning Rand, Eve, and their mansion, the ending forgoes the possibility of providing closure to some of the major strands of character and narrative.

Jones's scripts solve these issues in ingenious fashion. Building on Rand's definitive death in the July '78 script, Jones sets the long final sequence at Rand's funeral, which takes place at a mausoleum on his own private grounds. Visually, this creates the opportunity for more striking imagery than a dark room and Chance in the back of a limo. In terms of narrative, it allows for a clearer resolution of Rand's storyline, while also making room for final appearances by Eve, Dr. Allenby, and the president. The latter reads Rand's eulogy, including a selection of aphorisms from Rand's personal diary, which also provides a more intimate closure to Rand's character arc. During the funeral, Chance gets up from his seat and wanders away, walking across the grounds until he comes to a small wood, where he attends to some plants struggling to survive the winter. Eventually, concerned for Chance's well-being, Eve searches the grounds for him. She finds Chance, they embrace, she tells him she has been looking for him, and he tells her, "I've been looking for you, too, Eve." They embrace one more time, and the film ends. This ending provides closure for Rand (and some of his household staff, minor characters who can be seen at the funeral), as well as a strong sense of clarity about Chance and Eve's future together, even if the details remain ambiguous.

However, there are some significant differences between the two Jones drafts that serve as instructive examples of attentive revision. First, in the December '78 draft, the president's eulogy, including Rand's aphorisms, is presented as one long speech, roughly a full page of dialogue. It begins as soon as Chance leaves the ceremony, and when the speech ends, the script cuts to a large, empty auditorium where the shady businessmen are meeting in private. Jones shortens their dialogue, but maintains the key thrust from Kosinski—the men continue to see Chance as a potential candidate because of the absence of any background information on him, and the script maintains Kosinski's pun about Chauncey Gardiner being "our only chance." The entirety of their conversation follows, also for the length of a page. Thus, during the script's closing sequence, Chance is off-screen for two minutes, including a cut to an entirely new location. The result is stagnant in its presentation.

The final draft solves this with two efficient changes. First, Jones centralizes the discussion of the shady businessmen by having them act as Rand's pallbearers. They conduct the conversation in breathless whispers as they carry Rand's casket up the steps of the mausoleum. However, rather than present it as one long dialogue, it is now intercut with the scenes of Chance leaving the funeral and the president's eulogy. This allows for dynamic movement around Rand's grounds, as the sequence cuts back and forth from Chance among the trees, Eve and Dr. Allenby at the funeral listening to the president, and the pallbearers' secret conversation. The words of the president's eulogy remain diegetic across these cuts, acting as a sound bridge to connect all the scenes temporally, up to and including the final scene of Chance and Eve's embrace, which is also significantly rewritten. In Jones's first draft, Eve waits for the funeral to end before she goes looking for Chance. She has a chat with the president and his wife, and then, with Dr. Allenby in tow, she gets into a chauffeured limousine and searches for Chance from the car. Once she finds him and they embrace, she brings him back to the car, where he shakes hands with Allenby, before they all pile in and drive off to end the film. In Jones's second draft, Eve cannot wait for the end of the funeral. She goes off on her own, and on foot, to look for Chance. When she finds him and they embrace, they are alone. As she begins to lead him back with her, the president's final reading from Rand's diary can be heard, and the film ends.

By retaining the conversation of the shady businessmen, Jones maintains the thematic closure of Kosinski's scripts, but with this funereal setting, his drafts also provide clear narrative resolutions for other key characters as well, particularly Eve. Rather than the claustrophobic confines of a dark room and the backseat of a limousine, his script provides us with movement and action, and also the opportunity to see Chance in nature, attending to plants like the gardener he is. Visually, thematically, narratively, and for key characters, the final draft provides a much more cinematic, and a much more satisfying, resolution.

Being There is a highly original film narrative with a thoughtful, funny script. It is full of unusual characters and situations both hilarious and poignant. The script also provides a subtle but scathing critique of the intermingling of American media, political, and corporate power and the way that television often absolves the public's conscience of any sense of responsibility for what those intermingled powers are doing. Importantly, the final draft is also highly readable. But it took hard, dedicated work to fashion it as such. Over several years and several drafts, two primary writers in Kosinski and Jones, with the input of Ashby, would mold it into the shape that would allow Ashby, producer Braunsberg, and the cast to "see" the film. Examining the three drafts presented in this book will provide students and scholars key insights into the process of screenplay revision. While a strong script will allow its readers to see the film, it is my hope that a close reading of this book will help anyone interested in Hollywood scriptwriting to see the process of crafting such a script.

Notes

1. Kosinski's life and career have been shrouded in controversy since soon after his arrival in the United States. His accounts of his life during the Second World War have been called into question, and he has been the subject of repeated accusations that his books were cowritten or almost completely written by his assistants and translators, and in some cases that his work was the result of plagiarizing. It is not in the purview of this text to settle those questions, but for more on them, see James Park Sloan, *Jerzy Kosinski: A Biography* (New York: Plume, 1997), particularly chapters 4, 5, and 6.
2. For more on Kosinski's forays into the nightlife of 1970s New York, see Henry Dasko, "Kosinski's Afterlife," *The Polish Review*, 49, no. 1 (2004), 700–2.
3. Sloan, *Jerzy Kosinski*, 294.
4. To name but a few, Roger Angell in the *New Yorker*, Janet Maslin in the *New York Times*, Diane Jacobs in the *Soho Weekly*, and Roger Ebert in the *Chicago Sun-Times* all gave the film rave reviews. Andrew Sarris named it one of his top ten films of 1979.
5. Jerzy Kosinski, *Being There* (unproduced screenplay), August 1971, Box 1, Folder 2, Hal Ashby Papers, Margaret Herrick Library, Los Angeles.
6. A Yale University drama department catalogue from 1972 describes one of Kosinski's courses:

DRAMA 17, *The Temptation to Create: Film and Fiction*. This seminar will analyze the aesthetic processes involved in creating fiction and film. It will attempt to differentiate the ways of abstracting reality and aim at providing examples of those processes. Analyses will be made of the new "cinematic prose" of novels made into films, of the screenplay as metaphor, and of the evocative properties of both fiction and the world of film. Mr. Kosinski, *Bulletin of Yale University School of Drama*, Series 68, Number 12, June 15, 1972, 56.

7 Kosinski, *Being There* (unproduced screenplay), August 1971, cover page.
8 For example, early in a course titled *Death and the Modern Imagination*, Kosinski announced that by the end of the course, one of the students would be required to die. For other examples, see Sloan, *Jerzy Kosinski*, 300–4.
9 Ibid., 298.
10 For various versions of the early efforts to produce a film of *Being There*, see: Christopher Beach, *The Films of Hal Ashby* (2009), 35; Nick Dawson, *Being Hal Ashby: Life of a Hollywood Rebel* (2009), 147–8; Aaron Hunter, *Authoring Hal Ashby: The Myth of the New Hollywood Auteur* (2016), 125–7; Ed Sikov, *Mr Strangelove: A Biography of Peter Sellers* (2002), 317; Sloan, *Jerzy Kosinski*, 298–9.
11 See Sloan, *Jerzy Kosinski*, 291–2.
12 Dawson, *Being Hal Ashby*, 202.
13 The novel and Kosinski's first two drafts set events in Manhattan, and only with his third draft does the setting change to Washington, DC. According to most accounts, it was Ashby and his team (particularly production designer Mike Haller) who decided the film would benefit from a DC setting. However, as Sloan points out, Kosinski afterward took credit for the idea, as he would for many of the changes that Ashby, Haller, and screenwriter Robert C. Jones would make to the script. See Dawson, *Being Hal Ashby*, 208–9; and Sloan, *Jerzy Kosinski*, 348.
14 Hal Ashby, interview by Jordan R. Young and Mike Bruns (1980), *Hal Ashby Interviews*, ed. Nick Dawson (Jackson: University Press of Mississippi, 2010), 100.
15 Ibid.
16 Ibid.
17 Noël Carrol, *The Philosophy of Motion Pictures* (London: Blackwell, 2008), 69.
18 Ted Nannicelli, "Why Can't Screenplays Be Artworks?," *Journal of Aesthetics and Art Criticism*, 69, no. 4 (Fall 2011), 412.
19 I would love to take credit for this fantastic portmanteau word, but I first heard it from film scholar Catherine Grant in her video essay "The Haunting of *The Headless Woman*," *tecmerin multimedia*, no. 2, July 2019.
20 Gruner details the writer–director relationship—Waldo Salt and John Schlesinger—and how it informs the scripting process for *Midnight Cowboy* (United Artists 1969), as well as how that process was informed by James Leo Herlihy's original 1965 novel, 259–64.
21 Field's uses of this expression are too numerous for one citation, but see, e.g., the chapter "About Structure," in Syd Field, *The Screenwriter's Workbook* (New York: Delta, 2006), 26–41.
22 Blake Snyder, *Save the Cat: The Last Book on Screenwriting You'll Ever Need* (Studio City, CA: Michael Wiese Productions, 2005), 69.
23 Ibid., 70.
24 J. J. Murphy, *Me and You and Memento and Fargo: How Independent Screenplays Work* (New York: Continuum, 2007), 6.

25 Sometimes comically so, as in Snyder's frustrated exhortation, "screw *Memento*!" Snyder, *Save the Cat*, 91.
26 Field, *Screenwriter's Workbook*, 28.
27 Murphy, *Me and You and Memento and Fargo*, 100.
28 Steven Price, *A History of the Screenplay* (London: Palgrave Macmillan, 2013), 6.
29 See also Janet Staiger, "The Hollywood Mode of Production to 1930" and "The Hollywood Mode of Production 1930–1960," in *The Classical Hollywood Cinema: Film Style and the Mode of Production to 1960*, ed. David Bordwell, Janet Staiger, and Kristen Thompson (London: Routledge, 2002).
30 Janet Staiger, "Blueprints for Feature Films: Hollywood's Continuity Scripts," in *The American Film Industry*, ed. Tino Balio (Madison: University of Wisconsin Press, 1985), 178.
31 Price, *History of the Screenplay*, 6–7; and Staiger, "The Hollywood Mode of Production to 1930" and "The Hollywood Mode of Production 1930–1960," 85–155, 309–39.
32 Price, *History of the Screenplay*, 184.
33 Ibid., 9, 203.
34 Ibid., 236.
35 Several other scholars and critics have also performed valuable research on the history of the screenplay and its relationship to films and film production. See, e.g., Lizzie Francke, *Script Girls: Women Screenwriters in Hollywood* (London: BFI, 1994); Jill Nelmes, ed., *Analysing the Screenplay* (London: Routledge, 2011); Marc Norman, *What Happens Next: A History of American Screenwriting* (New York: Three Rivers Press, 2008); Tom Stempel, *Framework: A History of Screenwriting in the American Film* (1988), 3rd ed. (Syracuse, NY: Syracuse University Press, 2000).
36 There are, of course, exceptions—films in Hollywood history that entered production without completed scripts. These instances are rare, and the films they produce are generally seen as inferior. But there are also examples where filming began without a completed, locked script only to produce a successful film, from the serious drama of *Coming Home* (United 1979) to the blockbuster extravaganza of the first *Iron Man* (Marvel/Paramount 2008).
37 Ernest Hemingway, "The Art of Fiction No. 21," interview by George Plimpton, *The Paris Review*, 18 (Spring 1958), https://www.theparisreview.org/interviews/4825/the-art-of-fiction-no-21-ernest-hemingway.
38 Jack Boozer, *Authorship in Film Adaptation* (Austin: University of Texas Press, 2008), 5.
39 See Noël Carrol, "Defining the Moving Image," in *Philosophy of Film and Motion Pictures*, ed. Noël Carrol and Jinhee Choi (Malden, MA: Blackwell, 2006), 113–34; and Noël Carrol, *The Philosophy of Motion Pictures* (London: Blackwell, 2008).
40 Nannicelli, "Why Can't Screenplays Be Artworks?," 405–14.
41 Ted Nannicelli, "The Ontology and Literary Status of the Screenplay: The Case of 'Scriptfic,'" *Journal of Literary Theory*, 7, no. 1–2 (2013), 135–53.
42 Ibid., 138.
43 Ibid., 152.
44 Jack Epps Jr., *Screenwriting Is Rewriting: The Art and Craft of Professional Revision* (New York: Bloomsbury Academic, 2016), 3.
45 Ibid., 7.
46 Ibid., 4.

47 Price describes the evolution of the script's form as "being a matter for discussion between individuals, especially the writer, producer and director," 7.
48 Boozer, *Authorship in Film Adaptation*, 3.
49 For example, Mary Lazar's comparative analysis of the novel and film does not mention Bob Jones's contributions to the script and attributes every change between novel and film to Kosinski. Mary Lazar, "Jerzy Kosinsk's Being There, Novel and Film: Changes Not by Chance," *College Literature*, 31, no. 2 (2004), 99–116.
50 Epps, *Screenwriting Is Rewriting*, 230.
51 Ibid., 230–1.
52 James Chapman and Nicholas J. Cull provide useful insight into how a script's political undertones can shift dramatically over time, particularly when written against a backdrop of rapid historical and political change, in their chapter on John Huston's *The Man Who Would Be King*. James Chapman and Nicholas J. Cull, *Projecting Empire: Imperialism and Popular Cinema* (London: I.B. Tauris, 2009), 153–69.
53 Jerzy Kosinski, *Being There* (London: Black Swan, [1970] 1983), 9.
54 Jerzy Kosinski, *Being There* (unproduced screenplay), August 1971, Box 1, Folder 2, Hal Ashby Papers, Margaret Herrick Library, Los Angeles, 1–3.
55 This seems to have derived from an idea first suggested by Ashby's longtime production designer, Mike Haller; see Dawson, *Being Hal Ashby*, 208–9.
56 Kosinski, *Being There* (novel), 11.
57 For more on the script development of *Shampoo*, see Dawson, *Being Hall Ashby*, 152–64; and Peter Biskind, *Star: The Life and Wild Times of Warren Beatty* (London: Simon & Schuster, 2010), 185–6. See also, *Shampoo*, undated screenplay, Box 60, Folder 660, Hal Ashby Papers, Margaret Herrick Library, Los Angeles; and *Shampoo*, draft April 9, 1974, Box 60, Folder 664, Hal Ashby Papers, Margaret Herrick Library, Los Angeles.
58 Robert C. Jones, personal interview, Los Angeles, January 28, 2009.
59 Kosinski, *Being There*, screenplay, August 1971, 56.
60 Jerzy Kosinski, *Being There* (unproduced screenplay), July 1978, Box 1, Folder 2, Hal Ashby Papers, Margaret Herrick Library, Los Angeles, 59.
61 Kosinski, *Being There*, novel, 11.
62 Epps, *Screenwriting Is Rewriting*, 230.
63 This ending, based on Jones's January 1979 draft, is available as an extra on the Criterion Collection Blu-Ray of *Being There*.
64 Kosinski, *Being There*, novel, 104–5.
65 Ibid., 103.
66 Ibid., 104.

1

Jerzy Kosinski: January 1978

Introduction

Jerzy Kosinski wrote at least three drafts of the *Being There* script: the first, from August 1971, a spec script that he hoped would raise interest in a film production, but also used for a course he was teaching at Yale University on film adaptation; the second, from January 1978, which was his first submission to the *Being There* film production team; and a final one, from July of 1978. This latter included substantial revisions of the January draft, but even with those changes he did not satisfy the film's director, Hal Ashby, or his production team, who soon after requested the assistance of Bob Jones to rewrite the script and craft something more cinematic. Each of Kosinski's drafts offers insights for the screenwriting student or professional. His process of adaptation, his revision of his own first draft, and his response to the notes from Ashby and his production crew reveal a writer at first superficially familiar with the mechanics of screenwriting but unfamiliar with screenplay form and structure. As the film becomes a reality and then moves closer to production, Kosinski's reworked drafts begin to show a more thorough understanding of the requirements of Hollywood screenwriting. He sheds much, if not all, of his propensity to direct within the script—abandoning specific camera movements and editing choices and minimizing parenthetical acting directions.

For this book, I have chosen to include the middle draft, from January of 1978. Space permitting, it would be instructive to include the July '78 draft as well. That later draft displays Kosinki's most serious efforts to craft a script according to the demands of the production team.[1] For that reason, I was tempted to include it rather than the January draft; however, without the context of Kosinski's earlier stabs at the script, the revisions that come later—at the hands of both Kosinski and Jones—are more difficult to qualify. Thus, I chose to go ahead with the January draft for several reasons.

First of all, the January draft displays Kosinski's grandest vision for what a *Being There* film might look like. Rather than limit his story to the simple fable of Chance's stumble through the corridors of American power, Kosinski chooses to cast that narrative against a backdrop of national strife, riven with revolutionary fervor. The action regularly cuts away from Chance and his relationship with the Rands to scenes of social and political unrest, including protests at Rand factories and businesses. These instincts are not necessarily "bad"—the nation was in the midst of a tumultuous era at the end of the 1970s that would lead to the Reagan "revolution" just a year later. However, these additions must have come as something of a shock to a production team planning to make a film centered on the more localized narrative of Chance and the Rands, as depicted in the novel and in Kosinski's first draft from '71. In addition to moving the focus of attention away from Chance, these embellishments also slow the film's pace to a significant extent. As mentioned in the Introduction, it takes nearly twenty pages to get to the Old Man's death, whereas the novel makes it there in four pages. This padding likely led Ashby to believe that Kosinski did not have faith in the protagonist he had created

Furthermore, as mentioned previously, other cutaways expend abundant time on the biographies and backgrounds of secondary figures, both major and minor. For example, the script depicts Secret Service agents in extensive discussions about the route the president's motorcade will take when he visits New York (where the action is still set), as well as detailed descriptions of the lawyer Franklin and his wife arguing as they try to sell their car. It seems clear that Kosinski's aim with such scenes is to broaden the world of the film, to create a more lived-in universe. And to be sure, certain films benefit from efforts to include such cultural and historical context. In the case of *Being There*, however, they serve more to diminish the ethereality of the fable. Early in the novel, Kosinski describes the effect that watching TV has on Chance: "He sank into the screen. Like sunlight and fresh air and mild rain, the world from outside the garden entered Chance, and Chance, like a TV image, floated into the world, buoyed up by a force he did not see and could not name."[2] This sense of Chance floating, through the script, through the worlds of those he encounters, even through the screen into the thoughts and reactions of the film's viewers, is diminished by the inclusion of so much extraneous material.

This leads to a final reason for including this draft of the script, which is that the differences between it and Jones's draft are more dramatic than either of Kosinski's other two drafts. All three of his drafts have much in common—despite some editing and tweaking, the openings are very similar and the endings are virtually the same—but this draft offers the clearest example of how fundamental revision is to the process of screenwriting. Once the deal was made for *Being There* to go into production, this is the draft that Kosinski submitted—this is the version he thought best suited for a film production. Just over a year later, principal photography began on the film, and while the contours of its major narrative beats remain quite similar, the film that was shot is strikingly different in many ways from the film this draft would have birthed. Thus, it serves as an exemplary model of how an appealing, even very strong, idea for a film can benefit from the process of collaborative revision.[3]

BEING THERE

a screenplay

by

JERZY KOSINSKI

(c) Jerzy Kosinski
All Rights Reserved.

Inspired by the novel
BEING THERE by Jerzy Kosinski (c) 1971

Property of:
Jerzy Kosinski
c/o SCIENTIA-FACTUM, INC.   FIRST DRAFT
60 West 57th street,
New York, New York 10019   January 27, 1978

Not for reproduction, circulation
publication or distribution.
ALL RIGHTS RESERVED TO THE AUTHOR © 1977

BEING THERE

PRE-CREDITS

1. EXT: TOWNHOUSE GARDEN   DAY

Early Spring.

Period: The United States of the near future. NOTE: To preserve the character of this story nothing in it should identify the period too closely. Avoid stressing current fashion, car vintages, etc.

A typical, medium-size townhouse garden, dense with lovely greenery, still common to Manhattan's best residential areas. At the rear of the TOWNHOUSE, there are trees, a lot of bushes, but as yet no flowers in the garden. The trees are at least thirty years old.

The TOWNHOUSE was built around 1910 in a style reminiscent of English and French domestic architecture of the 18th century. Its imposing facade, its window sills and its immense main door are of the same period. The exterior of the TOWNHOUSE has clearly not been cleaned since it was built. There are curtains visible in the windows, and the brass fixtures of the main door are brightly polished.

An old, high brick wall, at least one story high, surrounds the garden. A solid iron gate as high as the wall is locked. Its corroded locks look as if the gate has never been opened.

Shown from above, a multi-directional TV antenna is protruding from the roof of the TOWNHOUSE; it looks almost out of proportion to the roof. Below stretches an exquisite Manhattan street, somewhere in the East Seventies with Park Avenue next to it. Central Park and the easily identifiable panorama of New York are in the background.

END PRE-CREDITS

A MAN strolls without apparent direction down the peaceful walkways of the TOWNHOUSE GARDEN.

CREDITS BEGIN

The MAN wears dark sunglasses and is dressed in a very well-tailored suit of plain dark cloth. Over his white shirt he wears a tie and vest. His wardrobe is of the fashion of the twenties; it looks quite up-to-date now. The MAN is also wearing gardening gloves and a gardener's apron over his suit.

His hands in gloves gently touch the newly emerged leaves as if testing their rigidity. He does the same with a new sprout of a branch. Now and then he carefully removes an old piece of bark or a dead leaf.

2. EXT. RAND TOOL FACTORY   DAY

(Few frames only) A surging crowd of unemployed men and women angrily besiege the Rand Factory somewhere in the U.S. The sign on the factory's gate declares: CLOSED. Many workers carry posters "BREAD AND WORK" "ENERGY CRISIS? NO!--LEADERSHIP CRISIS? YES!"; "WHITE HOUSE--OUT HOUSE!"; "NATIONALIZE RAND INDUSTRIES--NOW!" Heavy helmeted police riot units with protective shields and submachine guns stand at the ready. Behind them long lines of ambulances and chartered buses. On the side, a few TV crews calmly film the event.

3. EXT. TOWNHOUSE GARDEN   DAY
(Continued from Scene 1)

Three modern, brightly painted sprinklers are splashing water in various parts of the garden, as the MAN passes them by.

CREDITS CONTINUE

The MAN--this is CHANCE: He is tall, at least five feet eleven inches, approximately thirty-five to forty years old, fair, and masculine. CHANCE is a charismatic figure and his charisma is obvious to anyone. His pure looks are of those few blessed by good health, balanced and peaceful disposition and trust in what comes next in life.

In terms of his appearance and manner, CHANCE is an incarnation of the U.S. Corporate man's visual ideal.

The actor portraying CHANCE cannot display any scars, or artificial teeth, or any sign indicating that he ever received medical assistance. CHANCE always walks very erect, yet is not rigid. CHANCE personifies health, both physical and mental. He has all his hair, doesn't wear eyeglasses; he speaks contemporary American English, with no trace of any regional accent or idiom. Whatever CHANCE does, whether alone or with others, or in front of others, talking or being talked to, he does it effortlessly, almost casually; his face never shows any sign of profound interest in what he is engaged in at the moment, no emotion being absorbed. Even when CHANCE watches TV, and as often as he does, it appears he is not really watching it, but merely acknowledges its presence. Yet, CHANCE never projects an image of being rude or inattentive; if anything he is rather pensive, perhaps reflecting on what has taken place, perhaps pondering his reactions. He smiles easily, very often, and his <u>smile</u> is extremely natural, open-faced and <u>engaging</u>.

This <u>engaging</u> facet of his smile appears whenever CHANCE is confronted by a situation he had not experienced before. A repeating, sweet and gentle <u>music motif</u> appears from time to time when CHANCE is smiling, reinforcing the impact of CHANCE's charisma and his influence on us all. CHANCE's charisma and <u>his instant impact on others</u> are the most essential dramatic elements of the credibility of this story. The convincing charisma of this actor is crucial to making <u>Being There</u> convincing.

From time to time CHANCE looks toward the sky as if checking the time, then turns around and walks toward the rear of the TOWNHOUSE. On the way CHANCE turns off all the sprinklers.

                                                                          CUT TO:

4.   EXT. SUBURBIA   DAY

(Few frames only) A suburban scene: against a hazy Manhattan skyline, a never-ending row of hundreds of small low-income houses; each house with a pathetic mock of a garden. Pointing toward the community, a large road sign reads: BENJAMIN RAND HOUSING PROJECT.

                                                                          CUT TO:

5.   EXT. TOWNHOUSE GARDEN   DAY
     (Continued from Scene 1)

As CHANCE walks toward it, the rear of the TOWNHOUSE is now clearly visible. It is of the same quality as the front: there is only one door leading to the garden and a single large window on the ground floor next to the door. This is where CHANCE's quarters are. Once again CHANCE looks back at his garden. It is beautiful, quiet, bright and very green.

<u>CREDITS END</u>

                                                                          CUT TO:

6.   INT. HOSPITAL EMERGENCY ROOM   DAY

(Few frames only) After yet another urban disaster, about a dozen blood-covered, wounded men and women are brought in by police and firemen in rapid succession.

CUT TO:

7.   EXT. TOWNHOUSE GARDEN   DAY
(Continued from Scene 1)

CHANCE leaves his garden; he opens the door and enters the TOWNHOUSE.

CUT TO:

8.   INT. CHANCE'S QUARTERS   DAY

CHANCE is entering his room; its window looking out to the garden from which CHANCE has just come.

CHANCE takes off his gloves, his apron and his dark glasses, and opens the doors of a large wardrobe.

CUT TO:

9.   INT. WHITE HOUSE OFFICE OF THE SPECIAL ASSISTANTS TO THE PRESIDENT   DAY

A White House office of the Special Assistants to the President is in direct proximity to the office of the National Security Adviser, and to the Oval Room. It is furnished with numbers of files, two solid desks, several leather armchairs, a comfortable sofa, several elaborate telephones each equipped with a tape recorder, and three large TV sets, each one with its own system to tape and to monitor several channels at once.

BOB and JOHN, two special assistants to the President are planning the President's forthcoming trip to New York. BOB is black, in his early thirties; a dynamic, handsome man who exudes confidence on his way up, and a bit of a colorful dresser. JOHN is white, in his late thirties; and efficient executive type, dresses with casual restraint. JOHN in shirt with rolled up sleeves, is returning to his office, passing the Oval Room, the office of the National Security Adviser and enters the door to the office marked; "BOB D. FERGUSSON JOHN F. MORGAN SPECIAL ASSISTANTS".

Inside BOB is leaning over a detailed map of New York spread all over his desk cluttered with documents. JOHN passes him by on the way to one of the phones.

>   BOB
>   (to John)
>   There y'are! It's all set.
>   (he points at the map)
>   To avoid the demonstrations, from
>   Kennedy the Boss will take a
>   helicopter straight to Central
>   Park. From there--
>   (he glances at the map)
>   a six-minute drive through the
>   park to Park Avenue, then only
>   five blocks to the Financial
>   Institute ... The park will be
>   closed to the public, the five
>   blocks of Park Avenue triple
>   cordoned ...
>   (he lights up)
>   You know how these demonstrations
>   by the unemployed upset him! He
>   feels betrayed by them. Is it <u>his</u>
>   fault they are out of work?
>   (pauses)
>   Bu this time, there will be no
>   chance that the BOSS will even
>   hear their shouts!
>
>   JOHN
>   (a bit pensively)
>   Don't say that! There's always a
>   chance!

He reaches for the phone.

                                                    CUT TO:

10.   INT: CHANCE'S QUARTERS   DAY
      (Continued from Scene 8)

Inside the wardrobe are several suits, three or four pairs of gardening gloves on one shelf and a pile of freshly laundered shirts on another. CHANCE neatly places his gloves and apron in the wardrobe. He closes the wardrobe and turns toward the center of the room.

                                                    CUT TO:

11. INT: PUBLIC LIBRARY   DAY

   (Few frames only) An imposing, old-fashioned reading room of about 100 tables; every table occupied by a reader. Noiselessly, the librarians move around to deliver and pick up books. Relief on the marble wall reads: BENJAMIN RAND MEMORIAL LIBRARY.

   CUT TO:

12. INT: CHANCE'S QUARTERS   DAY
    (Continued from Scene 8)

   CHANCE walks through the room. It is a medium-size room, with a high ceiling. The furniture is large and heavy, of the Victorian style. A large brass (or copper) bed, dominates the room; it is neatly made. IN front of it is a heavy oak table with two heavy oak chairs. On a big oak chest of drawers sits the largest available modern TV set. The set is placed directly across from the bed and from the table. On the wall hang four old-fashioned Currier-and-Ives type lithographs depicting the four seasons: Spring, Summer, Fall, Winter. (The scenes dipicted [sic] in the lithographs should be limited to nature only--i.e., trees, flowers, hedges and snow, and the drawings are of a crude quality). To one side of the room a door is slightly ajar. Through the open door a sink and part of a bathtub can be seen; it is apparent that it is CHANCE's bathroom.

   CUT TO:

13. EXT. SLUMS   DAY

   (Few frames only) A skid row of addicts lined up and lolling about on a typical Bowery section of Manhattan. Some are young, some old, all displaying the tragic marks of defeat by life, the sense of which they had never been able to master. In the background towers a large modern building. The sign over the entrance reads: BENJAMIN AND EVE RAND REHABILITATION CENTER.

   CUT TO:

14. INT: CHANCE'S QUARTERS DAY
    (Continued from Scene 8)

   CHANCE walks toward the table and on his way he picks up the remote-control element from the TV set. He sits down on one of the chairs at the table directly facing the TV set, his hand on the table top, holding the remote control. His expression is blank.

CUT TO:

15. INT. NEW YORK RESTAURANT DAY

A "chic" midtown French restaurant. Luncheon. At one of the best tables, four white ladies enjoy their lunch. They are all in their late thirties, and early forties, dressed and bejeweled with solid elegance available to society's privileged few.

As the waitress and maitre d' serve them, the conversation now centers around and is directed to one of the LADIES. She is SOPHIE.

SOPHIE, is a slightly fat but still very feminine and beautiful woman in her forties, with an extreme decolletage, revealing a more than ample, firm bosom. She is heavily jeweled.

LADY NO. 1 A natural redhead, speaks with a slight French accent, to SOPHIE.

> LADY NO. 1
> And Benjamin Rand?--will he be as active in this election as he was in the last one?

The other LADIES turn to SOPHIE, suddenly curious.

> SOPHIE
> (replaces a glass of wine.
> She pretends to hesitate
> about whether to tell
> the truth)
> Benjamin Rand? Honestly I doubt it.

She sips her wine. The other LADIES are waiting to hear more from her.

> SOPHIE
> Benjamin has been taken to the hospital.
> (pauses, then ominously)
> For the last time, I think!

LADY NO. 2, an exotic beauty with a touch of gray in her dark hair. To SOPHIE, concerned but firm in her advice.

                    LADY NO. 2
               (with jealousy)
          Does this mean that our beautiful
          Elizabeth Eve Rand will soon
          inherit <u>all</u>?

                    SOPHIE
               (with wisdom)
          Who knows? But my dear, as the
          French say, "leave everything to
          Chance!"

                                                       CUT TO:

16. EXT. MANHATTAN STREET   DAY

     (Few frames only) Subway entrance and exit that services a
     gigantic modern building. Early morning. A mass of humanity
     enters the subway; a mass of humanity pours out of it onto the
     marble plaza in front of the building and is slowly swallowed
     by the giant entrance to the building. On the building: on a
     marble plate the sign: RAND BANK AND TRADE CENTER. The huge
     relief in the marble of the plaza: BENJAMIN RAND PLAZA.

                                                       CUT TO:

17. INT: FAMILY ROOM.   EVENING

     (Few frames only) A typical suburban low-income white middle
     class family room. Large TV (of the Sony-Advent video type)
     screen dominates the room's center. Watching it is the FATHER,
     a worn out, pale, baldish man in his thirties, who has just
     finished his TV dinner and pushed the tray aside, the MOTHER
     a stocky, plump woman with her hair-do stiffly lacquered into
     place, who is still eating.

     On the screen a <u>StarTrek</u>'s [*sic*] Dr. Spock-like character,
     is addressing a large gathering of peaceful Martians all
     waving American flags. To the right of the room, DAUGHTER NO.
     1, six years old, with pig-tails still eating her TV dinner
     is watching her own small size color TV set. On the screen,
     a cartoon bird just flattened by a car happily gets up,
     completely unharmed To the right of the room, DAUGHTER NO.
     2, bespectacled twelve year old, still eating her TV dinner
     is watching her own medium size color TV. On the screen, a
     handsome Clint Eastwood <u>Magnum Force</u> type character calmly
     slaps a dizzy blonde across her face.

                                                       CUT TO:

18. INT: CHANCE'S QUARTERS   DAY
    (Continued from Scene 8)

    CHANCE's fingers press the remote-control buttons.

    SOUND: CLICK of the activated TV remote-control.

    As CHANCE is looking directly into the TV set, we see his face as if he looked straight at us. He is peaceful and composed, almost expressionless. His stare is direct, almost vacant; his eyes blink occasionally.

    CUT TO:

19. INT: MODERN DEPARTMENT STORE   DAY

    (Few frames long fragment) On a floor of a large New York department store, at the Video Equipment Counter, a handsome middle-aged man flirts with a young and attractive salesgirl, perhaps his mistress. He moves closer to the counter, and in a moment of charged sexuality, he and the girl without upsetting their composures, discreetly touch and fondle each other.

    The latest Betamax-like tripple [sic] screen video recorder placed on the counter for advertising purposes is turned on, calmly filming the unsuspecting lovers and transmitting their image to all its three screens above the counter. Several passing customers having the choice to watch "live" the couple or the TV screen out of habit, keep watching the screen, involuntarily respecting the couple's intimacy.

    A large inscription on the wall identifies the establishment as RAND DEPARTMENT STORE--WORLD's LARGEST

    CUT TO:

20. INT: CHANCE'S QUARTERS   DAY
    (Continued from Scene 8)

    SOUND: TV AUDIO. CLICK. CHANCE's face does not react as he changes the channel. Variety show. The sound of laughter and audience applause, then laughter again.

    SOUND: TV AUDIO. CLICK. News program:

    >   NEWSCASTER (V.O.)
    > The heads of seventeen states are
    > meeting today in Washington. The
    > final reception and the morning
    > parting scene took place in the
    > White House garden.

As CHANCE keeps watching, TV NEWS now portrays several
distinguished heads of state at an international gathering.
The meeting has just ended. All heads of state are shaking
each other's hands in an exaggerated manner of friendship
and understanding. To catch the spirit of the meeting, the
TV news camera cuts to the scene of the clasped hands only;
in rapid succession, several handshakes are portrayed; some
heads of state use both hands to greet each other. CHANCE
looks thoughtful: the scene seems to have "sunk in" his mind.
Almost involuntarily affecting such a handshake CHANCE grips
one hand with his other one.

After a long moment CHANCE finally changes the channel.

CUT TO:

21. INT: CORPORATE CONFERENCE ROOM   DAY

A spectacular, oval shaped room of the Wall Street corporate
headquarters of The First American Financial Corporation.
The room's oval panoramic windows overlook Manhattan and the
sea. In the center an oval-shaped solid marble table with
twelve red-leather upholstered chairs. On the wall a life-
size magnificently framed portrait of Benjamin Rand (in his
sixties), the Corporation's current Chairman of the Board
(for Rand's looks see Scene)[sic]. Around the room slightly
smaller in size portraits of the recent Republican Presidents
of the United States with easily recognizeable [sic] Dwight
D. Eisenhower, Richard Nixon and Gerald Ford.

Three distinguished looking, middle-aged, well mannered [sic]
ARAB sheiks MEN, all turbaned and gowned, are hiding their
anxiousness; drinking coffee from small gold-plated cups; or
pacing the room, pretending to look at the portraits, or the
view through the windows. The ARAB BUSINESSMEN are tense and
nervous; they're glancing at the room's imposing oak door,
waiting.

MRS AUBREY enters.

Mrs. AUBREY is RAND's corporate personal secretary. She has
been with RAND at the First American Financial Corporation
for many years, and since the onset of his illness, she has
continued to work for him at this apartment. She has the old-
fashioned secretarial look; she is a slender spinster in her
fifties, always wears dark suits or dresses, usually trimmed
with white--i.e., White collar and cuffs, scarf, flower, etc.

                    AUBREY
              (energetically, as if
              ready to make an
              announcement.)
    Gentlemen!
              (she corrects herself
              quickly)
    Your Highnesses!

Unable to hide their impatience, ARAB SHEIKS gather around her, anxious to hear the news.

                    ARAB NO.1
              (bespectacled, youthful,
              in his forties, speaks
              with over pronounced
              Oxford accent. To MRS
              AUBREY)
    How is our dear friend, Benjamin?

                    AUBREY
              (in a business tone, her
              manner unchanged)
    It's all in the hands of our Lord.

                    ARAB NO.2
              (middle-aged, portly, very
              presentable, speaks with
              Harvard accent)
    Is it really that bad?

                    ARAB NO.3
              (the oldest of the three,
              tall and bony, speaks
              with a high-pitched
              Arabic-English)
    Has our most dear friend Benjamin--
              (raises his eyes,
              murmuring)
    Let Allah protect him
              (pauses, repeats slowly)
    Has our most beloved friend, Benjamin already appointed his successor?
              (raises his eyes,
               murmuring)
    Let Allah protect him too!

                    AUBREY
                (determined to make it
                 brief)
            Mr. Rand has not chosen, at this
            time, to chose [*sic*] his successor.
                (she pauses, then continues
                 in a stern manner)
            But your Highnesses might rest
            assured that whatever his decision,
            Mr. Rand will leave nothing
            to chance!

Nodding politely, the ARAB SHEIKS look at each other with despair.

                                                CUT TO:

22.   INT: CHANCE'S QUARTERS   DAY
        (Continued from Scene 8)

SOUND: TV AUDIO: A scene from a soap opera. As CHANCE keeps watching it, TV portrays a middle-aged businessman and his beautiful young wife dining in their elegant home. Two servants serve the meal. Inadvertently, the man drops his fork on the floor. The man picks up the fork and hands it to one of the servants. The servant takes the fork away and returns with a fresh one on a silver tray. The man picks up the fork and resumes eating. CHANCE looks thoughtful, the scene seems to have "sunk in" in his mind.

SOUND: A knock at the door--the TV SOUND is lowered.

CHANCE turns toward the door.

                    CHANCE
                Come in.

GERTRUDE, the maid enters. She is in her fifties, short, amply built, with chubby, rosy cheeks. She wears a white, heavily starched uniform. She is carrying a tray and speaks with a very strong German accent.

                    GERTRUDE
                (rigidly)
            Good morning. Here is your lunch.
            Good appetite.

She puts it in front of him.

                        CHANCE
                    (politely)
                Thank you.

23.   EXT. NEW YORK CAR DEALER   DAY

    A large car dealer outdoor display yard. Large sign
    above: GALAXY AUTO SALES, INC. A DIVISION OF RAND INDUSTRIES.
    In the background, the gasoline pump with the gas price
    sticker on its top, "GAS-REGULAR $3. gallon PREMIUM $3.75/
    gallon". In the yard, dozens upon dozens of big U.S. And
    foreign used and new cars are displayed with large price
    stickers standing on their roofs. Seen from afar, the year and
    make of cars are not readily identifiable. All stickers claim
    prices cut by 60-80%, all encourage sales for "only $5 down,
    $5 for the first month."

    A long line of about twelve cars driven by men and women who
    want to sell them has formed at the entrance to the yard. They
    are all middle class, rather well-dressed--yet anxious to get
    rid of the cars they can't afford to keep any longer. As they
    drive into the yard, FIVE DEALERS, three white, two black, all
    middle-aged, paunchy and tired, are handling the customers.
    The DEALERS are clearly reluctant to buy used cars when they
    can't sell their own stock.

    A couple has just stepped out of the immaculately kept, white
    Mercedes sedan.

    This is TOM FRANKLIN and his WIFE. FRANKLIN is a lawyer from
    a reputable Manhattan firm. He is in his thirties, dressed in
    a conservative gray business suit, white shirt, dark tie,
    and seems to be a bright and nice young man, fresh from a
    "blameless" East Coast law school.

    FKANKLIN's [sic] WIFE, a typical Vassar girl, is in her late
    twenties, ordinarily pretty, with short brown hair, regular
    features and a good figure. She has a quietly aggressive
    I-told-you-so manner.

    The FRANKLINS are greeted by the smileless DEALER NO.1.

                        DEALER NO.1
                    (off-handedly)
                Yeah? What can I do for you?

                        FRANKLIN
                    (ill at ease, as if
                    ashamed of himself.

>   He glances athis WIFE for
>   help, but she turns
>   away, masking her
>   anger.)
> We--
>   (corrects himself)
> that is I--would consider selling
> this
>   (FRANKLIN points at the
>   Mercedes and pauses,
>   waiting for a sign of
>   encouragement from the
>   DEALER. There is none.
>   Now FRANKLIN attempts a
>   nonchalant tone)
> It's a bit old. It already has
> fifteen thousand miles!
>   (he pauses, waiting for
>   the DEALER to encourage
>   him. The DEALER does
>   not. FRANKLIN's WIFE
>   glances at her husband
>   with poorly masked
>   disdain. FRANKLIN is
>   desperate. He looks up
>   at the DEALER.)
> How about--fifty?
>
>   DEALER NO.1
>   (pretends he did not hear)
> What?
>
>   FRANKLIN
> Fifty?
>
>   DEALER NO.1
>   (pretending he is ready to
>   leave)
> You must be kidding!
>
>   FRANKLIN
>   (upset)
> But--I paid eighty for this. Top
> of the line! Not even two years
> old, of fifteen thousand miles...

>   DEALER NO.1
>   Thirty-five!
>
>   FRANKLIN
>   But--the used-car Blue Book lists
>   this car at sixty!
>
>   DEALER NO.1
>   Then go and sell it to the Blue
>   Book!
>
>   FRANKLIN
>   (resigned)
>   O.K. Thirty-five!

FRANKLIN's WIFE cannot take it any longer. About to cry, she pats the shiny hood of the Mercedes for the last time and walks away, as FRANKLIN follows the DEALER into his office.

>   CUT TO:

24.   INT: CHANCE'S QUARTERS   DAY
      (Continued from Scene 8)

>   GERTRUDE
>   During the night, the Old Man kept
>   asking about you. I told him what
>   a great gardener you are.

She looks at CHANCE coquettishly. Unperturbed, CHANCE begins to eat very calmly. GERTRUDE leaves the room.

SOUND: TV AUDIO

A love scene. On a couch, an athletic, hispanic-looking [sic] young man wearing only swimming trunks moves next to a frail, Slavic-looking young woman who wears a bikini. She extends her hand lets it slide over the man's neck and chest, he picks her up and carries her across the room to the bed. Just as he lowers himself over her, and she strains to him, the scene dissolves, superceeded [sic] by stallions galloping in a field. CHANCE looks thoughtful: the scene seems to have "sunk" into his mind.

>   CUT TO:

25.   EXT: TOWNHOUSE GARDEN   DAY

Wearing dark glasses and a different suit, CHANCE tends the garden, dragging the green watering hose from one path to the next. Carefully, he washes off the dust that has settled on leaves. CHANCE treats plants as if they were people; in a close-up, under his touch they seem to come to life, looking bigger, juicier, healthier and more beautiful.

CUT TO:

26. INT: FACTORY DAY

    (Few frames long fragment) And endless assembly line in a modern, electronics factory. Faceless workers mechanically "feeding" parts that lifelessly move in front of them. Above them, painted on the wall in large letters: RAND INDUSTRIES INCORPORATED.

CUT TO:

27. EXT. TOWNHOUSE GARDEN DAY
    (Continued from Scene 25)

    Here and there CHANCE removes a disintegrated leaf, gently cuts out a decomposing branch, a decaying surfaced root.

    Suddenly, GERTRUDE is leaning out of a top-floor window, gesturing wildly.

    > GERTRUDE
    > (flaps her arms and
    > screams hysterically)
    > Mein Gott, mein Gott. The Old Man!
    > Come! Come quick!

    Reluctant to be separated from his garden, CHANCE looks up toward her. His face remains enigmatic but he waves an acknowledgement, then turns toward the house and, not rushing, walks to the door.

    GERTRUDE disappears from the window.

CUT TO:

28. INT: TOWNHOUSE BEDROOM DAY

    CHANCE enters the darkly-lit bedroom of the OLD MAN: It is enormous. Its walls are lined with built-in old-fashioned shelves filled with books. Old solid curtains are almost drawn, but there is enough light to see the interior. On the large old-American oak table, flat leather folders are spread around.

A huge painting of a young woman, gold brown skin and of great beauty hangs above the bed.

In the bed, the OLD MAN is propped against the stiff pillows and seems poised intently, as if he were listening. He is in his upper eighties; his face is ash white, the upper jaw overlaps the lower lip of his mouth. CHANCE is gazing at the OLD MAN, who opens his eyes with difficulty and sees CHANCE. He gestures at him to come closer. CHANCE moves toward him, then leans over the man.

>   OLD MAN
>   (points with difficulty at
>   the woman in the
>   painting above the
>   headrest)
> I loved her so much, so much ... (he strains) But, as she was black--we could never marry. The world didn't want our love. We ran away, and hid from the world here, in this house. Then--then you were born ... (he strains) And when you were born, we named you Chance--the child of our love--because it is by chance that you came to this world. (he strains) And when she died, you, my boy, were too young to remember your mother. And I too old to ever forget her, too weary to go back to the world that hated her so. (he strains) Just before your mother died I swore on the memory of our love to care for you as long as I live. (pauses) To shelter you, from that world full of hate.

With a blank expression CHANCE strains to hear better. The OLD MAN points next to the bed. There, on the night table, stands a large 11 x 14 framed photograph of the same young black woman holding a white baby boy in her arms; both are embraced by a handsome, slightly grayish white man in a business suit of the twenties. This was the OLD MAN about thirty years ago. The child was CHANCE: other yellowish photographs of the twenties and thirties show the OLD MAN at various times of his life. They portray him as a politician, at a rally, surrounded by Republican financial and business elite; with his partners in an old-fashioned Wall Street law firm. In this time, he was clearly a known and active public figure.

>   OLD MAN
>   Look at me then ... And at you, my
>   boy. You were such a nice boy,
>   Chance
>   (he pauses)
>   such a good boy ... Even though you
>   couldn't grasp the principles of
>   reading or writing, and so the
>   tender soil of your brain has
>   never been developed.
>   (he pauses)
>   The world
>   (pauses, with his hand,
>   indicated the
>   photographs at the night
>   table)
>   The world, that same world that
>   hated my love for your mother,
>   would call you retarded.
>   (pauses)
>   But, <u>it is the world that is
>   retarded--not you</u>.
>   (pauses, strains)
>   But I did my best to protect you
>   from them. You have your garden,
>   your own world which you love so.
>   And the television to remind you
>   of what the world has turned to. I
>   have made you a good life, haven't I?

Chance nods.

The OLD MAN turns to look at the photographs on the night table. In one of them, the OLD MAN is surrounded by his law partners--clearly taken in the TOWNHOUSE's GARDEN, about thirty years earlier, was taken in the late fall. The trees, half of their present size, have lost their leaves. Half of the photograph with another person on it had been torn out for reasons of secrecy. In yet another photograph the OLD MAN in his early thirties is bent, lecturing a child, CHANCE when he was a small boy. Behind them we recognize the GARDEN's iron gate. I was less rusty, but as now it was then already padlocked.

SOUND: The firm and youthful OLD MAN, as he was in his forties, is talking:

                    OLD MAN (V.O.)
        ... and as long as I live, you'll always find, my dearest boy, everything you need right here, in this house. You will stay here, with me, untroubled by the world, troubling no one. Until I die, you won't ever leave this place. Do you understand me, Chance?

                    BOY (V.O.)
        I understand.

CHANCE leans closer to hear the words of the dying OLD MAN.

                    OLD MAN (CONT.)
        All these years I've kept my promise. You've never gone out. I have protected you, kept you pure, unspoiled by the world, but now-- and I shall probably not live many more years--perhaps it is time to make some preparations for your future without me ... (he strains)

Suddenly, he is surprised by something he feels. He strains to live but it is too late. His shoulders slump down, his chest seems to collapse. In a second, he is dead.

CHANCE stares at his face, then looks up at the painting of his mother. He looks at her intently, and as his eyes meet her eyes, a tender, <u>engaging smile</u> appears on his face.

                                                               CUT TO:

29.   INT: TOWNHOUSE ATTIC   DAY

Dressed in yet another suit, CHANCE makes his way through the dust-filled attic cluttered with used early-twenties furniture, boxes and piles of books, encyclopedias, bound collections of newspapers, etc. There are also two early His Master's Voice record players, several broken radios, a typewriter of equally early vintage, two broken early-model TV sets, a pedal-operated Singer sewing machine, and several old suitcases and trunks. Careful not to soil his suit, CHANCE picks up an old, almost trunk-like leather suitcase, beautifully fitted with brass buckles and locks. He drags it to the large cedar closet in the attic's corner. There, he loads the suitcase with several suits, shoes, shirts, ties and other paraphernalia.

                                                          CUT TO:

30.   INT: TOWNHOUSE LIBRARY   DAY

Bookshelves full of bound leather volumes. Heavy drapes hang at the window, pulled back, and the room is flooded with sunshine. Ornate and highly polished mid-nineteenth century mahogany furniture and large heavy leather chairs fill the room with a certain grandeur. On the wall hang early American paintings and, in the room's center, yet another portrait of the same young woman (CHANCE's mother). Here she is portrayed standing in the TOWNHOUSE's GARDEN; in the background a rear entrance of the TOWNHOUSE that now serves as the entrance to the TOWNHOUSE that now serves as the entrance to CHANCE's quarters. Behind the desk in the center of the room, sits MR. FRANKLIN. Leaning against the desk is Ms. HAYES, his assistant.

Ms HAYES is in her languid twenties. She has the modern look and listless fashion of an efficient though overly eager secretary who perceives herself as a liberated woman.

Various papers are spread out on the top of the desk on which Mr. FRANKLIN is writing. Ms. HAYES is looking through a separate pile of papers.

In a corner of the library, TWO WORKERS are packing books into large wooden crates.

OFF CAMERA: Noise of a box being nailed closed.

CHANCE enters. He wears very large dark glasses that almost hide his expression and a dark suit of a similar cut to the ones described in the previous scenes but of a different color. Both his glasses and his suit make his look of the twenties even more pronounced.

CHANCE walks slowly toward the center of the room.

Mr. FRANKLIN gets up and takes a step toward CHANCE, his hand outstretched. The two men shake hands.

                    FRANKLIN
               (with instant sincerity)
          I'm Thomas Franklin and I
          representthe law firm handling
          this estate ...
               (he turns toward Ms.
                HAYES)
          ... and this is Miss Hayes, my
          assistant.

Ms. HAYES turns eagerly toward CHANCE.

                    HAYES
          How do you do.

                    FRANKLIN
               (after a short pause, he
                continues in a
                businesslike tone)
          Just before she left yesterday,
          Gertrude, the maid, said a man who
          was a guest lived in the rear of
          this house. ...

FRANKLIN looks down at the desk and shuffles the papers. Then he inclines his head toward CHANCE:

                    FRANKLIN (Cont.)
          However, we have no record of a
          guest residing in this house--how
          long have you been here?

An engaging smile brightens CHANCE's face.

                    CHANCE
               (his face quite blank now)
          How long? I have been here ever
          since I remember ...

CHANCE hesitates, but then continues easily.

Ms. HAYES looks at CHANCE with interest.

                    CHANCE (Cont.)
               (walks to the window and
                looks down at the
                garden. The garden is
                full of sunshine.)
          ... as long as this garden ...

> (CHANCE points at the
> garden. He hesitates
> again, as though
> searching for a more
> exact date. His voice
> does not change key.)
> ... ever since I was a child.

Ms. HAYES, touching her lower lip pertly with the tip of a pencil, continues to look at CHANCE.

> FRANKLIN
> (perplexed, disbelieving)
> You what? Since you were a child?
> (more matter-of-factly now)
> May I ask you your name?

CHANCE's voice does not hesitate.

> CHANCE
> My name is Chance.

> FRANKLIN
> Mr. Chance?

> CHANCE (nods)
> Yes. Chance. The gardener.

> FRANKLIN (uncertainly)
> Let's look through our records again.

FRANKLIN leans over the desk, picks up some of the sheets of paper heaped in front of him and reads them. Ms. HAYES is still looking at CHANCE.

CHANCE notices her staring and smiles engagingly at her. Ms. HAYES immediately responds and smiles back.

FRANKLIN is still looking into his inventories, then he looks up at CHANCE.

> FRANKLIN
> (expansively)
> Please sit down, Mr. Chance.

CHANCE turns around and effortlessly pulls a heavy leather
armchair closer to the desk. He sits down with poise and
self-assurance.

>   FRANKLIN
>   (chews his lip)
>   Your name does not appear anywhere
>   in our records.

He raises his head and looks gravely at CHANCE. CHANCE smiles
gently unconcerned.

>   FRANKLIN
>   (with lowered eyes)
>   No one by the name of Chance has
>   ever been connected with the
>   deceased.

Casually, CHANCE glances at the painting of the golden-brown
woman. Again (as in scene 28) his eyes meet hers; an engaging
smile softens his face.

FRANKLIN looks quickly at Ms. HAYES as if to reassure himself,
but she returns his look without expression. FRANKLIN pauses
and now talks as if also addressing Ms. HAYES:

>   FRANKLIN
>   The deceased gave up his political
>   career over thirty years ago. When
>   his bad health immobilized him, he
>   also retired from practicing law.
>   He cherished his privacy more than
>   anything, and to help him in this,
>   our firm has been in control of
>   all his affairs for over thirty
>   years now ... .

SOUND: OFF-CAMERA. Intermittent hammering of crates
being shut.

FRANKLIN pauses as if expected CHANCE to say something. CHANCE
gazes at him solemnly.

>   HAYES
>   After Miss Louise left, only
>   Gertrude, the imported maid was
>   taking care of the deceased. ...
>   There was no one else employed
>   here ... .

                    FRANKLIN
               (absent-mindedly)
          Who is Miss Louise?

                    HAYES
               (glancing at her papers)
          An old black maid from Alabama who
          used to work here for years.

     CHANCE's face brightens as if refreshed by memory:

                    CHANCE
          Louise knows me well. She was
          here, in this house, as long as I
          can remember. She used to cut my
          hair; Louise will tell you that I
          have lived and worked here. That I
          take care of the garden ...
               (reminisces) [sic] She used to call
          me her "Mr. Gard'iner" ...

                    HAYES
               (interrupting)
          Louise died, Mr. Chance.

                    CHANCE
               (as if unaware of what Ms.
               HAYES said)
          Louise left just before the
          flowers bloomed in our garden. She
          went away to ...

                    HAYES
               (with some concern, she
               leans forward in her
               chair and again
               interrupts CHANCE)
          Yes, Mr. Chance, but Louise fell
          ill and died. As you know,
          Gertrude came here to work from
          Europe only a short while ago.
          Gertrude assumed you were a guest
          in this house, and gardening was
          your hobby.

                    CHANCE
            (suddenly blank, almost
             expressionles s)
        I did not know that Louis [sic]
        had died.

                    HAYES (persistently)
        She did. And Gertrude is too new
        to know how long you had been here
        before her arrival.

                    FRANKLIN
            (becoming almost hostile)
        Can you recall being contracted as
        a gardener, Mr. Chance?
CHANCE does not answer.

                    FRANKLIN
            (a bit annoyed)
        Have you been contracted as a
        gardener here?

                    CHANCE (unsure)
        No.

                    FRANKLIN
            (cunningly)
        How much money did you make for
        your work?

                    CHANCE
            (answers easily)
        I didn't make money. I was given
        everything I needed here--
            (he reflects)
        I was even allowed to wear any of
        the Old Man's suits, coats, shirts
        and shoes that Louise used to
        bring to me from the attic ... .
            (in a gesture of
             explanation, CHANCE
             points at his suit)

                    HAYES
            (interjects suddenly)
        It's quite beautiful how stylish
        your clothes are, Mr. Chance--and
        how they fit you!

CHANCE smiles at her again. She responds, smiling.

In the background, the same TWO WORKERS begin to seal the room's windows.

FRANKLIN looks at his clothes and compare [sic] them with CHANCE's. He is a bit upset by comparison. He turns to CHANCE and speaks as if in a court of law.

> FRANKLIN
> It would simplify matters if you could produce some identification--you know: diplomas, bank receipts, driver's licence [sic], medicalinsurance records ...

> CHANCE
> (hesitatingly)
> I don't have any of those things. I've never needed them.

> HAYES
> (interjecting again with warmth)
> Perhaps your birth certificate?

CHANCE shakes his head.

> FRANKLIN
> (annoyed, hostile)
> You must have some receipts from a hospital, or a doctor, or a dentist. Surely there are other people who have known you here and elsewhere?

> CHANCE
> I have never been hospitalized. And I don't know any people. Only Louise ...

> FRANKLIN
> (categorically)
> We shall need some proof of your past residence and employment here.

>   CHANCE (determined)
>   You have me. I am here. What other
>   proof do you need?

Ms. HAYES and FRANKLIN laugh weakly. CHANCE smiles back at them.

>   FRANKLIN
>   (back to business)
>   As far as we know, the deceased
>   had no relatives and left no
>   beneficiaries. All his contracted
>   employees had been paid in full.
>   Now if you want to read and sign
>   this document.

FRANKLIN shuffles the papers on the desk and draws out one legal-size sheet filled with fine print. He hands it to CHANCE.

CHANCE picks up the sheet. He stares at it for a while with a look of concentration; he wrinkles his brow, scowls and holds his chin between the thumb and forefinger of his hand. Then he hands the sheet of paper back to FRANKLIN.

>   CHANCE
>   (with conviction)
>   I can't. I can't sign it.

>   FRANKLIN
>   (attempts to hide his
>   satisfaction)
>   As you wish.

FRANKLIN gathers all the papers together.

>   FRANKLIN
>   (firmly)
>   By tomorrow all doors to this
>   house will be sealed. I regret,
>   but under all the circumstances-as
>   I see it--and officially I have to
>   tell you this. You will have to
>   move out immediately and take your
>   belongings with you.

In an afterthought, FRANKLIN politely hands CHANCE his calling card.

                    FRANKLIN
            If, however, you want to make any
            claims against this estate, you
            can find me in my office.

    CHANCE takes the card from him but when FRANKLIN and Ms.
    HAYES do not look, casually drops it on the way to the door.

                                                        CUT TO:

31.   EXT. TOWNHOUSE GARDEN   DAY

    CHANCE emerges from his quarters carrying the extremely large
    brown leather suitcase he loaded in scene 29. He frequently
    shifts the suitcase from hand to hand with effort, as it seems
    to be heavy. CHANCE is dressed in a dark blue suit of the same
    fashion as his other suits and he is wearing dark glasses. He
    is also carrying a large old-fashioned iron key to the gate.

    As he crosses the garden, he looks around. Reluctantly,
    obviously uncertain, he inserts the key into the lock of the
    gate. Hesitating, he turns the corroded padlock. The lock
    opens with difficulty. The gate screeches as he forces it open.
    Leaving the key in the gate, CHANCE crosses the threshold. He
    is outside now.

                                                        CUT TO:

32.   EXT. UPPER MANHATTAN STREET   DAY

    It is a street of tall, residential apartment houses. There
    are some elegant shops, some restaurants, and moderate traffic.

    Carrying his heavy suitcase, CHANCE slowly walks to the
    sidewalk. He looks around with fascination, from time
    to time pausing to rest. He glances at the passersby and
    whenever he catches a stare of a passing man, or woman, or
    child, the <u>engaging smile</u> lights up his face, and they all
    respond smiling joyously back at him. Soon CHANCE passes a
    television store with dozens of various TV sets, small and
    large, displayed in the store window as if suspended from the
    branches of a large mock tree. All the sets are turned on (as
    they usually are in Manhattan TV stores during the day) and
    each one shows a different program in color.

    CHANCE is just about to pass the TV store when this window
    display attracts his attention. The video camera points
    outward from the upper left corner of the window setting and
    is focused at the sidewalk, to allow the window watchers to
    see themselves on TV. (It is a standard video monitoring

camera placed behind the cashiers in many banks and stores.) CHANCE backs up, stands in front of the window and suddenly, as he faces the window, his own face appears on several of the TV sets on display.

CHANCE places his suitcase down on the sidewalk. He looks for a second at his projected face as it appears on the screens of the TV sets, then removes his glasses. As he does it, he is watching himself removing the glasses on the TV sets. He raises his left arm, then his right, as if testing whether it is actually he himself who is appearing on these TV sets; he turns sideways.

Finally, as if bored but still unwilling to part with his image altogether, he picks up the suitcase and begins to walk backward toward the curb. CHANCE reaches the curb, but since his head is still turned backward looking over his shoulder at the TV sets he can't see it. His suitcase is in his right hand, his dark glasses in his left. CHANCE is stepping down off the curb between two parked cars, still looking over his shoulder at the TV sets in the display window.

One of the cars, a long, silverish custom made limousine, its midsection extended, slowly backs up. CHANCE does not see it moving. The rear of the car hits him and his suitcase. CHANCE falters, loses his glasses and drops his suitcase, which hits the street with a bang. Large drops of perspiration spring out on his forehead. He is caught between the two cars. The suitcase lies on the street, under the car's rear bumper. PETE, the chauffeur, half jumps out from the car, looks back, sees what has happened, panics, gets into the car again and moves it a few inches forward. Then he gets out again and runs to CHANCE. PETE is in his forties, uniformed, and throughout this incident clearly panic-stricken.

The sidewalk side of the accident. FIVE PASSERS-BY (a WOMAN, two BUSINESSMEN, a COUPLE) stop to watch. PETE helps CHANCE to the sidewalk. CHANCE leans against the car's trunk. A woman gets out of the back seat of the car. This is EVE RAND. First astonishment then slight panic show on her face.

EVE is in her late thirties. She has the look of a traditional New England lady; a natural blonde, tanned, with regular features, always fresh skin, with no trace of wrinkles. EVE is extremely feminine; many would consider her a quiet beauty. Her beige tweed suit is immaculately tailored, around her neck a dark brown silk scarf. She is also wearing a small gold pin, gold earrings and a large florentine [sic] gold bracelet. EVE is not too vivacious, nor is she cold-looking. She does not consciously strain to make an impression, she is not affected or conceited. At no time is there a trace of snobbishness or coquetry about her.

EVE rushes toward CHANCE, who is being supported by the visibly shaken PETE:

>   EVE (terrified)
> Oh dear God, oh dear God, I hope
> you're not badly hurt!

She looks at CHANCE's face expectantly. There are droplets of perspiration on his forehead. CHANCE calmly looks up at her.

>   CHANCE
>   (very calm)
> It's only my leg. I think it was
> hit by the car.

>   EVE
> Dear God! I hope nothing is broken.

She notices the onlookers and raises her voice a bit, as if to counteract their potential enmity.

>   EVE (Cont.)
> I can't tell you how sorry I am.
> Pete,
>   (she gestures at PETE)
> Our chauffeur, has never had an
> accident before
>   (she bends over CHANCE's
>   leg)
> Please raise your trouser leg so I
> can take a look.

CHANCE obediently pulls up his left trouser leg. EVE examines the bruise. Three inches in diameter, a red-bluish swollen blotch, is in the middle of the calf.

>   CHANCE
> It's all right.

>   EVE
> Thank God, nothing seems broken.
> Is it very painful?

                    CHANCE
          Not at all. Really, I can hardly
          feel it.

The PASSERSBY are leaving disinterestedly.

                    EVE
              (pondering aloud)
          Perhaps, perhaps we should call
          the ambulance to take you to a
          hospital. Of course, it would mean
          notifying the police
              (pauses, discomforted by
               the thought).
          Then, the photographers would
          come, there will be pictures in
          the papers.
              (she looks at CHANCE, who
               listens attentively. Now
               she asks with hope)
          We wouldn't want all that, would
          we?

                    CHANCE
              (picks up her mood)
          No, of course not.

                    EVE
          Can we drive you to your own
          physician?

                    CHANCE
              (calmly)
          I don't want to go to the
          hospital. And I don't have my own
          physician.

EVE straightens up, a concentrated look on her face, as she studies CHANCE. Wordlessly, the two of them look at each other; an <u>engaging smile</u> softens CHANCE's face.

                    EVE
              (now more at ease,
               reassured)
          Would you mind seeing our family
          doctor then?

                    CHANCE
                (as if not understanding)
            Your family doctor?

                    EVE
            My husband has been very ill. His
            doctor and nurses are staying with
            us.

                    CHANCE
                (directly)
            I wouldn't mind seeing your doctor.

                    EVE
                (addressing both CHANCE and PETE)
            Fine. Let's get started
                (to CHANCE)
            However, if the doctor thinks it
            necessary, we will then have to
            take you straight to the hospital.

CHANCE leans on the arm of PETE, who leads him to the limousine and installs him on the rear seat. EVE follows them. PETE returns to collect CHANCE's suitcase. He picks it up—it is a bit dented. Next to it, on the sidewalk, he notices the remnants of CHANCE's smashed sunglasses. PETE bends to examine the bits and collects carefully. While PETE collects the glass, the car's registration plate is in view: It reads: "RAND 1." PETE places the suitcase in the trunk, and quickly gets into the car.

Gently, the limousine pulls out into traffic.

                                                    CUT TO:

33.   INT: INSIDE RAND LIMOUSINE   DAY

In the rear seat, EVE turns slightly toward CHANCE and presses a button to raise the glass partition separating them from PETE.

SOUND: Noise of the traffic subsides.

                    EVE
            I'm Mrs. Benjamin Rand.
                (she pauses and adds in a
                lighter tone, always
                very natural),
            Elizabeth-Eve Rand. My friends
            call me Eve.

CHANCE looks at EVE as if recalling something; an <u>engaging smile</u> again brightens his face:

                CHANCE
          (still smiling)
    I am Chance.

As he plays with the electric window button he inadvertently lowers the window. Outside, a noisy group of strikers, carrying banners "work now!" is surrounded by police. For a moment, traffic noise blurs CHANCE's voice, as he repeats:

              CHANCE (Cont.)
Chance.
         (for a moment,
         involuntarily, he seems
         to be recalling what Old
         Louise used to call him.
         He repeats--)
Chance. The Gard'iner.

                EVE
         (pronounces the name very
         clearly as if having
         heard it before)
Mr. Chauncey Gardiner? But of course. I do recognize your name very well indeed.

                CHANCE
         (slightly surprised by her
         altering of his name,
         repeats after her)
Chauncey Gardiner!--

                EVE
Mr. Gardiner, my husband and I have been very old friends of Basil and Perdita Gardiner. We often visit their private island with them. It's such fun to be on a private island. So much interesting wildlife there!
         (she pauses)
Are you, a relative of theirs, by any chance?

                    CHANCE
               (softly, and at ease, a
               bit apologetic.)
          I don't have any relatives. I'm
          all alone.

                    EVE
               (pauses, moved by what he
               said)
          Would you like a little whisky or
          fruit juice?

                    CHANCE
          A fruit juice. Thank you

There is a small bar installed in the front of the rear
seat; next to it is a white telephone and a TV set. Through
the window CHANCE looks at the passing cars, then up at the
skyscrapers. He gets visibly dizzy from the view.

                    EVE
               (looking at CHANCE)
          I see that you are suffering ...

She hastens to open the bar. From a crystal decanter she pours
into a large monogramed crystal glass. She gives it to CHANCE
and pours whisky for herself.

The limousine slows down passing a group of men and women
demonstrating outside a large bank. Their banners read "RAND
SELLS USA TO SHEIKS", "SHEIKS GO HOME", "RAND-DON'T YOU OPEC
US". CHANCE looks out.

                    EVE
               (upset by the sight of the
               demonstration)
          These people--what do they expect?
          A miracle? To save the Corporation
          from bankruptcy Benjamin
               (she corrects herself--)
          my husband had to use every chance
          he got. What else could he do?

                    CHANCE (blandly)
          Nothing.

CHANCE sips his drink. EVE smiles and drinks hers. CHANCE--holds the glass in his hand as if not certain what to do with it. Suddenly, his eyes focus on the car's TV set. He replaces the glass, then looks at the TV set for a moment.

      CHANCE
    (pointing at the set)
  Does this work?

      EVE
  Yes, it does.

EVE leans forward and turns a dial. The mutters apologetically.

      EVE
  Reception is not always good ...

SOUND: TV AUDIO V.O.
  ... and here, at the Relief Center
  for the Unemployed, the President
  is talking with the unemployed.
  Some of them have been without
  a job for over two years now.

EVE turns TV to another channel.

SOUND: CLICK. TV AUDIO: Revival Group singing.

      EVE
  It may help to distract you, and
  take your mind off your pain. Is
  there anything you want to watch?

      CHANCE
  No, no thank you. I like to watch.
  This is fine.

            CUT TO:

34. INT: RAND DUPLEX ON UPPER PARK AVENUE IN MANHATTAN DAY

Large bedroom, good solid furniture of the contemporary "Country Estate" style. CHANCE's leg has just been examined by DOCTOR ALLENBY, who is standing beside the bed closing his medical bag and throwing away a disposable syringe he used to give CHANCE and injection.

DR. ALLENBY is in his fifties. A typical society doctor, he is personable, elegant and always at ease.

                    DR. ALLENBY
          As I suspected, there has been no
          injury to the bone, or to the
          muscles. Meanwhile, I'll instruct
          the nurse about your next
          injection.

     DR. ALLENBY leaves the room.

                                                    CUT TO:

35. INT: CORRIDOR RAND DUPLEX   DAY

     An imposing first-floor corridor in RAND's duplex apartment. DR.
     ALLENBY is descending the stairs; EVE, slightly apprehensive,
     waits for him at the foot of the stairs.

                    Dr. ALLENBY
                      (reassuringly)
          There's no serious injury to the
          leg at all. What Mr. Gardiner
          needs is simply to rest. I've
          prescribed some medicine to reduce
          the swelling and to ease the pain.
                      (he pauses and becomes
                       very concerned)
          However, I am not at all pleased
          with your husband's condition.
          This morning's electrocardiogram
          was not as good as ...

                                                    CUT TO:

36. INT: CORRIDOR RAND DUPLEX   DAY
     (Same corridor as in Scene 35)

     EVE with BONNIE, the household maid in the corridor. BONNIE is
     ordinary-looking and well into her thirties; she wears a smock
     and is highly trained, totally obedient, and accepts orders
     without ever questioning them.

                    BONNIE
          Yes, Madam. But I haven't found
          any wallet, or money, or anything
          in Mr. Gardiner's suit or pants ...

                    EVE
             (a bit taken aback)
          Oh, dear, he must have lost his

                    wallet when Pete ran into him on
                    the sidewalk ... .
                        (pauses)
                    Still, have all his suits and
                    shirts pressed immediately. His
                    suitcase must be sent out to be
                    repaired. ...
                        (as if on second thought)
                    There's a stack of Kosinski novels
                    the desk in my room--take them to
                    Mr. Gardiner. And also please have
                    the large television console moved
                    into Mr. Gardiner's room right
                    away.

                                                      CUT TO:

37.   INT: RAND'S BEDROOM   DAY

       A very large, imposing room, its walls covered with a soft,
       blue-gray watered-taffeta type of material. Heavy drapes are
       open beside the very tall windows. The room is furnished with
       a large bed, sofa, chests of drawers, armchairs, and the usual
       bedroom furnishings. In the left corner of the room stand
       tall, green oxygen tanks, with multiple gauges attached to
       their heads partially hidden behind a screen. Next to them
       stands a doctor's table with oxygen masks and a large modern
       electrocardiogram machine with its attachments. There are also
       various other pieces of emergency medical equipment scattered
       on the table--i.e., syringes, disinfecting dishes, sterile
       jars and bottles, assorted dishes, etc. An aura of emergency
       permeates the atmosphere.

       BENJAMIN RAND in a silk robe sits in an easy chair beside
       his bed. A glass of fluid is on a small silver tray beside
       him. EVE, still dressed in the clothes from the time of
       the accident, sits on the edge of the bed facing her
       husband: BENJAMIN RAND is the founder and majority shareholder
       of the RAND INDUSTRIES INCORPORATED, as well as Chairman
       of the Board of the First American Financial Corporation,
       and on the board of numerous other business, financial and
       philanthropic establishments.

       BENJAMIN RAND is well into his late seventies, gray-haired
       and substantially bald, with a clean, pale complexion. He is
       a bit portly and no taller than EVE. Now he looks very tired,
       yet in spite of his long illness there is still a quality of
       inner strength and of great dignity about him. RAND looks

at a person over the rims of his glasses directly into one's eyes, unflinchingly. His manner, however, is gracious, easy, free, and always attentive. He is an authentic, self-made man, a staunch Republican lord to the manner of his day and generation in the United States.

> EVE
> (talking to RAND)
> In any case, to spare me police interrogation--and to save you and me from all the public embarrassment the car accident could cause--Chauncey Gardiner refused even to go the hospital or to see his owndoctor!!
> (she pauses--RAND listens attentively)
> What's more, Gardiner lost his wallet in the accident--all his credit cards and money ... Our hospitality is the very least at this time that we can offer him.

RAND nods in understanding and concern while EVE talks.

> EVE (Cont.)
> But as he's allowed to get up, if you feel well enough, dear, perhaps the three of us could dine together tonight.

> RAND
> I'll be all right, my love, I'll be all right. The last electrocardiogram was quite satisfactory, I'm told. (pauses) Isn't your Chauncey Gardiner, one of the Gardiners we keep running into whenever we travel? ...

CUT TO:

38. INT: CHANCE'S ROOM RAND DUPLEX   DAY

CHANCE is leaning back on the bed, he is covered with a throw. EVE is sitting on a chair pulled close to the bed.

                    EVE
               (with emotion)
     ... I can't tell you how guilty
     and responsible I feel for this
     accident, Mr. Gardiner. I hope
     your staying with us does not
     inconvenience you too much?

                    CHANCE
               (looks at her a bit
                hesitantly)
     Please don't feel guilty; it
     doesn't inconvenience me at all.

                    EVE
               (breaks in)
     Now, is there anyone you'd like to
     notify about your accident? Your
     wife? Your family?

                    CHANCE
               (directly, slightly
                apologetic)
     I have no wife. No family.

                    EVE
               (slight relief in her
                voice)
     Perhaps your business associates
     then? (pauses) Please feel free to
     use Ben's office, the telephone,
     Telex, messengers ...
               (very eagerly, as a second
                thought)
     Would you need a secretary? My
     husband has been ill so long, and
     his staff here has very little to
     do.

                    CHANCE
     No, thank you. I have no business
     to do.

                    EVE
               (hesitating, a bit
                disbelieving)
     But there must be someone you
     would like to contact?

                    CHANCE
                 (softly)
            There is no one. I'm all alone.

EVE and CHANCE look at each other. In EVE's eyes there is a
trace of a newly born feeling.

                    EVE
                 (with great warmth)
            Mr. Gardiner,
                 (she pauses)
            Chauncey--if that's so--and I'm
            not just being polite--if you have
            no immediate business to attend
            to, please stay here with us until
            your leg is completely healed. As
            you see, we have lots of room and
            the best medical staff available
            right here. I do hope you won't
            refuse.

EVE looks at CHANCE pleadingly. CHANCE looks pensive

                    CHANCE
                 (an engaging smile appears
                  on his face)
            I won't refuse,
                 (he pauses)
            Eve.

                                                    CUT TO:

39.   INT: DINING ROOM RAND DUPLEX NIGHT

The dining room with a high ceiling, a large marble fireplace
and highly polished parquet floor. All furniture is mahogany,
highly polished, English eighteenth-century traditional--i.e.,
long dining table, high-backed chairs, and sideboard.

RAND, EVE and CHANCE are seated at a smaller round table,
covered with a snow-white cloth. Ornately cut crystal glasses
shine in the candlelight. MARIANNE, the waitress, is serving.
RAND is wearing a velvet smoking jacket and EVE an evening
hostess gown. Two fine droplet-shaped diamonds hang from her
ears on a fine chain. CHANCE is wearing one of his dark suits;
there is an evening look to it.

MARIANNE is about thirty years old, slim and delicate. Her
uniform is black and close-fitting with a small frilly half-
apron over it.

> RAND
> (to CHANCE, speaking
> slowly with barely
> perceivable difficulty)
> ... doesn't this accident prevent
> you from attending to your
> business?

> CHANCE
> (looks directly at RAND)
> My house has been closed. I had to
> leave. Now I have nothing to do.

With his impeccable manners, CHANCE cuts a piece of meat very carefully. He eats slowly and is at ease.

He raises his eyes and catches EVE's attentive stare. Inadvertently, he drops his fork on the floor. Aware he is being watched by both EVE and BENJAMIN, CHANCE behaves exactly like the man who dropped his fork in the TV soap opera (Scene 22). Under EVE's watchful stare, calmly, he picks up the fork and hands it to MARIANNE who takes the fork away. In a moment she returns with a fresh one on a silver tray. CHANCE picks up the fork and resumes eating.

RAND looks under his glasses at the food on his plate; he removes his glasses, breathers onto the lenses and polishes them with his handkerchief. Then he puts the glasses back on and stares at CHANCE over the rims.

> RAND
> (expectantly)
> When you say "your house has been
> closed," you mean to say, your
> business was shut down as a result
> of the Government's new Tax
> Reform. Just like that?

> CHANCE
> (directly)
> Yes. Just like that.

> RAND
> (moved, restraining his
> anger)
> You did put up a fight, didn't you?

                    CHANCE
               (hesitantly)
     All I did was tend to my garden.
     Then the lawyers came and asked me
     to . . .

                    RAND
               (angrily follows his own
                thoughts)
     The Federals? Did they throw the
     book at you?

                    CHANCE
               (recalling)
     Not even a book. A calling
     card...

                    RAND
     I know exactly what you mean.
     Today, the businessman is at the
     mercy of kid-lawyers from Security
     Exchange Commission. All they want
     is to regulate our natural growth!
     To them, a constitution is just
     another empty calling card.
               (ironic but desperate)
     A calling card, indeed ... .

CHANCE looks up at RAND and meets his curious gaze. He looks across the table and meets EVE's equally curious expression. An <u>engaging smile</u> softens his features and he looks directly at RAND:

                    CHANCE (softly)
     There isn't a garden left in which
     I could work and grow with the
     seasons.
               (he falters, as if a
                thought just dawned on
                him)

The smile leaves his face, and he returns to his meal. RAND leans across the table toward CHANCE.

                    RAND
               (with feeling, intently)
     Very well put, Mr. Gardiner--I
     hope you don't mind if I call you
     Chauncey ... .

>   (he pauses as if reflecting
>   on what CHANCE has just
>   said)
>   A gardener! Isn't that the perfect
>   description of what a <u>real
>   businessman</u> is--a person who makes
>   flinty soil productive, who waters
>   it with his own sweat, and creates
>   for the community. Yes, Chauncey,
>   what an apt statement you've just
>   made.
>
>   CHANCE
>   (humbly)
>   Thank you, Mr. Rand.
>
>   RAND
>   Ben. Please, do call me Ben.
>
>   CHANCE
>   (as if recalling something
>   very dear to him)
>   The garden I left, Ben, was such a
>   place--everything that grew there
>   I watered, and I watched it grow.

CHANCE pauses. EVE looks at CHANCE with dreamy eyes and a faint smile flickering across her lips.

>   CHANCE (Cont.)
>   (looking at RAND--sadly)
>   But now all is gone and all that
>   is left is the room upstairs.

With his head CHANCE indicates the upper floor of the DUPLEX.

>   RAND
>   (obviously moved, regards
>   CHANCE gently)
>   As the saying goes, "All dressed
>   up--and no where to go." But you
>   are young, Chauncy [sic] ...
>   (almost reprimandingly)
>   Why do you have to talk about <u>the
>   room upstairs</u>--that's where I'm
>   going soon.

                    (he pauses and murmurs
                    sadly)
            You could be my son, you are so
            young! You and Eve: both of you so
            young!

                         EVE
                    (shaking her head)
            Ben, dear ...

                         RAND
                    (a bit impatient)
            I know, I know, you don't like me to
            bring up our ages.

MARIANNE, the waitress approaches and pours some more wine.
CHANCE's glass is still full--he has not touched it. MARIANNE
withdraws. She casts an admiring glance at CHANCE. EVE notices
it and looks at her sternly. MARIANNE quickly averts her gaze.

RAND notices CHANCE is not drinking. Directly
to CHANCE.

                         RAND
            Well, if you can't find a good
            opportunity soon, how will you
            take care of your family?

                         CHANCE
                    (flatly)
            I have no family.

                         RAND
                    (shaking his head
                    impressed)
            Your responsibilities were that
            demanding?

                         EVE
                    (breaks in pleadingly)
            Ben, please--

                         RAND
                    (to EVE, slightly
                    reprimanding her)
            I'm sure Chauncey doesn't mind
            answering my questions.
                    (turns to CHANCE)
            Do you?

                    CHANCE (politely)
Of course not.

                    RAND
          (persistently, looking at
          CHANCE)
Well--didn't you ever want a
family?

                    CHANCE
          (stressing what he says)
I don't know what it is to have a
family.

                    RAND
          (nods in sadness and then
          murmurs)
They certainly wiped you out,
didn't they?
          (reassuringly)
But I tell you, I loved a lot, saw
a lot of little men who forgot
that we enter naked and exit
naked. That's it: No accountant
can audit life in our favor!
          (pauses, murmurs angrily)
Meanwhile, that man in the White
House!

CHANCE does not answer. He eats, chewing slowly. RAND
exchanges a meaningful look with EVE. Both are visibly
saddened by CHANCE's silence. RAND stops eating, turns to
CHANCE and tries again.

                    RAND
          (speaks with great
          conviction)
I am an old man, Chauncey, and I
speak to you frankly. There's
honesty about you that I like. You
don't beat around the bush, don't
use weasel words ... You're down to
earth ...

They have finished eating and are slowly getting up from the
table. CHANCE leans on a cane.

                                              CUT TO:

40. INT: WHITE HOUSE OFFICE OF THE SPECIAL ASSISTANTS TO THE PRESIDENT   DAY

(Same as in Scene 9)

Wearing a safari-like suit, BOB FERGUSSON, all excited, stands in front of a large graphic map of New York. A thick red line that runs over the map indicates PRESIDENT's route to the meeting at the Financial Institute. JOHN MORGAN, in a tweed jacket, sits in a chair calmly watching FERGUSSON.

> FERGUSSON
> (picks up a red marker)
> Rand is too ill to attend! The Boss decided to visit the old man in his New York apartment. We have to--
> (with the marker, he crosses out part of the planned route. Instead, he draws a bypass to RAND's apartment building)
> jump a bit sideways!

> MORGAN
> (still calm, but clearly concerned)
> But--the security has already been set up. There's just not enough time to start it all over again--

> FERGUSSON
> We'll do the spot check just before the Boss lands in Central Park. That's the chance we have to take.

> MORGAN
> (resigned, a bit upset now)
> I don't like leaving things to chance!

CUT TO:

41. INT: LIBRARY RAND DUPLEX NIGHT

RAND and CHANCE seated in the library. MARIANNE is serving an after-dinner drink from a cut-crystal carafe.

The library is a fairly large room located on the first floor of the duplex; its double doors lead to the corridor. The library is paneled in wood and leather and its bookshelves are filled mostly with leatherbound and legal-size volumes. There is an ornate old-fashioned desk, with leather folders and a gold-encrusted inkwell set on its top. On the desk is a custom-made telephone, and two others are discreetly tucked into the shelves behind RAND's desk. The sofa and four deep armchairs are either tapestry or leather, and there is a large Persian carpet on the floor. A marble fireplace dominates on wall. All windows are high, with heavy, dark maroon drapes.

          RAND
     (in the middle of his
     conversation with
     CHANCE--proudly)
... and so, because of my role in the Rand Industries and as the Chairman of the Board of The First American Financial Corporation--thelargest of its sort in the nation--I have just started a loan program to assist American Businessmen so harassed by the Government's repressive measures to control inflation, its over-taxation, and union extravagances.

RAND sips his liqueur. CHANCE listens in an attentive pose:

          RAND
We at the First American know how to offer a helping hand to the business community--
    (he pauses, searches for a
    word)
--to use your phrase, all the gardeners of this despairing garden of ours ... .

SOUND: The telephone rings. RAND picks up the receiver and listens:

          RAND
     (impatiently)
Yes, yes, I'll talk to him now...

                    (turns to CHANCE)
                ... forgive me Chauncey, but this
                can't wait.

CHANCE nods understandingly.

                    RAND
                (into the telephone)
                I'm fine, thank you. ... No, no.
                    (speaks very firmly with
                    considerable effort)
                ... I have decided that I shall
                not address the Annual Meeting of
                the Financial Institute tomorrow.
                Doctors orders? Of course not! You
                know me, Jonathan--I don't obey
                doctors!
                    (laughing)
                But sure I obey pain! (seriously)
                We're hoping the President will
                come to address the Institute, as
                he promised to do. So far it's
                been green light from the White
                House ... .
                    (he listens for a minute)
                I certainly will ... . (pause)
                Thank you, Jonathan.

RAND hangs up, and turns to CHANCE.

                                                    CUT TO:

42.   INT: CHANCE'S ROOM RAND DUPLEX   DAY
      (Same room as in Scene 38)

Next morning, BILL, the butler, has just helped CHANCE with
his jacket. While dressing, CHANCE keeps watching TV. BILL
is in his fifties, ordinary, nondescript, very pedantic and
efficient. While BILL examines CHANCE's final appearance very
carefully (a small whisk brush in his hand) CHANCE reluctantly
parts with the TV and looks at himself in the mirror.

SOUND: Phone ringing. BILL answers it.

                    BILL
                Hello? Yes, Mr. Rand, Mr. Gardiner
                is here.

                    (turns to CHANCE)
                    It is for you, Sir. Mr. Rand
                    calling from his bedroom.

CHANCE takes the receiver:

                    CHANCE
                Yes, Mr. Rand.
                    (he hesitates, corrects
                    himself)
                Yes, Benjamin ... . (pause) ...
                certainly. I'll come right down.

                                                    CUT TO:

43.   INT: RAND'S BEDROOM DAY

RAND sits in bed, just finishing his breakfast. CHANCE is
sitting in a chair near the bed.

                    RAND
                    (in the middle of a
                    sentence)
                ... and so ...
                    (very excited)
                he simply telephones me from
                Kennedy, where he's just landed.
                Everyone's excited that the
                President is going to address the
                annual meeting of the Institute
                today. The whole nation will be
                listening!
                    (excitedly)
                When he learned I was ill and
                unable to preside over the meeting
                as scheduled, he apparently
                decided to visit me here, at home,
                on his way to the luncheon. That's
                nice of him, don't you think?
                Well, he'll be here in less than
                an hour.
                    (with sudden emotion)
                A Democrat, true, but he is also a
                decent and open-minded man. I want
                you to meet him, Chauncey.

ALINE, a nurse, comes into the room with a tray of injections
and pills.

ALINE is a plain, chubby woman in her middle thirties--
stern and efficient, dressed in starched white uniform, cap,
stockings and shoes. ALINE approaches the bed. CHANCE gets up
to leave.

CUT TO:

44. INT: CHANCE'S ROOM RAND DUPLEX   DAY

CHANCE sits on his bed watching TV.

SOUND: TV AUDIO   ANNOUNCER (V.O.)
 ... at Kennedy Airport. The
 President was mobbed by over a
 hundred thousand angry unemployed
 who have staged a massive
 demonstration against his
 Administration. Later in the day
 the President will address the
 luncheon at the Financial
 Institute, ...

CHANCE's expression does not change.

SOUND: CLICK of TV remote control.

CUT TO:

45. INT: LIBRARY RAND DUPLEX   DAY

RAND is sitting behind his desk dressed in a black faintly
pinstriped business suit. He is handing a leather folder to
Mrs. AUBREY.

AUBREY
(in the middle of her talk
with RAND—matter-of-factly)
... by the way, Sir, the gentlemen
from the Secret Service have just
arrived and have begun their
duties. The President should be
here in about thirty minutes.

CUT TO:

46. INT: CORRIDOR RAND DUPLEX DAY

SECRET SERVICE MEN 1 and 2, with earplugs in, are examing
[sic] the walls, drapes and furniture in the corridor. They are

both in their thirties, strong, average-looking functionaries, wearing regular off-the-rack gray business suits.

CUT TO:

47. INT: CHANCE'S ROOM RAND DUPLEX DAY

    (Continued from Scene 44)

    CHANCE still watching TV. His expression is blank.

    SOUND: TV AUDIO   ANNOUNCER (V.O.)

    > ... and now we see the Presidential motorcade moving slowly up Park Avenue. Following his visit to Benjamin Rand. ...

    SOUND: CLICK of TV remote control.

    SOUND: TV AUDIO   ANNOUNCER (V.O.)

    > ... later in the day, the President will fly to Tennessee, his home state, to address the National convention of ...

CUT TO:

48. INT: MRS. AUBREY'S OFFICE RAND DUPLEX   DAY

    This is one of the rooms in RAND's apartment that, for the duration of RAND's illness, have been turned into temporary offices. This office, occupied by Mrs. AUBREY and her staff, is next to the LIBRARY: its door leads to the CORRIDOR. In the office there are three desks, each equipped with the latest-model electric typewriter, calculators, Dictaphone and multiple-button office telephones—one of them has the small-version desk-switch-board. A medium-size, mahogany-finished Telex machine and the latest electronic silent ticker-tape machine, with its constantly changing rows of stock quotations, stand in a corner of the room. The room also contains several brand-new first-quality file cabinets.

    Mrs. AUBREY is on the phone. In the background move SECRET SERVE MEN 3, 4 and 5. MEN 3 and 4 are examining the room. MAN 5 is at the window, watching the outside.

                    AUBREY
               (speaking into telephone)
          ... If you are ready, Mr. Gardiner,
          you could come down now to join
          Mr. Rand in the library. In the
          meantime, the gentlemen from the
          Secret Service will be able to do
          your floor ... .

                                                    CUT TO:

49.   INT: LIBRARY RAND DUPLEX   DAY

RAND, sitting behind his desk, has just finished drinking his
medicine from a small glass handed to him by ALINE. CHANCE
sits on the sofa, poised and at ease. GREG is leaning against
the mantelpiece. ALINE leaves the room.

GREG, chief of the SECRET SERVICE MEN, is in his late thirties
and dressed like the other men. His hair is cut very short and
he carries himself with a certain authority. RAND has dealt
with GREG during previous meetings with the President.

                    GREG
               (to RAND, continuing what
               was interrupted by the
               nurse's entry)
          ... I hope you don't mind all this
          moving around, Sir.

                    RAND
               (warmly)
          Go ahead—let your men do their jobs!

GREG opens his jacket and presses a small cigarette-box size
walkie-talkie cleverly hidden behind his trouser belt. Enter
SECRET SERVICE MEN 6 and 7. Each of them carries a small
instrument resembling a Geiger counter. They hunch their
shoulders and swiftly move around the room, running the
instrument along wall, shelves and drapes.

The door opens. SECRET SERVICE MAN 8 enters:

                    MAN 8
               (in a low voice to GREG)
          Everything's O.K.! The President's
          here!

SECRET SERVICE MAN 8 leaves, followed by 6 and 7; they close the door behind them.

>   GREG
>   (as he is about to leave
>   the library, he nods
>   slightly)
>   Thank you, Mr. Rand ... Mr.
>   Gardiner,
>   (turns to RAND)
>   It was a pleasure to see you
>   again, Sir.

>   RAND
>   (warmly)
>   Thank you, Greg, thanks you.

GREG leaves the room.

RAND quickly pulls a small silver pillbox from his pocket and nervously retrieves a pill. He swallows the pill and drinks some water from a glass which he then conceals in the shelves behind his desk. The door is being held open. THE PRESIDENT enters.

THE PRESIDENT of The United States is in his late fifties, of medium height and wears a dark suit similar to the one RAND's wearing. A mid westerner, he seems to be a man of exceptionally rugged constitution. His head is square and his features well-molded. His voice is low, his eyes scrutinizing. He is courteous, though a bit impatient, and he expects those he talks to to reach their point quickly and briefly. The PRESIDENT raises both arms as he walks across the room toward RAND. His face is all smiles. CHANCE gets up, and stands totally at ease.

>   PRESIDENT
>   (exclaiming)
>   Benjamin, my dear friend, how nice
>   to see you again.

>   RAND
>   (just about to rise)
>   Mr. President ...

>   PRESIDENT
>   (halts RAND with a gesture
>   of his arm)

Don't get up, Ben, please don't.
I know you're a bit overworked.

          RAND
     (very moved)
Mr. President! It is good to see
you. How thoughtful of you to come
all this way to look in on a dying
man.

        PRESIDENT
     (embraces RAND)
Nonsense, Benjamin, nonsense!
Let's talk about life.

The PRESIDENT turns toward CHANCE.

          RAND
Mr. President, I want to introduce
my very special friend, Chauncey
Gardiner.

RAND indicates CHANCE with his arm. As the PRESIDENT turns
to greet CHANCE, CHANCE, at ease, an engaging smile on his
face, meets him halfway. As if subconsciously imitating the
hand-shakes of the heads of state on the TV program CHANCE
watched in Scene 20, CHANCE reaches for the PRESIDENT's hand,
and shakes it with both his hands in a most friendly manner.
PRESIDENT is now convinced he must have met CHANCE on several
other occasions.

        PRESIDENT
Chauncey Gardiner! Of course! How
nice to see you again, my friend!

         CHANCE
     (warmly, at ease)
So nice to see you again, Sir!

CHANCE remains standing, totally at ease, an engaging smile on
his face. The PRESIDENT sits in an armchair close to RAND's
desk. CHANCE remains standing.

        PRESIDENT
     (friendly to CHANCE)
Sit down, Chauncey, sit down—and
let's both reprimand Benjamin for
locking himself behind these
walls.

                            (to RAND)
                    You'll be missed at the meeting of
                    the Institute.
                            (looking around)
                    Let me have your thoughts on the
                    subject I'll be covering today.

                                                        CUT TO:

50.   INT: CORRIDOR RAND DUPLEX   DAY

                            GREG
                            (in the middle of chatting
                            with Mrs. AUBREY)
                    ... Mr. Rand doesn't look too good
                    to me.

                            AUBREY
                            (sadly)
                    He's trying hard--very hard, but
                    his heart and his age are against
                    him.

        She stretches her hands in a gesture of doubt. GREG changes
        the subject as if not wanting to upset Mrs. AUBREY anymore.

                            GREG
                    And where is the beautiful Mrs.
                    Rand?

                            AUBREY
                    Mrs. Rand left early this morning
                    to inaugurate a new center for
                    retarded children in Boston ...
                            (she pauses)
                    She loves children so much! What a
                    pity she doesn't have her own ... .

                                                        CUT TO:

51.   INT: DOCTOR'S ROOM RAND DUPLEX   DAY

        A medium-sized room, well-furnished--this is a guest room now
        occupied by the DOCTOR and NURSES on duty at RAND's. Some
        medical objects, blood pressure apparatus, nurses' uniforms,
        etc., Are scattered about.

        Dr. ALLENBY wearing his white coat, paces the room nervously.
        ALINE is sitting next to the phone.

                    ALLENBY
                (looks at his watch--as if
                to himself--nervously)
            I hope he remembered to take his
            medicine on time!

He continues pacing the room:

                    AlLENBY
                (turns to ALINE)
            Just in case, prepare an injection.
ALINE rises.

                                            CUT TO:

52   INT: KITCHEN RAND DUPLEX   DAY

The kitchen is large and very modern, all built in stainless
steel and formica [sic]. Oversized stoves, ovens, and three
enormous refrigerators indicated a large kitchen staff. A TV
set is standing on a rolling stand and is being watched by the
COOK, MARIANNE, BILL, BONNIE, ALINE, (all in their working
uniforms) and SECRET SERVICE MAN 9.

SOUND: TV AUDIO

                    WOMAN (V.O.)
                (soap opera type)
            ... I am in love with you ...
                (pause)
            I love you and I want you ...
                (pause)
            and I know that you know it ...
                (pause)
            ... and I am grateful that you
            love me.
                (pause)
            ... But we have to be wise.
                (pause)
            And so I shall go.
                (pause)
            I won't see you anymore
                (pause--crying, sobbing
                and nose blowing ...)

MARIANNE is on the verge of tears. She blows her nose into a
handkerchief. The COOK and BILL are also moved but pretend

that they aren't. SECRET SERVICE MAN 9, seeing BONNIE concealing her tears, is checking his own emotion and quickly turns away to the window.

CUT TO:

53. INT: LIBRARY RAND DUPLEX DAY
(Continued from Scene 49)

RAND is pale and perspiring. He is clearly not feeling well.

> RAND
> (to the PRESIDENT--in a
> tired voice)
> "... all the wasted effort to contain spiraling prices and wages by means of central instead of directing full attention to stimulating a national pride and desire to progress and to secure a dramatic increase in our productivity."
> (PRESIDENT listens, nods,
> RAND pauses, very tired
> seems to be finished.)

The PRESIDENT, who is by now a bit bored, quickly turns to CHANCE.

> PRESIDENT
> (directly)
> And you, Chauncey? What do you think about this bad season?

> RAND
> (attempts to insert his own
> complaints)
> Like all of us, Mr. President, Chauncey has also felt the harsh impact of the Government's Tax Reform ... The massive uprooting of business.

CHANCE stares pensively at the PRESIDENT, but his stare is blank. After a pause.

> CHANCE
> (a thought dawns on him)
> Yes, there's a lot of uprooting--

> but we all know in nature
> everything has its season: there
> are spring and summer, but there
> are also fall and winter.
> (he pauses)
> ... And then spring and summer
> again. As long as the roots are
> not severed and we are strong, the
> plants survive the winter.

RAND looks at CHANCE and nods his head approvingly. The PRESIDENT also looks at CHANCE. An <u>engaging smile</u> lights CHANCE's face.

> PRESIDENT
> (seizes the chance to
> avoid clashing with
> RAND)
> I must admit, Chauncey, that what
> you've just said is one of the
> most refreshing thoughts I've
> heard in a very long time!

He rises and stands erect, his back to the fireplace, facing RAND and CHANCE:

> PRESIDENT
> (reflecting on what CHANCE
> has just said)
> Given our understanding of its
> mechanics, our economic system
> remains--like nature, in the long
> run--stable and rational.
> (he pauses for a moment
> then turns to RAND)
> We welcome the inevitable seasons
> of nature, yet even you, the
> mighty Republicans, are so quickly
> upset by the seasons of the
> economy. The country must realize
> that a President can't cause an
> economic miracle. ...

The PRESIDENT turns and now looks admiringly at CHANCE.

> PRESIDENT
> (gesturing toward CHANCE)
> As always, I keep admiring

>   Chauncey's good, solid sense. This
>   bi-partisan quality is just what
>   we lack--in the media, as well as
>   on Capitol Hill.

The PRESIDENT glances at his watch. RAND attempts to rise. CHANCE rises and stands at ease. The PRESIDENT's gesture to RAND stops him.

>   PRESIDENT
>   (attentively, with concern
>   to RAND)
>   No, no, Benjamin, you rest. I'll
>   see you again soon, my friend.
>   When you are better, you and Eve
>   must visit us in Washington.
>   (turns to CHANCE and
>   speaks with vigor)
>   And you, Chauncey? Will you come
>   again to see me and my family? We
>   will all look forward to that!

CHANCE stands at ease. An _engaging smile_ on his face. The PRESIDENT turns toward the exit.

>   CUT TO:

54. INT: DOCTOR'S ROOM RAND DUPLEX   DAY
    (Continued from Scene 51)

    SECRET SERVICE MEN 10 and 11 are leaving.

    Dr. ALLENBY collects his medical bag, gestures at ALINE to follow him and rushes out in a hurry. ALINE picks up a tray with syringes and follows him.

>   CUT TO:

55. INT: CHANCE'S ROOM RAND DUPLEX   DAY

    CHANCE sits on his bed. He is watching TV:

    SOUND: TV AUDIO   ANNOUNCER 1 (V.O.)
                             We are all on standby, here at the Financial
                             Institute of America, to hear what measures the
                             President will propose ...

    SOUND: CLICK

>   CUT TO:

56. INT: MRS. AUBREY'S OFFICE DAY

   Mrs. AUBREY is at her desk watching television.

   SOUND: TV AUDIO   ANNOUNCER 3 (V.O.)
        The President is arriving in our city in an
        atmosphere of high tension following the
        disclosure of the rise in national unemployment
        to an unprecedented level of over <u>twenty</u> percent.
        A massive demonstration against the administration
        is planned by ...

                                                    CUT TO:

57. INT: KITCHEN RAND DUPLEX DAY
   (Continued from Scene 52)

   The COOK, MARIANNE, BILL, BONNIE and ALINE--are
   watching the TV set.

   SOUND: TV AUDIO   ANNOUNCER 4 (V.O.)
        The White House announced today that, after his
        high-level consultations with members of the
        Cabinet, House and Senate, and with prominent
        leaders of the business community, the President is
        expected to ...

                                                    CUT TO:

58. INT: RAND'S BEDROOM NIGHT

   RAND in bed, very drawn, pale, clearly exhausted by the
   PRESIDENT's visit. An oxygen tank stands next to the bed, and
   an oxygen mask hangs within RAND's reach. The electrocardiogram
   machine stands on its own rolling stand at the foot of the bed,
   its cords and connectors hanging loosely on its side, as if just
   used. RAND is talking to EVE:

                    RAND
              (speaking very slowly but
              glowingly)
        ... credit and tight money as
        I presented it to the President ...
              (he breathes heavily and
              brightens for a moment)
        ... but <u>what Chauncey said</u> pleased
        the President very much. (pause)
        The President hears my kind of
        argument from just about everyone,

> but <u>Chauncey's bipartisan honesty,
> seldom, if ever</u> ... even though,
> the President seems to know
> Chauncey quite well ...

From across the room, not seen by RAND, Dr. ALLENBY is silently gesturing to EVE. EVE kisses RAND's forehead and leaves the room.

CUT TO:

59. INT: CORRIDOR RAND DUPLEX   DAY

Dr. ALLENBY to EVE, speaking very gravely:

> AlLENBY
> ... particularly now that the
> President's unexpected visit left
> Benjamin exhausted. No cause for
> alarm, yet. But we must be
> prepared. ... After all ...

He gestures with resignation. EVE is authentically saddened. For a moment she is lost in thought, then regains her usual composure.

CUT TO:

60. INT: EVE'S BEDROOM   DAY

EVE's room is a medium-size, oval room with walls covered in pale pink-silk and soft rose drapes. There is a queen-size bed, with a pale pink cover. Near the bed stand a console and a writing table lined with silk--all of the furniture is small and delicate, made of gilded wood and upholstered to match the walls. In the background, barely visible, are eight panels of canvas paintings. Here and there are large pieces of Sevres porcelain two chests of drawers, and a marble bust of Benjamin Rand. In the far corner, a circular table draped in a pink silk circular cloth that hangs to the floor, is covered with many different-size family photographs, all framed in silver.

EVE, pensive, sits in front of her writing table and is very upset by what she has just heard from DR. ALLENBY. She hesitates, then picks up the telephone and dials.

CUT TO:

61.   INT: CHANCE'S ROOM RAND DUPLEX   DAY

CHANCE in an armchair watching TV. His injured leg rests on a hassock.

SOUND: TV AUDIO: Sound of car race.

SOUND: The phone rings.

CHANCE picks up the receiver, his eyes still staring in the direction of the TV set in front of him.

SOUND: TV AUDIO: Sound of car crashing.

>   CHANCE
>   (into the phone)
>   I'm watching television . . . .
>   (pause--with no obvious
>   emotion)
>   Yes, Eve, I would like to see you too.

CHANCE replaces the receiver and continues watching TV, motionless and peaceful, his leg still stretched out on the hassock.

SOUND: TV AUDIO: Sound of multiple car crashes and screams.

EVE walks in, dressed as in Scene 60. Before CHANCE manages to get up to greet her, she sits down on the hassock, beside his leg.

SOUND: TV AUDIO: TV stays on, muffled sounds of a car race continue throughout this scene.

>   EVE
>   (looks at CHANCE--very
>   moved, anxious)
>   I'm so sorry that we had no advance notice of the President's visit, and I wasn't home with you and Benjamin to greet him. I think that, in spite of his views, he is a most intelligent man ... .

CHANCE nods in agreement.

>   EVE
>   Benjamin told me how impressed the president was by what you said, and how much the President valued

                    your judgment. He's such a nice
                    man, the President, isn't he?

                              CHANCE
                         (his eyes turned to TV set)
                    Yes, he is, though he looks so
                    much bigger on television.

                              EVE
                    I see what you mean. Ben would
                    agree with you.
                         (she pauses ready to
                         change the subject.
                         Tenderly)
                    How is your leg?

EVE gently touches CHANCE's leg. Almost involuntarily
he puts his hand on hers;

                              CHANCE
                         (with an engaging smile)
                    When you touch it, it doesn't hurt
                    me at all, Eve ... .

EVE removes her hand and glances shyly at CHANCE.

                              EVE
                         (with an outburst of
                         suppressed emotion)
                    Even though I feel guilty for your
                    accident, Chauncey, I'm so happy
                    to have you here! You're the only
                    person, the only man ...
                         (she recovers her poise)
                    I myself have very few friends,
                    and most of Benjamin's are almost
                    all of his generation ...
                         (pauses)
                    ... and he's been ill for so long.
                         (she saddens)
                    Dr. Allenby just told me that
                    Benjamin's condition is worsening.
                    There's not much hope.

EVE (as if unaware) puts her hand again on CHANCE's leg.

                              EVE
                         (hesitates)
                    I'm--

>   (pauses)
>   I'm very grateful that you're
>   here, with us--
>   (pauses)
>   --with me, Chauncey.

                                                    CUT TO:

62.   INT: LAW FIRM   DAY

   Room of Wasp-ish Park Avenue law firm in Manhattan. FRANKLIN
   and FOUR other LAWYERS, are intently watching a TV program.

   SOUND: TV AUDIO: ANNOUNCER 5 (V.O.)
             ... in his long-awaited speech to the Financial
             Institute in New York, the President reassured the
             nation that inflation would prune the dead limbs
             of savings, thus enlivening the vigorous trunk of
             industry. In this context ...

                                                    CUT TO:

63.   INT: CHANCE'S ROOM RAND DUPLEX   DAY

   CHANCE in an armchair watching TV.

   SOUND: TV AUDIO   ANNOUNCER 6 (V.O.)
             ... The President said that before making his
             historical speech he had engaged in a most fruitful
             discussion with Benjamin Rand and Chauncey
             Gardiner ...

   CHANCE's face does not change when these names are mentioned.

   SOUND: TV AUDIO   ANNOUNCER 6 (V.O.)
             The industrialist and financier, Benjamin Rand, has
             been for over a decade Chairman ...

   SOUND: Click of the TV remote control.

   SOUND: TV AUDIO   ANNOUNCER 7 (V.O.)
             ... The President pointed out to his Republican
             critic the need for a massive bipartisan effort to
             save the nation from the worst economic crisis in
             its history. However, the President agreed with Mr.
             Chauncey Gardiner, one of Benjamin Rand's closest
             associates, who stated that as long as the roots of
             industry remain firmly planted in the national soil,
             the economic prospects are undoubtedly sunny ...

                                                    CUT TO:

64. INT: MRS. AUBREY'S OFFICE RAND DUPLEX   DAY

Mrs. AUBREY, wearing the same suit as in Scene 56. She picks up the receiver of the ringing telephone.

                    AUBREY
               (listens to the phone)
          Yes, it is ...
               (pause)
          I'm sorry, Mr. Courtney. Mr. Rand
          cannot speak to you now, Sir.
               (pause)
          Yes, if you wish. I'll try to
          connect you with Mr. Gardiner ... .

Mrs. AUBREY presses the hold button on the telephone, then presses another button and dials two digits.

                    AUBREY
               (pause, then speaks very
                firmly)
          Mr. Gardiner? This is Mrs. Aubrey.
          Congratulations, Sir, on being
          quoted by the President. Mr.
          Thomas Courtney the financial
          editor of The New York Times is on
          the line. Would you talk to him?

                                                    CUT TO:

65. INT: CHANCE'S ROOM RAND DUPLEX   DAY

                    CHANCE
               (his eyes on the TV set--
                speaks into the
                receiver)
          I'll talk to him.

SOUND: TV AUDIO. The voices of THREE FINANCIAL ANALYSTS discussing the President's speech on a television news special, can be distinctly heard from the TV set in CHANCE's room.

                                                    CUT TO:

66. INT: THE NEW YORK TIMES OFFICE   DAY

TOM COURTNEY sits behind his desk with a telephone receiver in his hand and listens intently. He is in his fifties, slightly balding, wearing a worn-out wool jacket, puffing on his pipe.

SOUND: TV AUDIO: The filtered, heavily muffled, voices of
the THREE ANALYSTS from CHANCE's TV set. On COURTNEY's end
they sound as if they are coming from persons sitting with and
around CHANCE:

>   1st ANALYST (Filtered)
> ... inflationary measure ...
>
>   2nd ANALYST (Fil.)
> ... nevertheless, the accelerated
> tax reductions and a compulsory
> arbitration ...
>
>   COURTNEY (D.V.)
>   (with exaggerated
>   cordiality)
> Hello, Mr. Gardiner. This is Tom
> Courtney, of the New York Times
> financial page. Thank you for this
> opportunity to talk to you, Sir ...
>   (pauses--listens
>   attentively for a
>   moment)
> I'm sorry to interrupt you during
> the conference which I can hear
> taking place ...

                                                        CUT TO:

67.   INT: WHITE HOUSE   NIGHT

In his tastefully furnished sitting room, alone and obviously
anxious, the PRESIDENT OF THE UNITED STAES quickly put on a
robe and, rushing, settles to watch the nightly NCB-TV News
program. The program's already on. On the screen are MIKE
STETSON and JOANNE DAVIDS, the NCB's formost [sic] newscasting
couple.

MIKE STETSON, a middle aged, albino blond and heavily
moustached [sic] is energetic, known for his staccato speech
manner and "to the point attitude". JOANNE DAVIDS, is a
golden-brown stereotypical beauty.

>   MIKE STETSON
> ... the lowest level of popularity
> of any public figure in this
> country. Sheltered by police from
> the largest demonstration of the

unemployed this city has seen in its entire history, fighting for his political life the President went to make peace with Benjamin Rand, the brain, power and purse behind the growing business community opposition to the Government's measures that by freezing the Stock Market thaw, drove countless businesses to close their gates. Joanne ...
    (turns to JOANNE DAVIDS)

        JOANNE DAVIDS
During the tumultous [sic] press conference, following his speech at the Financial Institute of America, the President revealed that it was the pressure of history and <u>not</u> political expediency that forced him to consult the outstanding leaders of the business opposition to his policies noteably [sic], Benjamin Rand and Chauncey Gardiner.
    (turns to STETSON)

        MIKE STETSON
NCB learned that the youthful Chauncey Gardiner, until recently a highly secretive financial wizzard [sic], (a SKETCH of CHANCE fills the screen behind STETSON for a moment) has been given a chance to succeed the ailing Benjamin Rand as Chairman of the First American Financial Corporation, the giant multinational conglomerate that owns among others, the Rand Industries. Following this revelation, the stock of the First American rose by the unprecedented 22%, a dramatic reversal of its steady three year decline. Joanne ...

                        CUT TO:

68. INT: CHANCE'S ROOM RAND DUPLEX   DAY

   CHANCE on the phone as in Scene 65, his face is expressionless; he is watching TV while listening to the receiver.

   SOUND: TV AUDIO CHANCE's SET: the ANALYSTS' talk continues:

>   1st ANALYST (V.O.)
>   (ominously)
>   If you recall, back in 1929 ...
>
>   2nd ANALYST (V.O.)
>   ... and what about last week's drop of sales in that sector from thirty-seven to eleven percent?
>
>   3rd ANALYST (V.O.)
>   ... the complete unpredictability of the market and, its susceptibility to purely psychological influences ...

                                                            CUT TO:

69. INT: THE NEW YORK TIMES OFFICE   DAY
   (As in Scene 66)

>   COURTNEY
>   (continues his talk with CHANCE)
>   ... and since the President quoted you Mr. Gardiner, in his speech, we're wondering whether, perhaps, you would be willing to comment on the nature of your relationship with the First American Financial Corporation?

                                                            CUT TO:

70. INT: CHANCE'S ROOM RAND DUPLEX   DAY
   (Continued from Scene 68)

>   CHANCE
>   (flatly--as the voice of the ANALYSTS on his TV

                        are heard in thebackground)
                    I cannot comment.

                                                    CUT TO:

71.   INT: THE NEW YORK TIMES OFFICE   DAY
        (Continued from Scene 69)
        COURTNEY strains to hear the background voices in
        CHANCE's room.

                        1st ANALYST (Filtered)
                    ... the over-the-counter prices
                    have been steadily ...

                            COURTNEY
                        (insistently)
                    Mr. Gardiner, Sir, would you care,
                    at least to comment on the nature
                    of the discussion that took place
                    among yourself, Mr. Rand and the
                    President?

                                                    CUT TO:

72.   INT: CHANCE'S ROOM RAND DUPLEX   DAY
        (Continued from Scene 70)
        The voices of the TV ANALYSTS are heard in the background:

                            CHANCE
                        (watching TV)
                    The President is an awfully nice
                    man. I enjoyed the meeting.

                                                    CUT TO:

73.   INT: THE NEW YORK TIMES OFFICE   DAY
        (Continued from Scene 71)
        SOUND: TV VOICES (FILTERED) from CHANCE's room continue:

                            COURTNEY
                        (a bit annoyed)
                    Good, Sir, and so, it seems, did
                    the President. But Mr. Gardiner,
                    we'd like to update our profile of
                    you.

>   (pauses)
>   First of all, what exactly is your
>   business? That is, what <u>particular</u>
>   line of business are you engaged
>   in at the moment, if you see what
>   I mean?

                                                    CUT TO:

74.   INT: CHANCE'S ROOM RAND DUPLEX   DAY
      (Continued from Scene 72)
      TV VOICES (FILTERED) continue in the background.

>   CHANCE
>   (watching TV, flatly)
>   I don't see what you mean. You
>   ought to be talking to Mr. Rand or
>   to the President.

                                                    CUT TO:

75.   INT: THE NEW YORK TIMES OFFICE   DAY
      (Continued from Scene 73)

>   COURTNEY
>   (restraining impatience)
>   Yes, of course, but since Mr. Rand
>   is ill, and the President is
>   rather busy, I am taking the
>   liberty of asking <u>you</u>.

                                                    CUT TO:

76.   INT: CHANCE'S ROOM RAND DUPLEX   DAY
      (Continued from Scene 74)
      TV VOICE (FILTERED) continued in the background.

>   CHANCE
>   (politely)
>   I don't think I have anything to
>   say. Good-by!

CHANCE hangs up the telephone.

                                                    CUT TO:

77.   INT: THE NEW YORK TIMES OFFICE   DAY
(Continued from Scene 75)
COURTNEY frowns, listens to the silence on the phone and hangs up.

                                             CUT TO:

78.   INT: EVE'S ROOM   DAY

Dressed only in a very revealing negligee, that reveals her figure, EVE reclines on a sofa. She is absorbed in reading a book titled Being There. When the telephone intercom starts to flash, she reluctantly picks it up, and speaks into the phone.

                    EVE
               Yes?
                    (pauses, listens then
                    visibly lights up)
               Please ask him to come to see me
               here.

She hangs up and, closing the book, on first impulse intends to dress. But after studying herself in the mirror she decides to remain in the neglige [sic] that is more seductive.

CHANCE knocks and enters the room. He is wearing another of his splendid suits. EVE is streted [sic] casually on the sofa.

                    EVE
               It's so nice to see you!

                    CHANCE
                    (looks at her with
                    natural admiration)
               You look so beautiful, Eve!

                    EVE
                    (slightly uncertain of
                    herself points at the
                    book, Being There that
                    rests in her lap)
               Have you read this?

CHANCE glances at the book but as EVE makes no attempt to pass it to him, he gets up, and, natural as always, reaches for it, his hand brushing against her thighs as he picks the book up. EVE tenses at his touch. Gently, he returns to his seat. CHANCE glances at the title, then at the Author's photo on the book's back cover.

                        CHANCE
            No. But I saw him (points at the
            Author's photo) on television.

                        EVE
                (at ease now)
            You have such a staggering recall,
            Chance [sic]. Do you also remember
            other people in your past?

    CHANCE looks at her expectantly.

                        EVE
                (more to the point)
            Women you had?

                        CHANCE
                (looks up directly at EVE)
            I don't know what it is to have a
            woman, Eve ...

    Uncertain what he means, EVE looks at him wordlessly.

                                                    CUT TO:

79.   INT: CHANCE'S ROOM RAND DUPLEX   DAY

        CHANCE is watching TV, his foot on the hassock.

        SOUND: Phone rings. TV AUDIO in the background.

        CHANCE picks up the receiver.

                                                    CUT TO:

80.   INT: MRS. AUBREY'S OFFICE RAND DUPLEX   DAY

        Mrs. AUBREY on the telephone.

                        AUBREY
                (a bit excited)
            Mr. Gardiner, Sir, the executives
            of NCB television just phoned to
            sk if you would appear on their
            show tonight. They apologize for
            such short notice, but the Vice-
            President was scheduled to
            elaborate on the President's
            speech and they have just learned
            that he will be unable to appear
            on the show. And as Mr. Rand is
            ill, and it is you whom the

President quoted, they want you to be the replacement.

CUT TO:

81. INT: THE NEW YORK TIMES OFFICE   DAY

COURTNEY is seated at his desk in the midst of briefing his THREE STAFFERS; with an air of certainty and nonchalance COURTNEY leans back in his chair. The THREE STAFFERS are all in their twenties: ONE a bit hippie-like; TWO black, straight from Brooklyn College; THREE a woman, a rather masculine, women's-lib type.

> COURTNEY
> (self-assuredly)
> ... Well, I just got through talking to Chauncey Gardiner, the man quoted by the President ...
> (pauses--then continues as if he knows a lot about Gardiner)
> As you know, Gardiner is an influential financier, who has business investments and other interests with the First Financial Corporation, among others. He is now participating non-stop in the high-level talks taking place at Rand's apartment.

COURTNEY looks at his STAFFERS. The THREE STAFFERS look at COURTNEY as if expecting to hear more.

> COURTNEY
> (dismissingly)
> Gardiner was in the middle of a conference when he talked to me, so he had to be rather abrupt. Anyway, we don't have time to round up all the information for tomorrow's front page. Go ahead and play up his expected affiliations, the photographs, the captions--you know, the routine stuff.

CUT TO:

82. INT: MRS. AUBREY'S OFFICE RAND DUPLEX   DAY
    (Continued from Scene 80)

    Mrs. AUBREY continues her conversation with CHANCE.

    >   AUBREY
    >   (reassuringly)
    >   ... You don't have to do anything,
    >   Mr. Gardiner.
    >   (cheerfully)
    >   The NCB producer will collect you,
    >   Sir, in time for the show. It's a
    >   live program, but you will only to
    >   be at the studio twenty minutes
    >   before it goes on the air. Tonight
    >   you're going to be the show's main
    >   attraction and the other networks
    >   don't have anyone as important as
    >   you scheduled for their shows.

                                                    CUT TO:

83. INT: CHANCE'S ROOM RAND DUPLEX   NIGHT

    CHANCE (As in Scene 79) watches TV. His leg is stretched out on the hassock. BILL the butler enters.

    SOUND: TV AUDIO: A musical.

    >   BILL
    >   Mrs. Aubrey sent me to assist you in
    >   getting ready for your
    >   television appearance, Sir.

    BILL goes to the closet and returns with a freshly pressed dark suit. He holds it up for CHANCE's inspection and approval.

                                                    CUT TO:

84. INT: LIBRARY RAND DUPLEX   NIGHT

    >   EVE
    >   (talking to Mrs. AUBREY who
    >   stands with an open steno
    >   pad in her hands. Deftly)

>   ... Oh, yes! Since Mr. Gardiner
>   will be absent tonight, I will
>   dine in Mr. Rand's bedroom. Would
>   you please have the large
>   television set brought to the
>   bedroom so we can watch Mr.
>   Gardiner's television appearance?
>
>   AUBREY
>   (pedantically making a
>   note on her steno pad)
>   Certainly, Mrs. Rand.
>
>   CUT TO:

85.   EXT: OUTSIDE RAND APT. BLDG. NIGHT

       CHANCE and the PRODUCER emerge from the lobby of RAND's building.

       The PRODUCER is in his forties, short, very modishly dressed, with a suit of a similar cut to CHANCE's but of an inferior quality. The PRODUCER, a typical slick New Yorker, speaks quite fast, is eager to please and ready to accommodate.

       FOUR PHOTOGRAPHERS are waiting outside, their cameras and flash bulbs ready.

       The DOORMAN, an old man in a uniform, tries to keep ahead of them as they move toward the network car waiting at the curb. THREE other building ATTENDANTS (ELEVATOR and DESK) are seen near the door. A large TV antenna protrudes from the car roof. The DRIVER jumps out and opens the door before the DOORMAN can get there.

       When CHANCE appears, all four PHOTOGRAPHERS take several shots in rapid succession. CHANCE does not seem to pay any attention to them, but the PRODUCER is quite pleased and eager to be photographed.

       CHANCE and PRODUCER enter the limousine and depart.

                                                          CUT TO:

86. INT: INSIDE NETWORK LIMOUSINE   NIGHT

CHANCE and PRODUCER on rear seat. A TV set is installed in front of them; the TV is on and its sound is barely audible, its light washing over the two men.

TV AUDIO: SOFT MUSIC

               PRODUCER
     (impressed, admiringly--
     turned toward CHANCE)
... can't tell you how grateful we are that you have agreed to be a guest on our show. NO other public figure wanted to be committed to any statement about our current economic disaster. Everyone's afraid to say anything ... anything at all.
     (he pauses)
I guess it's because they think people don't like the messengers of bad news, huh?
     (he chuckles a bit)
But you, Sir, you don't mind telling the people what's <u>really</u> going on, do you?

CHANCE watches the TV; then turns toward the PRODUCER and <u>smiles engagingly</u>:

               PRODUCER
     (even more admiringly)
... of course, occupying as you do a position of intimacy with Mr. Rand, the President, and the world of finance, you're best suited to provide millions of our viewers with an explanation they can all understand ...
     (he pauses, then stresses)
With an explanation they can <u>watch</u>!

CHANCE leans forward and changes the channel on the TV set.

SOUND: TV AUDIO: Wildlife program.

SOUND: TV AUDIO: A deodorant commercial.

              PRODUCER
    (almost recites)
THIS EVENING show has more viewers each night than all people who saw all the theater plays combined in the last forty years--and more people than went to the movies or a drive-in in the last twenty-five years ... .
    (pauses for effect)
... Nevertheless, Mr. Gardiner, you talk to sixty-five million people tonight, you can be as outspoken as you wish.
    (pauses. impressed [*sic*]
    by his own figures)
Sixty-five million people will love watching your conversation with the host!

CHANCE leans forward and again changes the channel on the TV set.

SOUND: TV AUDIO: Intermittent laughter and applause.

              PRODUCER
    (slowly, already instructing)
... the host will not interrupt you while you're talking, but if he wants to stop you, or to give you a chance to reply, he'll let you know by raising his left forefinger to his left eyebrow. Then you'll stop, and he'll comment on what you've said or ask you a question. Then, you will speak again ...

                                          CUT TO:

87.   INT: CHANCE'S ROOM RAND DUPLEX   NIGHT

Inside CHANCE's room (looking toward the door). COOK (we know him from Scenes 52, 57) enters in a hurry and visibly nervous. He rushes to the closet and opens it.

COOK goes through every pocket in all of CHANCE's jackets, pants and vests, examining each article of clothing for labels or other markings. Everything CHANCE has was brought with him when he left the TOWNHOUSE, most of the clothes, though they fit CHANCE extremely well, had belonged to the OLD MAN. They were all made before 1929 and are of solid quality, carefully tailored by one of the best tailors of that happy era. When the COOK can't find what he is looking for, he runs to the dresser and goes through all the drawers. He is about to give up when he finds a manufacturer's label on one of the suit jackets. He retrieves a small knife and carefully cuts out the label, then hides it in his pocket. Quickly, he examines one of CHANCE's shoes. When he finds a name of the shoemaker he quickly copies it in his notebook.

CUT TO:

88. INT: MAKE-UP ROOM OF STUDIO NIGHT

Medium-size standard TV studio make-up room, with the usual assortment of mirrors, Kleenex boxes, cream jars, brushes, make-up trays, etc. The MAKE-UP MAN (who is medium height, in his forties, slender, slightly effeminate, gentle, and shy of manner) is completing the final touches of CHANCE's make-up. The PRODUCER stands next to him and watches him work:

MAKE-UP MAN
(to CHANCE)
Will you be making many television appearances, Sir?

CHANCE
(directly)
I don't know. But I like to watch.

MAKE-UP MAN and PRODUCER chuckle politely at his modesty.

PRODUCER
Don't we all!
(he offers CHANCE a
cigarette)

CHANCE
No thank you. I don't smoke

The PRODUCER turns to a small side-wall bar.

PRODUCER
Aren't you lucky! How about a drink then?

```
                        CHANCE
              No thank you. I don't drink.

                        PRODUCER
              A healthy habit! Perhaps a glass
              of juice? Milk?

                        CHANCE
              Milk, thank you.
```

The PRODUCER takes a glass, pours milk from a paper carton into it and hands it to CHANCE. CHANCE drinks it quickly and puts the glass on the make-up counter.

```
                        MAKE-UP MAN
                   (applying final touch to
                   CHANCE's eyebrow and
                   closing his case)
              Good luck, Sir!
```

CHANCE gets up from the chair and leaves the room. The PRODUCER follows him.

As soon as they are both outside, the MAKE-UP MAN locks the door behind them. Quickly he removes a chamois cloth from his pocket and wraps it around the glass left on the counter by CHANCE, taking care not to erase CHANCE's fingerprints. He hides the glass in the inner pocket of his raincoat.

                                                    CUT TO:

89. INT: TV STUDIO (BEHIND MAIN STAGE)   NIGHT

CHANCE and the PRODUCER stand behind a thick partition separating them from the main stage, the cameras and the live studio audience. To their side stands a large bulky TV monitor that shows all the action on stage. TWO MALE TECHNICIANS move in the background (Both men are in their thirties,. They wear casual work clothes, jeans, overalls, etc.)

SOUND: A loudly applauding audience can be heard from the other side of the partition. Simultaneously, an image appears on the monitor, which CHANCE and the PRODUCER are watching.

SOUND: TV AUDIO: The sound from the monitor merges with the LIVE SOUND from the audience on the other side of the partition. CHANCE detecting the source of the LIVE SOUND, turns toward the partition as if uncertain what is happening.

                        PRODUCER
                    (noticing CHANCE's mild
                    interest, whispers
                    reassuringly)
                No rush, Sir. You still have about
                seventeen second!

The HOST appears on the monitor.

The HOST is in his forties, of medium height, with curly,
soft fair hair parted in the middle. He is a picture of the
smart lover from the popular middle-class novel, dressed in an
exaggerated fashion of today.

CHANCE moves a bit closer to see the screen.

SOUND: TV AUDIO and HOST's LIVE VOICE OVER simultaneously:

                        HOST (V.O.)
                    (pompously)
                Tonight, in place of the Vice-
                President, who is unable to be
                with us, we are very honored to
                have as our special guest Mr.
                Chauncey Gardiner, the
                distinguished financier, and a man
                quoted only today by the
                President.

CHANCE is watching on the TV set. He is at ease, no emotion
shows on his face.

The PRODUCER quickly touches CHANCE's shoulder and indicates
that CHANCE should follow him. They walk toward the partition
and he escorts CHANCE to the opening in it, indicates
the opening and gently pushes CHANCE toward it. Without
hesitation, CHANCE spreads open the partition and crosses the
threshold from shadow to light.

SOUND: HOST (V.O.)
                    (raising his voice)
                Ladies and gentlemen--our very
                special guest--Mr. Chauncey
                Gardiner!

                                                    CUT TO:

90.   INT: TV STUDIO ON STAGE NIGHT

Standard talk-show stage with a formica desk, a chair behind it, and some easy chairs next to the desk. A large backdrop "This Evening Show" is behind them. Two full-size rolling TV cameras and their crews, lights, microphones, and studio band are visible. There is a live audience of about three hundred. Almost directly across from the HOST's desk stand a large TV monitor, another is diagonally across from the guests [*sic*] seats, on which the HOST and his guests can see themselves while they are on the air.

From the AUDIENCE P.O.V.: Immediately after the HOST's announcement, CHANCE, appears from behind the partition into the full glare of the lights. Two TV cameras slowly roll toward him, pushed by their CREWS.

The HOST walks toward CHANCE to greet him. Simultaneously CHANCE's image appears on the monitors which hang on both sides above the stage, facing the audience. These are the sets on which the studio audience can monitor the show, in addition to being able to see it live directly in front of them.

As CHANCE walks toward the HOST, a flashing sign appears on the large prompter above the stage facing the audience: "Applause! Applause!" The audience responds to the prompting by applauding.

The HOST guides CHANCE with a gesture of his hand toward the chair next to the desk, inviting CHANCE to sit down. CHANCE sits down, composed and at ease. The HOST sits behind the desk.

SOUND: APPLAUSE CONTINUES

CHANCE looks at himself on the monitor, in a corner of the stage diagonally across from where he is sitting.

SOUND: APPLAUSE ENDS

     HOST
Mr. Gardiner--first, let me thank you, Sir, in the name of the millions of Americans who are watching "This Evening Show" tonight, for filling in on such short notice for the Vice-President.

CHANCE watches the HOST's face on the monitor on which he had been watching himself. Looking at the monitor gives CHANCE a pensive look--he seems to be staring across the stage, as if thinking. Suddenly, his own face again appears on the monitor CHANCE <u>smiles engagingly</u> and sees his own smiling face on the monitor, and CHANCE turns to the HOST, who leans toward CHANCE from behind his desk.

The HOST glances at the notes spread on his desk.

          HOST
          (looking at CHANCE)
I will be direct, Mr. Gardiner: do
you agree with the President's
view of the economy?

          CHANCE
          (Calmly looks at the HOST)
Which view?

SOUND: AUDIENCE LAUGHTER

The HOST, a bit confused, quickly glances at the notes spread in front of him on his desk.

SOUND: LAUGHTER DIES

          HOST
          (with less certainty)
The view the President set forth
today in his major address at the
Financial Institute of America.
Apparently, before his speech, the
President consulted with you,
among others ...

          CHANCE
          (noncommitting)
  Among others!

SOUND: AUDIENCE LAUGHTER

          HOST
          (hesitates again--glances
          at his notes)
What I mean is ...
          (he pauses and looks at
          this notes again--now
          speaks with energy)

>   Well, the President predicted that
>   despite the decline in national
>   productivity,
>
>   (he stumbles)
>   a season of growth will follow. As
>   in a garden ...
>   (he touches his eyebrow
>   with his forefinger
>   signaling it is now
>   CHANCE's turn to talk)

CHANCE looks across the stage at his own image on the monitor; an <u>engaging smile</u> again appears on his face.

>   CHANCE
>   turns slightly to the
>   audience while
>   continuing to look at
>   his own image on the
>   monitor to his right.
>   (Firmly)
>   I know this garden very well. I
>   have worked in it all my life ...
>   (with conviction)
>   ... it is a <u>good</u> garden.
>   (pauses, as if reflecting)
>   Its trees are healthy, and so are
>   its hedges and flowers, as long as
>   they are trimmed and watered in
>   the right season.
>   (he pauses)
>   All they need is someone to tend
>   this garden! To take care of it--
>   not just to--
>   (he searches for a word)
>   to talk and do nothing!

On the prompter above the stage facing the audience a sign flashes: "Applause! Applause!"

SOUND: AUDIENCE erupts with applause

CHANCE sees his own face on the stage monitor. An <u>engaging smile</u> lights up his face.

SOUND: The APPLAUSE continues.

                                                            CUT TO:

91.   INT: FRANKLIN BEDROOM   NIGHT

It is a middle-income bedroom, furnished in modern style. FRANKLIN's WIFE is in bed. She is watching TV on a console facing the bed.

SOUND: TV AUDIO: AUDIENCE APPLAUDING

FRANKLIN is just coming into the bedroom.

SOUND: TV AUDIO: APPLAUSE is heard (This is the sound of the audience applauding CHANCE in Scene 90) FRANKLIN takes off his jacket, sits down on the bed, his back turned to the TV set; he begins to undress. He hears the applause on the TV and looks over his shoulder at his WIFE.

> FRANKLIN
> What did he say, dear?

> WIFE
> (exclaiming)
> Wow! You missed it? Gardiner just said that the economy is doing fine. ... He said the economy is supposed to be something like a garden: you know, things grow and things wilt. It's only a mild frost in the garden. A new direction is needed, that's all.

SOUND: TV AUDIO of the set in front of her. The applause is dying down.

92.   INT: TV STUDIO ON STAGE   NIGHT
(Continued from Scene 90)

SOUND: TV APPLAUSE dying down (this is the same applause heard on FRANKLIN's TV set in Scene 91)

The HOST leans toward CHANCE.

CHANCE is staring at the image of the HOST which has just appeared on the stage monitor. The HOST wears a thoughtful expression.

> HOST
> (attempting to be precise,
>   glances at his notes again)

>   It is your view then, Mr.
>   Gardiner, that the highest
>   unemployment in our history, the
>   fastest inflation we have ever
>   known,--that all this is just
>   another phase, another dry season,
>   so to speak, in the growth of our
>   national garden, so to speak ...
>
>   CHANCE
>   (directly to the camera)
>   It is in my view.
>
>   HOST
>   (a bit at a loss)
>   But, to use your figure of speech,
>   is the current bad season the
>   fault of, so to speak, our garden-
>   -or of our gardener?--so to speak?
>
>   SOUND: AUDIENCE LAUGHTER

                                                           CUT TO:

93.   INT: LIVING ROOM OF MS. HAYES'S APT.   NIGHT

An East-side apartment, typical single woman's "pad" furnished with miscellaneous furniture, toward the Scandinavian-modern style. Mrs. HAYES, wearing a robe, sits on a sofa watching TV with a drink in her hand. At the dining table, watching TV, sit TWO ROOMMATES.

ROOMMATE 1, smoking a cigarette, is blond, in her twenties, tall and slender, wears shorts and Hermes shirt, is talkative.

ROOMMATE 2, drinking a sugar-free diet drink (i.e., TAB), is red-haired, in her early thirties, a bit plump, wears jeans and blouse.

On a TV set the HOST turns to CHANCE. In a close-up, an <u>engaging smile</u> lights up CHANCE's face.

>   HAYES
>   (turns to the others
>   pointing at CHANCE)
>   Now, that's what I call a stunner!
>   Come to think of it,
>   (she pauses, startled by a
>   reminiscence)

he looks like someone I met recently by chance ... .

        ROOMMATE 1
     (watching CHANCE with a romantic gleam in her eyes)
Oh? And where is he now?

        HAYES
     (as if wakened from a daydream)
Who?

        ROOMMATE 1
that [sic] "someone" you met by chance.

        HAYES
     (watching CHANCE's performance, speaks dreamily)
I don't know. The more I think about him, the more I think that he never exited ... .

        ROOMMATE 2
     (watches CHANCE with a concentrated expression. Repeats, imitating Hayes)
"He never existed!"
     (she exclaims)
And how!

Ms HAYES, ROOMMATE 1 and ROOMMATE 2 now watch TV. CHANCE's face fills the screen.

SOUND: TV AUDIO. APPLAUSE ENDS.

CHANCE on TV screen.

        CHANCE
     (with conviction)
It is the fault of the gardener. There is plenty of room for new trees and new flowers of all kinds. All that is needed is someone to tend this garden,

>   someone who loves it and cares for
>   it. Someone
>   (he pauses, saddens)
>   who, like me, has no other place
>   to go to, because he lost all that
>   he once had ...

SOUND: APPLAUSE from the AUDIENCE.

CUT TO:

94.   INT: FRANKLIN BEDROOM   NIGHT
(Continued from Scene 91)

The HOST's face appears on FRANKLIN's TV set.

SOUND: TV AUDIO: the APPLAUSE mounts.

FRANKLIN's WIFE is watching the set. FRANKLIN, wearing pajamas, is hanging his trousers in the electric pants presser beside the bed.

FRANKLIN's WIFE sits straight up in bed and looks at FRANKLIN.

>   WIFE
>   (ruefully)
>   I told you there was no need to
>   sell the Long Island house so
>   quickly. And no need to get rid of
>   the Mercedes! When people like
>   Gardiner get into the act after
>   the election, they'll have the act
>   together! Honestly, you're always
>   the first to panic.

FRANKLIN returns to bed and looks at the TV set. He leans forward, straining to see better. He is staring at the TV set very intently.

CHANCE's face is now on the screen.

SOUND: TV AUDIO: The APPLAUSE continues.

>   WIFE
>   (curiously)
>   what [*sic*] are you thinking about?

>   FRANKLIN
>   (pensively)
>   I think I know that man--

>   (indicating CHANCE on the
>   TV set--he thinks for a
>   moment)
>   Yes, I do! He was at Yale! At the Law
>   School, of course. A great
>   athlete ...
>
>   WIFE
>   And what a personality! The
>   President says all kinds of things
>   he doesn't mean, but this man,
>   Gardiner, means every word he
>   doesn't say.
>   (she reflects pensively)
>   And, what's more, he's awfully
>   good-looking too ...

                                                          CUT TO:

95. INT: TV STUDIO ON STAGE   NIGHT
     (Continued from Scene 92)

CHANCE and the HOST. CHANCE is just finishing his speech:

>   CHANCE
>   (sadly)
>   The roots in my garden have always
>   been strong and every Spring the
>   blossoms grew stronger and more
>   beautiful. This garden needs a good
>   man. If you love your garden,
>   find such a man and next year you
>   will surely see the garden bloom.
>   (he pauses, reflects)
>   I could not let my garden die. I
>   loved it too much.

SOUND: TV AUDIO. The APPLAUSE mounts to an uproar.

Without any anxiety, an <u>engaging smile</u> on his face, CHANCE looks at the audience. Many members of the audience are waving warmly to him, the majority still applauding. The HOST calms down the audience with his hands.

>   HOST
>   (turns to CHANCE--loudly)
>   Thank you
>   (almost drowned out in
>   uproar, repeats)

>   thank you, Mr. Gardiner, thank
>   you. Yours is the spirit we all
>   need so much!
>   (turns to audience)
>   Let's hope that such spirit will
>   bring spring into our troubled
>   garden. Ladies and gentlemen--Mr.
>   Gardiner is a very busy man and
>   has other important business to
>   attend to. Let's all thank him for
>   being with us tonight ...
>   (gesturing toward CHANCE
>   with his hand)
>   A great American!
>
> SOUND: Roar of APPLAUSE

CUT TO:

96.   INT: CORRIDOR RAND DUPLEX   NIGHT

CHANCE is returning from This Evening Show. BONNIE greets him in the corridor:

>   BONNIE
>   (almost spontaneously)
>   Mr. Gardiner, if I may say so,
>   Sir, you were simply splendid!
>   (she calms herself)
>   Mr. and Mrs. Rand are waiting for
>   you in Mr. Rand's bedroom.

CHANCE, at ease, <u>smiles engagingly</u> at her.

CUT TO:

97.   INT: RAND'S BEDROOM   NIGHT

A dinner table with some remaining dishes and glasses is pushed off to one side of the room. A large dormant TV set on its own stand is placed directly in front of RAND's bed. RAND rests in bed. EVE sits in an armchair beside the bed. CHANCE is sitting close by.

>   RAND
>   (in the middle of a
>   sentence, speaking with
>   emotion)

... I hope the whole country
watched you tonight, the whole
country! You have a great gift,
Chauncey, a great gift indeed.
   (he pauses, smooths the
   blanket on his bed)
A gift of being one with the
people. Today that's the mark of a
true leader.

RAND looks at EVE, who is nodding in agreement, barely concealing her pleasure.

          RAND
Eve almost cried when she saw you
being so articulate, coming across
so well, so loved by the people.
She almost cried, didn't you Eve?

          EVE
   (to RAND, blushing, embarrassed)
Ben, dear ...

          RAND
   (to CHANCE with warmth)
By the way, Chauncey there's a
reception tomorrow at the U.N. Eve
is on the Hospitality Committee.
Since I won't be able to escort
her, I'd like you to go in my
place. Together, the two of you
will make quite a stir
there ...
   (he smiles, please with
   himself)
I can already hear the gossip!

          EVE
   (to RAND, a bit
   embarrassed by his
   directness)
Ben, dear ...

                    CHANCE
               (an engaging smile on his
               face)
          I'd be glad to go with Eve, Benjamin.
               (he turns to EVE,
               the smile still on his face)

EVE looks at CHANCE with obvious feeling. RAND notices
her enchantment and he looks at the two of them with
fatherly love.

                                             CUT TO:

98.   INT: WHITE HOUSE ROOM   DAY

A round-table conference with SIX MEN and the PRESIDENT of the
United States. The decor of the room indicates it is in the
White House. The SIX MEN are in their late forties and middle
fifties. They are all distinguished-looking Congressmen and
Senators wearing dark business suits. TWO wear eyeglasses.

The conference has just ended. In an almost relaxed manner,
the SIX MEN are pushing back their char-is, ready to leave.
The PRESIDENT turns to his personal SECRETARY, who is standing
beside him with an open steno pad.

The SECRETARY is an above-average Harvard graduate, in his
thirties, tall and well-built, has dark, medium-short hair,
eyeglasses, and is dressed in a very conservative "Ivy League"
suit. He is exceptionally efficient and attentive in his
manner.

                    PRESIDENT
               (a bit absent-midedly
               [sic] still preoccupied
               with something else)
          ... And yes, ask them to send me
          the file on Chauncey Gardiner,
          will you? I know I've met him
          several times, but I can't think
          where, or with whom.

                    SECRETARY

          Right away, Mr. President

                                             CUT TO:

99.   INT: UN MAIN RECEPTION ROOM   DAY

The reception at the United Nations takes place in a large room with small cocktail tables and chairs placed near its walls. There are about one hundred people, one-fifth of whom are women, milling about. The mood is exuberant: this is an event celebrating the creation of the UN, and the socialites mingle freely with the diplomats. The guest are mainly diplomats, functionaries of the United Nations Secretariat, press and news people, outside V.I.P.s, of all races and colors of skin. Some men and women are wearing their native costumes--mostly African and Indian diplomats. PHOTOGRAPHERS No. 1,2,3,4 and 5 are scattered around. THREE TV CAMERAMEN No. 1,2,3, representing three major national TV networks carrying portable video recorders move around freely. During the course of the party the crowd grows slightly with the new arrivals.

EVE and CHANCE walk through the crowd, accompanied by the UN CHIEF OF PROTOCOL (a Scandinavian-looking man in his forties). Various diplomats bow to EVE--she responds in turn. EVE and CHANCE are led to a most visible table slightly off center, and are seated. The CHIEF OF PROTOCOL summons a WAITER.
A WAITER arrives with a tray of champagne. EVE and CHANCE each take a glass.

A broad and portly man, dressed in a dark suit, passing by notices EVE and approaches the table, his hand outstretched in an exaggerated friendly greeting. This is AMBASSADOR SKRAPINOV of the Soviet Union, Chief of the Soviet Mission to the United Nations and the Senior Soviet diplomat in the United States, said to be the likely successor to the post of Head of the Soviet Government.

SKRAPINOV is in his fifties, with a healthy reddish complexion; he is a substantial-looking man of peasant stock, who dresses in the Western fashion but whose manner is that of Russian exuberance. SKRAPINOV speaks loudly, laughs easily and is basically of a good-humored disposition.

SKRAPINOV is at the table now and gallantly kisses EVE's hand. The CHIEF OF PROTOCOL gently leaves the table and disappears in the throng. CHANCE rises and stands at EVE's side, quite at ease; an <u>engaging smile</u> lights his face.

                    EVE
               (turns slightly toward
                CHANCE formally)
          Chauncey, dear, let me introduce
          you to His Excellency Vladimir
          Skrapinov, Ambassador of the
          Soviet Union. Ambassador Skrapinov
          ... Mr. Chauncey Gardiner, a close
          friend of Benjamin's and mine.

                    SKRAPINOV
               (all smiles)
          Delighted, delighted, so pleased
          to know you, Mr. Gardiner.
               (in a heavy Russian accent)
          I had the pleasure of seeing you,
          Mr. Gardiner, on the television
          last night. I admire your down-to-
          earth philosophy. Like American
          people, the Russian people would
          love what you say. They would eat
          out of your hand, if you forgive
          this expression. You are a very
          fine speaker; you understand about
          common people if I may take the
          liberty to compliment you.

                    EVE
               (addressing SKRAPINOV)
          My husband is ill but he sends you
          his regards, Mr. Ambassador.
          Benjamin recalls with pleasure the
          fascinating talks he has had with
          you in Moscow and in Washington.

SKRAPINOV nods, all smiles. EVE notices and old friend passing
by in the crowd.

                    EVE
               (concern on her face--as if
                suddenly recalling
                something)
          Please excuse me for a moment,
          gentlemen, I have to attend to my
          duties as a hostess.

EVE leaves the table and joins a couple of diplomats in the crowd. SKRAPINOV and CHANCE are now alone at the table. People pass by in the background, slightly out of focus.

One after another, PHOTOGRAPHERS No. 1,2,3,4 and 5 eagerly approach and photograph CHANCE and SKRAPINOV sitting together. All PHOTOGRAPHERS are in their thirties, and carry three or four cameras suspended on their shoulders, camera bags, etc. Their flashbulbs attract attention, and there is a stir of obvious interest among many guests who watch SKRAPINOV and CHANCE.

SOUND: Faint party noises.

As PHOTOGRAPHERS No. 1,2,3,4 and 5 take pictures, SKRAPINOV moves his chair closer to CHANCE's. THREE TV CAMERAMEN, each with a helper, now move closer to the table, pointing their video recorders at CHANCE and SKRAPINOV. They start recording. Around them excitement builds up. The meeting between CHANCE and SKRAPINOV becomes and event of the reception. SKRAPINOV is fully aware of this and makes the most of it.

                SKRAPINOV
I am so sorry we have not met sooner, but tell me, Mr. Gardiner, how serious is Mr. Rand's illness? I did not want to upset Mrs. Rand by asking her.

                CHANCE
Mr. Rand is ill. Very ill.

                SKRAPINOV
  (eagerly)
So I understand, so I understand. Mr. Gardiner, may I be candid with you?
    (he looks at CHANCE who
     <u>smiles engagingly</u>)
Considering the grave economic condition in your country--such inflation, such unemployment--such financial crisis--
    (he pauses)
shouldn't we the diplomats, and you, the businessmen, get together more often? I noticed that in your television speech you alluded to

> politics indirectly--but you made
> your point quite clear ...

PHOTOGRAPHER No. 4 approaches and quickly takes a photograph of the two men.

> SKRAPINOV
> (he lowers his voice)
> ... because, in fact, we are not
> so far from each other, not so
> far.

> CHANCE
> (an engaging smile lights
> his face. He repeats
> after SKRAPINOV)
> Not so far ...
> (CHANCE points with his
> head at the distance
> between the chairs)

SKRAPINOV looks intently at CHANCE, then lights up in response.

> CHANCE (cont.)
> ... our chairs almost touch!

SKRAPINOV laughs aloud and, spontaneously, pats CHANCE on his shoulder.

> SKRAPINOV
> (exclaims)
> Bravo. Bravo! Very good!
> (ominously)
> Our chairs indeed almost touch and
> ...
> (he inclines cunningly
> toward CHANCE)
> ... how shall I put it? We both
> want to remain seated, don't we?
> With all the military around ready
> to invent another war, when one
> chair goes, so does the other
> chair
> (pauses)
> and then ...
> (very loudly)

>   BOOM! We are both down! As we say
>   in Russian ...

SKRAPINOV bends closer to CHANCE and speaks a phrase in Russian which we barely hear. An <u>engaging smile</u> lights CHANCE's face.

>   SKRAPINOV
>   (notices CHANCE's smile
>   and something dawns on
>   him: he looks
>   astonished)
>   But of course! You do understand
>   Russian, Mr. Gardiner, do you not?

CHANCE continues to smile

>   SKRAPINOV (Cont.)
>   (looks proudly at CHANCE)
>   I knew it all along. I know an
>   educated man when I meet one.

EVE returns to the table with TWO OTHER DIPLOMATS, who just begin to introduce themselves to CHANCE and SKRAPINOV. Both DIPLOMATS No. 1 and No. 2 are in their forties, in dark suits, quite rigid in manner. SKRAPINOV is now surrounded by the TV CAMERAMEN and poses himself with dignity for a quick interview.

EVE and CHANCE leave SKRAPINOV at the table and walk away. As they start, we hear SKRAPINOV pompously pronouncing:

>   SKRAPINOV (V.O.)
>   Like the Soviet people, my dear
>   friend Mr. Gardiner also
>   understands the thread of the new
>   war as a remedy for American
>   economic crisis. As he is
>   intimately familiar with those in
>   power, Chauncey Gardiner knows
>   that ...

SKRAPINOV's voice fades out as CHANCE and EVE make their way through the crowd. On three occasions EVE stops to shake hands with DIPLOMATS NO. 3, 4, and 5. (We assume from her gestures and CHANCE's handshaking that quick general introductions are being made.)

EVE and CHANCE are approached by REPORTER 1, who whispers something to EVE; she nods in agreement. EVE and CHANCE follow

REPORTER 1 toward the UN Foyer, which is an extension of the UN Main Reception Room.

CUT TO:

100. INT: ROOM IN THE FBI COMPUTER CENTER, FBI HEADQUARTERS, WASHINGTON, D.C. DAY

Three FBI AGENTS, all in their mid-thirties, in business suits are leaning over a giant fingerprint-date retrieving computer. A large 11 x 14 transparency of several fingerprints marked on the bottom CHAUNCEY GARDINER, AGE ? is just being fed into the computer. The FBI AGENTS wait anxiously as the computer "digests" the print. After a few seconds the computer ejects an 5 x 7 index card. FBI AGENT 1 grabs it eagerly as AGENTS 2 and 3 bend over to see it. The card is blank. The FBI AGENTS look at each other in utter disbelief, then AGENT 2 feeds the transparency into the computer again. Again the computer ejects a blank card. Now FBI AGENT 3 feeds into another computer an 11 x 14 transparency marked CHAUNCEY GARDINER, AGE ? containing both a full face and a profile of CHANCE taken clearly by one of the photographers either in front of RAND's residence, at the TV studio, or at the UN party.

Anxiously, AGENT 3 activates the computer. After a while, the computer ejects a blank index card. The FBI AGENTS are openly distressed.

> FBI AGENT 1
> I don't believe it. I just don't believe it?
> (he pauses, looks at the others in utter resignation. With his chin he points at CHANCE's photograph)
> It's as if he had never existed!

Reluctantly, he reaches for the red phone marked "Top Priority Only" and asks the operator for "The White House." On the desk in front of him lies a fresh manila folder marked FBI: CHAUNCEY GARDINER, AGE ? Waiting for The White House, FBI AGENT 1 mechanically opens the folder. It contains nothing. Meanwhile, FBI AGENT 2 looks up at a life-size portrait of J. EDGAR HOOVER hanging on the wall. He turns to FBI AGENT 3:

                        FBI AGENT 2
            If he ...
                  (he points at the portrait of
                   J. EDGAR HOOVER)
            ... if he only knew what's going on
            in this country now that he's no
            longer with us!
                  (he gestures in despair)

                                                        CUT TO:

101.   INT: CHANCE'S ROOM RAND DUPLEX   DAY

       CHANCE in yet another of the OLD MAN's suits, this time beige,
       is watching TV.

       SOUND: A knock on the door.

       EVE enters, dressed to go out, wearing a light bluish tweed
       suit. CHANCE lights up when he sees her.

                        EVE
            Chauncey, dear, I'm about to do some
            errands for Benjamin, and
            some household shopping ... .
                  (she hesitates)
            Would you like to go with me?

                        CHANCE
            I would love to, Eve.
                  (he turns off TV set and
                   gets up)

       SOUND: There is a knock at the door.

                        CHANCE
            Come in.

       Mrs. AUBREY enters, as always, efficient in manner, a steno
       pad in her hand.

                        AUBREY
                  (addressing CHANCE)
            Sir, there is quite a group of
            gentlemen from the press and TV
            waiting for you outside. They
            wonder whether you wouldn't answer
            some of their ...

> EVE
> (to Mrs. AUBREY
> interjects)
> Mr. Gardiner will accompany me
> this morning, Mrs. Aubrey. Please
> have the car ready!
>
> AUBREY
> (to EVE)
> Certainly, Mrs. Rand
> (pauses, to CHANCE)
> However, if at this time you
> prefer not to speak to the press,
> it might be better to leave the
> building through the side exit.
> The car could wait there ...
> (while facing CHANCE, she
> looks up at EVE as if
> expecting her to decide)
>
> CHANCE
> I don't mind ...
>
> EVE
> (interjects)
> Mr. Gardiner and I will meet the
> reporters on our way.
>
> CUT TO:

102. EXT: OUTSIDE RAND APT. BLDG.   DAY

Outside Rand's Park Avenue residence a group of REPORTERS and CAMERAMEN had staged a veritable vigil waiting for an interview with CHANCE.

There are two portable television cameras on tripods and about TEN CAMERAMEN and PHOTOGRAPHERS and SEVEN REPORTERS waiting. The REPORTERS stand and talk to each other; they are generally in their thirties or early forties, and all wear neat business suits. The PHOTOGRAPHERS are older, and more disheveled, in casual clothing, carrying heavy equipment bags and satchels on their shoulders.

CHANCE and EVE emerge from the building on their way to the RAND limousine. The REPORTERS and TV CAMERAMEN politely block their path. EVE is smiling and at ease. CHANCE shows no emotion.

> REPORTER 1
> (steps forward)
> Would you be so kind as to answer
> a few questions, Mr. Gardiner?

As he looks around, CHANCE <u>smiles engagingly</u>. The REPORTERS nearby light up in response.

EVE steps slightly in front of CHANCE. There is a sudden firmness about her.

> EVE
> (loud enough for all the
> reporters to hear her)
> Let's get this straight right now,
> gentlemen. Like my husband, whom
> you know so well, Mr. Gardiner is
> a busy man. You will not keep him
> too long. Agreed?

THREE of FOUR (V.O.) almost simultaneously:

>> VOICE 1 -- Yes, Mrs. Rand.
>> VOICE 2 -- All right, beautiful!
>> VOICE 3 -- O.K.
>> VOICE 4 -- (mumbles) What's the rush?

> REPORTER 2
> (addressing CHANCE)
> After reading the Times editorial
> about the President's speech in
> which you were quoted, do you have
> anything to say, Sir?

CHANCE looks at EVE, and she returns his look without expression.

> CHANCE
> (flatly)
> I didn't read it.

Stirred up by his answer, the REPORTERS surround CHANCE. They now direct all their questions at CHANCE, firing them off rapidly one after the other. TV CAMERAMAN 1, films the scene, a couple of REPORTERS point microphones closer to CHANCE's face, while FOUR PHOTOGRAPHERS take pictures.

                  REPORTER 3
            (astonished)
      Sir, you did not read the Times editorial on the President's address?

                  CHANCE
            (with a smile)
      I did not.

REPORTERS 5, 6, and 7 look at each other, astounded by his answer. EVE looks at CHANCE with astonishment, which quickly turns to admiration.

                  REPORTER 2
      But, Mr. Gardiner ...
            (persisting, as if
             attempting to save
             CHANCE's face)
      ... you must at least have glanced at it?

                  CHANCE
            (still smiling)
      I did not.

                  REPORTER 3
      In its editorial, the Washington Post spoke of your "crude brand of populism." Did you read that?

                  CHANCE
            (still smiling--at ease)
      I did not.

                  REPORTER 2
      Well, what about the phrase, "crude brand of populism"?

                  CHANCE
            (at ease)
      It's a brand I don't use.

ALL REPORTERS laugh. EVE uses this as a pretext to interject.
She steps forward:

>   EVE
>   (loudly--slightly
>   apologetic)
>   Mr. Gardiner has many
>   responsibilities--especially
>   since--as you all know, my
>   husband, Mr. Rand, has been ill.
>   When necessary, Mr. Gardiner finds
>   out what is in the papers from our
>   staff's briefings.
>
>   REPORTER 4
>   (an older man--politely to
>   CHANCE)
>   Mr. Gardiner, Sir, what papers do
>   you read when you're less busy.
>
>   CHANCE
>   I do not read any newspapers.
>   (pauses)
>   I watch television.

TV NEWSCASTER 1, a blond, feminine, good-looking woman in her
twenties, poses in front of the TV camera. To interview CHANCE she
moves forward sexily.

>   TV NEWSCASTER 1
>   Mr. Gardiner, now that you appear
>   to be the spokesman for your party
>   in the forthcoming elections,
>   would you care to tell our viewers
>   which state can claim you as its
>   son?
>
>   CHANCE
>   The garden state.
>   (an <u>engaging smile</u> softens
>   his face)
>
>   TV NEWSCASTER 1
>   The Garden State!

>   (she reflects, then
>   exclaims)
>   Oh! New Jersey, of course! They
>   must be proud of you over there.
>   Well, Sir, where then is your
>   home?
>
>   CHANCE
>   Here!
>   (he points behind at the
>   building he and EVE have
>   just come out of, and
>   turns away to answer the
>   next reporter)

GERARD FONZI TV NEWSCASTER. Good-looking, dark wavy hair, in his mid-thirties. Neat light-colored business suit.

>   FONZI
>   Mr. Gardiner, do you mean, Sir,
>   that <u>you</u> find television coverage
>   of the news sufficient?
>
>   CHANCE
>   (faces the TV camera, an
>   <u>engaging smile</u> lights up
>   his face)
>   As I have said, I don't read. I
>   just watch.
>
>   FONZI
>   Thank you, Mr. Gardiner. Few men
>   in public life have the courage
>   not to read--none have the guts to
>   admit it!
>   (turns to camera)
>   This is Gerard Fonzi, NCB News, in
>   front of the Manhattan hide-a-way
>   of the newest Presidential
>   hopeful--Chauncey Gardiner!

GROUP SHOT--ALL the REPORTERS look at each other, clearly uncertain of how to react. CHANCE smiles engagingly.

                                                  CUT TO:

103. INT: OFFICE OF EDITOR-IN-CHIEF THE WASHINGTON POST   DAY

A solidly furnished newspaper office. Journalistic trophies--prizes, diplomas, awards, plaques from various social and political associations all inscribed to AUSTIN STURGESS stand on the enormous desk and hang on the walls.

AUSTIN STURGESS, the Post's Editor-in-Chief is in his early fifties. Gray-haired, healthy-looking, casually dressed, in tweed jacket and slacks, he exudes energy, strength of conviction, and easy familiarity. He has just finished talking on the phone.

> STURGESS
> (into the phone)
> Send them in. Right away.

Waiting, he paces the room. Enter CLEMY and BERNIE, two Washington Post crack reporters. CLEMY in his thirties, dark-haired, very casually dressed in pullover and jeans, rapid speaking, and restless. BERNIE, same age, blond, carefully attired (tweedy jacket, shirt and tie) speaks with phlegm.

STURGESS, cordially, rushes to them, patting them on the arms and shoulders.

> STURGESS
> That's fast, my hounds, that's very fast. Let's have it all!

He places himself behind his desk and gestures for CLEMY and BERNIE to sit down. BERNIE sits down, sinking in an easy chair.

> STURGESS
> (very impatient, questioningly)
> Bernie? Clemy? C'mon, my hounds--lets' have it!

> CLEMY
> (standing nervously, very restless)
> All the traces--established beyond a doubt--
> (he glances at BERNIE)

                    BERNIE
              (calmly)
          Doubtlessly established ...

                    CLEMY
          ... that Gardiner--is--
              (pauses for effect)

                    BERNIE
              (staccato)
          ... a p-r-i-v-a-c-y f-r-e-a-k!

                    CLEMY
              (elaborating for STURGESS)
          A post-Watergate ... privacy
          freak! A new brand of public
          figure ...

                    BERNIE
          And a p-h-e-n-o-m-e-n-a-l comeback
          for the Populist Republicans!

                    STURGESS
              (as if perceiving new
              journalistic triumphs--
              speaks potential
              headlines that he
              already visualizes in
              his paper)

          "Populist Politician Succeeds in
          Erasing All Traces! ..."

                    BERNIE
              (ominously)
          Of course, Gardiner could not get
          rid of his family, his
          connections, his past, <u>all</u> on his
          own. There must be others, many
          others, <u>important others</u> ...

                    CLEMY
          Who helped him to erase <u>all</u> ...
              (pauses)
          as if he had never existed!

> BERNIE
> And who decided to take a chance--
> to <u>launch</u> him only now ...

> STURGESS
> (walking around the room
> all excited, murmurs)
> Others, others ... What a s-t-u-p-
> e-n-d-o-u-s cover-up ... .

He clearly perceives possibilities for a scoop for his paper. Pleased with himself, he moves to embrace his hounds, who eagerly submit to his fatherly arm.

> STURGES [*sic*]
> (on second thoughts,
> proudly)
> And one day what a book this will
> make for my hounds!
> (he embraces them even
> more fondly)
> And what a movie about what's in
> the book! Starring, let's see. ...

CUT TO:

104. INT: RAND'S LIMOUSINE   DAY

EVE and CHANCE sit in the rear seat. The car is moving through Manhattan streets.

> EVE
> (very pleased)
> I have never seen anyone who
> handles the media better than you
> do. ... You're cool, detached--
> almost as if you were born to it
> ... .

<u>Engaging smile</u> lights CHANCE's face.

> EVE
> It was simply magnificent watching
> you with the reporters. They all ate
> out of your hand.

EVE watches him tenderly. Slowly, she puts her hand on his thigh. Her hand rests there. CHANCE does not react.

                              EVE
                    (slightly discouraged by
                    his passivity,
                    pleadingly)
               Would you go with me tonight,
               Chauncey, to a dinner party at the
               home of a very close friend of
               mine? Now that you've been on TV
               and had your picture in the
               papers, she's all excited and
               thinks you're marvelous. Would you
               mind?

                              CHANCE
                    (warmly)
               I'd be glad to go.

                              EVE
               To make her a bit jealous, I told
               her you and I have been friends
               for quite some time.

Her hand moves an inch or two higher on CHANCE's thigh. He does not seem to notice.

                                                            CUT TO:

105.   SKRAPINOV'S OFFICE DAY   [*SIC*]

It is a medium-size room at the Soviet Mission to the UN in Manhattan, with thick, red wall-to-wall carpeting, and large portraits of Marx, Engels, Lenin, and two more portraits of the most recent Chiefs of Soviet State. The room's bookshelves are filled with a multi-volume bound Soviet encyclopedia and endless volumes of the collected works of Marx, Engels, and Lenin. A large desk in the corner commands the room. On its top sit an elaborate inkwell set, with a miniature rocket pointing to the sky, a silver statuette of Lenin to its left, and, to the right of a row of white telephones, a black-and-white photograph of SKRAPINOV's wife and three children.

SKRAPINOV sits behind his desk and is in the middle of giving instructions to KARPATOV.

KARPATOV, an intelligence officer and one of SKRAPINOV's subordinates, is in his thirties. He is slender, pale, and almost bald and constantly hunches his shoulders. His manner is that of a fearful, obedient, overeager bureaucrat.

KARPATOV is standing in front of the desk. He also speaks with a Russian accent:

>KARPATOV
>(with some apprehension)
>... nevertheless, we have been able to establish <u>beyond doubt</u> that the White House is <u>also</u> eager to find out more about Gardiner. Clearly, such interest on their part is of <u>great political significance</u> ...

SKRAPINOV glares coldly at KARPATOV and waits for KARPATOV to finish his report. KARPATOV fidgets nervously but says no more.

>SKRAPINOV
>
>And?

>KARPATOV
>(pretends not to understand the prompting)
>And?

SKRAPINOV gets up and, without a word, begins to pace back and forth across the room, barely containing his anger. Finally, he explodes, emphatically--slowly.

>SKRAPINOV
>I wanted one answer from your department, and one answer: the answer to the question, <u>who is Gardiner</u>? Where are <u>the facts</u> I asked for?
>(he raises his voice, almost screaming)
>Where are the facts, Karpatov?

>KARPATOV
>(upset--stands almost at attention)
>Comrade Ambassador!--until now we have encountered great

difficulties with Gardiner. We have activated all our agents, but so far we just haven't been able to crack this Chauncey Gardiner's cover. ... In the entire history of our intelligence operations in the United States our agents have never come across such well-organized total blackout of a politician's past!

                                                                      CUT TO:

106.   EXT. NEW YORK CENTRAL PARK ZOO   DAY

A sunny afternoon. As dozens of people mingle about them, EVE and CHANCE are watching a CHIMPANZEE. The CHIMPANZEE plays in his cage, which is fitted with a few pathetic trees, when, among the zoo visitors, it suddenly notices a VISITOR with a working portable TV set. The CHIMPANZEE--fascinated--begins to watch the program, a game show. Amused by the CHIMPANZEE's interest the VISITOR, a young man in his early twenties, presses the TV set against the cage so the animal can see the program better. The CHIMPANZEE begins to respond to the game show: it gets excited, it saddens, it jumps with utmost joy when the prize is revealed. CHANCE and EVE watch the CHIMPANZEE, EVE amused, CHANCE slightly saddened.

                CHANCE
          (nodding toward the
          CHIMPANZEE)
He's like me. He also lost his garden!

                EVE
          (also saddened, cuddles
          against CHANCE's strong
          arm)
One day--one day, when you will feel like, you'll tell me all about your life.
     (she presses tenderly
      against him)
I know--I can sense that you have gone through a lot.

>   (she is overcome by
>   feeling)
>   But, if you tell me nothing about
>   it, I'll understand. You see, Chauncey,
>   (she hesitates to say it)
>   I feel so close--so safe with you--it
>   is--it is as if you've always
>   existed for me! If I knew your
>   past it would change nothing!

CHANCE looks at her and <u>smiles engagingly</u>. Just then he is noticed and clearly recognized by other BY-STANDERS. THREE or FOUR smile at him appreciately [*sic*].

>   BY-STANDER 1
>   (a middle-aged woman)
>   I saw you on TV. You're a great
>   guy. I hope you win! Good luck to
>   you, Gardiner!
>
>   BY-STANDER 2
>   (an older woman, low-
>   income class)
>   You're Mr. Gardiner, aren't you!
>   You're the one to save our garden,
>   to find jobs for us! God bless
>   you, Chauncey!

CHANCE <u>smiles engagingly</u>. EVE is moved to tears.

>   BY-STANDER 3
>   (an eighteen-year-old
>   girl, suburban type)
>   Hello, Chauncey Gardiner! My
>   parents say you're going to be our
>   next President.
>   (she smiles coquettishly)
>   I'll vote for you! You're
>   handsome!

CHANCE <u>smiles engagingly</u>.

>   BY-STANDER 4
>   (with an Instamatic
>   camera, a good-looking
>   middle-class housewife,

>   all smiles, approaches
>   CHANCE)
>   You're the politician I saw the
>   other day on TV?
>   (she moves closer)
>   Can I have your autograph?
>   (she is about to open her
>   bag to retrieve a
>   notebook and pen)
>
>   CHANCE
>   (with a smile, pointing at
>   her camera)
>   Wouldn't you rather take a picture?
>
>   By-STANDER 4
>   I sure would!
>   (excitedly)
>   Thank you!

She takes a picture of CHANCE and is about to continue the conversation when EVE moves forward protectively.

>   EVE
>   (a bit annoyed)
>   This is Mr. Gardiner. You might
>   have seen his photograph in the
>   papers.
>
>   BY-STANDER 4
>   (as she leaves)
>   I don't read papers. I watch TV!

EVE looks at CHANCE admiringly.

>   EVE
>   It's amazing, Chauncey, how well
>   you understand the common people,
>   and how openly they react to you!

CHANCE smiles engagingly.

                                                      CUT TO:

107.   INT: SKRAPINOV'S OFFICE   NIGHT

SKRAPINOV behind his desk, drumming the top with his fingers. KARPATOV enters, visibly terrified.

KARPATOV approaches the desk and stiffens:

>   SKRAPINOV
>   (commandingly)
>   Major Karpatov, the facts! Begin ...
>
>   KARPATOV
>   (wetting his lips)
>   Comrade Ambassador: we have not
>   succeeded in discovering the
>   slightest information about his
>   past--as I said, <u>it's almost as if
>   he had never existed</u> ...

SKRAPINOV puffs up like a frog, rises and smashes the desk top with his fist: the statuette of Lenin topples to the floor. KARPATOV trembling, picks it up with reverence and puts it back on the desk.

>   SKRAPINOV
>   (screaming, still standing)
>   You can't palm off such nonsense
>   on me, Karpatov, I won't accept
>   it.
>   (mimicking his tone)
>   <u>As if he had never existed</u>. Are
>   you mad? Do you realize that only
>   hours ago I mentioned Gardiner in
>   <u>my speech</u> to the New York Chamber
>   of Commerce?
>   (pauses)
>   Thank God ...
>   (corrects himself)
>   ... what luck the American
>   President had quoted him also! Do
>   you realize that Gardiner is on
>   the way to becoming one of <u>the
>   most important men</u> in this country
>   and ...

> the biggest, most powerful
> industrial state in the world! And
> you dare to tell me--<u>As if had had
> never existed</u>!
> > (pauses; is exhausted,
> > begins to lecture a bit)
> Gardiner is a businessman, a
> brand-new type of Republican
> politician, a protégé of Benjamin
> Rand's, one of the most powerful
> men in America (whispers) possibly
> an architect of a coup d'Etat
> [*sic*]!
> > (reflects, then proclaims)
> Men like Gardiner decide the fate
> of <u>millions of simple people every
> day</u>!

CUT TO:

108. INT: DINNER PARTY   NIGHT

    The dinner party given by EVE's friend, SOPHIE, has ended. Drinks are being served in an extremely large living room filled with paintings, sculptures, and glass cabinets containing small art objects. An enormous chandelier hangs on a golden rope and resembles a tree whose leaves have been replaced by flickering candles.

    GUESTS are scattered, sitting and standing around. Most evening clothes. WAITERS and WAITRESSES are moving through with trays of coffee and after-dinner drinks.

    EVE arrives accompanied by CHANCE. EVE in a long gown, CHANCE in another of the OLD MAN's suits that looks very evening-ish. At the door they are greeted by SOPHIE, the hostess.

    EVE wears an impressively simple evening gown, modestly jeweled. SOPHIE throws her head back a bit and brazenly measures CHANCE up and down, while EVE shyly looks down.

    > SOPHIE
    > He's even more handsome than on
    > television. <u>Now I know why</u> you've
    > never mentioned him to me before ...

                    EVE
                (afraid that someone might
                overhear)
            Sophie, please ...

                    SOPHIE
                (mockingly resigned)
            I'll shut up, don't worry.

SOPHIE is still laughing; EVE seems to be a bit embarrassed by SOPHIE's grossness.

                    SOPHIE
                (to CHANCE)
            Do forgive me, Mr. Gardiner. Eve
            and I always laugh like
            schoolgirls when we're together.

            You're even handsomer than your
            pictures ... .

CHANCE looks at her, an <u>engaging smile</u> on his face. SOPHIE moves a bit away from CHANCE and measures him again:

                    SOPHIE
            Of course, with your height and
            broad shoulders and narrow hips
            and long legs and such obvious
            health and sheer strength ...

                    EVE
                (breaks in slightly
                embarrassed)
            Sophie, please ...

                    SOPHIE
            I'll be quiet now, I will ...
                (energetically)
            Do come with me, Mr. Gardiner.
            Everybody's been dying to meet you
            ...

While EVE remains surrounded by other guests, SOPHIE leads CHANCE into the crowd.

On the way, CHANCE is approached by a PUBLISHER: He is a short, well-dressed man in his forties. SOPHIE leaves the two men to each other.

                    PUBLISHER
               (eager but respectful)
          Mr. Gardiner--may I introduce
          myself. I am Ronald Steigler of
          Eidolon Publishing Company. Last
          night I watched your TV
          performance and tonight, while
          driving here, I heard on my car
          radio that the Soviet Ambassador
          mentioned the talks he had
          conducted with you at the UN.

                    CHANCE
               (with an engaging smile)
          On the radio? You don't have a TV
          in your car?

                    PUBLISHER
               (embarrassed but
                pretending to be amused)
          Well, no, but I hardly even listen
          to my radio-- traffic is so hectic
          ... .

PUBLISHER snatches a drink from the tray of a passing WAITER and props himself up against the wall. He gulps the drink quickly.

                    PUBLISHER
               (moves closer to CHANCE)
          Mr. Gardiner, my editors and I have
          been wondering if you'd consider
          writing a book for us? Something
          timely, on the theme you spoke of on
          TV. We could bring it out in
          mass paperback in six weeks.

CHANCE does not react.

                    PUBLISHER
          At this time, when your popularity
          is about to be sky-high, such a
          book could influence the outcome
          of the elections ... .
               (pauses)

We could draw up a contract in a
day or two and I could promise you
right now a high six-figure
advance--for the hard-cover rights
only! Then ...
    (pauses)
a seven-figure advance for
paperback ...

          CHANCE
    (directly)
But I can't write!

          PUBLISHER
    (smiles deprecatingly)
Of course not! Who has the time!
One glances at things, one talks,
listens, watches television ...
    (saddens)
You know, because of all this,
publishing books isn't exactly a
flowering garden these days.

          CHANCE
    (with mild interest)
What kind of garden is it?

The PUBLISHER is about to answer when they are separated by other guests. Suddenly CHANCE is cornered by an obviously EFFEMINATE MAN, about fifteen years older than CHANCE. His hair is long, silky, and combed neatly straight from his forehead to the nape of his neck. His eyes are large and expressive, shaded with unusually long eyelashes. EFFEMINATE MAN looks closer at CHANCE, then leans across and whispers something into CHANCE's ear.

CHANCE does not answer; an <u>engaging smile</u> lights his face. EFFEMINATE MAN, as if encouraged by CHANCE's reaction, moves even closer and whispers into CHANCE's ear once more. CHANCE retains a <u>smile</u> on his face.

          EFF. MAN
    (whispering to CHANCE)
We could do it <u>now</u>. We can go
upstairs together.

>   CHANCE
>   (a blank, vacant
>   expression on his face)
>   I like to watch.
>
>   EFF. MAN
>   (astonished)
>   <u>Watch</u>? You mean ... <u>just</u> watch?
>
>   CHANCE
>   (with bland expression)
>   Yes. To watch. Just watch ...
>
>   CUT TO:

109   INT: CIA DIRECTOR'S OFFICE WASHINGTON, D.C.   DAY [SIC]

An imposing room, furnished with first-quality leather and wood furniture, supermodern [sic] desk, discreetly containing various switches, built-in telephones, etc. On one wall an enormous life-size portrait of John Foster Dulles; on the other, smaller 16 x 20 paintings of Roosevelt, Truman, Eisenhower, Kennedy, a reduced 11 x 14 black-and-white photograph of Nixon, paintings of Ford, Carter, and of the (U.S. President of the time the story of BEING THERE unfolds).

The CIA DIRECTOR is very tall, in his sixties, impeccably dressed in tweeds.

>   CIA DIRECTOR
>   (in the middle of phone
>   conversation)
>   No, General, we haven't been able
>   to ...
>   (pauses)
>   But I can assure you, Gardiner is
>   definitely not a foreign-power
>   plant ...
>   (pauses, listens)
>   I said he is <u>not</u> a foreign power
>   plant ...
>   (pauses, listens. He
>   spells it)
>   plant, p-l-a-n-t, like in a garden
>   ...

>   (pauses, listens)
>   No, General, he does not appear to
>   be Jewish. Our Arab friends have
>   nothing to fear ... .
>   (pause, listens)
>   No, he does not appear to be
>   Mormon. In Salt Lake City they
>   have records of all Mormons who
>   have ever lived--he is not listed
>   there ... .
>   (pauses, listens)
>   Our Jewish friends have nothing to
>   fear ...
>   (with conviction-pauses,
>   listens)
>   Yes, General, he might be one of
>   the candidates ... Yes, he could.
>   Yes, he might. Elected, yes,
>   that's what I mean, General
>   (listens)
>   Do I trust the good instinct of
>   our people, General! Half our
>   population is honest--
>   (pauses)
>   Of course, it's not always the
>   same half ... .
>
>   CUT TO:

110.   INT: CHANCE'S ROOM RAND DUPLEX NIGHT

>   The room is lit solely by the light emanating from the TV
>   set. CHANCE sits on top of his bed. EVE sits on the hassock
>   next CHANCE's knees, between CHANCE and the TV set. CHANCE
>   and EVE are still in their party clothes (as in Scene 108).
>
>   SOUND: TV AUDIO male soloist.
>
>   EVE
>   (whispering in short
>   bursts)
>   You don't mind my coming in here, to
>   your room, do you, Chauncey?

>   CHANCE
>   (looks straight ahead
>   toward TV. Light from
>   the TV plays on his
>   face)
>   No. I don't. I like to see you
>   here.

EVE sits down next to CHANCE on the bed. She leans toward him and her hair brushes his face. She presses her body against his; her fingers tightly gripping his shoulders.

SOUND: TV AUDIO:

>   1st FEMALE VOICE (V.O.)
>   I won't do it, I won't

EVE begins to kiss CHANCE's neck and face.

SOUND: TV AUDIO: 2nd MALE VOICE (V.O.)
>   Please ... I beg you.

EVE kisses CHANCE's neck and his cheeks. CHANCE neither moves nor resists. Suddenly, EVE goes limp and lets her head fall on his chest.

>   EVE
>   (a bit desperate)
>   Don't you want me? Don't you feel
>   <u>anything</u> for me--<u>anything at all</u>?

CHANCE sits up at the edge of the bed and looks at her, surprised and hurt by her outcry.

>   EVE
>   (in despair)
>   You don't want me.
>   (sadly, in a low voice)
>   I am right, aren't I?

SOUND: TV AUDIO -- muffled dialogue of MALE and FEMALE voices continue throughout this scene.

CHANCE keeps looking at EVE thoughtfully. <u>Engaging smile</u> softens his features:

                    CHANCE
               (pauses, searching for
               words)
          I do want ... to watch you.

EVE sits up, gasping for breath.

                    EVE
               (astonished)
          To watch me?

                    CHANCE
          Yes, to watch you, Eve. You're so
          beautiful.

                                                  CUT TO:

111.   INT: HOSPITAL TV ROOM   NIGHT

TV ROOM in a smalltown [sic] Southern hospital, for the poor
and homeless. It is late evening. The large TV set in the
room's center stands on a wooden table. Watched by patients,
four women (three black) and two men (one black, one white)
all sleepy and weary, all in hospital robes.

TV is on, its flickering light playing on the fatigued viewers
and decrepit walls of the room. The late evening news program
reports the news of the day. Full screen head shot of CHANCE
fills the screen for several seconds.

SOUND: TV AUDIO.   NEWSCASTER (V.O.)
               ... on the national scene, the
               emergence of Chauncey Gardiner, the
               wizardly [sic] financier who until
               recently remained virtually unknown,
               was greated [sic] with universal
               excitement by business and labor
               alike. Gardiner is expected to
               succeed Benjamin Rand as ...

One of the black women is Miss L the old maid from the OLD
MAN's HOUSE. Very dignified in her old age, she is sick and
moves with difficulty, but now, seeing CHANCE, life rushes
through her with new strength. LOUISE gets up with difficulty
and screaming rushes toward the TV

                    LOUISE
        Chance, ma sweet Chance, m'a sweet
        boy!

She pushes through the others knocking them off their chairs. One chair hits the table with the TV: the image and sound disappears [sic]. To bring the image back, LOUISE starts hitting the TV set, screaming and crying incoherently. OTHERS try to calm her down. Suddenly, tired and exhausted she collapses on the floor, sobbing quietly. As OTHERS lean over her, she looks up at them, as if reflecting.

                    LOUISE
                (almost with a whisper)
        M'a sweet boy, ma Chance, a big man
        now!

She smiles through the tears as OTHERS help her to stand up and lead her to the door.

                                                    CUT TO:

112.   INT: CHANCE'S ROOM RAND DUPLEX   NIGHT
        (Continued from Scene 110)

CHANCE and EVE in the room, EVE now sitting on the floor, leaning against CHANCE's calves. CHANCE keeps watching the same program as in Scene 110.

SOUND: TV AUDIO   FEMALE VOICE (V.O.)
            You repulse me. Leave me alone.

SOUND: TV AUDIO   MALE VOICE (V.O.)
            You have no choice. It's now or never!

                    EVE
        To watch me? When I ... <u>Just</u> to
        watch?
            (she looks at him unsure
            of herself)

                    CHANCE
            (turns toward TV set with
            a soft expression on his
            face)
        Yes, I like to watch. Just to
        watch ...

> EVE
> (uncertain)
> Is that <u>all</u> you want ...
> (almost submissive)
> ... to <u>watch me</u>?

> CHANCE
> Yes to watch. To watch you.

> EVE
> I don't understand. You just want to watch me?
> (slowly, understands)
> Watch me? You mean ... when ... when ... when I?

EVE gets up and paces swiftly up and down the room, crossing between the TV set and CHANCE.

Suddenly, she makes a decision and returns to the bed. Hesitating she slowly undoes her gown. In the bluish light emanating from the TV, her gown falls to the floor. She sits down at CHANCE's feet, hiding her nakedness.

CHANCE stares blankly at the TV in front of him. EVE sees his vacant gaze and, as if prompted by it, she stretches out on her back on the carpet in front of the TV set. The TV casts uneven shadows of light on EVE; her body can be seen only dimly. She begins to move her hands along her body. She trembles and a tremor continues to run through her. Then her bare feet involuntarily kick the carpet several times.

CUT TO:

113. INT: RAND'S BEDROOM   DAY

RAND, sits in his bed, propped against pillows, pale and a bit shakey [sic]. Standing beside him is MRS AUBREY operating a large dictaphone [sic] machine placed next to the bed. RAND has just finished dictating.

> RAND
> (a bit resigned, pointing
>   at the machine)
> It's all there now, please have it transcribed and included in my Last Will. I will sign it later
> (pauses) Oh, yes, ask Finley to

>   have proper witnesses ready for my
>   signing.
>
>   AUBREY
>   (very moved, almost in
>   tears, but tries to hide
>   it)
>   Certainly, Mr. Rand.
>
>   RAND
>   (cheered by his thought)
>   This should make Chauncey
>   sufficiently independent
>   financially to stick to his views
>   (pauses, smiles knowingly)
>   and to rejoin his garden!
>
>   AUBREY
>   (about to cry, quickly
>   dries her tears)
>   You are--you are the most generous
>   man in the world, Mr. Rand!
>
>   RAND
>   (a bit curtly)
>   The dead need no savings. All are
>   on easy street.
>   (quickly changes the
>   subject)
>   After I sign my Will, all Members
>   of the Board should wait in my
>   library to meet with me--and to
>   meet my successor ...

MRS AUBREY raises her eyes, surprised.

>   RAND (cont.)
>   Don't you think it's about time?
>   (does not wait for an
>   answer and announces)
>   Chauncey Gardiner, who else?

MRS AUBREY lights up. RAND looks up at her questioningly.

>   RAND
>   Well, what do you think!

                        AUBREY
              (with a rare outburst of
              feelings)
         A very wise choice!

                                            CUT TO:

114.   INT: WHITE HOUSE ROOM   DAY

     The PRESIDENT presses a button on his desk. His SECRETARY
     enters. The PRESIDENT picks up a folder from his desk and
     hands it to his SECRETARY.

                        PRESIDENT
              This isn't what I asked for ...
                   (slightly irritated)
              ... these are only recent press
              clippings, photographs, and some
              useless information about
              Gardiner's accident and residence
              at Rand's. I know all this
              already! I specifically requested
              the <u>standard file</u> on Gardiner.
                   (impatiently)
              Where is it?

     PRESIDENT's SECRETARY fidgets uneasily.

                        SECRETARY
              I'm sorry, Mr. President, but I
              consulted <u>all our standard
              sources</u>. They don't have a
              standard file on Gardiner's past.
              <u>It's as if he never existed</u>.

                        PRESIDENT
                   (mutters sarcastically and
                   points tensely at the
                   file)
              <u>As if he never existed</u>?

                        SECRETARY
                   (mechanically)
              That's correct, Sir.

>   PRESIDENT
>   (sternly)
>   You mean to tell me that none of our
>   agencies know anything about a man
>   with whom I spent half an hour face
>   to face? <u>A man I quoted in my policy
>   speech</u>!
>   (pauses)
>   Not to mention a man befriended--and
>   thank God, <u>also quoted</u>--by Skrapinov,
>   the Soviet Ambassador to the United
>   Nations?
>
>   SECRETARY
>   As I said, Sir, I tried all our usual
>   sources ...
>   (he twitches nervously)
>   ... but I'll certainly keep trying.
>
>   PRESIDENT
>   (sarcastically)
>   I would appreciate that.

SECRETARY [*SIC*]

CUT TO:

115. INT: SKRAPINOV'S OFFICE   DAY

SKRAPINOV sits behind his desk. In front of him, sitting stiffly, are KARPATOV, dressed in a different suit from the one he wore in Scene 107, and COLONEL SULKIN. SULKIN is the highest Soviet Intelligence official in the United States. He is in his forties, wears steel-rimmed glasses and is short, flabby, and insignificant looking.

>   SULKIN
>   (in mid-sentence)
>   ... investigating Gardiner has
>   already resulted in the loss of
>   one of our best agents. Yet,
>   except for Gardiner's accident, we
>   have still not been able to
>   uncover anything significant--who
>   he is, where he is from, who <u>was</u>

>   he as recently as one
>   week ago!

SKRAPINOV swallows nervously.

>   SULKIN
>   (continues aware of the
>   importance of his words)
>   No doubt, his past was <u>very
>   carefully</u> camouflaged, but we
>   don't even know who helped him in
>   this task. For example, his
>   leather suitcase was made in 1918
>   in Chicago. The artisan who made
>   it went out of business in 1929
>   and killed himself soon afterward!
>   (pauses for effect)

Sweating from excitement, SKRAPINOV, brushes his forehead with his sleeve.

>   SULKIN (cont.)
>   His shirts were made in 1928! The
>   factory where they were made
>   burned down in 1930.
>   (pauses, then breathes
>   deeply in despair)
>   Meanwhile, our team of linguistics
>   has even analyzed tapes of
>   Gardiner's voice, recorded by our
>   agents in Manhattan. It is
>   impossible to ascribe his accent
>   <u>to any single community in the
>   entire United States</u>.

SKRAPINOV looking at SULKIN in bewilderment, is visibly shaken and, pretending nonchalance, pulls a pitcher of water toward himself.

>   SULKIN
>   We believe--(he pauses)--we
>   believe Gardiner is--must be--a
>   leading member of an American
>   elitist faction which has for some
>   years been planning a <u>coup d'etat</u>
>   [*sic*] ...

>   SKRAPINOV
>   Did you say coup d'Etat [*sic*]?
>
>   SULKIN
>   (with authority)
>   I did, indeed, Comrade, indeed. <u>A
>   coup d'etat</u> [*sic*]. Do you doubt
>   the possibility?
>
>   SKRAPINOV
>   (hastily reassuring him)
>   Well, no, of course not. After all
>   Lenin himself foresaw it.
>
>   SULKIN
>   (leaning toward SKRAPINOV,
>   menacingly)
>   Still, your Chauncey Gardiner
>   remains, to all intents and
>   purposes, a ...
>   (once again pauses for
>   effect)

Terrified, SKRAPINOV watches every move SULKIN makes. SULKIN snaps the lock of his attaché case, opens it very slowly, aiming at effect, draws out a slim manila folder. He spreads the folder and pulls out a blank page of white paper.

SULKIN holds up the pages by the corner with his finger and thumb, then turns it around as if to display its blank entirety.

>   SULKIN
>   (exclaims)
>   ... <u>a blank page</u>!
>
>   SKRAPINOV
>   (sweats in disbelief)
>   A blank page, Colonel Sulkin?
>
>   SULKIN
>   (echoes threateningly)
>   That's correct, <u>blank page</u>! <u>Our</u>
>   name for <u>your</u> Chauncey Gardiner.

SKRAPINOV, extremely nervous, reaches hurridly [sic] for a glass of water with a hand which now shakes noticeably.

CUT TO:

116. INT: LIBRARY RAND DUPLEX   DAY

CHANCE sits on a sofa. RAND, looking pale and drawn, sits behind his desk in his robe.

> AUBREY
> (in the middle of a sentence to CHANCE)

... also all major television networks have asked for exclusive prime-time interviews ... .
> (she pauses)

Apparently your appearance scored the highest "alert-excitement" rating in the network's history ... .

> RAND
> (interjects, amused)

Does the "alert-excitement" rating mean Chauncey has alerted them?

> AUBREY
> (explains pedantically)

Well, not quite, Mr. Rand. "<u>Alert-excitement</u>" rating is based on the number of people so excited by a TV program they watch ...
> (she points toward CHANCE)

--in this case, Mr. Gardiner's appearance--that they called other TV viewers to make sure they wouldn't miss it ...

Impressed, RAND nods.

> AUBREY
> (turns to CHANCE)

<u>Fortune</u>, <u>Time</u>, <u>Newsweek</u>, <u>Esquire</u>, <u>People</u>, and <u>House and Garden</u>,

>   would like to do profiles on you.
>   The BBC is ready to fly you to
>   London for a TV special. The
>   Directors of the All-Arab Stock
>   Exchange want you to be their
>   keynote speaker at the
>   inauguration of the newest All-
>   Arab Information Retrieving Center
>   in Cairo ...

CHANCE, a blank look on his face, does not answer.

>   AUBREY
>   (looks at him expectantly)
>   Just a final point. This morning's
>   Wall Street Journal predicts your
>   imminent appointment to the Board
>   of the First American Financial
>   Corporation, and the paper would
>   like to have a statement from you.

Mrs. AUBREY glances quickly at RAND. Nodding, RAND smiles knowingly. Both RAND and Mrs. AUBREY look at CHANCE.

>   CHANCE
>   (with no emotion)
>   I cannot give them any statement.

>   RAND
>   (very pleased)
>   You don't give in to press easily,
>   Chauncey, do you? Good, good!
>   I like that.

>   CHANCE
>   (an engaging smile on his
>   face)
>   Thank you, Benjamin.

                                                          CUT TO:

117.   INT: SKRAPINOV'S OFFICE   DAY
       (Continued from Scene 115)

SKRAPINOV gulps down the water and, with a shaking hand, puts the glass down.

SKRAPINOV
(swallows nervously and
smacks his lips)
I beg your pardon, Colonel Sulkin,
but when I took it upon myself
first to talk to Gardiner and then
to allude to him in my speech, I
naturally assumed that he was a
member of the Wall Street elite.
After all, <u>Benjamin Rand, the
President, the television, the
press</u>--he seems to be <u>one of them</u>!

SULKIN
(admonishing)
<u>Seems</u>? What makes you, Comrade
Skrapinov, think that this
Gardiner is <u>not</u>, in fact, one of
them?

SKRAPINOV
(removes drop of sweat
from his eyebrow--
mutters)
Well, you said he is nothing but a
<u>blank page</u> ...
(he gestures with his head
toward the page on his
desk)
... the lack of <u>any substance</u>

SULKIN
(parodying SKRAPINOV's
tone of despair)
"The lack of any substance"! But,
Comrade Skrapinov!
(he assumes a tone of
authority)
I am here to <u>congratulate</u> you on
your Marxist instinct--Soviet
Government has no doubt--no doubt
whatever!--that Chauncey Gardiner
is in fact a <u>plant</u> of a big-
business Republican power group.
... A plant designed to regain ...

                    SKRAPINOV
               (uncertain he has
               understood)
          A plant?

                    SULKIN
               (impatiently)
          A plant! P-l-a-n-t.
               (he spells it)
          Like in a garden ...

                    SKRAPINOV
               (enlightened)
          A plant, of course!

                    SULKIN
          And that power group, led by
          Gardiner, will soon be taking over
          the American Government.
               (he pauses for effect then
               lowers his voice,
               staccato)
          ... Gardiner is of such importance
          to this group that it masked every
          detail of his identity until,
          under the pretext of a minor car
          mishap he emerged at Rand's home
          three days ago.
               (he pauses, murmurs to
               himself)
          A new type of political leader.
          What a figure! Fascinating!!

                                               CUT TO:

118. INT: WHITE HOUSE ROOM   DAY
      (As in Scene 114)

      The PRESIDENT is talking with his SECRETARY

                    PRESIDENT
               (very annoyed)
          ... Let's stop this nonsense. Have
          you asked Benjamin Rand about
          Gardiner?

SECRETARY
We have tried, Sir. Unfortunately, Mr. Rand has had a serious relapse, is under sedation, and cannot talk. His doctors agree that it's unlikely that he will recover sufficiently to be articulate enough ...

PRESIDENT
(interrogating)
Did you speak with Mrs. Rand?

SECRETARY
Yes, Sir, we did. Mrs. Rand was at her husband's bedside. She said that she respects Mr. Gardiner's privacy. She simply refuses to say anything more.

PRESIDENT
(in a voice of authority)
What about our investigative sources? Have you talked to Walter?

SECRETARY
(eagerly)
I did, Mr. President. They haven't been able to find a single thing. Gardiner has never been hospitalized, carries no insurance, nor, for that matter, any other document or identification ... no credit cards, no checks, he doesn't seem to own any property.
(as if recalling an important detail)
... Gardiner's clothes were all custom-made, but none after 1930! None can be traced to <u>a buyer</u>! But there is no doubt that, at this time, he has not done anything or

made any statement that anyone can object to.
(he pauses for effect, then lowers his voice)
Mr. President, our men snooped a bit on Gardiner in New York: Gardiner doesn't talk business or politics on the phone or at Rand's home, where he is still a guest. <u>All</u> he does is watch television-- even when he and Mrs. Rand are in his bedroom, Sir ...

PRESIDENT
(interrupts angrily)
What? What did you say?

SECRETARY
(fidgeting a little)
I said he watches television ... all channels ... practically all the time--<u>even at night when Mrs. Rand is with him in his bedroom</u>, Sir.

PRESIDENT
(cuts in sharply, very upset)
There's no excuse for such unauthorized surveillance, no excuse at all, and, damn it, who the hell cares what Gardiner does in his bedroom!

CUT TO:

119. INT: SOPHIE'S APARTMENT   DAY

An elegant living room impeccably furnished with French period furniture (Empire). EVE and SOPHIE are in the middle of afternoon tea.

SOPHIE
(a bit conspiratorial)
But you still haven't said a word about <u>how is he</u>?

              EVE
         (slightly annoyed)
    You don't understand: Chauncey is
    not that kind of a man!

              SOPHIE
    That's what I want to know: what
    kind of a man is he?
         (giggles)

              EVE
         (disregards SOPHIE's
          giggling)
    He is very brainy, very cerebral--
    a man of restraint. He knows that
    with one touch--just one touch, I
    would open to him.

              SOPHIE
         (can't wait to hear more)
    Yes? And, and do you?

              EVE
         (disregards SOPHIE's
          question)
    But he doesn't want to exploit me.
    He respects my love for Benjamin ...

              SOPHIE
         (disappointed)
    Your love for Benjamin?

              EVE
         (as if analyzing CHANCE
          for herself)
    Chauncey wants to conquer me from
    within my very self ...

              SOPHIE
         (getting desperate)
    From within?

              EVE
         (as if daydreaming)
    Chauncey ... he uncoils my wants.
    Desire flows within me and--when

>   he watches me--I reveal myself to
>   myself.

As if she had never seen her friend in such a stat. SOPHIE looks at EVE entirely baffled.

>   SOPHIE
>   (incredulous)
>   When he <u>watches</u> you?
>
>   EVE
>   (peaceful and natural)
>   Yes. He makes me free.
>   CUT TO:

120.   INT: RAND'S BEDROOM   DAY

Group shot--RAND very sick in bed. CHANCE and EVE sit at his bedside. Mrs. AUBREY with a steno pad stands next to them.

>   RAND
>   (speaks with great
>   difficulty)
>   I am sorry to trouble you,
>   Chauncey ...
>   (he breathes heavily)
>   ... but I want you to meet some of
>   my friends and business
>   associates. They also have been
>   eager to meet with you. Later
>   today they'll be meeting
>   informally ... perhaps you could
>   attend ...
>
>   CHANCE
>   (willingly)
>   Yes, Benjamin, I will go.

EVE looks at CHANCE with love and fulfillment.

>   RAND
>   (mobilizes the rest of his
>   energy)
>   And now, Eve, please ...
>   (he looks at CHANCE)

>   I want to be left alone with
>   Chauncey.

EVE promptly gets up and gently leaves the room. Mrs. AUBREY follows. RAND gestures for CHANCE to approach his bedside. CHANCE moves toward him, then leans over the dying man (same movements mood, etc. as in Scene 28)

>   RAND
>   (point with difficulty at
>   the large portrait of
>   EVE that hangs over his
>   bed)
>   She is the only treasure that I
>   have, Chauncey. Now, with me gone,
>   there will be no one to protect
>   her.
>   (strains)
>   And I am about to be gone ... .

CHANCE strains to hear better.

>   RAND
>   (continues in a whisper)
>   And you, Chauncey ...
>   (straining)

RAND places his shriveled hand on CHANCE's.

>   RAND
>   I feel you are the son I never had
>   ...
>   (he pauses, swallows with
>   difficulty, then speaks
>   with remaining force)
>   Promise me, promise me ...
>
>   CHANCE
>   (gently)
>   I promise, Benjamin.
>
>   RAND
>   Promise you will stay with ...
>
>   CHANCE
>   (gently)
>   I promise, Benjamin.

                    RAND
          Thank you, my son. Thank you!

RAND's shoulders slump down, his chest seems to collapse.

CHANCE stares at his face, then looks up at the portrait of EVE (similar movements, mood, etc. to Scene 28) As his eyes meet her eyes, the <u>engaging smile</u> appears on his face.

                                              CUT TO:

121.   INT: SMOKING ROOM   DAY

It is a large beamed room, furnished with numerous comfortable sofas and armchairs. There are solid, light-colored drapes at the windows, (windows are made up of many small pieces of glass edged in lead--Tudor like), a grand piano in one corner, and a deep fireplace.

In the room are SEVEN MEN we have not seen before, all in their late forties and middle fifties and dressed in the best quality dark business suits, white shirts, and conservative ties. They all have the look of the upper rung of American corporate ladder. They sit in easy chairs around the room, smoking cigars and drinking coffee. All SEVEN MEN face the MAN ON THE SOFA whose face we will not see but whose voice resembles--<u>and may or may not be</u>--the voice of the Republican Candidate for President of the United States.

                    MAN ON SOFA (V.O.)
                (addressing all men in the
                room--in the middle of a
                sentence)
          ... some of you already know that
          Duncan has withdrawn because of
          the facts about his role in the
          Security Exchange coverup [*sic*]
          that couldn't have surfaced ...
                (he pauses)
          at a worst time ...

                    MAN 1
                (interrupts politely)
          Sir, it wasn't easy to come up
          with even Duncan, and let's not

>   kid ourselves: whom can we possibly get
>   at this late date?

Silence in the room.

>   MAN 2
>   What about George?
>
>   MAN 3
>   Too sick. He just had another
>   operation; the second in three
>   months. He's an obvious health
>   risk. And anyway, he's writing his
>   memoirs ... .

>   CUT TO:

122. EXT: RAND'S LIMOUSINE   DAY

The car (same as in Scenes 32 and 33) moves smoothly toward Washington, D.C. exurbia, passing by the familiar Washington skyline. Car's registration plate: "RAND 1." A man's figure is silhouetted in the window.

In the car's rear seat sits CHANCE watching the TV.

SOUND: TV AUDIO -- Sound of gangster shootout.

DRIVER (not the chauffeur PETE we saw in Scene 32) is in his thirties, of medium height, with a clean, honest face, and he wears a new brown uniform and new pigskin gloves.

>   DRIVER
>   (looks over his shoulder)
>   I'm sorry, Mr. Gardiner, but the
>   traffic's pretty bad. Still we
>   should be there in twenty minutes.

<u>Engaging smile</u> appears on CHANCE's face.

SOUND: TV AUDIO: Shooting continues.

>   CUT TO:

123. INT: SMOKING ROOM   DAY
      (Continued from Scene 121)

MAN 4 sitting in the farthest corner of the room. We cannot see his face, which is hidden by MAN 6, who sits in front of him.

```
                    MAN 4
              (almost quietly)
        ... I think I have someone ...

When he speaks all the MEN in the room turn in his
direction.

                    MAN 4 (Cont.)
        Chauncey Gardiner!

                    Man ON SOFA (V.O.)
        We don't know much about this
        Gardiner. Nothing has been brought
        to light regarding the man. He
        just keeps popping up on TV ...

                    MAN 4
              (with conviction)
        He hasn't said anything that could
        possibly be used against him ...

                    MAN 2
        ... or against anyone in the Party
        ...

                    MAN ON SOFA (V.O.)
        Let's face it, since his emergence
        he hasn't said anything. Period.

                    MAN 5
        That's Gardiner's greatness. He's
        got a knack for making a statement
        without making an enemy. With the
        press on our back, he doesn't even
        say enough to be misquoted!

                    MAN 1
        Never mind what he says! The
        minute Gardiner went on
        television, he got the highest
        rating ever ... the newspapers
        that carried his picture on their
        front page were sold out in hours.
        ... He's already a symbol, a
        national hero of sorts ...
```

                    MAN 6
          Why?

                    MAN 2
          Gardiner scored the highest rating
          ever for being silent while on TV.
          He never speaks unless he can
          improve on his silence!

                    MAN 4
          In his last will Rand left half of
          his estate to Gardiner--the other
          half to his widow.
               (pauses)
          If Gardiner is on our ticket,
          there will be a substantial
          financial contribution ...

                    MAN ON SOFA (V.O.)
               (hesitantly, as if
                pondering)
          I think you just tapped something.
          Something big ... Gardiner,
          Gardiner. Hm ...

                                                  CUT TO:

124.   EXT: COUNTRY ESTATE   DAY
       (Continued from Scene 122)

       RAND's limousine pulls into the immaculately kept driveway
       of a country estate. There is an enormous park-like garden
       surrounding the house, which is an imposing colonial,
       built around 1920, carefully restored and maintained.
       Seven long limousines (all American-made) are already
       parked in the driveway, one behind another. In each car,
       its DRIVER sits waiting.

       RAND's limousine stops in front of the entrance to the
       house. The DRIVER jumps out and opens the rear door.
       CHANCE gets out, looks around and walks toward the house.
       The DRIVER closes the car door.

       CAMERA FOLLOWS CHANCE

       SOUND: DRIVER (V.O.)
                 I'll wait for you in the car, Sir.

Reverse angle from the garden: As the camera keeps backing, CHANCE, at ease, is walking toward the house.

SOUND: Crunching of the gravel path.

The camera keeps backing: a few steps before the entrance to the house, CHANCE slows down, attracted by the full view of the estate's splendid garden, still sunk in repose.

CHANCE glances at the house, then at the garden, hesitates, then veers a bit and stops amidst the first bushes and trees.

                                                    CUT TO:

125.   INT: SMOKING ROOM   DAY
       (Continued from Scene 123)

                    MAN 6
           All public-opinion experts we
           talked to agree that Chauncey
           Gardiner is a new phenomenon
                (he pauses)
           a political figure for the
           eighties!
                (he pauses for effect)
           a totally non-self-incriminating
           type, to be sure ... a new deal
           for the American people! To start
           the era of good feeling again!

                                                    CUT TO:

126.   EXT: OUTSIDE COUNTRY ESTATE   DAY
       (Continued from Scene 124)

       CAMERA STATIONARY: CHANCE, still amidst the greenery.

       The bushes and trees lie calm as CHANCE (as in Scene 1) gently touches their taught branches laden with fresh buds anwd shoots, careful not to shake-off the droplets of water that nestled upon the slender stems and tiny buds that shot upward.

                                                    CUT TO:

127. INT: SMOKING ROOM   DAY
      (Continued from Scene 125)

                    MAN ON SOFA (V.O.)
                  (repeats slowly)
            A new deal for the American people
            ... The era of good feeling ...
                  (pauses reflecting, then
                   speaks emphatically)
            Then, perhaps Chauncey Gardiner is
            our chance!

                                                    CUT TO:

128. EXT: OUTSIDE COUNTRY ESTATE   DAY
      (Continued from Scene 126)

   CHANCE amidst the greenery; still reluctant to leave it
   not knowing whether he will enter the HOUSE. Slowly,
   CHANCE's face, enigmatic but seductive, his stare almost
   hypnotic, fills the entire screen.

   CREDITS APPEAR

   An engaging smile lights CHANCE's face, reinforced by the
   musical motif that has always accompanied it.

   CREDITS END

                          THE END

Notes

1 In a note to Hal Ashby accompanying the July '78 draft of the script, producer Andy Braunsberg described it as "a great improvement over the last two scripts." Memo, Andrew Braunsberg to Hal Ashby, July 31, 1978, Box 1, Folder 6, Hal Ashby Papers, Margaret Herrick Library, Los Angeles.
2 Jerzy Kosinski, *Being There* (novel) (London: Black Swan, [1970] 1983), 11.
3 On the cover page of the script that follows, Kosinski has written "First Draft." However, he had already produced the draft of 1971 while at Yale. It is unclear whether he submitted the '71 draft to the production before submitting the January '78 draft, or if there was another draft between this one and the July '78 draft. See endnote 1 regarding Braunsberg's reference to the July '78 draft being better than the "last two scripts."

2

Robert C. Jones: December 1978

Introduction

Throughout his career, as both an editor and a director, Hal Ashby had a propensity to form lasting collaborative relationships with cast and crewmembers who shared his ideas about filmmaking and films as a form of socially progressive entertainment. Cinematographer Haskell Wexler, who shot four of the films that Ashby directed as well as two of the films he edited for director Norman Jewison,[1] described their approach to filmmaking: "We did have strong feelings about what America was and what we could be, and we felt our responsibilities as artists and citizens."[2] When Ashby met a like-minded individual with whom he also worked well, he tended to maintain the collaborative partnership, and when somebody was not available to work on a particular film, Ashby was likely to approach them again one or two films later. A few examples of Ashby's frequent collaborations include three films with writer Robert Towne, two with editor Don Zimmerman (who had trained as an editorial assistant on several earlier Ashby films), and six films with production designer Mike Haller. Haskell Wexler's son Jeff worked in various capacities in the sound department on almost all of Ashby's films. Ashby also worked on repeated occasions with actors like Lee Grant, Jack Warden, and Jon Voigt on two films, and Randy Quaid on three.

One of Ashby's longest creative relationships was with Bob Jones. Jones had begun his career as an editor in Hollywood at roughly the same time as Ashby had, and they both spent the early- to mid-1960s rising through the editorial ranks. In 1968, both were nominated for Academy Awards for editing, Jones for *Guess Who's Coming to Dinner* (Columbia Pictures) and Ashby for *In the Heat of the Night* (Mirisch Corporation/United Artists), which Ashby won. While they had come up in the same field at roughly the same time, the two did not meet until Ashby was looking for somebody to edit his third film as director, *The Last Detail* (Columbia 1973). Producer Gerald Ayers, who had worked with Jones on *Cisco Pike* (Columbia 1972), suggested him to Ashby and the two quickly found they worked well together.[3] Jones, who also had fruitful collaborative relationships with directors Arthur Hiller (seven films), Stanley Kramer (three films), and Warren Beatty (two films), would go on to edit *Shampoo* (Columbia 1975), *Bound for Glory* (United Artists 1976), and the theatrical release of *Lookin' to Get Out* (Lorimar/Paramount 1982).[4]

It was while working on *Bound for Glory* that Jones, with Ashby's encouragement, began to forge a second career path, as a writer. Jones had written an adaptation of Saul Bellow's *Henderson the Rain King*, and Ashby, impressed, asked him to work on rewrites of *Bound* for Glory.[5] After editing that film, Jones would spend the rest of the decade working on two scripts for Ashby that would never be realized: Bellow's *Henderson* and an adaptation of Richard Brautigan's "unfilmable" *The Hawkline Monster*, which became a passion project for both Jones and Ashby.[6] It was on *Coming Home*, Ashby's follow-up to *Bound for Glory*, that Jones first became publically known as a writer. As has been detailed in many places, the script production process for *Coming Home* was a long and, at times, fraught endeavor. Originally conceived of by Jane Fonda as a film based on the Ron Kovic memoir *Born on the Fourth of July*, the first drafts of the script were written by Nancy Dowd.[7] For reasons that are still contested, Dowd was removed from the project and veteran screenwriter Waldo Salt was brought in to substantially rework the script.[8] When the film went into production, the script still was not to the satisfaction of Ashby or producer Jerome Hellman, who had worked with Salt on *Midnight Cowboy* (United Artists 1969) and *The Day of the Locust* (Paramount 1975), so Ashby turned to Jones once again for rewrites, this time much more extensive than those he had done for *Bound for Glory*.[9] The resultant work won Dowd, Salt, and Jones jointly the Academy Award for Best Original Screenplay in 1979.[10]

Thus, by autumn of 1978 Jones had over a decade's experience as a Hollywood editor in addition to a burgeoning writing career, the combination of which endowed him with a finely developed sense of timing, pace, and narrative development. When Ashby believed that the *Being There* scripts that Kosinski was submitting were less than cinematic, it made sense he would call on a long-standing friend and collaborative colleague whose instincts he trusted.

It is important to note that it was never Ashby or Jones's intention to completely rewrite or reinterpret *Being There*. Rather, Ashby had been enamored of the novel since Sellers first sent it to him in 1971. He and Jones were concerned that Kosinski's efforts to extend cinematic grandeur to his ethereal fable had detracted from the deceptive simplicity of Chance's journey through the corridors of American power. They wanted to redraft a script much more closely in line with the novel. *Being There* remains very much Kosinksi's story, but the film as produced could only have come into being after Jones's work on the script. With the novel and Kosinski's drafts in hand, Jones's tasks for the rewrite appear to have been threefold: restore the novel's fable-like quality; remove and rewrite the extensive literary descriptions, asides, and in-script directions that Kosinski's drafts lean upon so heavily; and provide a greater sense of cinematic unity to the film's narrative and character development.

On the first score, Jones cut anything resembling backstory, including Chance's. For example, Kosinski includes a long deathbed speech from the Old Man (see 56) in which he details Chance's parentage and childhood, robbing the narrative of vital ambiguity as the investigation into Chance's background becomes increasingly central in the film's second half. Jones also dramatically reduced the number of scenes in which secondary characters appear without Chance, retaining only those that depict discussions about or investigations into the life and background of the protagonist. As a result, even when he is off-screen Chance remains the central presence in the film. This allows Jones time and space in the script to reinscribe the character with endearing quirks that help the viewer develop an empathy bond with Chance, which is vital to his reception. As mentioned in the

Introduction, Chance changes very little through the course of the narrative, which results in an atypical Hollywood protagonist. Part of what makes him appealing to viewers is his offbeat way of interacting with the world, such as his comical reaction to his first elevator ride or the numerous occasions when he mimics something he sees on television (aided of course by the understated flair of Peter Sellers's performance). Centralizing Chance like this is fundamental to the film's success.

The effect of Jones's removal of the overly literary descriptions becomes apparent on the first page and remains throughout the script. The Introduction includes my comparative analysis of the three drafts' treatment of the film's opening and how much more quickly and efficiently Jones introduces Chance and his environs, provides an effective visual account of Chance's life in the house, introduces Louise, and announces the death of the Old Man. Such trimming abounds throughout Jones's draft. For example, here is Kosinski's description of the office of Mrs. Aubrey, Rand's executive secretary (see 90):

```
This is one of the rooms in RAND's apartment that, for the
duration of RAND's illness, have been turned into temporary
offices. This office, occupied by Mrs. AUBREY and her staff,
is next to the LIBRARY: its door leads to the CORRIDOR. In
the office there are three desks, each equipped with the
latest-model electric typewriter, calculators, Dictaphone
and multiple-button office telephones--one of them has the
small-version desk-switch-board. A medium-size, mahogany-
finished Telex machine and the latest electronic silent
ticker-tape machine, with its constantly changing rows of
stock quotations, stand in a corner of the room. The room
also contains several brand-new first-quality file cabinets.
```

Here is the description from Jones's first draft (see 248):

```
The nerve center of the Rand Enterprises since he has
become ill. Four or five desks, all the latest electronic
office equipment, three TV's with video taping facilities,
countless telephones. MRS. AUBREY, Rand's senior secretary,
is at her desk, answers her phone.
```

Jones cuts nearly sixty words of description from the scene, including the room's geographical location vis-à-vis other rooms inside the mansion, but manages to convey the same sense of bustling importance. He would cut it even further for the final draft (see 386):

```
MRS. AUBREY is Rand's executive secretary, but her office is
the Nerve Center of Rand Enterprises.
```

Jones then uses the unfolding of events and actions within the office to depict any necessary design or props. For students of scriptwriting this is a fine example of the power of revision. There is nothing necessarily "wrong" with Kosinski's description: he sees Mrs. Aubrey's office in his head, has specific ideas about how the office looks, and writes those details into his script. But unless such information is absolutely vital to the progression of the narrative, it is unnecessary—the director and production designer will have clear ideas about what an office-as-nerve-center will look like, and will design and shoot it accordingly. In that sense, what Jones has produced is a much more shoot-able script.

Finally, in terms of narrative unity, by reworking major and minor details Jones achieves just the sort of lived-in universe that Kosinski was going for, only much more subtly so. In the Introduction, I discuss his decision to end the film with Rand's funeral, which creates a more satisfying resolution of the narrative as well as the character arcs of Chance, Rand, and Eve. But seemingly minor changes also provide the script with a greater cinematic unity, for example, Jones's handling of the character of Thomas Franklin. In fact, Franklin in Jones's script exemplifies how well Jones excels at all three of these tasks. Franklin is the lawyer who arrives at the Old Man's house and, when unexpectedly coming across Chance (for whom there is no record in the Old Man's papers), must evict him. As such, he functions mainly as a plot device: Chance needs to be evicted, so Franklin evicts him. In the novel, Franklin appears one further time, when his wife is watching Chance's television appearance, and Franklin thinks he might recognize him. This acts as a satisfying callback to his first appearance, and also implies that there is somebody in the world who might know Chance's true identity, but the novel does not follow up on this possibility. Kosinski expands on the character in the script, including his and his wife's efforts to sell their car (52) as one of the scenes intercut with Chance's long introduction. In action descriptions and parentheticals, Kosinski portrays how little Franklin's wife thinks of him. When the callback comes (123, 126), her disdain for her husband is played against her admiration for Chance on TV. In this iteration, Franklin thinks he recognizes Chance, but decides he must be somebody he knew at Yale, "a great athlete!" Again, this is his last appearance in the narrative.

In Jones's draft, the car sale is cut completely, as are all the opening intercut scenes. Franklin remains the lawyer who evicts Chance, and he turns up again when his wife is watching Chance's television appearance. This time, however, Franklin recognizes Chance for who he is. He later meets his assistant, Ms. Hayes, who had accompanied him on the first visit to the Old Man's house, and they discuss whether Chance was trying to fool them at the house that day (284), adding to the air of mystery that surrounds Chance in the second half of the film. It is with Franklin's final appearance, though, that Jones displays his awareness of how to get the most out of a secondary character. Dr. Allenby, Rand's personal physician, has heard Chance mention the lawyer Thomas Franklin on two occasions. Allenby is the only person in the script who is suspicious about Chance and who he really is (in Kosinski's drafts, he has no such suspicions). He eventually looks Franklin up, calls him, and they arrange to meet. At that meeting (307), Franklin relays to Allenby everything that happened at the house the day he and Chance met; he assumes what he has seen on TV about Chance is true—that he is some sort of wealthy mastermind—but it is his confirmation to Allenby that Chance insisted on showing them his garden that peaks Allenby's interest. Later, immediately after Rand dies, Allenby gently confronts Chance about his true identity, while also realizing that Chance loves Eve in his way and is maybe an innocent actor in the mistaken identity, rather than a manipulative conman. The film implies that Allenby will keep the information to himself, especially in Jones's first draft, which ends with both Eve and Allenby searching for Chance after Rand's funeral. This is a deft move on Jones's part. It ties up the loose end of Franklin being out in the world and one day possibly revealing Chance's true identity. But also, in showing a close friend to the Rands such as Allenby accept Chance even when he learns of his true identity, it conveys to the viewer that Chance is likely to remain in his new position, even if the world does eventually discover who he truly is. Thus it is Franklin who acts both to push Chance out into his new world and then, albeit inadvertently, to help secure his place in it. With this move, Jones deepens Franklin's role in the narrative to a much greater, more satisfying extent than does Kosinski's description of his financial and marital woes.

Such instances abound in Jones's draft. While his second draft is an even tighter, more accomplished script, comparing this first draft with Kosinski's provides a deeply illustrative example of the difference between what literary and cinematic writing looks like in a script and why the latter is more effective in helping a reader "see" the film, but also more desirable to producers and directors looking to turn the script into a film.

```
                        BEING THERE













                         Screenplay

                            by

              Jerzy Kosinski and Robert C. Jones










                                            December 16, 1978
```

FADE IN:

EXT. TOWNHOUSE GARDEN - WASHINGTON, D.C. - AFTERNOON

An afternoon in late November, the leaves have left the trees, and the early darkness of a winter dusk approaches. The garden is long and narrow, guarded on either side by a high brick wall. At one end stands the rear of a three-story brick townhouse; at the other, a one story brick building. CLASSICAL MUSIC is heard in the distance. A MAN, handsomely dressed in a well-tailored suit of the 1920's, works in the garden. A gardener's apron protects his suit from the earth as he turns the loam along one of the walkways. He works slowly, precisely, obviously engrossed in his surroundings. This man is called CHANCE. Chance stops working for a moment, takes a pocket watch from inside his coat, checks the time. He looks to the darkening skies, returns the watch to his pocket. As Chance starts toward the one story brick building, he takes a spotless rag from his apron pocket and wipes the dirt from the tines of his pitchfork.

INT. GARAGE - AFTERNOON

The sound of the music increases as Chance enters the garage from the garden. A gleaming 1921 TOURING CAR is revealed as he walks through the garage and leans the pitchfork against a wall. Chance takes a neatly folded cover from a shelf, carefully puts it over the car. When he finishes covering the car for the night, Chance picks up the pitchfork, leaves the garage through a side entry.

INT. POTTING ROOM - AFTERNOON

The Potting Room is filled with the tools of the gardener, everything arranged in an orderly fashion. Rows of small pots are on tables, young plants sprouting from some of them. A small, 1940's table model black-and-white TV rests on a shelf. It is playing, tuned to the BOSTON POPS ORCHESTRA. Attached to the front of the screen is a wheel containing colored gels. The wheel spins, creates an early form of color TV. As Chance enters, his attention is on the television set. He watches it as he oils the tines of the pitchfork and puts it away. Chance turns off the TV and leaves the room, but the sound of the Boston Pops continues.

INT. CHANCE'S ROOM - AFTERNOON

A room adjacent to the Potting Room. A large screen remote control color television set dominates the room. It is on, tuned to the Boston Pops. In contrast to the new TV, the rest of the room is sparsely but tastefully decorated with expensive furniture of the twenties. There are no books, magazines, newspapers or reading matter of any kind to be seen. Chance comes in, watches the TV with a detached gaze as he removes his apron. He changes the channel with the remote control as he puts his apron and the pitchfork rag into a laundry bag. He takes off his suit jacket, hangs it in the closet where it is accompanied by several others, all of like quality. Chance changes the channel once again.

EXT. GARDEN - NIGHT

Chance, wearing a different suit and carrying the laundry bag, crosses from the rear building to the main house.

INT. MAIN HOUSE - REAR ENTRANCE/HALLWAY - NIGHT

The interior of the main house has the mustiness of age, the warmth of oak. White dropcloths and sheets cover all of the furniture. Chance enters, walks through the hallway.

INT. MAIN HOUSE - DINING ROOM - NIGHT

A large dropcloth is over the dining room table and chairs. It is neatly folded back at one end, leaving one chair and place setting uncovered. A small portable color TV is next to the place setting. Chance enters, puts his laundry bag on a covered table near the doorway. He sits at the dining room table, turns on the TV, and carefully unfolds his napkin, puts it on his lap as he watches the screen. LOUISE, an elderly black maid, enters with a tray of food and Chance's clean laundry.

      LOUISE
    (sets dinner before
    Chance)
... Evening, Chance.

      CHANCE
    (slowly, perfect diction,
    no accent of any kind)
... Good evening, Louise.

Louise sets Chance's clean clothes on the small table, picks up his laundry bag.

> LOUISE
> ... The Old Man is getting weaker, Chance.

> CHANCE
> (begins to eat)
> I see.

> LOUISE
> I'm afraid he's slippin' a bit with every hour that goes by ...

Chance, his manners impeccable, concentrates on the TV as he eats. A buzzer SOUNDS, Louise looks upstairs.

> LOUISE (CONT'D)
> ... Back up those stairs - damn ... That Man's needin' me more and more just before he never needs me again ...

> CHANCE
> (still watches TV)
> Is his back feeling better? Louise gives Chance a look.

> LOUISE
> ... Gobbledegook ... You and your gobbledegook. You're gonna be the death of me yet, Chance ...
> (she turns to leave)
> ... Unless those stairs are ... The Good Lord's liable to snatch up two unwillin' souls at the same time if I keep on trampin' up those stairs ... I don't want none of that ...

Louise disappears through the doorway. Chance continues to eat and watch TV.

INT. CHANCE'S ROOM - DAWN

Chance is asleep, lying on his back. His eyes slowly open, and, with no change of expression, he sits up and turns on the TV with the remote control. Chance gets out of bed, goes to the dresser and takes his pocket watch out of a drawer, checks the time. He crosses to the closet, his eyes never straying from an early morning show on television. He puts on a bathrobe and leaves the room.

INT. POTTING ROOM - DAWN

Chance enters, turns on the TV with the spinning color wheel, then waters a few of the pots with a sprinkling can. He turns off the TV and exits.

INT. GARAGE - DAWN

Chance comes into the garage, takes the cover off of the touring car, folds it and puts it on a shelf. He leaves the garage.

INT. CHANCE'S ROOM - DAWN

Chance returns to his room, changes channels on the television, takes off his robe and hangs it back up in the closet, then goes into the bathroom.

EXT. GARDEN - MORNING

A light snow is falling. The door to the small building opens, Chance peeks out, then goes back inside. A few seconds pass and Chance reappears, this time with an umbrella. Smartly dressed in suit and tie, he crosses to the main house.

INT. MAIN HOUSE - REAR ENTRANCE/HALLWAY - MORNING

Chance opens the door, shakes off and closes the umbrella before entering. He hangs the umbrella on a doorknob, then heads for the dining room.

INT. DINING ROOM - MORNING

Repeating his ritual, Chance enters the dining room, sits, turns on the TV, carefully spreads his napkin on his lap. He watches the screen for a moment, then turns, expecting Louise. She doesn't appear, so he turns back, watches TV. After a few beats, Chance hears Louise's footsteps hurrying down the stairs. She comes into the dining room, visibly distraught. Chance looks up, smiles.

> CHANCE
> Good morning, Louise.

> LOUISE
>   (out of breath)
> He's dead, Chance! The Old Man's dead!

> CHANCE
>   (flatly, turns back to TV)
> ... I see.

> LOUISE
> Must of happened durin' the night,
> I don't know ... Lord, he wasn't
> breathin' and as cold as a fish.
> I touched him, just to see, and you
> believe me, Chance - that's doin'
> more than I get paid to do ... Then
> I just covered him up, pulled the
> sheet over his head ...

> CHANCE
>   (nodding)
> Yes. I've seen that done.

> LOUISE
> Then I got the hell out of that
> room and called the doctor and I
> think I woke him probably, he
> wasn't any too alert. He just
> said, 'Yeah, he's been expectin'
> it and said he'd send somebody
> over ...' Lord, what a mornin'!

> CHANCE
>   (watches news, flashes of
>   season's first snowfall)
> ... Yes, Louise, it's snowing in
> the garden today. Have you looked
> outside and seen the snow? It's
> very white.

A beat of silence from Louise, then anger.

> LOUISE
> Dammit, Boy! Is that all you got
> to say? More gobbledegook?
>   (Chance smiles, is silent)
> That Old Man's layin' up there

                    dead as hell and it just don't
                    make any difference to you!

                              CHANCE
                        (with a smile, accepting
                         death)
                    Yes, Louise. I have seen it often.
                    It happens to old people.

                              LOUISE
                    Well, ain't that the truth ...

                              CHANCE
                    Yes. It is.

Louise throws back the cover from a chair next to Chance and
sits, softening a bit toward him.

                              LOUISE
                    Oh, Lord, Chance - I don't know
                    what I was expectin' from you ...
                    I'm sorry for yellin' like
                    I did ... No sir, I just don't
                    know what I was expectin' ...
                        (Chance doesn't react,
                         watches TV)
                    ... I 'spose I'd better gather up
                    some breakfast for you ...

                              CHANCE
                        (a turn to her)
                    Yes, I'm very hungry.

                              LOUISE
                        (rises, looks upstairs)
                    Well, no more stewin' those prunes
                    every mornin', that's somethin', I guess ...
                        (she starts out, stops
                         by the door)
                    ... what are you goin' to do now,
                    Chance?

                              CHANCE
                        (gazing at TV)
                    I'm going to work in the garden.

Louise gives Chance a long look, then turns to leave.

                        LOUISE
                    (as she goes)
                ... I'll get you some eggs.

Chance nods in approval, then changes the channel on the TV.

INT. MAIN HOUSE - SERVANT'S STAIRWAY - MORNING

An enclosed stairway. Chance enters, proceeds up the stairs.

INT. MAIN HOUSE - UPSTAIRS HALLWAY - MORNING

Chance comes out of a doorway adjoining the main staircase. He moves off down the hall.

INT. MAIN HOUSE - OLD MAN'S ROOM - MORNING

The furniture in this room is not covered with sheets but the Old Man is. There is a polite knock at the door, then Chance enters the room. As Chance moves slowly to the Old Man's bed, we sense a feeling of respect from Chance, as well as a bit of curiosity. Chance stands by the side of the bed for a moment, then he reaches down and gently pulls the sheet back from the Old Man's face. He touches the man's forehead, lightly, briefly, then replaces the sheet. Chance moves to the TV (like the one in his own room) and turns it on. He sits in an easy chair next to the Old man's bed and watches a movie from the early forties. Chance puts an arm out, rests it on the Old Man's covered body. With the other, he changes the channels with the remote control. He returns to the channel with the forties movie and seems to become absorbed in a scene in which a gentleman tips his hat to a lady. The scene seems to have 'sunk into' his mind.
EXT. GARDEN - MORNING

It has stopped snowing. Chance, wearing a hat, the gardening apron over his suit and boots, putters in the garden. Louise comes out of the main house. She is dressed warmly, a scarf over her head, a heavy coat. Chance sees her, tips his hat to Louise exactly like the man he saw on television.

                        LOUISE
                ... Well, ain't you the gentleman
                this mornin' ...
                    (a pause)
                ... gotta go now, Chance ...

                    CHANCE
               (resumes working)
          Yes.

                    LOUISE
          You're gonna need somebody,
          someone's gotta be around for you,
          boy ...
               (he keeps working)
          ... You oughta find yourself a
          lady, Chance ...
               (she smiles slightly, with
                caring)
          But I guess it oughta be an old
          lady, 'cause you ain't gonna do a
          young one any good, not with that
          little thing of yours ...
               (she reaches out, puts a
                hand on his shoulder)
          ... You're always gonna be a
          little boy, ain't you?
               (he smiles, keeps working)
          ... Goodbye, Chance ...

Louise gives his shoulder a squeeze, turns and moves toward the house.

                    CHANCE
               (as she goes)
          Goodbye, Louise.

Louise waves as she enters the townhouse. Chance tips his hat once again as she disappears.

INT. MAIN HOUSE - FRONT HALLWAY - MORNING

Louise enters the hallway, picks up a couple of suit cases waiting by the door. She stops as she sees TWO MEN in white carrying a stretcher down the main staircase. She notices the ease with which they bring the Old Man's body down the stairs.

                    LOUISE
          ... He used to be a big man...
          'Spose he wasted away to about
          nothin' ...
               (a beat - then she talks
                to the body of the old Man)

>   ... I guess I'll be goin' off to
>   find me some folks, Old Man ... I'm
>   not batty enough to stay around
>   this neighborhood any longer ...

The stretcher bearers move to the front door. Louise steps in front of them.

>   LOUISE (CONT'D)
>   (to stretcher bearers)
>   Wait up! I'm goin' out that door first.

Louise takes one more look at the covered body, then opens the front door, leaves.

INT. CHANCE'S ROOM - DAY

The TV plays offstage as Chance washes up in the bathroom. He finishes, comes into the bedroom, takes a pair of house slippers from his closet, turns off the television and leaves the room.

EXT. GARDEN - DAY

Chance, carrying his slippers, crosses through the layer of fresh snow to the townhouse.

INT. DINING ROOM - DAY

Chance, wearing the slippers, enters and sits at his place. He turns on the TV, puts the napkin on his lap. He watches TV for a moment, then turns, looks for Louise. She does not appear so he resumes watching TV. He changes channels, views a wildly exciting FOOTBALL game. At a peak in the excitement, he again switches channels. Chance watches TV News coverage of the PRESIDENT of the United States greeting foreign dignitaries at the White House. CLOSE SHOTS on television reveal that the President uses a two-handed handshake when meeting his guests. Unconsciously, Chance grips one hand with the other, the scene on TV seeming to have 'sunk into' his mind.

INT. TOWNHOUSE - FRONT HALLWAY - DAY

A key is heard in the lock. The door opens and THOMAS FRANKLIN and SALLY HAYES enter. Franklin, an attorney, is in his late thirties, carries a large briefcase. Hayes is younger, attractive, also an attorney. She totes a briefcase, has

the look of a modern, liberated woman. Hayes appears to be
surprised at the interior of the house.

                    HAYES
               (looks around)
      ... This is another world, Tom - I
       never would have believed it ...

                  FRANKLIN
      Yeah... He and my father used to
      ride together back in the
      thirties ... Fox hunting ... Before
      I was born ...

                  HAYES
      ... Would you take me on a tour?

                  FRANKLIN
      Gladly ...
          (he smiles)
      ... The safe is in Mr. Jennings'
      bedroom, that'll be stop number
      one.

Franklin puts a hand on Hayes' shoulder as they go off down
the hall.

INT. DINING ROOM - DAY

Chance still watches TV, waits for Louise to serve him.
Franklin and Hayes appear in the doorway of the dining room.
They are both surprised to see Chance.

                  FRANKLIN
      ... Why ... Hello, we thought we
      heard something ...
          (moves to Chance, hand
           outstretched)
      I'm Thomas Franklin.

Chance remains seated, takes Franklin's hand warmly in both of
his like the President did on TV.

                  CHANCE
      Hello, Thomas ... I'm Chance, the
      gardener.

                    FRANKLIN
               (a beat)
          ... The gardener?
               (thinks it's a joke,
               laughs)
          ... Yes, of course ... Mr. Chance,
          this is Ms. Hayes.

Hayes moves to shake Chance's hand.

                    HAYES
          Mr. Chance, I'm very pleased to
          meet you.

                    CHANCE
               (doesn't rise, again
               shakes with both hands)
          Yes.

Chance turns back to the TV and Hayes and Franklin
exchange looks.

                    FRANKLIN
               (after an uneasy pause)
          ... We're with Franklin, Jennings
          and Roberts, the law firm handling
          the estate.

                    CHANCE
               (a smile, totally at ease)
          Yes, Thomas - I understand.

Another period of silence. Franklin and Hayes seem
perplexed.

                    FRANKLIN
          ... Are you waiting for someone?
          An appointment?

                    CHANCE
          Yes. I'm waiting for my lunch.

                    FRANKLIN
          Your lunch? You have a luncheon
          appointment here?

CHANCE
Yes. Louise will bring me lunch.

FRANKLIN
Louise? ... The maid? ...
    (a look to Hayes)
But she should have left earlier today ...

CHANCE
    (smiles at Hayes)
I see ...

FRANKLIN
    (a beat)
... You've quite a sense of humor, Mr. Chance - but all kidding aside, may I ask just what you are doing here?

CHANCE
I live here.

FRANKLIN
You live here?
    (a look to Hayes)
... We don't have any record of that.

CHANCE
Yes. It's very cold outside today, isn't it, Thomas?

FRANKLIN
    (a beat)
... How long have you been living here?

CHANCE
Ever since I can remember, since I was a child.

FRANKLIN
    (doubting)
Since you were a child?

CHANCE
Yes, Thomas. I have always been here. I have always worked in the garden.

HAYES
... Then you really are a gardener?

CHANCE
Yes.

HAYES
Your appearance doesn't suggest that at all, Mr. Chance.

CHANCE
Oh. Thank you.

FRANKLIN
Do you have any proof of your employment, Mr. Chance - any checks from the deceased, any contracts or documents?

CHANCE
No.

FRANKLIN
How were you compensated for these duties you say you performed?

CHANCE
Compensated ...?

FRANKLIN
How were you paid?

CHANCE
I was given meals, and a home ...

HAYES
What about money?

CHANCE
I never needed money.

Franklin steps to the TV, turns it off.

     FRANKLIN
Mr. Chance, perhaps you could show us some identification with your address -- a Driver's License, a credit card, checkbook?

     CHANCE
No, I do not have any of those.

     FRANKLIN
Then how about medical records? Could you give us the name of your doctor, or your dentist?

     CHANCE
I have no need for a doctor or dentist. I have never been ill. I have never been allowed outside of this house, and, except for Joe, I have never had any visitors.

     FRANKLIN
... Joe? Who's Joe?

     CHANCE
  (turns TV back on)
Joe Saracini. He was a mason that did some repairs on the brickwork at the rear of the house. That was in 1952.

     FRANKLIN
1952 ... ?

     CHANCE
  (changes channels)
Yes. I remember when he came. He was very fat and had short hair and showed me some pictures from a funny little book.

     HAYES
Some pictures ...?

     CHANCE
Yes. Of men and women.

                    HAYES
          ... Oh.

                    FRANKLIN
          Mr. Chance, that was twenty-seven
          years ago.

                    CHANCE
          Yes and the Old Man used to come
          to my garden. He would read and
          rest there.

                    FRANKLIN
          Come now, Mr. Jennings had been
          bedridden for thirty-five years,
          since he fractured his spine.

                    CHANCE
          Yes, Thomas, that is correct.
          Then he stopped visiting my garden.

                    FRANKLIN
              (a beat)
          ... We shall need some proof of
          your having resided here, Mr.
          Chance.

                    CHANCE
          You have me, I am here. What more
          proof do you need?

Franklin and Hayes exchange looks.

INT. TOWNHOUSE - REAR ENTRANCE/HALLWAY - AFTERNOON

Chance puts on his snow-boots as Franklin and Hayes continue their questioning.

                    FRANKLIN
          Have you served in the Army?

                    CHANCE
          No, Thomas. But I have seen the
          Army on television.

                    HAYES
          How about taxes, Mr. Chance,
          surely you must have paid taxes?

                    CHANCE
          No.

Chance picks up his slippers and leads the attorneys outside.

EXT. GARDEN - AFTERNOON

Chance describes his garden with pride as they walk toward the rear building.

                    CHANCE
               (points)
          Those trees were very young when I
          first arrived.

                    FRANKLIN
          Are you related to the deceased,
          Mr. Chance?

                    CHANCE
          No, I don't think so. And I have
          planted and shaped all the hedges,
          and in the springtime you will be
          able to see my flowers.

                    HAYES
          Might you have a birth
          certificate, Mr. Chance?

                    CHANCE
          No.
               (points to wall)
          That's where Joe fixed the bricks.

They arrive at the rear building and Chance opens the door to the garage. Franklin and Hayes follow him inside.

INT. GARAGE - AFTERNOON

Franklin and Hayes are taken aback by the touring car.

FRANKLIN
                        (admires car)
                    ... Do you drive this, Mr. Chance?

                    CHANCE
                    No, Thomas. I have never been in
                    an automobile.

                    HAYES
                        (amazed)
                    You never been in a car?

Chance is silent for a moment, he blushes slightly.

                    CHANCE
                    ... Well ... From time to time I
                    did sit in it ... Just in here ...
                    It hasn't been outside since the
                    Old Man hurt himself.
                        (he turns)
                    I live in here.
Chance moves toward his room, Franklin and Hayes follow.

INT. CHANCE'S ROOM - AFTERNOON

Chance sits on the bed to remove his boots as Hayes and
Franklin inspect the room.

                    CHANCE
                    The Old Man gave me nice
                    television sets, this one has
                    remote control.
                        (he turns it on with the
                        remote)
                    He has one just like it.

                    FRANKLIN
                    Mr. Chance, the fact remains that
                    we have no information of your
                    having any connection with the
                    deceased.

                    CHANCE
                    Yes, I understand.

Chance puts on his slippers, crosses to the closet, opens the
door. It is filled with men's wear.

> CHANCE (CONT'D)
> I am allowed to go to the attic and select any of the Old Man's suits. They all fit me very well. I can also take his shirts, shoes and coats.

> HAYES
> It is quite amazing how those clothes have come back into style.

> CHANCE
> Yes. I have seen styles on television.

> FRANKLIN
> (getting back to business)
> What are your plans now, Mr. Chance?

> CHANCE
> I would like to stay and work in my garden.

Chance turns to watch TV. Franklin takes Hayes to a side of the room.

> FRANKLIN
> (quietly)
> ... What do you make of all this?

> HAYES
> I really don't know, Tom - he seems so honest and simple ... In a way, he's quite charming ...

> FRANKLIN
> (looks at Chance)
> ... Yeah ...

> HAYES
> ... It's very bizarre - I don't know what to think ...

> FRANKLIN
> Well ... He's either very, very bright or very, very dense - he's hard to figure ...

>   (he unzips briefcase)
>   ... Let's just keep everything
>   legal.

Franklin takes out some papers, approaches Chance.

>   FRANKLIN (CONT'D)
>   Mr. Chance, assuming what you say
>   is the truth, I would like to know
>   what sort of claim you are
>   planning to make against the
>   deceased's estate.
>
>   CHANCE
>   (does not understand)
>   I'm fine, Thomas. The garden is a
>   healthy one. There is no need for
>   a claim.
>
>   FRANKLIN
>   Good. That's good. Then if you
>   would please sign a paper to that
>   effect.

Franklin hands the release to Chance but Chance does not take it.

>   CHANCE
>   No, Thomas. I don't know how to sign.
>
>   FRANKLIN
>   Come now, Mr. Chance.
>
>   CHANCE
>   (smiles)
>   I have no claim, Thomas.
>
>   FRANKLIN
>   But you won't sign, correct?
>
>   CHANCE
>   Correct.
>
>   FRANKLIN
>   Very well, Mr. Chance - if you
>   insist on dragging this matter
>   on ... But I must inform you this

> house will be closed tomorrow at
> noon. If indeed, you do reside
> here, you will have to move out.
>
>   CHANCE
> Move out? I don't understand, Thomas.
>
>   FRANKLIN
> I think you do, Mr. Chance.
> However, I will reiterate, this
> house is closed and you must
> leave ...
>   (he gives Chance his
>   business card)
> Call me if you change your mind
> about signing.
>   (turns to Hayes)
> C'mon, Sally - let's grab a bite ...
>
>   HAYES
>   (a smile to Chance)
> Good day, Mr. Chance.
>
>   CHANCE
>   (returns smile)
> Good day, Sally.

Chance watches as they leave, then puts Franklin's card on a desk without ever looking at it and turns to stare at television.

INT. TOWNHOUSE - ATTIC - AFTERNOON

A large attic filled with the Old Man's possessions of the past. Chance enters, turns on an old black-and-white TV with a magnifying lens attached to the front. As it plays, he selects a fine leather suitcase from several, takes a hand made [*sic*] suit from a long rack.

INT. CHANCE'S ROOM - AFTERNOON

The TV is on as Chance packs his belongings.

EXT. GARDEN - AFTERNOON

Chance, very nicely dressed, comes out of the rear building carrying his suitcase. He stops on occasion to inspect his garden as he walks toward the townhouse.

INT. TOWNHOUSE - FRONT HALLWAY - AFTERNOON

Chance is reluctant to open the front door. After some hesitation, he gathers up his courage, opens it and steps outside, closing the door behind him.

EXT. FRONT OF TOWNHOUSE - AFTERNOON

Chance stops short on the front steps; the townhouse is situated in a decaying ghetto. The snow is a dirty grey, houses adjoining have their windows shattered, are smeared with grafitti [*sic*]. Chance tries to return to the safety of the townhouse, but the door is locked. He stands on the steps for a moment, then moves to the trash laden sidewalk. He stops, ponders which way to go, finally makes up his mind and moves off to his left.

EXT. GHETTO STREET - AFTERNOON

The buildings are crumbling, rusted out cars line the street. A group of Black people huddle together in threadbare stuffed furniture on the sidewalk, a fire burning between them for warmth. Chance rounds the corner, walks up to them. He stands by them, smiles. They stare back, no sign of friendship in their faces. Chance nods politely to them, then walks away down the sidewalk.

EXT. GHETTO STREET - WASHINGTON, D.C. - AFTERNOON

A group of eight to ten hard-core ghetto youths hang out on a corner. Other passersby give them a wide berth, they are unapproachable. Chance nears the group, approaches.

>   CHANCE
>   (friendly)
>   ... Excuse me, would you please
>   tell me where I could find a
>   garden to work in?

They turn to him as one, silent, amazed that this White trespasser would intrude on their jiving.

>   CHANCE (CONT'D)
>   (after a beat)
>   ... There is much to be done
>   during the winter, I must start

>   the seeds for the spring, I must
>   work the soil ...

One of the Black youths, LOLO, interrupts Chance.

>   LOLO
>   What you growin', man?

The leader of the gang, ABBAZ, shuts up Lolo with an elbow and moves menacingly forward.

>   ABBAZ
>   (nose to nose with Chance)
>   ... What you doin' here, boy?
>
>   CHANCE
>   I had to leave my garden. I want
>   to find another.
>
>   ABBAZ
>   Bullshit. Who sent you here, boy?
>   Did that chickenshit asshole
>   Raphael send you here, boy?
>
>   CHANCE
>   No. Thomas Franklin told me that I
>   had to leave the Old Man's house,
>   he's dead now, you know ...
>
>   ABBAZ
>   Dead, my ass! Now get this, honkie
>   - you go tell Raphael that I ain't
>   takin' no jive from no Western
>   Union messenger! You tell that
>   asshole, if he got somethin' to
>   tell me to get his ass here
>   himself!
>   (edges closer to Chance)
>   You got that, boy?

Chance smiles at Abbaz and reaches into his pocket.

>   CHANCE
>   Yes. I understand.
>   (he takes out his remote
>   control TV changer)
>   If I see Raphael I will tell him.

Chance points the changer at Abbaz and clicks it three times, tries to change the picture. Abbaz immediately pulls out a switchblade, whips the blade open.

>   ABBAZ
>   (holds knife at Chance)
> Now, move, honkie! Before I cut
> your white ass!

Chance, disappointed that the changer did not work, returns it to his pocket.

>   CHANCE
> Yes. Of course.
>   (as he leaves)
> Good day.

Abbaz, Lolo and the gang watch him go, then begin to buzz with excitement: "Who the fuck died?" "Why'd he pull that changer on us, man?" "The Old Man died, must be Papa Joe!" "He's some weird honkie, man."

EXT. CHINATOWN - WASHINGTON, D.C. - AFTERNOON

A Bulletin board affixed to a storefront in Chinatown. Chance gazes at the notes pinned to it, written in Chinese. Smiling, he turns from it, walks on through the area.

EXT. PORNO AREA - WASHINGTON, D.C. - AFTERNOON

A street lined with adult book stores, X-rated movies and strip joints. An elderly Black woman approaches carrying a bag of groceries. Chance steps in front of the woman, stops her.

>   CHANCE
> I'm very hungry now. Would you
> please bring me my lunch?

The woman looks up to Chance, becomes very frightened. She turns and half-runs into a sleazy bar for safety. Chance watches after her for a moment, then continues along.

EXT. PARK - WASHINGTON, D.C. - AFTERNOON

Chance stands looking through a chain-link fence watching some
teenage boys playing basketball. He bangs on the fence, calls
to them.

                    CHANCE
        I have seen your game! I have
        watched Elvin Hayes play it many
        times! They call him "Big E!"

The boys ignore him, Chance walks away.

EXT. WASHINGTON, D.C. STREET - LATE AFTERNOON

Chance walks down the center meridian of a divided street. He
seems oblivious to the automobiles passing on either side. In
the background can be seen the Washington Monument.

EXT. WASHINGTON, D.C. STREET - LATE AFTERNOON

Chance seems stumped on which way to go. He looks up one
street, then the other, has no idea where they lead. He turns,
looks behind him and sees a large statue of Benito Juarez
pointing. Chance smiles and goes off in the direction that
Benito points.

EXT. REAR OF THE WHITE HOUSE - DUSK

Tourists are gathered around gaping through the fence at the
White House. Chance is turned the other way, inspecting the
branches of a dying tree. Chance moves to a POLICEMAN standing
nearby.

                    CHANCE
        Excuse me ...
            (points to tree)
        ... That tree is very sick. It
        should be cared for.

The Policeman looks at the tree, then at Chance, figures a man
dressed that well must be important.

                    POLICEMAN
        Yes sir. I'll report it right
        away.

                    CHANCE
          Yes. That would be a good thing to
          do. Good day.

                    POLICEMAN
          Good day.

The Policeman takes out his walkie-talkie as Chance
walks away.

EXT. BUSINESS DISTRICT - EVENING

A fashionable area. Expensive shops, well-kept streets and
sidewalks. A television store has caught Chance's eye. He
stands by the display window, looks in at a dozen or so color
TVs, all turned on, playing various channels. A video camera
points outward from a corner of the window and is focused on
the sidewalk to allow potential customers to see themselves
live on an Advent TV. Chance is intrigued by his own image. He
poses, lifts one arm, then the other to make sure that it is
really him on television. He moves forward, smiles, then moves
slowly backward, notices himself become smaller on the screen.
He steps back off the curb, frowns as his likeness disappears
from frame on the Advent. Standing between two parked cars,
Chance takes out his remote control, clicks it at the Advent.
Four or five other sets in the window change channels, but he
does not reappear on the giant screen. As he does this, the
car to his left, a large, American-made limousine, backs up.
The car bumps Chance, pins him against the car to his right.
Chance cries out in pain, drops his suitcase, his changer, and
bangs his hand on the trunk of the limo. The chauffeur, DAVID,
and the liveryman, JEFFREY, immediately jump from the car, run
back to Chance.

                    DAVID
          I'm very sorry, sir ... I ...

David and Jeffrey reach out to help, but Chance is wedged
solidly between the two cars.

                    CHANCE
               (in pain)
          ... I can't move ... My leg ...

                    DAVID
               (rushes back to limo)
          ... My Lord ...

                    JEFFREY
          This is terrible, sir - I hope
          you're not badly injured ...

                    CHANCE
          No. I'm not badly injured. But my
          leg is very sore.

David pulls the car forward, freeing Chance. A few bystanders
begin to gather as Jeffrey helps Chance to the sidewalk.

                    JEFFREY
          Can you walk? It's not broken, is it?

                    CHANCE
               (leans against limo, holds leg)
          It's very sore.

David gets out of the car, comes back.

                    DAVID
          Perhaps I should call an ambulance.

A BYSTANDER interrupts.

                    BYSTANDER
          Somebody ought to call the police!

                    CHANCE
               (looks over, smiles)
          There's no need for police, it's
          just my leg.

During this, the rear door of the limo opens and EVE RAND
steps out. Eve is in her late thirties, has the look of a
traditional New England lady. She watches as Jeffrey tends to
Chance.

                    JEFFREY
          I don't think we should call
          anyone just yet, it may not even
          be all that serious.

                    CHANCE
               (obviously hurting)
          I agree.

JEFFREY
Let's have a look, do you mind?

CHANCE
Of course. I would like to look.

Chance bends, raises his trouser leg. A red-bluish swollen bruise, three inches in diameter, is forming on his calf.

JEFFREY
It's starting to swell, is it painful?

CHANCE
Yes.

Eve moves closer to Chance, looks at the bruise.

EVE
(to Chance)
... Won't you let us do something for you? Your leg should be examined, we could take you to a hospital.

CHANCE
(smiles at Eve)
There's no need for a hospital.

EVE
Why, there certainly is. You must see a doctor, I insist on it. Please, let us take you.

Eve turns to get back into the limo. David goes with her to hold the door.

DAVID
I'm terribly sorry, Mrs. Rand, I never saw the man.

EVE
Oh, I don't think it was anyone's fault, David.

DAVID
Thank you, ma'am.

Chance is hesitant about getting in the car. Jeffrey offers a helping hand.

                    JEFFREY
              Please, sir.

                    CHANCE
              I've never ridden in an
              automobile.

                    JEFFREY
                (a beat)
              I assure you, sir, David is a very
              careful driver. Please, won't you
              let us take you?

                    CHANCE
                (looks at the car, then decides)
              ... Yes. You can take me.

                    JEFFREY
              Very good.

Jeffrey assists Chance into the rear seat of the limo.

                    CHANCE
                (as he gets in)
              ... My suitcase.

                    JEFFREY
              Yes sir. I'll take care of that.

Jeffrey closes the door, goes back to pick up Chance's suitcase, does not notice the remote control. As Jeffrey puts Chance's bag into the trunk, we see the personalized license plate "RAND 1."

INT. LIMOUSINE - EVENING

Chance and Eve settle in the back seat. As they talk, David starts up the limo, Jeffrey joins him in front and the limo pulls out into traffic.

                    EVE
              I hope you're comfortable.

                    CHANCE
              Yes. I am.

EVE
These can be such trying
situations everyone seems to make
such a to-do over a simple little
accident. Of course, they can be
very frightening, and I must
apologize for David, he's never
had an accident before.

CHANCE
Yes. He's a very careful driver.

EVE
... Why, yes, he is ... Is your leg
feeling any better?

CHANCE
It's feeling better, but it's
still very sore.

EVE
I see.
    (a thought)
... Say, would you mind seeing our
family doctor?

CHANCE
    (doesn't understand)
Your family doctor?

EVE
Yes. My husband has been very ill.
His doctor and nurses are staying
with us. Those hospitals can be so
impersonal - why, it might be
hours before you are treated ...

CHANCE
I agree.

EVE
Fine, it will save a lot of
unnecessary fuss and it will be so
much more pleasant for you ...
    (leans forward)
David, we'll just go on home.
Jeffrey, would you call and let
them know?

                         JEFFREY
                Yes ma'am.

Eve presses a button, the glass partition closes. As the
window rolls up behind him, Jeffrey dials the limo telephone.
There is a moment of silence. Eve, still a bit on edge from
the accident and feeling a bit uncomfortable with a stranger
in the car, presses another button. The limo's bar moves out,
revealing a row of decanters and glasses.

                         EVE
                Would you care for a drink?

                         CHANCE
                Yes. Thank you.

As Eve pours cognac into a monogrammed crystal glass, Chance
notices the limo's TV set.

                         CHANCE (CONT'D)
                I would like to watch television.

                         EVE
                    (a bit surprised)
                Oh? Certainly ...

She hands Chance the cognac, turns on the TV.

                         EVE (CONT'D)
                Oh, by the way - I'm Eve Rand.

                         CHANCE
                Hello, Eve.

Chance takes a sip of the cognac, is not accustomed to
alcohol, coughs. There is another moment of silence.

                         EVE
                May I ask your name?

                         CHANCE
                    (with a slight cough)
                My name is Chance.

                         EVE
                Pardon me, was that Mr. Chance?

                    CHANCE
               (still indistinct)
          No. I'm a gardener.

                    EVE
          Oh ... Mr. Gardiner ... Mr. Chauncey
          Gardiner ... You're not related to
          Basil and Perdita Gardiner are
          you?

                    CHANCE
          No, Eve. I'm not related to Basil
          and Perdita.

                    EVE
          Oh. Well, they're just a wonderful
          couple, we've been friends for
          years. We visit their island quite
          often.

Chance reaches out to change the channel on the TV, suddenly
realizes he doesn't have his remote control. He starts going
through his pockets, searches for it.

                    EVE (CONT'D)
          Did you lose something?

                    CHANCE
          Yes. I lost my remote control.

                    EVE
          Oh ... Well, I'm very sorry...

Another pause, Chance reaches out, changes channels on TV.

                    EVE (CONT'D)
          ... I'll feel so relieved after
          Dr. Allenby examines your leg.
          After that, David can run you on
          home, or to your office or
          wherever you'd prefer ...
               (Chance still watches TV)
          ... Is there anything special you
          would like to watch?

                    CHANCE
          I like to watch. This is fine.

Chance watches the news. Eve sips on her cognac
as David eases the limo out of the city of Washington.

EXT. HIGHWAY - WOODED AREA - NIGHT

The limo approaches, then turns into the entrance-way of the
Rand Estate. Two guards stand on either side of the open gate,
salute as the car passes through.
EXT. RAND DRIVE - NIGHT

The drive runs alongside a stream, then turns and crosses
a large meadow. The limousine passes, still no sign of the
house. It is a very, very long driveway.

INT. LIMOUSINE - NIGHT

Chance is glued to the TV, switches channels, again watches the
news. Eve takes his fascination with television as a sign of
intelligence.

>   EVE
>   I can see that it must be very
>   important for you to stay informed
>   of all the latest events.
>
>   CHANCE
>   Yes.
>
>   EVE
>   I admire that in a person. As for
>   myself, I find there is so much to
>   assimilate that it can become
>   quite muddling at times ...

Chance nods, changes the channel, watches a Mighty Mouse
cartoon. Eve looks at him perplexed, then takes it for a joke
and smiles.

EXT. RAND MANSION - NIGHT

Two uniformed valets, WILSON and PERKINS, await the limousines
by the front door of the Rand mansion. Wilson stands behind
a wheelchair. As the limo parks, Perkins and Jeffrey assist
Chance into the chair. Wilson turns to Eve as she gets out of
the limo.

                    WILSON
          Good evening, Mrs. Rand.

                    EVE
          Good evening, Wilson.

                    WILSON
          I shall take the gentleman to the
          third floor [sic] guest suite,
          ma'am. Dr. Allenby is standing by.

                    EVE
          Thank you, Wilson. That will be fine.

Perkins and Jeffrey carry Chance in the chair up the steps and
into the house. Eve and Wilson follow.

INT. RAND MANSION - FRONT HALLWAY - NIGHT

Once inside the house, Wilson takes over wheeling Chance. A lady,
GRETA, is waiting to take Eve's coat.

                    EVE
          Thank you, Greta.
              (to Wilson)
          I'll be with Mr. Rand if I'm
          needed.

                    WILSON
          Yes, ma'am.

                    EVE
              (to Chance)
          I'll see you after the doctor has
          a look at your leg, Mr. Gardiner.

                    CHANCE
              (looking around mansion)
          Yes, I think he should examine my
          leg.

Eve watches as Wilson wheels Chance around a corner.

INT. ELEVATOR - NIGHT

The doors open, Wilson pushes Chance into the elevator. As
Wilson pushes a button and the doors close on them, a strange
look comes over Chance's face.

                    CHANCE
               (looks to Wilson)
          ... I've never been in one of these.

Wilson thinks that Chance is talking about the wheelchair.

                    WILSON
               It's one of Mr. Rand's. Since he's
               been ill ...
Chance looks around the elevator.

                    CHANCE
               Does it have a television?

                    WILSON
                 (laughs)
               No - but Mr. Rand does have one
               with an electric motor, that way
               he can get around by himself.

                    CHANCE
               I see.

Chance again checks out the elevator.

                    CHANCE (CONT'D)
               How long do we stay in here?

                    WILSON
               How long? I don't know, see what
               the doctor says ...

The elevator stops on the third floor.

INT. RAND MANSION - HALLWAY - NIGHT

A hallway adjoining a large, glass-enclosed room. Eve passes through the hall, enters the room.

INT. BENJAMIN RAND'S HOSPITAL ROOM - NIGHT

Eve enters into a hermetically sealed area, set up with all the latest hospital emergency gear; oxygen, EKG machine, X ray machine, transfusion equipment, sterilizers, etc. BENJAMIN RAND, wearing a silk bathrobe, lies in a king-sized bed in the

center of the room. A nurse, CONSTANCE, is attending to her
duties in the room, looks up as Eve comes in.

                CONSTANCE
        Good evening, Mrs. Rand.

                EVE
        Good evening, Constance.

Ben Rand perks up as he sees Eve crossing to him. He is in his
sixties, maintains an inner strength and dignity despite the
sapping effects of his illness.

                RAND
           (with weakness)
    ... Eve ...

Eve kisses him, holds his hand.

                EVE
        Oh, Ben - I miss you so when
        I'm out ... How are you feeling?

                RAND
        Tired ... And I'm getting tired of
        being so tired. Other than that,
        I'm doing very well.

                EVE
        No headaches?

                RAND
        No, it's been a good day - better
        than yours, from what I've been
        told.

                EVE
           (holds his hand against her cheek)
        You heard?

                RAND
        I may be a shut-in, but I do not
        lack for news. I'm sorry you had
        to go through all that.

                    EVE
          Oh, it wasn't all that bad,
          darling. We were fortunate that
          Mr. Gardiner turned out to be so
          reasonable.

                    RAND
          Reasonable? Good, I'd like to meet
          a reasonable man. Why don't you
          ask this Gardiner to join us for
          dinner?

                    EVE
            (sits on the side of the bed)
          Do you feel well enough for that?

                    RAND
            (smiles)
          Hah! ... Tell me the truth, Eve -
          if I wait until I feel better,
          will I ever meet the man?

There is silence from Eve. Rand squeezes her hand, turns to
Constance.

                    RAND (CONT'D)
          Constance! I want new blood
          tonight, I'm getting up for
          dinner.

                    CONSTANCE
          But, Mr. Rand ...

                    RAND
          Don't argue, tell Robert I want
          new blood!
              (turns to Eve)
          ... Ask him to dinner.

Rand pulls Eve's hand close, kisses it.

INT. EAST WING GUEST SUITE - NIGHT

An enormous bedroom, filled with 18th Century antique furniture.
DR. ROBERT ALLENBY dabs Chance's ass with a piece of cotton

soaked in alcohol, prior to an injection. Chance stands with his pants to the floor, looks to the television which is not turned on.

>   ALLENBY
> The injection will ease the pain
> and swelling, Mr. Gardiner.

>   CHANCE
> I understand. I've seen it done
> before.

>   ALLENBY
> Now, you'll barely feel this. It
> won't hurt at all.

Allenby administers the injection, Chance reacts from the pain.

>   CHANCE
> You were wrong, it did hurt.

>   ALLENBY
>   (a chuckle)
> But not for long ...

As Allenby puts a band-aid [sic] on Chance's ass, Chance spots a remote control for the TV on the bedside table. He reaches out, picks it up.

>   ALLENBY (CONT'D)
> It's good that there was no
> apparent damage to the bone.

>   CHANCE
> Yes. I think so, too.

>   ALLENBY
> However, with injuries such as
> this, I have run into minor
> hemorrhaging, which really isn't
> too serious at the time, but can
> cause secondary problems if not
> looked after.

                    CHANCE
          I see.

Chance turns on the TV.

                    ALLENBY
               (a look to the TV, then to
               Chance)
          You can pull your trousers up,
          now.

                    CHANCE
          Oh, fine.

                    ALLENBY
               (as Chance pulls up pants)
          Just to take the proper
          precautions, Mr. Gardiner, I'd
          recommend we take you downstairs
          and X-ray your leg.
               (no reaction from Chance,
               Allenby takes a long
               look at him)
          ... By the way, Mr. Gardiner, I
          would like to ask you something
          straight out.

                    CHANCE
               (doesn't understand)
          ... Straight out?

                    ALLENBY
          Yes. Are you planning on making
          any sort of claim against the
          Rands?

                    CHANCE
               (after a beat)
          Claim ...? ... Oh, claim, that's
          what Thomas asked me.

                    ALLENBY
          Thomas? Who's Thomas?

                    CHANCE
          Thomas Franklin, an attorney.

                    ALLENBY
          An attorney?

                    CHANCE
               (turns back to TV)
          Yes.

                    ALLENBY
               (suddenly very cold)
          Then you wish to handle this
          matter through your attorneys?

                    CHANCE
          There's no need for a claim, the
          garden is a healthy one.

                    ALLENBY
               (gives Chance a look)
          Oh, I see ...
               (warms up)
          ... Well, then ... You're a very
          funny man, Mr. Gardiner. You
          caught me off guard, I must
          admit ...

                    CHANCE
               (changes channels, sits on bed)
          Thank you.

                    ALLENBY
          Good, keep your weight off that
          leg, Mr. Gardiner. In fact, it
          would be best if you could stay
          here for a day or two, if that
          would be possible. Since
          Benjamin became ill we have our
          own hospital downstairs. I can
          promise you the finest in care,
          unless, of course, you would
          prefer to go elsewhere.

                    CHANCE
          Yes, I could stay here. Thank you.

                    ALLENBY
          Fine. Would you like me to speak
          to your personal physician?

                    CHANCE
          No.

Allenby waits for Chance to say more, he does not. Finally,
Allenby picks up his bag, heads for the door.

                    ALLENBY
              (stops by door)
          I'll send Wilson up to take you
          for X-rays, Mr. Gardiner. Feel
          free to use the telephone, and
          please let me know if you have any
          discomfort.

                    CHANCE
              (clicking changer)
          Yes, I will.

Allenby gives him a look, then leaves. Chance watches an old
movie of a man lighting a cigar. The man enjoys the cigar,
blows out smoke. The scene seems to 'sink into' Chance's mind.

EXT. MANSION - PATIO - NIGHT

Eve sits next to a roaring patio fireplace with a steaming cup
of tea. Allenby comes outside, joins her.

                    ALLENBY
          Good God, Eve - you'll freeze out
          here.

                    EVE
          I wanted some fresh air, Robert.
          How is Mr. Gardiner?

                    ALLENBY
          A rather large contusion, but I
          don't feel there is any serious
          damage. I'd like to keep an eye on
          him, though - I suggested that he
          stay here for a couple of days.

                    EVE
          Stay here? Is that necessary?

                    ALLENBY
          Not necessary, but preferable. I
          don't think he'll be a bother, he
          seems like a most refreshing sort
          of man.

                    EVE
          Yes, he is different ... Not the
          kind of person one usually meets
          in Washington.

                    ALLENBY
          How true. Mr. Gardiner may be a
          welcome change of pace.

                    EVE
          He's very intense, and internal,
          don't you think?

                    ALLENBY
          At times, yes. But that's not an
          uncommon reaction to such an
          accident. Actually, I found him to
          have quite a sense of humor.

                    EVE
          Good. It might be pleasant for a
          couple of days.
              (Eve puts down her tea)
          ... Robert ... Is there any
          improvement ...?

                    ALLENBY
          No, Eve ... I'm sorry.

Eve is silent for a moment, looks out to the
darkness.

                    EVE
          ... Sometimes when I see Ben I
          could swear that he's getting
          stronger ... Something that he
          might say, the way he moves, or a
          look in his eyes - makes me feel

>   that this is all a nightmare and
>   that he'll be better soon ... It's
>   just so hard to believe what's
>   really happening ...

Allenby reaches out, holds Eve's hand.

INT. RAND MANSION - FIRST FLOOR HALLWAY - NIGHT

The elevator door opens, Wilson guides Chance in the wheelchair into the hallway.

>   CHANCE
>   (looks back to elevator)
>   ... That is a very small room.
>
>   WILSON
>   (laughs)
>   Yes sir, I guess that's true
>   smallest room in the house.
>
>   CHANCE
>   (glancing around)
>   Yes. It seems to be.

Wilson takes this as another joke, chuckles as he wheels Chance toward Rand's hospital room.

INT. RAND'S HOSPITAL ROOM - NIGHT

CONSTANCE and another nurse, TERESA, stand by as Rand is being given a transfusion. Rand lifts his head as Wilson wheels Chance into the room.

>   RAND
>   Welcome to Rand Memorial Hospital,
>   Mr. Gardiner.
>
>   CHANCE
>   (looks around room)
>   ... I see.

Wilson pushes Chance to the X-Ray machine, where the technician, BILLINGS, a Black man, waits. As Wilson and Billings help Chance onto the X-Ray table, Chance's face brightens up.

                    CHANCE (CONT'D)
          I feel very good in here.

                    RAND
          Sure you do. This ward is air
          tight, I have a little extra
          oxygen pumped in, keeps my spirits
          up.

                    CHANCE
          Yes. I like that very much.

                    BILLINGS
              (lining up Chance's leg)
          This won't take long, Mr.
          Gardiner. Please hold still when I
          ask.

Chance stares at Billings, reacts to him being Black.

                    CHANCE
              (to Billings)
          Do you know Raphael?

                    BILLINGS
          No sir, I don't believe I do.

                    CHANCE
          Oh. I have a message for him.

                    BILLINGS
          Yes, sir.

                    CHANCE
          A Black man gave me the message.

                    BILLINGS
          Well, I still don't believe I know
          the man, Mr. Gardiner. Now, hold
          still.

Rand looks over as Billings takes the X-Ray.

                    RAND
          Aplastic anemia, Mr. Gardiner -
          aplastic anemia.

Chance smiles to Rand.

                    RAND (CONT'D)
          Failure of the bone marrow to
          produce red blood cells ... Not a
          damn thing they can do about it.
          Oh, they can make me comfortable,
          prolong my life with steroid
          therapy and transfusions ... And
          what makes my blood boil, what
          little I have left, that is, Mr.
          Gardiner - is that it's generally
          a young person's disease ... Here I
          am, getting on in years and about
          to die of a young person's
          disease ...

                    CHANCE
             (still smiles at Rand)
          Yes. You look very sick.

                    BILLINGS
          Hold still, please, Mr. Gardiner.

                    RAND
             (a laugh)
          I am very sick, and, as you can
          see by all this paraphernalia, I
          am very wealthy. I think I would
          rather be wealthy and sick than
          poor and sick.

                    CHANCE
             (looks around the room)
          I understand. I've never seen
          anything like this on television.

                    BILLINGS
          Please, hold still, Mr. Gardiner.

                    CONSTANCE
          You too, Mr. Rand, you must stay
          quiet.

Rand lays his head back.

                    RAND
          ... We're prisoners, Mr. Gardiner
          - we're prisoners of tubes and
          technology.

                    CHANCE
               I agree.

                    RAND
                 (flat on his back)
               ... You will join us for dinner,
               won't you, Mr. Gardiner?

                    CHANCE
                 (also flat on his back)
               Yes. I am very hungry.

                    RAND
               ... So am I, my boy - so am I.

INT. RAND DINING ROOM - NIGHT

THURMAND, a waiter, and MARIANNE, a waitress, enter into the Rand dining room carrying trays of food. The dining room is immense, a 70-foot ceiling, huge fireplace. Allenby, Eve, Rand, and Chance (both in wheelchairs) sit around the table. Rand speaks slowly, with obvious weakness.

                    RAND
               I know exactly what you mean.
               Today the businessman is at the
               mercy of kid-lawyers from the SEC.
               All they want to do is regulate
               our natural growth! It's happening
               across the country!

                    ALLENBY
               To everyone, I'm afraid. The
               Government controls are so
               restricting that the Medical
               Profession, as we know it, is
               being legislated out of existence.

                    RAND
               Of course! By kid-lawyers!

Eve turns to Chance.

                    EVE
               Won't your injury prevent you from
               attending to business, Mr.
               Gardiner?

                    CHANCE
          No. It won't do that.

                    EVE
          ... Would you like us to notify
          anyone for you?

                    CHANCE
          No. The Old Man died and Louise
          left.

There is a moment of silence.

                    EVE
          Oh. I'm very sorry. Well, if you
          have any need for any of our
          facilities, please do not hesitate
          to ask.

                    RAND
          Do you need a secretary?

                    CHANCE
          No, thank you. My house has been
          closed.

                    RAND
          Oh. When you say 'Your house has
          been closed', you mean to say that
          your business was shut down?

                    CHANCE
          Yes. Shut down and locked by the
          attorneys.

                    RAND
          What'd I tell you? Kid-lawyers!
          The S.E.C.! Damn them!

                    EVE
          I hope that staying here won't be
          an inconvenience for you.

                    CHANCE
          No. I like it here.

                    RAND
          That's good, Mr. Gardiner. Or may
          I call you Chauncey?

                    CHANCE
               (agreeable to being called
                Chauncey)
          Yes. Chauncey is fine.

                    RAND
          And I'm Ben.

                    ALLENBY
               (smiles to Chance)
          ... And please call me Robert.

                    CHANCE
          Yes, Robert. I will.

                    RAND
          So tell me, Chauncey, what are
          your plans now?

Chance looks around the room.

                    CHANCE
          Does this house have a garden?

Allenby gives Chance a look.

                    RAND
          Do we have a garden? Hah!
          Tomorrow, Chauncey, you will see
          our gardens.

                    CHANCE
          I see. I would like to work in
          your garden.

                    EVE
               (laughs)
          Oh, I know exactly what you mean.
          I sometimes enjoy puttering around
          myself, such a pleasant way to
          forget one's troubles.

                    CHANCE
I am a very good gardener.

                    RAND
A gardener! Well put, Chauncey
excellent! Isn't that what a
businessman is? A gardener? A
person that makes flinty soil
productive with the labor of his
own hands, who waters it with the
sweat from his own brow, and who
creates a place of value for his
family and community? Yes,
Chauncey, what a brilliant
metaphor -- yes, indeed, a
productive businessman is a
laborer in his own vineyard.

                    CHANCE
Thank you, Ben. The garden that I
left was such a place. Everything
which grew there was with the
labor of my own hands. I planted
seeds and watered them and watched
everything grow.

                    RAND
        (weakly)
Bravo!

                    CHANCE
But I don't have that any more ...
        (points to ceiling)
... All that's left for me now is
the room upstairs.

                    RAND
Now, wait a minute, Chauncey you
are young, you are healthy, for
God's sake don't give up on
yourself! You have to fight! You
can't let those bastards keep you
down! I don't want to hear any
more from you about the 'Room
Upstairs'. That's where I'm going
soon.

There is a long pause. Chance looks up, then smiles at Rand.

>   CHANCE
>   It's a very pleasant room, Ben.

>   RAND
>   (laughs)
>   Yes, I'm sure it is. That's what
>   they say, anyway.

Another period of silence. The servants bustle around the room as Allenby studies Chance.

INT. RAND'S POOL ROOM - NIGHT

Allenby opens the door. Rand enters in his electric wheelchair followed by Chance being pushed by Wilson.

>   RAND
>   ... I don't know what you've heard
>   about me, Chauncey, but I'm sure
>   you know everything there is to
>   know. Cigar?

Rand holds out humidor to Chance.

>   CHANCE
>   Yes, thank you.
>   (takes cigar)
>   No Ben. I don't know everything
>   about you.

Rand smiles as he takes a cigar for himself.

>   RAND
>   ... No, of course you don't.
>   Excuse me for being so
>   presumptuous. No man knows
>   everything about another man -
>   however, very few are honest
>   enough to admit it.

>   ALLENBY
>   That is so true. You're different,
>   Chauncey ... Quite different than
>   most men.

                    CHANCE
               Thank you, Robert.

Rand lights his own cigar, then hands an ornate lighter to
Chance.

                    RAND
               (picks up pool cue, weakly
                strokes the balls)
               ... You know, Chauncey, there are
               thousands of American businessmen,
               large and small, that share your
               plight. I've been concerned with
               the situation for some time now.

Chance, not knowing to bite off the tip, tries to light the
cigar like the man on TV. It will not light.

                    RAND (CONT'D)
               So I've been thinking about
               beginning a financial assistance
               program, Chauncey, to help out
               American businessmen that have
               been harassed by inflation,
               excessive taxation, unions and
               other indecencies ...

Allenby watches Chance trying to light the cigar as Rand
speaks on, shooting pool as he talks.

                    RAND (CONT'D)
               ... I'd like to offer the decent
               'Gardeners' of the business
               community a helping hand. After
               all, they are our strongest
               defense against the pollutants who
               so threaten our basic freedoms and
               the well-being of our middle
               class. Tell me, would you have any
               thoughts on such a program?

Chance puts the unlit cigar in the ashtray, smiles at Allenby,
then answers Rand.

                    CHANCE
               No, Ben.

                    RAND
               (a smile)
          Reluctant to speak, eh, Chauncey?
          Well, I can understand that. When
          a man loses everything, anger has
          a tendency to block out reason for
          a time. Just give it some thought,
          work with the idea, I'm sure
          you'll have plenty to say in a few
          days.

                    CHANCE
          I could give it some thought, Ben,
          but my leg is very sore.

                    RAND
          ... Oh?
               (looks to Allenby)
          Robert, take a look, would you?

                    ALLENBY
          Some pain is to be expected ...
               (bends to Chance, looks at leg)
          ... And I think what would be best
          for the two of you is a good
          night's rest.
               (checks watch)
          ... It's late, I'm afraid it's
          time for my patients to prepare
          for bed.

                    RAND
               (puts down pool cue)
          We have common foes, Chauncey -
          kid lawyers and our physician!

                    CHANCE
          I agree.

Allenby laughs as he takes Rand's cigar from him, snuffs it in the ashtray.

INT. MANSION - ELEVATOR - NIGHT

Wilson stands behind Chance in the wheelchair. Chance glances slowly and inquisitively around the elevator. When his eyes meet Wilson's, the valet breaks out in laughter.

>   WILSON
>   (laughing, trying to apologize)
>   ... Sorry, sir - I just couldn't
>   contain myself ... I knew you were
>   going to come out with another one
>   of your jests about the
>   elevator ... Excuse me, sir ...

The elevator stops, the door opens.

INT. MANSION - THIRD FLOOR HALLWAY - NIGHT

Wilson wheels Chance out of the elevator.

>   CHANCE
>   (looks back as the door closes)
>   ... Hmmm ... Elevator.

>   WILSON
>   (laughs again)
>   ... Yes sir - elevator!

Wilson stops laughing, becomes the stone-faced servant once again as he notices Eve coming out of her bedroom. Wilson stops wheeling Chance, stands stiffly at attention as Eve and Chance talk.

>   EVE
>   Chauncey, I wanted to tell you how
>   dreadful I feel about the accident
>   today, but that I'm delighted that
>   you are staying with us.

>   CHANCE
>   Thank you, Eve - I like this house
>   very much.

>   EVE
>   ... And Ben is just mad about you
>   - you've lifted his spirits so -

>   it's just ... Well, it's just a
>   real pleasure having you with us.
>
>   CHANCE
>   Ben is very ill, Eve - I've seen
>   that before.
>
>   EVE
>   Yes ... I know, Chauncey.
>
>   CHANCE
>   I like Ben very much ... He reminds
>   me of the Old Man ...
>
>   EVE
>   He does ...?
>
>   CHANCE
>   Yes. Are you going to leave and
>   close the house when he dies?

Eve is not prepared for such a question.

>   EVE
>   ... Why ... No, I don't think so ...
>
>   CHANCE
>   That's good.

Chance smiles at Eve and there is a moment of silence before Eve steps back into her bedroom.

>   EVE
>   ... Good night, Chauncey.
>
>   CHANCE
>   Good night, Eve.

Eve closes the door. Wilson wheels Chance down the hallway toward the guest room.

EXT. FRONT OF RAND MANSION - MORNING

Eve comes out of the house, Jeffrey holds the door for her as she gets into "RAND 1." Jeffrey gets in and the limo pulls away. Chance comes out of the front door, walking with a limp. His first view of the Rand grounds in the daylight, he is taken

by the extent of the greenery. An attendant, LEWIS, hurries to
Chance.

>   LEWIS
>   Did you want a car, sir?
>
>   CHANCE
>   Yes. I would like a car.
>
>   LEWIS
>   Yes, sir.

Lewis goes to his post, picks up a phone. As Chance looks
at the surroundings, Allenby and Wilson, with Chance's
wheelchair, come out of the house.

>   ALLENBY
>   (frowns as he sees Chance walking)
>   Chauncey, there you are. What are
>   you doing on that leg?
>
>   CHANCE
>   It's fine today, Robert.
>
>   ALLENBY
>   Shame on you, Chauncey - you
>   should let me be the judge of
>   that.
>   (motions to Wilson)
>   Please, sit in the chair.

Wilson pushes the wheelchair to Chance, he sits.

>   ALLENBY (CONT'D)
>   (checks leg)
>   I swear, Chauncey, between you and
>   Benjamin, I've got my hands
>   full ...
>   (looks at calf)
>   ... Say, that is coming along, the
>   swelling has gone down
>   considerably ...
>   (pokes a spot)
>   ... Any pain here?

                    CHANCE
          Yes, Robert. But it's not bad.

A limousine pulls up to the front of the mansion, waits for Chance.

                    ALLENBY
               (continues examining)
          ... Benjamin has been hounding me
          to allow him to address the annual
          meeting of his Financial Institute
          today, but obviously, the strain
          would be impossible ... How about
          here, Chauncey, any soreness?

                    CHANCE
          Hardly any, Robert.

Lewis, the attendant, interrupts.

                    LEWIS
          Your limousine, sir.

                    CHANCE
          Oh, thank you.

                    ALLENBY
               (reacting to limo)
          ... Were you going somewhere?

                    CHANCE
          No, Robert.

                    ALLENBY
               (a beat)
          ... Oh.
               (checks leg)
          ... My God, I only wish that
          Benjamin had your recuperative
          powers ... Anyway, the President
          offered to sit in for Ben at the
          meeting, quite a nice gesture,
          I felt. He's due here soon, I
          believe.

                    CHANCE
          Yes, Robert. I know about the
          President.

                    ALLENBY
                (mildly surprised)
            ... Oh? You've heard?

                    CHANCE
            Yes. Ben called me. He wants me to
            meet the President.

                    ALLENBY
                (stands)
            He does, does he?

                    CHANCE
            Yes, Ben told me to be in his room
            at ten o'clock.

                    ALLENBY
            Why, that's terrific, Chauncey.

                    CHANCE
            How do I know when it's ten
            o'clock?

A long look from Allenby, then he looks at his watch.

                    ALLENBY
            ... It's five of, you'd best get
            on in there.

                    CHANCE
            Thank you, Robert.

Wilson begins to push Chance.

                    CHANCE (CONT'D)
            I would like to walk today.

                    ALLENBY
            Hell yes - walk. You're meeting
            the President, aren't you?

                    CHANCE
                (gets out of chair)
            Oh, really?

Allenby, a bit puzzled, watches as Chance goes into the house.

INT. RAND MANSION - HALLWAY - MORNING

Chance limps aimlessly through a hallway. He stops, admires a large tapestry on the wall. A servant, SMYTHE, notices Chance appears confused, approaches him.

          SMYTHE
May I help you, Mr. Gardiner?

          CHANCE
    (with a smile)
Yes. I would like to go to Rand Memorial Hospital.

          SMYTHE
    (a pause)
... Sir?

          CHANCE
Yes.

There is another long pause.

          SMYTHE
... Did you wish to see someone, sir?

          CHANCE
Yes, I would like to see Ben.

          SMYTHE
Oh, Mr. Rand, of course. Right this way, sir.

Chance follows Smythe down the hall.

INT. RAND'S HOSPITAL ROOM - MORNING

Rand is in an easy chair, dressed for his meeting with the President. The two nurses are working at the disinfecting table. Rand smiles as Chance is shown into the room by Smythe.

          RAND
Chauncey, up and around this morning, are you?

                    CHANCE
          Yes, Ben. My leg is not very sore.

                    RAND
          Well, that's good news, my boy.

                    CHANCE
          You're looking much better today,
          Ben.

                    RAND
          Hah! It's all make-up, Chauncey ...
          I asked nurse Teresa to fix me up,
          I didn't want the President to
          think I was going to die during
          our talk.

                    CHANCE
          I understand.

                    RAND
          No one likes a dying man, my boy -
          because few know what death is.
          All we know is the terror of it.
          But you're an exception, Chauncey
          - that's what I admire in you,
          your marvelous balance. You don't
          stagger back and forth between
          fear and hope - you're a truly
          peaceful man.

                    CHANCE
          Thank you, Ben.
               (looks at Rand closely)
          ... The nurse did a very good job,
          Ben.

The nurses turn, look at Chance.

EXT. FRONT RAND MANSION - MORNING

Wilson is at the head of eight servants lined up on the front
steps. Two black PLYMOUTH SEDANS pull up and park. EIGHT MEN
in grey business suits get out. One of them, WOLTZ, goes
directly to Wilson.

                    WOLTZ
          Good morning, Mr. Wilson.

                    WILSON
          Good morning, Mr. Woltz, nice to
          see you again.

                    WOLTZ
          Thank you. How have you been?

                    WILSON
          Fine, thank you.
              (hands Woltz paper)
          We have an additional guest with
          us today, Mr. Chauncey Gardiner.

                    WOLTZ
              (reads list)
          I see ...
              (turns to other men)
          Okay, let's go to work.

The eight servants pair up with the eight men in suits and go into the house.

INT. RAND MANSION - THIRD FLOOR HALLWAY - MORNING

Allenby gets off the elevator, stands and thinks for a moment, then heads off down the hallway in the direction of Chance's room.

INT. RAND'S HOSPITAL ROOM - MORNING

Chance watches television as Rand speaks.

                    RAND
          Yes, when I was younger I had
          thoughts about public office ...
          But I found, Chauncey - that I was
          able to contribute more as a
          private citizen ... of course, my
          wealth provided me with
          considerable influence, but I've
          tried, believe me, not to misuse
          that power ... It's extremely
          important, Chauncey, when one is

>   in a position of eminence, that he
>   does not allow himself to become
>   blinded to the needs of the
>   country ... The temptations are
>   strong, and I've been labeled a
>   'kingmaker' by many, but I have
>   tried to stay open to voices of
>   the people ... I have tried to
>   remain honest to myself ...
>
>   CHANCE
>   (changing channels)
>   I see, Ben.
>
>   RAND
>   ... Maybe one day you shall find
>   yourself in a similar position,
>   Chauncey ... Maybe one day ...

EXT. FRONT RAND MANSION - MORNING

Two black limousines followed by a station wagon with small holes in the side pull up in front of the mansion. As men from the first limousine and the station wagon jump out and take positions around the driveway, Lewis hurries to his post, picks up his phone.

INT. RAND MANSION - MRS. AUBREY'S OFFICE - MORNING

The nerve center of the Rand Enterprises since he has become ill. Four or five desks, all the latest electronic office equipment, three TV's with video taping facilities, countless telephones. MRS. AUBREY, Rand's senior secretary, is at her desk, answers her phone.

>   MRS. AUBREY
>   (into phone)
>   Yes ... Oh, very good, Lewis, thank
>   you.

Mrs. Aubrey hangs up, picks up another phone, pushes a button.

INT. RAND'S HOSPITAL ROOM - MORNING

Rand smiles at Chance as the phone rings.

                    RAND
          He's here.
               (into phone)
          Yes, Mrs. Aubrey?
               (listens)
          Fine. Show the President to the
          library, we'll be along in a few
          minutes.

Rand hangs up the phone, turns to Chance with a twinkle in his eyes.

                    RAND (CONT'D)
          It's an old habit that goes along
          with power -- keep them waiting ...

Teresa brings Rand's wheelchair to him.

                    RAND (CONT'D)
               (stands, very weak)
          Not now, Teresa. I'm seeing the
          President on my own two feet.

                    TERESA
          But, Mr. Rand ...

                    RAND
               (puts an arm around Chance
               for support)
          Shall we go, Chauncey?

                    CHANCE
          Yes, Ben. That's a good idea.

Rand walks slowly, clings to the limping Chance tightly as they leave the room.

EXT. HALLWAY - MORNING

Secret Service Men are seen in the background as Rand stops outside Mrs. Aubrey's office, leans in.

                    RAND
          Mrs. Aubrey, have you received the
          papers on the Caracas agreement?

                    MRS. AUBREY
          Yes, sir. They're ready for you to
          sign.

                    RAND
          Excellent.
              (turns to Chance)
          A good woman, Mrs. Aubrey.

                    CHANCE
              (seeing her for first
              time)
          I agree, Ben.

They shuffle off down the hallway. Chance smiles at the Secret
Service men that they pass.

INT. RAND MANSION - HALLWAY BY LIBRARY - MORNING

Woltz and Wilson wait by the library door. Woltz takes a small
metal detector from his pocket as Rand and Chance approach.

                    WOLTZ
          Good morning, Mr. Rand.

                    RAND
          Woltz, how have you been?

                    WOLTZ
              (passes detector over
              Rand's body)
          Just fine, thank you, sir.
              (turns to Chance)
          And you must be Mr. Gardiner.

                    CHANCE
          Yes.

                    WOLTZ
              (passes detector over
              Chance)
          Just a formality, Mr. Gardiner.

                    CHANCE
              (as he finishes)
          Thank you very much.

Wilson knocks lightly, then opens the library door, Rand and Chance enter.

INT. RAND LIBRARY - MORNING

Rand and Chance come into the Library and the President goes to Rand with both hands outstretched.

>   PRESIDENT
>   Ben!
>
>   RAND
>   (very weak)
>   ... Mr. President, how good to see
>   you.
>
>   PRESIDENT
>   It's so good to see you too, Ben,
>   you look terrific!
>
>   RAND
>   (barely able to stand)
>   I'm not convinced of that, Mr.
>   President, but your visit has
>   raised my spirits ...
>
>   PRESIDENT
>   Well, I'm delighted to be here, my
>   friend. I've missed you.
>   (guides Rand to chair)
>   Here, sit down, get off your feet.

As Rand sinks into the chair, Chance approaches the President with both hands outstretched.

>   CHANCE
>   Good morning, Mr. President.
>
>   PRESIDENT
>   (smiling)
>   ... Hello.

Chance and the President exchange a two-handed handshake. Rand, still weak from standing, catches his breath and introduces Chance.

                    RAND
          Mr. President, I'd like you to
          meet my dear friend, Mr. Chauncey
          Gardiner.

                    PRESIDENT
          Mr. Gardiner, my pleasure.

                    CHANCE
          You look much taller on
          television, Mr. President.

                    PRESIDENT
              (a beat)
          ... Oh, really ...

                    RAND
              (smiling)
          You will find that my house guest
          does not bandy words, Mr.
          President.

The President gives Chance a look, then laughs.

                    PRESIDENT
          Well, Mr. Gardiner, that's just
          fine with me - I'm a man that
          appreciates a frank discussion ...
          Be seated, please, Mr. Gardiner ...

                    CHANCE
              (sitting)
          Yes, I will.

                    PRESIDENT
              (also sits)
          Now, Ben, did you happen to get a
          chance to ...

Chance perks up at the mention of his name, interrupts.

                    CHANCE
          Yes?

There is a beat as the President looks at Chance quizzically,
then he continues.

                    PRESIDENT
          I just wondered if you had gone
          over my speech, Ben.

                    RAND
          Yes, I did.

                    PRESIDENT
          ... Well?

                    RAND
          Overall - pretty good. But, Mr.
          President, I think it's very
          dangerous to resort to temporary
          measures at this stage of the
          game.

                    PRESIDENT
          Well, Ben ... I ...

                    RAND
          I sympathize with your position,
          Mr. President, I know how
          difficult it is to be
          straightforward, the reaction to
          such a speech could be chaos.

                    PRESIDENT
          That's too big a risk, I can't
          take the chance.

                    CHANCE
               (again perks up)
          Yes?

Once again, the President gives Chance a puzzled look.

INT. RAND MANSION - THIRD FLOOR HALLWAY - MORNING

Perkins accompanies Secret Service Agent RIFF as he checks out the third floor. Riff knocks on each door, looks inside, then moves in.

INT. CHANCE'S ROOM - MORNING

Allenby is searching through Chance's clothes looking for some sort of identification. There is a knock at the door, Allenby pulls back from the closet as Riff opens the door, looks inside.

                    ALLENBY
               Oh ... Hello.

                    RIFF
                 (entering)
               Good morning. I'm Riff, Secret
               Service.

                    ALLENBY
               ... Yes. Of course.

Perkins watches curiously as Riff passes the metal detector over Allenby's clothing.

INT. LIBRARY - MORNING

The President is worried about what Rand is telling him. He paces, smokes a cigarette. Chance smiles through it all.

                    RAND
               ... There is no longer any margin
               for inflation, it has gone as far
               as it can, you've reached your
               limits on taxation, dependence on
               foreign energy has reached a
               crisis, and, from where I see it,
               Mr. President, the Free Enterprise
               System has reached the breaking
               point. We are on the brink of
               another crash from which recovery
               might not be possible.

                    PRESIDENT
               It's that serious, huh?

                    RAND
               I'm afraid so.

The President now looks nearly as bad as Rand. He sits, turns to Chance.

                    PRESIDENT
               Do you agree with Ben, Mr.
               Gardiner? Are we finished? Or do
               you think we can stimulate growth
               through temporary incentives?

                    CHANCE
              (a beat)
         As long as the roots are not
         severed, all is well and all will
         be well in the garden.

                    PRESIDENT
              (a pause)
         ... In the garden?

                    CHANCE
         That is correct. In a garden,
         growth has its season. There is
         spring and summer, but there is
         also fall and winter. And then
         spring and summer again ...

                    PRESIDENT
              (staring at Chance)
         ... Spring and summer ...
              (confused)
         Yes, I see ... Fall and winter.
              (smiles at Chance)
         Yes, indeed ...
              (a beat)
         Could you go through that one more
         time, please, Mr. Gardiner?

                    RAND
         I think what my most insightful
         friend is saying, Mr. President,
         is that we welcome the inevitable
         seasons of nature, yet we are
         upset by the seasons of our
         economy.

                    CHANCE
         Yes. That is correct.

                    PRESIDENT
              (pleased)
         ... Well, Mr. Gardiner, I must
         admit, that is one of the most
         refreshing and optimistic
         statements I've heard in a very,
         very long time.

The President puts out his cigarette, rises.

PRESIDENT (CONT'D)
... Many of us forget that nature and society are one! Yes, though we have tried to cut ourselves off from nature, we are still a part of it! Like nature, our economic system remains, in the long run, stable and rational. And that is why we must not fear to be at its mercy!
   (he smiles at Chance, who
   is absorbed in looking around
   the room at the books)
... I envy your good, solid sense, Mr. Gardiner - that is precisely what we lack on Capitol Hill.
   (glances at watch)
I must be going.
   (holds out hand to Chance)
Mr. Gardiner, this visit has been enlightening ...

Chance rises and shakes the President's hand.

CHANCE
Yes. It has.

PRESIDENT
... You will honor me and my family with a visit, won't you?

CHANCE
Yes. I will.

PRESIDENT
Wonderful, we'll all look forward to seeing you.
   (turns to Rand)
Is Eve around? I'd like to say hello.

RAND
No, she flew up to Boston for another charity event. She'll be sorry to have missed you.

                    PRESIDENT
I'm sorry, too. Well, Nancy wanted
me to send along her best to the
two of you - and, Ben, I want to
thank you for your time and
thoughts.

                    RAND
Nonsense, Mr. President - I thank
you for coming to spend time with
a dying man.

                    PRESIDENT
Now, Ben, I won't have any of
that. Why don't you listen to your
good friend Chauncey this is a
time to think of life!

The President clasps Rand's hand.

                    RAND
You're right, Mr. President I
don't like feeling sorry for
myself.

                    PRESIDENT
Take care of yourself, Ben.

                    RAND
You take care too, Bobby.

                    PRESIDENT
          (as he turns to go, a
           smile to Chance)
Mr. Gardiner ...

The President leaves the library and Chance sits back down.

                    RAND
          (as the door closes)
He's a decent fellow, the
President, isn't he?

                    CHANCE
Yes, Ben - he is.

                    RAND
          He was quite impressed with your
          comments, Chauncey - he hears my
          sort of analysis from everyone,
          but yours, unfortunately - seldom
          if ever at all.

                    CHANCE
          I'm glad he came, Ben. It was nice
          talking to the President.

EXT. RAND MANSION - MORNING

An aide, KAUFMAN, waits by the front door of the Rand mansion.
As the President comes out, he speaks quietly to Kaufman.

                    PRESIDENT
          Kaufman, I'm going to need
          information on Mr. Chauncey
          Gardiner's background.

                    KAUFMAN
              (makes note of name)
          Gardiner, yes, sir.

                    PRESIDENT
          And put it through on a Code Red -
          I want it as soon as possible.

                    KAUFMAN
          No problem, Chief.

They head toward the waiting limousines.

INT. RAND MANSION - HALLWAY - MORNING

Rand has an arm around Chance, hangs on for dear life as the two
of them walk through the hall. Behind them, Wilson and Perkins
push empty wheelchairs.

                    RAND
              (very weak)
          ... You know, Chauncey, there's
          something about you ... You're
          direct, you grasp things quickly
          and you state them plainly. You
          don't play games with words to
          protect yourself. I feel I can
          speak to you frankly ... You know

> what I was talking to you about
> last night?

              CHANCE
       (blankly)
> No, Ben.

              RAND
> Oh, sure you do, the financial
> assistance program. I think you
> might be just the man to take
> charge of such an undertaking. I'd
> like you to meet with the members
> of the Board, we'll be able to
> discuss the matter at greater
> length at that time.

              CHANCE
> I understand.

              RAND
       (stops outside his door)
> And, please, Chauncey - don't rush
> your decision. I know you're not a
> man to act on the spur of the
> moment.

              CHANCE
> Thank you, Ben.

              RAND
> And now, Chauncey, I'm afraid you
> must excuse me - I'm very tired
> all of a sudden.

Wilson and Perkins leave the wheelchairs, assist Rand into his hospital room.

              CHANCE
       (as they go in)
> I'm sorry that you are so sick, Ben.

The door closes, Chance limps off down the hall.

EXT. RAND MANSION - GARDEN - DAY

Chance, with a limp, walks down a pathway in the garden, admires the greenery. In the background, coming from the house, we see Eve.

                  EVE
        (approaches Chance, calls)
Chauncey!

                CHANCE
        (stops, turns)
Hello, Eve.

                  EVE
Your leg must be getting better.

                CHANCE
Yes. It's feeling much better now.

                  EVE
Good. I'm glad to hear that.
    (they walk together)
... How did you like meeting the President?

                CHANCE
Fine. He's very nice.

                    EVE
Yes, he is. I'm sorry I didn't get to see him.

They walk along in silence for a moment. Chance sees a huge greenhouse not far from them, heads toward it. Eve turns to him, hesitates, then questions.

                EVE (CONT'D)
... Chauncey ... Last night you mentioned an old man, that died.

                CHANCE
Yes.

                  EVE
Was he a relative? Or an intimate friend?

                    CHANCE
               (looking at greenhouse)
          He was a very wealthy man,
          he looked after me since I was young.

                    EVE
          Oh, I see ... Your mentor, perhaps?

                    CHANCE
               (quizzically)
          ... Mentor ...?

Eve takes his uncertainty as a reluctance to discuss the Old Man.

                    EVE
          Forgive me, Chauncey - I didn't
          mean to pry. You must have been
          very close to him.

                    CHANCE
          Yes. I was.

                    EVE
          I'm sorry ...
               (getting more to the point)
          ... And what about Louise? YOU
          mentioned that she had gone, were
          you close to her also?

                    CHANCE
          Yes. I liked Louise very much.
          She was his maid.

                    EVE
               (relieved)
          Oh, his maid! ... Stupid me, I
          thought perhaps she was someone
          that you may have been
          romantically involved with.

                    CHANCE
          Oh, no. She brought me my meals.

                    EVE
               (pleased)
          Of course.

Eve edges slightly closer to Chance. Chance edges slightly closer to the greenhouse, is fascinated by it.

> CHANCE
> What is that?

> EVE
> Our greenhouse.

> CHANCE
> (pleased)
> Oh, I like that very much.

> EVE
> Yes, so do we.

Chance peeks through one of the windows.

INT. RAND'S BEDROOM - DAY

Rand is in bed. Eve, Chance and Allenby are seated around him, the two nurses standing to one side. They all watch the President's address to the Financial Institute on TV. Chance inhales deeply, enjoys the oxygen in the room. Rand is looking weaker. Every so often, Allenby casts a concerned glance his way.

> PRESIDENT'S VOICE
> ... And there are so many of you that have proclaimed that we are on the brink of the worst financial crisis in this nation's history. And there are so many of you demanding that we put into effect drastic measures to alter its course. Well, let me tell you, gentlemen, I have been conducting multiple-level consultations with members of the Cabinet, House and Senate. I have conducted meetings with prominent business leaders throughout the country. And this very morning I had an in-depth discussion with your founder and Chairman-Of-The-Board, Mr. Benjamin Turnbull Rand and his close friend and advisor Mr. Chauncey Gardiner ...

Rand perks up a bit at this mention. Allenby manages a smile, once again looks at Rand, checking his condition. Eve looks proudly at Chance, who continues to enjoy the oxygen.

>   PRESIDENT'S VOICE (CONT'D)
> ... Well, gentlemen, I found this
> to be a most rewarding
> conference ... To quote Mr.
> Gardiner, a most intuitive man,
> 'As long as the roots of industry
> remain firmly planted in the
> national soil, the economic
> prospects are undoubtedly sunny.'

Rand starts coughing, breathing heavily. Allenby and the nurses rush to his bedside. Allenby shoots a quick look to Eve and Chance.

>   ALLENBY
>   (motioning toward door)
> Excuse us, please.

Eve and Chance leave the room as Allenby administers aid to Rand.

>   PRESIDENT'S VOICE
> Gentlemen, let us not fear the
> inevitable chill and storms of
> autumn and winter, instead, let us
> anticipate the rapid growth of
> springtime, let us await the
> rewards of summer. As in a garden
> of the earth, let us learn to
> accept and appreciate the times
> when the trees are bare as well as
> the times when we pick the fruit.

EXT. RAND MANSION - PATIO - DAY

Eve and Chance sit in silence on the patio. Eve's eyes are swollen, red, she has been crying. She turns to Chance, reaches out, touches his hand.

>   EVE
>   (hesitates)
> ... I'm ...
>   (pause)
> ... I'm very grateful that you're

>   here, Chauncey ...
>   (pause)
>   ... With us ...
>
>   CHANCE
>   So am I, Eve.

Allenby comes out the door, his mood is serious, professional. Eve turns quickly, awaits his news.

>   ALLENBY
>   (sits alongside Eve)
>   ... Eve - this has been an
>   exhausting day for Ben ...
>
>   EVE
>   (anxious)
>   ... But he's ...?
>
>   ALLENBY
>   He's resting comfortably now.
>   There's no cause for alarm, yet ...

Mrs. Aubrey comes out of the house.

>   MRS. AUBREY
>   Mr. Gardiner, I have a telephone
>   call for you. Sidney Courtney, the
>   financial editor of the Washington
>   Post.
>
>   CHANCE
>   (not moving)
>   Thank you.
>
>   MRS. AUBREY
>   Would you care to take it, sir?
>
>   CHANCE
>   Yes.

Chance still does not move. Eve mistakes Chance's not moving for concern for herself. She puts a hand on his shoulder.

>   EVE
>   I'll be all right, Chauncey you go
>   ahead with Mrs. Aubrey ...

                    CHANCE
               (rising)
          Yes, Eve. You'll be all right.

Chance follows Mrs. Aubrey into the house. Eve watches him go, then turns to Allenby.

                    EVE
          ... He's such a sensitive man,
          so considerate ...

INT. RAND MANSION - MRS. AUBREY'S OFFICE - DAY

Mrs. Aubrey leads Chance to a phone at one of the desks. The three television sets are on, attract Chance's attention.

                    CHANCE
               (picks up phone, looks at TVs)
          Hello.

INT. WASHINGTON POST - COURTNEY'S OFFICE - DAY

SID COURTNEY, a Black man in his fifties, wears a rumpled wool jacket, smokes a pipe.

                    COURTNEY
          Hello, Mr. Gardiner. This is Sid
          Courtney, Washington Post.

INTERCUT - MRS. AUBREY'S OFFICE / COURTNEY'S OFFICE

                    CHANCE
          Hello, Sid.

                    COURTNEY
          I'm sorry to disturb you, Mr.
          Gardiner, I know you must be very
          busy.

                    CHANCE
               (looking from one TV to
               the other)
          No. I'm not busy.

                    COURTNEY
          Then, I'll be brief. I covered the
          President's speech at the
          Financial Institute today, and

> since the Post would like to be as exact as possible, we would appreciate your comments on the meeting that took place between Mr. Rand, the President and yourself.

> CHANCE
> The President is a nice person. I enjoyed it very much.

> COURTNEY
> Good, sir. And so, it seems, did the President - but we would like to have some facts; such as, uh ... What exactly is the relationship between yourself and that of the First American Financial Corporation?

> CHANCE
> I think you should ask Mr. Rand that.

> COURTNEY
> Of course. But since he is ill I'm taking the liberty of asking you.

> CHANCE
> Yes, that is correct. I think you should ask Mr. Rand that.

Courtney doesn't understand but continues his questioning.

> COURTNEY
> I see. Then one more quick question, Mr. Gardiner; since we at the Post would like to, uh - update our profile on you - what exactly is your business?

> CHANCE
> I have nothing more to say.

Chance hangs up the phone, watches the TVs. Courtney listens to the dial tone, then puts the receiver down.

                    COURTNEY
                (to himself)
            Typical - no wonder he's so close
            to Rand ...

INT. RAND MANSION - HALLWAY - DAY

Chance comes out of Mrs. Aubrey's office, notices the service elevator.

                    CHANCE
            Hmmm. Elevator.
            He gets in the elevator.

INT. ELEVATOR - DAY

Chance looks at the row of buttons, presses one. He smiles as he feels the elevator move.

INT. RAND MANSION - BASEMENT - DAY

One of Mrs. Aubrey's secretaries, JENNIFER, waits with an arm load of paperwork for the elevator. The door opens, Chance smiles at her as he steps out.

                    JENNIFER
                (surprised to see him)
            Why, hello, Mr. Gardiner - are you
            looking for someone?

                    CHANCE
            No.

Jennifer gets in the elevator, the doors Close. Chance looks around the basement, puzzled. He had expected to be on the third floor.

INT. MRS. AUBREY'S OFFICE - DAY

Mrs. Aubrey is at her desk, buzzing her inter-house phone. As Jennifer enters, Mrs. Aubrey hangs up in frustration.

                    MRS. AUBREY
            I can't find Mr. Gardiner anywhere.

                    JENNIFER
            He's in the basement.

                    MRS. AUBREY
            What's he doing in the basement?

                    JENNIFER
          I don't know, Mrs. Aubrey.

Mrs. Aubrey grabs a notepad, leaves the office.

INT. RAND MANSION - BASEMENT - DAY

Mrs. Aubrey comes out of the service elevator, hurries through the basement. She checks: The boiler room. The electrical room. The photographer's studio (Eve is sitting for a portrait) The gym (Allenby is working out).

INT. RAND MANSION - BASEMENT BOWLING ALLEY - DAY

Chance stands in the middle of the two-lane bowling alley, totally confused. Mrs. Aubrey enters, he smiles at her.

                    MRS. AUBREY
          Oh, Mr. Gardiner, I've been
          looking all over.

                    CHANCE
          Oh, yes.

                    MRS. AUBREY
          Morton Hull, the producer of 'This
          Evening' just called.

                    CHANCE
          Yes, I have seen that show on
          television.

                    MRS. AUBREY
          Of course. They would like you to
          appear on the show tonight. The
          Vice President was scheduled, but
          he had to cancel, and they asked
          if you would be interested.

                    CHANCE
          Yes. I would like to be on that
          show.

                    MRS. AUBREY
          Fine. They felt that since you had
          such close ties with the
          President, you would be a splendid
          choice.
               (Chance nods, there is a pause)

>   ... Can I help you? Are you
>   looking for something?
>
>   CHANCE
>   No. I like this attic very much.

Mrs. Aubrey gives him a look, leaves.

EXT. SKY - DUSK

AIR FORCE 1 passes through the clouds.

INT. AIR FORCE 1 - DUSK

The President sits on a couch in one of the compartments on the jet. Before him, stand six of his STAFF, Kaufman included.

>   PRESIDENT
>   ... Gentlemen, I quoted this man
>   on national television today he is
>   obviously a financial sophisticate
>   of some reknown [sic].
>
>   KAUFMAN
>   Yes, sir - we are aware of all
>   that, but still, we haven't been
>   able to ...
>
>   PRESIDENT
>   (interrupts)
>   He's an advisor and close personal
>   friend of Rand's! For Christ
>   sakes, they have volumes of data
>   on Benjamin!
>
>   KAUFMAN
>   Yes, Mr. President, we attempted
>   to contact Mr. Rand, but he was
>   too ill to ...
>
>   PRESIDENT
>   (again interrupts)
>   I do not want Benjamin Rand
>   disturbed! You have other ways of
>   gathering information than to
>   trouble a dying man. Use whatever
>   agencies are necessary to put
>   together a detailed history of
>   Chauncey Gardiner, if you run into

>   problems, alert Honeycutt.
>   (he stands)
>   I'll be in the office at seven in
>   the morning and I would like to
>   have it at that time.
>   (he starts for door)
>   I've got to take a leak.
>
>   KAUFMAN
>   Right, Chief.

As the President goes to the Men's Room, two of the aides reach for telephones.

INT. CHANCE'S ROOM - EVENING

Chance wears a velvet bathrobe, watches TV. Perkins lays out a suit, shirt, tie, etc. on the bed.

>   PERKINS
>   I believe these garments will be
>   quite appropriate, Mr. Gardiner.
>
>   CHANCE
>   (eyes on TV)
>   Yes. They are fine. There is a
>   knock at the door.
>
>   PERKINS
>   Excuse me, sir.

Perkins answers the door, it is Eve.

>   EVE
>   (entering)
>   Chauncey ...
>
>   CHANCE
>   (rises)
>   Hello, Eve.
>
>   EVE
>   Chauncey, I just wanted to wish
>   you well. I know you'll be
>   smashing.
>
>   CHANCE
>   Thank you, Eve.

                    EVE
          And Benjamin sends along his best
          wishes.

                    CHANCE
          How is Ben feeling?

                    EVE
          He's tired, Chauncey - but he's
          going to watch you tonight. We'll
          both be watching.

                    CHANCE
          That's good. I like to watch, too.

                    EVE
          I know you do - you and your
          television ...
               (a pause)
          ... Good luck, Chauncey.

Eve impulsively steps forward, kisses Chance on the cheek. Chance smiles at her, and Eve, slightly embarrassed, turns and leaves the room. Chance sits back down, watches TV as Perkins attends to his clothes with a whisk broom.

INT. WASHINGTON POST - STAFF ROOM - NIGHT

Courtney heads a meeting of his four staffers. One man, KINNEY, a research assistant, sits behind a stack of paperwork, has a downcast expression as he listens to Courtney.

                    COURTNEY
          ... Gardiner is laconic, matter-of
          fact. The scuttlebutt is that he's
          a strong candidate for one of the
          vacant seats on the board of First
          American. But before we can do any
          sort of a piece on the man, we're
          going to need facts on his
          background ...
               (turns to Kinney)
          ... Kinney, what did you come up with?

                    KINNEY
               (after a pause)
          ... Nothing.

```
                    COURTNEY
            (sighs, taps pencil on table)
        ... Skip the levity, Kinney -
        what have you got?

                    KINNEY
            (another pause)
        ... I realize this sounds banal
        but there is no information of any
        sort on Gardiner. We have no
        material on him - zilch ...
```

The room is quiet except for the tapping of Courtney's pencil.

EXT. TELEVISION STATION - NIGHT

The RAND 1 limousine parks in front of the station. As Jeffrey opens the door for Chance, MORTON HULL steps to the limo.

```
                    HULL
        Mr. Gardiner, I'm Morton Hull, the
        producer of 'This Evening.'

                    CHANCE
            (as they shake hands)
        Hello, Morton.
```

Hull takes Chance into the station.

INT. RAND MANSION - CHANCE'S ROOM - NIGHT

Constance, Rand's nurse, enters Chance's room, goes to the closet.

INT. TV STATION - CORRIDOR - NIGHT

Chance is intrigued by the surroundings as Hull guides him through the corridor.

```
                    HULL
        Of course, Mr. Gardiner, the fact
        that you occupy such a position in
        the world of finance makes you
        ideally suited to provide our
        millions of viewers with an
        explanation of this nation's
        economic crisis.
```

                    CHANCE
          I see.

                    HULL
          Do you realize, Mr. Gardiner, that
          more people will be watching you
          tonight than all those who have
          seen theater plays in the last
          forty years?

                    CHANCE
          Yes. It's a very good show.

                    HULL
          I'm glad you like it, Mr. Gardiner.

Hull takes Chance into the MAKE-UP room.

INT. RAND MANSION - CHANCE'S ROOM - NIGHT

Constance is in the closet, searching through Chance's pockets, finding nothing. She takes out a small knife, cuts a label from one of the jackets. Quickly, she examines one of Chance's shoes, copies the name of the shoemaker in a notebook. Constance hurries to the dresser, continues her search.

INT. TV STATION - CORRIDOR/MAKEUP ROOM NIGHT

COLSON, the makeup man, comes through the corridor carrying a glass of water. He turns into the makeup room, goes to Chance who sits in front of the lights. Hull sits next to Chance, briefs him on the show. Chance has his eyes on a TV monitor, watches the guest preceding him on "This Evening."

                    COLSON
              (gives Chance water)
          Here you go, Mr. Gardiner.

                    CHANCE
          Thank you. I'm very thirsty.

                    COLSON
          Yes, sir - it's hot under those
          lights.

Colson applies finishing touches to Chance.

>   HULL
>   Now, if the host wants to ask you
>   a question, he'll raise his left
>   forefinger to his left eyebrow.
>   (Chance watches TV)
>   Then you'll stop, and he'll say
>   something, and then you'll answer.

On the TV, WILLIAM DUPONT, the host, wraps up his talk with his guest.

>   COLSON
>   (a last-minute dab)
>   Okay, Mr. Gardiner, you're all
>   set.

Hull leads Chance out of the makeup room. Colson closes the door, then carefully picks up Chance's water glass, wraps it in Kleenex, puts it in his overcoat pocket.

INT. TV STATION - "THIS EVENING" STUDIO - NIGHT

William Dupont introduces Chance.

>   DUPONT
>   Ladies and gentlemen, our very
>   distinguished quest [*sic*], Mr.
>   Chauncey Gardiner!

The BAND plays as Chance comes onto the stage. An audience of about three hundred applauds Chance as he appears. Two TV cameras move with him as he walks, with a smile and a limp, to center stage. Dupont shakes Chance's hand, Chance holds Dupont's hand with both of his own.

>   DUPONT (CONT'D)
>   Mr. Gardiner, how very nice to
>   have you with us this evening.

>   CHANCE
>   Yes.

>   DUPONT
>   (showing Chance to chair)
>   I'd like to thank you for filling
>   in on such short notice for the
>   Vice President.

CHANCE
   (sits)
You're welcome.

DUPONT
   (also sitting)
I always find it surprising, Mr. Gardiner, to find men like yourself, who are working so intimately with the President, yet manage to remain relatively unknown.

CHANCE
Yes. That is surprising.

DUPONT
   (a beat)
... Well, your anonymity will be a thing of the past from now on.

CHANCE
   (doesn't understand)
I hope so.

DUPONT
Yes ... Of course, you know, Mr. Gardiner, that I always prefer an open and frank conversation with my guests, I hope you don't object to that.

CHANCE
No. I don't object.

DUPONT
Fine, then let's get started. The current state of our country is of vital interest to us all, and I would like to know if you agree with the President's view of the economy?

CHANCE
Which view?

Applause and laughter from the audience. Dupont accustomed to parrying with his guests, asks again.

> DUPONT
> Come now, Mr. Gardiner, before his speech at the Financial Institute the President consulted with you and Benjamin Rand, did he not?

> CHANCE
> Yes. I was there with Ben.

> DUPONT
> I know that, Mr. Gardiner.

> CHANCE
> Yes.

> DUPONT
> (a beat)
> Well, let me rephrase the question; the President compared the economy of this country to a garden, and stated that after a period of decline a time of growth would naturally follow. Do you go along with this belief?

> CHANCE
> Yes, I know the garden very well. I have worked in it all my life. It is a good garden and a healthy one; its trees are healthy and so are its shrubs and flowers, as long as they are trimmed and watered in the right seasons. The garden needs a lot of care. I do agree with the President; everything in it will grow strong, and there is plenty of room in it for new trees and new flowers of all kinds.

The audience applauds Chance's apparent metaphor. Dupont waits for it all to subside, then asks another question.

INT. RAND'S HOSPITAL ROOM – NIGHT

Rand is in bed. Eve sits in a chair next to the bed, squeezes Rand's hand in excitement as they both watch Chance on television. Teresa, the nurse, watches in the background.

> DUPONT
> (over TV)
> ... Well, Mr. Gardiner, that was very well put indeed, and I feel it was a booster for all of us who do not like to wallow in complaints or take delight in gloomy predictions.

INT. WHITE HOUSE - PRESIDENT'S BEDROOM - NIGHT

The President and First Lady are in bed together watching the show.

> PRESIDENT
> Gloomy predictions? That insolent son of a bitch!

> DUPONT
> (over TV)
> Let's make it clear, Mr. Gardiner, it's your view that the collapse of the Stock Market, the dramatic increase in unemployment, you feel that this is just another season, so to speak, in the garden?

The First Lady cuddles close the President, ruffles his hair, tries to cheer him up.

INT. TV STUDIO - "THIS EVENING SHOW" - NIGHT

Chance answers.

> CHANCE
> In a garden, things grow - but first some things must wither; some trees lose their leaves before they grow new leaves...

INT. CIA ROOM - NIGHT

A small, dark room. A videotape machine is running. Also, a machine is turning that records the harmonics of Chance's voice. TWO CIA MEN run the equipment, watch as a needle charts Chance's voice onto paper.

>   CHANCE
>   (over TV)
>   ... Then they grow thicker and
>   stronger and taller. Some trees
>   die, but fresh saplings replace
>   them. Gardens need a lot of care
>   and a lot of love.

INT. THOMAS FRANKLIN'S BEDROOM - NIGHT

Franklin, the attorney that evicted Chance, comes out of the bathroom brushing his teeth. His wife, JOHANNA, is in bed absorbed in "This Evening." Franklin sits on the end of the bed, watches the show.

>   CHANCE
>   (over TV)
>   ... And if you give your garden a
>   lot of love, and if you work very
>   hard and have a lot of patience,
>   in the proper season you will see
>   it grow to be very beautiful ...

More applause from the TV. Franklin leans closer to the set.

>   FRANKLIN
>   (puzzled)
>   It's that gardener!

>   JOHANNA
>   Yes, Chauncey Gardiner.

>   FRANKLIN
>   No! He's a real gardener!

>   JOHANNA
>   (laughs)
>   He does talk like one, but I think
>   he's brilliant.

>   DUPONT
>   (over TV)
>   I think your metaphors are quite
>   interesting, Mr. Gardiner, but,
>   haven't we seen seasons that have
>   been devastating to certain
>   countries?

INT. PRESIDENT'S BEDROOM - NIGHT

The President and First Lady continue to watch.

> DUPONT
> (over TV)
> Such as disastrous winters, prolonged droughts that have wiped out crops, hurricanes that have all but swept away island communities? Doesn't a country need to have someone in charge that can see it through such crises?

> PRESIDENT
> ... That bastard ...

The First Lady moves closer to him.

INT. CHANCE'S ROOM - NIGHT

The TV, its volume low, plays in the background as Constance, with a pair of tweezers, plucks a hair from Chance's pillow, puts it into a small vial.

> DUPONT
> (over TV)
> Don't we need a leader capable of guiding us through the seasons? The bad as well as the good?

> CHANCE
> (over TV)
> Yes. We need a very good gardener.

INT. TV STUDIO - NIGHT

Dupont continues his questions.

> DUPONT
> Do you feel that we have a 'Very good gardener' in office at this time, Mr. Gardiner?

At the end of the question, Dupont glances over Chance's shoulder to look at the monitor.

                          CHANCE
                    (a beat)
                  I understand.

Chance turns to see what Dupont is looking at, sees the back of his own head on the TV screen.

                          DUPONT
                  I realize that might be a
                  difficult question for you, Mr.
                  Gardiner - but there are a lot of
                  us around the country that would
                  like to hear your thoughts on the
                  matter.

Chance is still turned to the monitor.

                          CHANCE
                  Oh, yes. It is possible for one
                  side of the garden to be flooded,
                  and the other side to be dry ...

INT. RAND MANSION - ALLENBY'S BEDROOM - NIGHT

Allenby watches Chance on television. The camera that covered Dupont in close-up has now pulled back, includes Dupont and Chance, both looking into camera. Allenby is concerned, he is unsure of Chance.

                          CHANCE
                    (over TV)
                  ... Some plants do well in the
                  sun, and others grow better in the
                  cool of the shade.

INT. HOTEL LOBBY - NIGHT

A group of ELDERLY BLACK PEOPLE sit in the lobby, watch "This Evening" on an old black-and-white TV.

                          CHANCE
                    (over TV)
                  ... It is the gardener's
                  responsibility to take water from
                  the flooded area and run it to the
                  area that is dry. It is the
                  gardener's responsibility not to
                  plant a sun-loving flower in the
                  shade of a high wall ...

During the preceding speech, Louise, the maid from the Old Man's house, chatters.

> LOUISE
> Gobbledegook! All the time he talked gobbledegook! An' it's for sure a White man's world in America, hell, I raised that boy since he was the size of a pissant an' I'll say right now he never learned to read an' write - no sir! Had no brains at all, was stuffed with rice puddin' between the ears! Shortchanged by the Lord and dumb as a jackass an' look at him now! Yes, sir - all you gotta be is white in America an' you get whatever you want! Just listen to that boy - gobbledegook!

There is a chorus of "Amens" as she finishes.

INT. TV STUDIO - NIGHT

Chance continues.

> CHANCE
> ... It is the responsibility of the gardener to adjust to the bad seasons as well as enjoy the good ones. If the gardener does his job, everything will be fine.

INT. RAND'S HOSPITAL ROOM - NIGHT

Audience applause is heard over TV. Rand claps weakly along with the TV sound. Eve and Teresa also clap.

> RAND
> (smiling)
> Splendid. Just splendid ...

Rand looks up as Constance comes into the room.

> RAND (CONT'D)
> Damn, Constance, get in here! You shouldn't miss any of this!

Constance hurries to Teresa's side. Rand turns to Eve.

> RAND (CONT'D)
> I'm becoming quite attached to
> Chauncey - quite attached...
>   (Eve smiles)
> ... And so are you, aren't you, Eve.

> EVE
>   (a beat)
> ... Yes, I am, Ben.

> RAND
>   (reaches out, takes her
>   hand)
> That's good ... That's good.

> DUPONT
>   (over TV)
> Well, Mr. Gardiner, from the sound
> of our audience, I'd say that your
> words are a most welcome respite
> from what we've been hearing from
> others ...

> CHANCE
>   (over TV)
> Thank you.

INT. TV STUDIO - NIGHT

Dupont asks another question.

> DUPONT
> I'm sorry to say that our time is
> running short, but before we
> close, I'd like to ask one final
> question. What sort of gardener,
> sir, would you be?

> CHANCE
>   (with confidence)
> I am a very serious gardener.

INT. PRESIDENT'S BEDROOM - NIGHT

More applause over the TV. The President pales.

                    PRESIDENT
          Oh, Jesus ...

He rolls over in bed. The First Lady reaches out, puts a
comforting hand on his shoulder.

INT. FRANKLIN'S BEDROOM - NIGHT

Franklin holds a phone to his ear with one hand, shuts off the
TV with the other.

                    FRANKLIN
          Okay, I'll see you in twenty
          minutes.

Franklin hangs up the phone, scurries around getting dressed.
His wife, Johanna, sits grimly in bed.

                    JOHANNA
            (coldly)
          ... Business, bullshit! Going out
          in the middle of the night to meet
          that bitch in a bar ...

                    FRANKLIN
          Sally Hayes is not a bitch - she's
          a damn fine attorney! I've got to
          talk to her about this Gardiner ...

                    JOHANNA
            (turns over in bed)
          Good night.

                    FRANKLIN
          Look, Johanna ...

                    JOHANNA
            (cuts him off)
          I said good night!

Franklin gives up, hurries from the room.

INT. TV STATION - CORRIDOR - NIGHT

Colson, carefully carrying his overcoat, walks with Chance
through the corridor. A delighted Hull walks behind them.

                        COLSON
            Marvelous! Just marvelous, Mr.
            Gardiner! What spirit you have,
            what confidence! Exactly what this
            country needs!

Chance smiles at well-wishers as they continue on through the corridor.

INT. PRESIDENT'S BEDROOM - NIGHT

The First Lady is snuggled up close to the President, caresses his body. After a moment, it becomes clear to her that he is not up to the occasion.

                        FIRST LADY
            ... Darling ... What's wrong?

                        PRESIDENT,
            ... I can't ... I just can't right
            now ... I'm sorry, dearest ... I
            just can't ...

The First Lady looks at him for a beat, then turns, lies on her back and stares at the ceiling.

INT. COCKTAIL LOUNGE - NIGHT

An 'in' meeting place for the upper-middle Washington, D.C. crowd. Thomas Franklin and Sally Hayes sit at a table, drinks in front of them.

                        FRANKLIN
            ... It didn't make any sense to me
            at all. I didn't know what the
            hell he was talking about ...

                        SALLY
            He wasn't making a speech to us,
            Tom - he was talking to the
            masses. He was very clever,
            keeping it at a third grade [*sic*]
            level - that's what they
            understand ...

                        FRANKLIN
            Yeah? Well, I don't understand
            what was up his sleeve when he
            pulled that stunt with us? What
            was he doing? And why?

>   SALLY
> Who knows ...? Maybe the government
> had something to do with it.
>
>   FRANKLIN
> You know, Sally - I really feel
> like I've been had, and you know
> what that means, don't you? ... It
> means that any political future I
> had is right down the toilet!

The CAMERA begins to slowly move away from the table, the sound of Franklin's voice continues.

>   FRANKLIN (CONT'D)
> ... Jesus, the thought of spending
> the rest of my life as an
> attorney, that is really a
> downer ... And, Christ, Sally, I
> almost forgot Johanna is starting
> to think something's going on
> between...

Franklin's voice fades into the background hubbub. The voice of Kinney, the research assistant from the Washington Post is heard as the camera settles on a table occupied by Sidney Courtney and his staff.

>   KINNEY
> ... Sid, be reasonable - I've been
> everywhere, there's no place left
> to check!
>
>   COURTNEY
> Try again.
>
>   KINNEY
> Sure, try again - where? There's
> nothing, it's like he never
> existed!
>
>   COURTNEY
> Try again.
>
>   KINNEY
> Sid, it's useless!

                    COURTNEY
          I said - try again.

Kinney stands, shoves his paperwork across the table.

                    KINNEY
          Up yours, Sid. You try again,
          I quit!

Kinney takes his drink with him as he leaves the lounge.

EXT. RAND MANSION - NIGHT

The household staff is lined up on the front steps, applauding Chance as he steps from the limousine. Chance accepts the plaudit, though does not understand the reason. As he nears the steps, Perkins and Wilson step forward.

                    WILSON
          An outstanding speech, sir.

                    PERKINS
          May I take your coat, Mr. Gardiner?

                    CHANCE
          Yes. Thank you, Perkins.

Perkins nods, takes Chance's overcoat, allows everyone to enter the house ahead of him. Alone on the steps, Perkins quickly searches through the pockets of the coat, finds nothing.

INT. RAND'S HOSPITAL ROOM - NIGHT

Rand is in bed. Eve sits on the edge, looks warmly to Chance who stands nearby. Allenby prepares an injection for Rand, and occasionally glances curiously at Chance. Chance breathes deeply, enjoys the oxygen.

                    RAND
                (with some effort)
          ... You possess a great gift,
          Chauncey, of being natural. And
          that, my boy, is a rare talent,
          the true mark of a leader. You
          were strong and brave, yet did not
          moralize. I hope the entire
          country was watching you tonight,
          the entire country ...

Allenby crosses to Rand, needle in hand.

>   ALLENBY
> And you, Benjamin, must be strong
> and brave for me. Turn over,
> please.
>
>   RAND
>   (holds up hand)
> In a minute, Robert - in a
> minute ... Chauncey, I would like
> to ask a favor of you ...
>
>   CHANCE
> Certainly, Ben.
>
>   RAND
> Senator Rowley's widow, Sophie, is
> hosting an evening reception
> tomorrow evening honoring
> Ambassador Skrapinov of the Soviet
> Union ... I think it's rather
> obvious that Robert won't allow me
> to attend, so - would you go in my
> place, and escort Eve?
>
>   CHANCE
> Yes. I would like to escort Eve.
>
>   RAND
> Good. Together, the two of you
> should create quite a stir - I can
> already hear the gossip.
>
>   EVE
>   (with a blush)
> ... Ben, really ...
>
>   RAND
>   (reaches out a tired hand
>   to Chance - Chance holds
>   it)
> ... Thank you, Chauncey ... Thank
> you very much.
>   (takes back hand)
> ... All right, Robert, I'm all
> yours.

Eve and Chance quietly leave the room. Allenby watches Chance go, then readies Rand for the injection.

INT. RAND MANSION - THIRD FLOOR HALLWAY - NIGHT

The elevator door opens, Eve and Chance come into the hallway. Chance looks back at the elevator for a beat, then the two walk quietly down the hall.

> EVE
> (stopping by bedroom door)
> ... You don't happen to have a tuxedo in your suitcase, do you?

> CHANCE
> No, thank you.

> EVE
> Oh. Well, we can fix up one of Ben's for you tomorrow night. Sophie insists on Black Tie.

> CHANCE
> I see.

> EVE
> (a pause, softly)
> ... I have very few friends, Chauncey ... And Benjamin's friends are all quite a bit older ...

Eve gives Chance a long look, then kisses him on the lips. She steps back, smiles.

> EVE (CONT'D)
> ... Good night, Chauncey.

> CHANCE
> Good night, Eve.

Eve goes into her bedroom, closes the door. Chance heads for his room as though nothing had happened.

INT. WHITE HOUSE - OVAL OFFICE ANTE ROOM - MORNING

Kaufman and the five other Aides nervously await the President's arrival. The door opens, the President briskly enters the room.

> PRESIDENT
> Good morning, gentlemen.

> AIDES
> (as one)
> Good morning, sir.

The President leads the way into the Oval Office.

INT. OVAL OFFICE - MORNING

As the President goes to his desk, Kaufman hands him a folder. The President sits, reads it quickly, it is very brief.

> PRESIDENT
> (to Kaufman)
> This is not what I requested.

> KAUFMAN
> No, sir.

> PRESIDENT
> This information goes back three days. I want the standard file, you know that.

> KAUFMAN
> Right, Chief.

> PRESIDENT
> So ...? Where the hell is it?

> KAUFMAN
> We ... uh, have been unable to come up with any information before the man appeared at Mr. Rand's home ... and, uh ...

> PRESIDENT
> What the hell are you talking about, Kaufman?

> KAUFMAN
> Well, we do have data from Honeycutt's sources, Chief - but it isn't pertinent.

> PRESIDENT
> I'd like to hear that data, Kaufman.
>
> KAUFMAN
> Yes, sir.

Kaufman takes a clipboard from the man at his right.

> KAUFMAN (CONT'D)
> (reading)
> Suits hand-made by a tailor in Chicago in 1918. The tailor went out of business in 1929, then took his own life.
> ... His shoes were hand-made in 1928. The cobbler has long since been dead. Underwear, all of the finest cloth, factory destroyed by fire in 1938. The man carries no identification; no wallet, no driver's license, no credit cards.
> ... He carries one item along with him, a fine Swiss pocket-watch crafted at the turn of the century; so far they have been unable to ascertain where or when purchase was made.
> ... He has never dyed his hair.
> ... Computers have analyzed Gardiner's vocal characteristics; it is impossible to determine his ethnic background, they feel his accent may be northeastern, but they will not commit to that.
> ... Fingerprint check proved negative, no identification possible.
> (a pause)
> ... That's it, Mr. President.

The President stares at Kaufman for a beat, then speaks into his intercom.

> PRESIDENT
> (into intercom)
> Miss Davis - I'd like my eggs poached this morning, please.

A quick "Yes sir" from Miss Davis over the intercom. The
President leans back in his swivel chair, looks at Kaufman.

                PRESIDENT (CONT'D)
... So what does all that add up to?

                KAUFMAN
Well, sir - it occurred to us that
he might be an agent of a foreign
power. But, we ruled that out, as
they invariably are provided with
too much documentation, too much
American identity ... We,
uh ... don't quite know what to make
of it yet, sir ... But we'll keep
on top of it, Mr. President -
we'll come up with the answer.

                PRESIDENT
        (with sarcasm)
I would appreciate that.

The Aides quickly leave the office.

INT. CHANCE'S ROOM - MORNING

Chance is in bed, a bed tray on his lap, eating breakfast.
A pile of the morning's newspapers lies at the foot of the
bed, untouched. The TV is playing, Chance watches as he eats.
There is a knock at the door.

                CHANCE
        (without turning from TV)
   Come in!

Eve enters, wearing a robe over her nightgown.

                EVE
Chauncey! Have you seen the
papers?

                CHANCE
No, Eve. I don't read the papers.

                EVE
        (moving to bed)
Well, it seems you've been
described as one of the architects

of the President's speech. And
your own comments from the
'This Evening' show are quoted side by
side with the President's.

     CHANCE
I like the President. He is a very
nice man.

     EVE
  (sits on bed)
I know ...
  (a moment)
... So are you, Chauncey ...
  (another moment, Chance
  watches TV)
... Do you mind my being here,
like this?

     CHANCE
  (a bite of toast)
No, Eve. I like you to be here.

Eve smiles, moves a little closer to Chance.

     EVE
... You know, Chauncey ... I want
us to be ...
  (with difficulty)
I want us... You and I to
become ... close ... I want us to
become very close, you know ...?

     CHANCE
Yes, Eve. I know that.

Eve suddenly begins to cry, sobbing quietly at first, then losing control, the tears flowing freely. To comfort her, Chance puts his arm around her shoulder, nearly tipping his breakfast tray. Eve responds to his touch, draws closer, holds Chance tightly. Chance does his best to avoid spilling his breakfast, keep an eye on the TV, and to comfort Eve. She gives in to her desires, begins to caress Chance, running her hand over his body. She kisses him, his eyes, his neck, his lips, his ears. Chance does not return the lovemaking, and Eve eventually catches hold of herself, stops. She lies quietly beside Chance for a time, regains her demeanor, then speaks.

                    EVE
          ... I'm grateful to you,
          Chauncey ... I would have opened to
          you with a touch, and you know
          that ...
               (Chance, confused, turns
               to her)
          ... But you're so strong - I can
          trust myself with you. I'm glad,
          Chauncey - I'm glad that you
          showed so much restraint ...

                    CHANCE
          Yes, Eve. I'm very glad that you
          didn't open.

                    EVE
          I know you are, Chauncey ...
               (a pause)
          ... You conquer a woman from
          within herself, you infuse in her
          the need and desire and the
          longing for your love.

                    CHANCE
               (another bite of toast)
          Yes. That could be true.

                    EVE
               (sits up)
          ... I guess I may as well be
          honest about my feelings,
          Chauncey, as I know you are I am
          in love with you ... I love you and
          I want you ... And I know that you
          know it and I'm grateful that
          you've decided to wait until
          ... Until ...

Eve cannot bring herself to finish the sentence. She rises,
straightens her robe and moves toward the door.

                    EVE (CONT'D)
               (stopping by door)
          ... I do love you, Chauncey.

A knock at the door startles Eve. She turns, opens it to MAGGIE, the seamstress. Maggie carries one of Rand's tuxedos.

> EVE (CONT'D)
> Oh, come in, Maggie.

> MAGGIE
> (entering)
> Yes, ma'am.

> EVE
> Chauncey, Maggie will alter Ben's tuxedo for you now.

> CHANCE
> Fine.

Eve leaves. Maggie stands by patiently as Chance eats his once-warm scrambled eggs and watches "Mr. Rogers Neighborhood" on TV.

INT. RAND MANSION - ALLENBY'S ROOM - DAY

Allenby is at his desk, searching through the Washington, D.C. telephone book. He finds a number, dials.

> ALLENBY
> (into phone)
> Mr. Thomas Franklin, please.
> (a wait)
> Is Thomas Franklin in?
> (a beat)
> Yes, this is Dr. Robert Allenby, would you please tell Mr. Franklin that I would like to talk to him? It concerns Chauncey Gardiner.

INT. RAND'S HOSPITAL ROOM - DUSK

Teresa and Constance work in a corner of the room. Rand is in bed, very still, deep in thought.

EXT. SOPHIE'S - EVENING

The RAND 1 limousine pulls up to Sophie's house. Jeffrey opens the door for Eve and Chance. He wears Ben's tuxedo, Eve is in a formal gown. The press is waiting, a couple of reporters, 5 photographers and a mini-cam crew from local TV station gather around Eve and Chance.

                    REPORTER #1
          Mr. Gardiner, what did you think
          of the Post's editorial on the
          President's speech?

                    CHANCE
               (smiling for photogs)
          I didn't read it.

                    REPORTER #2
               (surprised)
          But sir - you must have at least
          glanced at it.

                    CHANCE
          No. I did not glance at it.

                    REPORTER #3
          Mr. Gardiner, the New York Times
          spoke of your 'Peculiar brand of
          optimism,' what was your reaction
          to that?

                    CHANCE
               (continues to pose for pictures)
          I did not read that either.

                    REPORTER #3
          Well, how do you feel about that
          phrase, 'Peculiar brand of
          optimism?'

                    CHANCE
          I do not know what it means.

                    REPORTER #2
          Sorry to persist, sir, but it
          would be of great interest to me
          to know what newspapers you do
          read.

                    CHANCE
          I do not read any newspapers. I
          watch TV.

There is a moment of silence as the reporters digest this. The
TV Reporter smiles, questions Chance.

                    TV REPORTER
            ... Do you mean, Mr. Gardiner,
            that you find television's
            coverage of the news superior to
            that of the newspapers?

                      CHANCE
               (flatly)
            I like to watch TV.

                    TV REPORTER
               (pleased))
            Thank you, Mr. Gardiner, for what
            is probably the most honest
            admission to come from a public
            figure in years. Few men in public
            life have the courage not to read
            newspapers none have the guts to
            admit it.

                      CHANCE
            You're welcome.

Eve and Chance walk toward the front door, leaving the newsmen to talk among themselves.

                       EVE
            I've never seen anyone handle the
            media as well as you, Chauncey.
            You're so cool and detached -
            almost as if you were born to it.

                      CHANCE
            Thank you, Eve.

The front door is opened for them by an attendant.

INT. SOPHIE'S - EVENING

The Black Tie [sic] reception is in progress. The house is crowded, possibly a hundred guests, mostly foreign ambassadors and other such dignitaries. Eve and Chance enter, are greeted by DENNIS WATSON, a State Department official.

                      WATSON
            Mrs. Rand, how good to see you.

                    EVE
          Mr. Watson.

                    WATSON
               (looks to Chance)
          And you must be Mr. Gardiner,
          correct?

                    CHANCE
          Yes.

                    EVE
          Chauncey, this is Mr. Dennis
          Watson of the State Department.

                    CHANCE
               (they shake)
          Hello, Dennis.

                    WATSON
          A pleasure to meet you, sir.

                    CHANCE
          Yes. It is.

SOPHIE, an older woman bedecked with jewelry, approaches,
embraces Eve.

                    SOPHIE
          Eve, child! How nice of you to
          come.

                    EVE
          Hello, Sophie.

Sophie steps back, looks at Chance.

                    SOPHIE
          And look who you brought with!

                    EVE
          Sophie, this is Chauncey
          Gardiner ...

                    SOPHIE
               (hugs Chance)
          Oh, I've been just dying to meet
          you, Mr. Gardiner!

                    EVE
          Chauncey, this is Mrs. Sophia
          Rowley.

                    CHANCE
               (being hugged)
          Hello, Sophia.

                    SOPHIE
               (steps back, admires Chance)
          Sophie, please - call me Sophie!

Sophie pulls them both into the party, leaving Dennis looking
after Chance as he walks away.

                    SOPHIE (CONT'D)
               (as they go, to Chance)
          You just have to let me introduce
          you to some of the exciting people
          here ... Why, Pat Boone and his
          daughter may drop by later!
They disappear into the crowd.

INT. WHITE HOUSE - OVAL OFFICE - NIGHT

The President is hunched over his desk, absorbed in
constructing a model airplane, a World War II flying fortress
bomber. The First Lady sits nearby, plays solitaire on a small
table. The President glances to her, then back to his work.

                    PRESIDENT
               (gluing the wing)
          ... How are the kids getting along?

                    FIRST LADY
          Oh. Well, I just talked to Cindy
          this morning. She loves
          California, but to quote her, she
          says, 'The Secret Service is
          getting to be a drag.' I guess she
          wants her privacy ...

                    PRESIDENT
          Huh ... I'm glad they're along with
          her, if you know what I mean ...
          How about Jack?

FIRST LADY
Well, I think Jack needs some time
alone with you, darling ...
He's getting to that age, you know ...
He really misses you ...

PRESIDENT
Yeah ... I'll have a talk with him
as soon as ...

A KNOCK at the door interrupts the President.

PRESIDENT (CONT'D)
(calls out)
... Yes, come in!

Kaufman enters.

KAUFMAN
Sorry to disturb you, chief but we
have new developments.

PRESIDENT
Oh? What?

KAUFMAN
We have word that the Soviets have
put out a top priority alert for
information on Gardiner's
background. So far, they haven't
come up with a thing - what's
more, as a result of their
eagerness, one of their ablest
agents blew his cover, we have him
in custody at this time.

PRESIDENT
Good. Anything else?

KAUFMAN
Yes, chief - eight other foreign
powers have put Gardiner under
surveillance. We're around-the-
clock now, sir - I'll keep you
posted.

The President nods, Kaufman leaves. The President puts
some more glue on the wing.

INT. SOPHIE'S - NIGHT

Sophie pulls Eve and Chance to AMBASSADOR SKRAPINOV and his WIFE. Skrapinov smiles as he sees Eve.

                    SKRAPINOV
          Mrs. Rand. How delightful.

Skrapinov kisses Eve's hand.

                    EVE
          It seems like ages, Mr.
          Ambassador.
              (a nod to his wife)
          Mrs. Skrapinov.

Mrs. Skrapinov returns the nod as Sophie introduces Chance.

                    SOPHIE
          Mr. Gardiner, let me introduce you
          to our guest of honor, His
          Excellency Vladimar Skrapinov,
          Ambassador of the Soviet Union.

Chance warmly shakes Skrapinov's hand with both of his own.

                    CHANCE
              (stumbles over name)
          Hello... His... His...

                    SOPHIE
          Ambassador Skrapinov, this is Mr.
          Chauncey Gardiner.

                    SKRAPINOV
          Delighted. Delighted.

                    SOPHIE
          And this is Mrs. Skrapinov.

Chance smiles at Mrs. Skrapinov as The Ambassador puts an arm around him.

                    SKRAPINOV
          You must sit with us, my friend,
          we have much to discuss.

                    CHANCE
          I agree.

SKRAPINOV
(to Eve)
How is my dear friend Benjamin feeling?

EVE
He's doing as well as could be expected, Mr. Ambassador. He still speaks of the stimulating discussions he's had with you.

SKRAPINOV
Ah, Yes. Please give him my regards.

EVE
Of course.

SOPHIE
(tugs at Eve)
Come on, Eve. Let's let the men talk, there are so many people that have been asking about you.

EVE
(to Chance and Skrapinov)
Would you two excuse me for a moment?

SKRAPINOV
Regretfully, Mrs. Rand - I shall yield the pleasure of your company to others.

CHANCE
Yes, Eve. I shall yield too.

EVE
(smiling)
I'll be back soon ...

Eve and Sophie leave. Skrapinov leads his wife and Chance to their table.

SKRAPINOV
(as they walk)
I'm sorry we haven't met sooner,

> Mr. Gardiner. I had the pleasure of seeing you on television last night and I listened with great interest to your down-to-earth philosophy. I'm not surprised that it was so quickly endorsed by the President.
> (quietly)
> ... Tell me, Mr. Gardiner, just how serious is Benjamin's illness? I did not want to upset Mrs. Rand by discussing it in detail.

CHANCE
Ben is very ill.

SKRAPINOV
Yes, so I've heard, a shame ... As you know, we in the Soviet Union have the keenest interest in developments of the First American Financial Corporation ... We are pleased to hear that you may fill Benjamin's place should he fail to recover.
(arrive at table)
Be seated, please, Mr. Gardiner.

Chance sits between Skrapinov and Mrs. Skrapinov.

SKRAPINOV (CONT'D)
(moves chair close to Chance)
... Mr. Gardiner, I wish to be quite candid - considering the gravity of your economic situation, shouldn't we, the diplomats, and you, the businessman - get together more often?

CHANCE
Yes, I agree, I think so too.

SKRAPINOV
To exchange our thoughts - what does a Russian know about

business? On the other hand, what does an American know about diplomacy?

          CHANCE
Yes, I understand.

          SKRAPINOV
And I have noticed in you a certain reticence regarding political issues - so why not a coming together? An interchange of opinion? We may find, my friend, that we are not so far from each other, not so far!

          CHANCE
   (an engaging smile)
We are not far ...
   (motions at nearness of
   their chairs)
... our chairs almost touch.

          SKRAPINOV
   (laughs)
Bravo! Bravo! Our chairs are indeed almost touching! And we want to remain seated on them, correct? We don't want them snatched from under us, am I right? Because if one goes, the other goes, and then - boom! Boom! And we are both down before our time, you see? And neither of us wants that, do you agree?

          CHANCE
I certainly do.

          SKRAPINOV
Yes. Tell me, Mr. Gardiner - do you by any chance enjoy Krylov's fables? I ask this because there is something ... there is something Krylovian about you.

                    CHANCE
          Do you think so? Do you think so?

                    SKRAPINOV
          So you know Krylov!

Skrapinov pauses, then leans close to Chance, speaks softly
in Russian. Chance, having never heard this language, raises
his eyebrows and laughs. Mrs. Skrapinov remains impassive.

                    SKRAPINOV (CONT'D)
              (amazed)
          So you know your Krylov in
          Russian, do you? Mr. Gardiner, I
          must confess I had suspected as
          much all along - I know an
          educated man when I meet one!

                    CHANCE
          Oh, good.

                    SKRAPINOV
          Yes, it is very good!

                    CHANCE
          Yes, it is.
              (beat)
          Would you tell me your name again,
          please?

                    SKRAPINOV
              (slaps Chance on the back)
          Ho! Ho! A dash of American humor!
          Vladimar Skrapinov!

                    CHANCE
          Yes. I like that name very much.

                    SKRAPINOV
          And yours, sir - Chauncey
          Gardiner!
              (in Russian)
          How poetic! Chauncey, a name of
          uncertain meaning! And Gardiner,
          a bit of the French, a suggestion
          of a stroll through the flowers! A
          beautiful name, my friend!

As he speaks in Russian, Eve comes to the table, taps
Skrapinov on the shoulder.

>   SKRAPINOV (CONT'D)
>   (immediately rises)
>   Mrs. Rand! You have returned to us!
>
>   EVE
>   Only to steal Mr. Gardiner away,
>   if I might.
>   (to Chance)
>   Everyone wants to meet you.
>
>   CHANCE
>   Yes, Eve. That would be good.
>
>   SKRAPINOV
>   (shakes Chance's hand)
>   We must speak again, Mr. Gardiner,
>   many times!
>
>   CHANCE
>   Thank you.

As Eve and Chance leave, Skrapinov turns and nods to a MAN
standing a short distance away. The man, KARPATOV, hurries to
the table.

>   SKRAPINOV
>   Yes? What have you found?
>
>   KARPATOV
>   (in Russian)
>   We have nothing on him, Ambassador
>   Skrapinov.
>
>   SKRAPINOV
>   (holds up hand, looks around)
>   Quietly, please. Mr. Gardiner, for
>   one, understands our language.
>
>   KARPATOV
>   (in English, softly)
>   Sorry, Comrade Ambassador.

                    SKRAPINOV
          What do you mean there is nothing?
          That's impossible.

                    KARPATOV
          There is no information available
          on the man before he moved into
          Benjamin Rand's. It has proven to
          be such a difficult task that it
          has resulted in the loss of one of
          our agents to the United States
          Government.

Mrs. Skrapinov strains to overhear the conversation.

                    SKRAPINOV
          But ... Where was this man Gardiner
          before last week?

                    KARPATOV
          Apparently the White House shares
          our curiosity - they have also
          launched an investigation, and,
          according to our sources, neither
          the F.B.I. nor the C.I.A. has met
          with success.

                    SKRAPINOV
          I see. Clearly, such interest on
          their part is of great political
          significance.

                    KARPATOV
          Clearly, yes comrade.

                    SKRAPINOV
          Hmmm ... Take this down.
              (Karpatov takes out notepad)
          I want this quote included in the
          Tass coverage; 'Chauncey Gardiner,
          in an intimate discussion with
          Ambassador Skrapinov, noted that
          "Unless the leaders of the
          opposing political systems move
          the chairs on which they sit
          closer to each other, all of their
          seats will be pulled from under

them by rapid social and political changes."

                    KARPATOV
          Very good, Your Excellency.

Karpatov leaves the table.

INT. WASHINGTON, D.C. COCKTAIL LOUNGE - NIGHT

The same lounge as before. Sidney Courtney sits at the same table as earlier, only this time with the editor of the Washington Post, LYMAN STUART. Courtney puffs on his pipe as he speaks.

                    COURTNEY
          ... It's strictly rumor at this
          stage, Lyman - just something in
          the wind ...

                    STUART
          Something rather big in the wind,
          I'd say. So whose files were
          destroyed? The CIA's or the FBI's?

                    COURTNEY
          I don't know. Like I said, it's
          just rumor so far, but we should
          start nosing around, see if we can
          talk to some people ...

The CAMERA begins to slowly MOVE AWAY from their table.

                    STUART
          ... But why? The question is why?
          Why would they destroy Gardiner's
          files? What is it about his past
          they are trying to cover up?
                    (his voice fades)
          ... A criminal record? A
          membership in a subversive
          organization? Homosexual, perhaps?

The SOUND of Stuart's voice dissolves into Thomas Franklin's as the CAMERA SETTLES on Dr. Allenby and Franklin sitting at a table nearby.

FRANKLIN
... And he told us that he had been living there since he was a child, working as a gardener. He showed us a room in the garage, where he said he stayed, and I ... Well, I didn't really believe him, of course - but why the act?

ALLENBY
I have no idea ...

FRANKLIN
Another thing that baffles me, Doctor - what was his connection with the deceased? Major financial dealings, obviously - but our firm has no record of any such transactions.

ALLENBY
Hmmm. You say he showed you his garden?

FRANKLIN
Well, he said it was his, he walked us through it.

ALLENBY
I see.
   (leans close to Franklin)
Mr. Franklin, I must ask you and Miss Hayes to keep this incident with Mr. Gardiner to yourselves. There's no telling what he was involved in, and the matter may be extremely confidential. So please, not a word.

FRANKLIN
Of course, Doctor, I understand.

ALLENBY
Fine. Thank you, Mr. Franklin.

FRANKLIN
Certainly, glad to be of help.

Allenby rises, leaves the bar.

INT. SOPHIE'S HOUSE - DINNER PARTY - NIGHT

Eve and Sophie are talking to a small group. Chance moves away to get an hors d'oeuvre and is approached by RONALD STIEGLER, a publisher.

>   STIEGLER
> Mr. Gardiner, I'm Ronald Stiegler, of Harvard Books.
>
>   CHANCE
>   (a two-handed handshake)
> Hello, Ronald.
>
>   STIEGLER
> Mr. Gardiner, my editors and I have been wondering if you'd consider writing a book for us? Something on your political philosophy. What do you say?
>
>   CHANCE
> I can't write.
>
>   STIEGLER
>   (smiles)
> Of course, who can nowadays? I have trouble writing a post card to my children! Look, we could give you a six figure [sic] advance, provide you with the very best ghostwriter, research assistants, proof readers ...
>
>   CHANCE
> I can't read.
>
>   STIEGLER
> Of course not! No one has the time to read! One glances at things, watches television ...
>
>   CHANCE
> Yes. I like to watch.

                    STIEGLER
          Sure you do! No one reads! ...
          Listen, book publishing isn't
          exactly a bed of roses these
          days ...

                    CHANCE
               (mild interest)
          What sort of bed is it?

INT. RAND'S HOSPITAL ROOM - NIGHT

Rand is in bed. Sitting nearby are two attorneys, MONROE and
TOWNSEND. Mrs. Aubrey stands to one side and Constance and
Teresa prepare an IV for Rand.

                    RAND
               (speaks slowly, with effort)
          Everything. I said everything and
          that's exactly what I mean.

                    MONROE
          But, Mr. Rand, the holdings are so
          extensive, I would like to be more
          precise in ...

                    RAND
               (interrupts)
          What could be more precise than
          everything ...?

Allenby enters the room, stands by the door, unnoticed.

                    MONROE
               (turns to Townsend)
          Everything to Mrs. Rand.

                    TOWNSEND
               (drafting a will)
          Right - everything.

                    RAND
          You two don't have to lecture me
          on the complexities of the
          situation, no one knows that
          better than myself ... But you must
          understand that I have an endless
          faith in Mrs. Rand's abilities - I

>   know that she will select the
>   right person for guidance when she
>   has the need ... She has shared my
>   life, gentlemen, she has given me
>   far more pleasure than any of my
>   so called [sic] assets ... Life has
>   suddenly become very simple for me
>   now - I may be older than my
>   years, and you might think me to
>   be somewhat feeble ... But I am
>   still in love, gentlemen, thank
>   God for that ...

Allenby silently leaves the room.

INT. SOPHIE'S HOUSE - DINNER PARTY - NIGHT

Dennis Watson, of the State Department, talks with Chance in a corner of the living room. Dennis whispers something into Chance's ear and Chance gives him an innocent smile. Dennis is encouraged by the smile.

>   DENNIS
>   We could do it now, we can go
>   upstairs.
>   (no reaction from Chance)
>   ... Please, it's time for us. Come
>   upstairs.
>
>   CHANCE
>   (blankly)
>   I like to watch.
>
>   DENNIS
>   Watch? You mean just watch me?
>   Doing it alone?
>
>   CHANCE
>   Yes. I like to watch very much.
>
>   DENNIS
>   Well, if that's what you want,
>   then I want it too.
>   (takes Chance's arm)
>   We can go this way.

                              CHANCE
                    I want to tell Eve.

                              DENNIS
                    Tell Eve? You mean Mrs. Rand?

                              CHANCE
                    Yes.

                              DENNIS
                         (pulling Chance)
                    Oh, you can tell her later. She'll
                    never miss you in this crowd.

Dennis leads Chance out of the crowded room.

INT. WHITE HOUSE - PRESIDENT'S BEDROOM - NIGHT

A light from the adjoining bathroom filters into the darkened bedroom. The President and the First Lady are in bed. They each lie on their backs, a distance apart and are silent.

                              FIRST LADY
                         (after some time)
                    ... Maybe you should talk to
                    somebody, darling.

                              PRESIDENT
                    No, that won't do any good.

                              FIRST LADY
                         (another pause)
                    ... Is it me? Is there something
                    I've done?

                              PRESIDENT
                    Oh, no, sweetheart - it's not
                    you ...

                              FIRST LADY
                         (another pause)
                    It's your damn job. It never
                    happened when you were a
                    senator ...

                              PRESIDENT
                    It's not that, I just ...

The inter-White House phone rings, the President reaches for it.

                  PRESIDENT (CONT'D)
            (into phone)
  Yeah, Kaufman - what is it?

                  KAUFMAN'S VOICE
            (over phone)
  Chief, we have a break in the case. Our man at the Washington Post says they are working on a story that either the CIA or the FBI destroyed Gardiner's files before anyone could get to them.

                  PRESIDENT
  What? Why?

                  KAUFMAN'S VOICE
            (over phone)
  I can't say at this time - neither agency will admit to a thing.

                  PRESIDENT
            (getting out of bed)
  Okay, get both Directors over here, I'll be right down.

The President hangs up the phone as the First Lady stares at the ceiling.

INT. SOPHIE'S HOUSE - UPSTAIRS ROOM - NIGHT

A small room exquisitely decorated in pale lilac tapestry. The lights are very dim, and Dennis, who we cannot see, is lying on the floor. Dennis' clothes are draped over a chair. Chance sees a very small pocket television on a desk. He turns the TV on.

                  DENNIS' VOICE
            (softly)
  Can you see well?

                  CHANCE
            (squints at small screen)
  Yes, very well, thank you.

                    DENNIS' VOICE
              Do you like it?

                    CHANCE
              Yes. It's very tiny, but it's
              good.

                    DENNIS' VOICE
                (disappointed at it being 'tiny')
              ... Are you sure you like it?

                    CHANCE
              Yes, I do, it's very good.

                    DENNIS' VOICE
                (excited)
              Really? Really!!!

Chance reacts to the change in tone of Dennis' voice, turns to look at him on the floor. Hearing the groans and heavy breathing, Chance thinks Dennis is ill.

                    CHANCE
              Do you need a doctor? I could call
              Robert ...

                    DENNIS' VOICE
              I don't want Robert.

                    CHANCE
              I see.

                    DENNIS' VOICE
                (through the groans)
              Your foot! Give me your foot!!

Dennis reaches out with his free hand, grabs Chance's foot, pulls it to himself.

                    CHANCE
                (some pain)
              Thank you. But my leg is still a
              little sore.

Chance watches as Dennis goes through some spasms, then his body relaxes. Chance is concerned for Dennis' health.

CHANCE (CONT'D)
Are you sure you're not ill?

We hear a contented sigh from the man on the floor.

EXT. SOPHIE'S - NIGHT

A long, black limousine with a Red Star on the door pulls away from Sophie's house.

INT. RED STAR LIMOUSINE - NIGHT

ALEXIS NOVOGROD, a high-ranking KGB officer, and two of his underlings are in the limousine, along with Skrapinov, his wife and Karpatov. Novogrod and his men wear heavy clothing, fresh from Moscow. They all drink vodka. (Dialogue in Russian, English subtitles)

NOVOGROD
The rank-and-file in the FBI feel he is FBI, but others feel he is a CIA man who knows how to destroy FBI files.

SKRAPINOV
That could be possible ...

NOVOGROD
But we are quite certain, comrade, that this man Gardiner is a leading member of an American elitist faction planning a coup d'etat [sic].

SKRAPINOV
A coup d'etat [sic]! Of course, that was foreseen by Lenin himself!

NOVOGROD
That is correct, Comrade Skrapinov. We have ascertained that Gardiner heads a big-business power group that will soon be taking over the American government.

SKRAPINOV
Big business. I could work with that faction quite nicely, Colonel Novogrod.

NOVOGROD
You have proven that already, Comrade Skrapinov, you are to be congratulated for recognizing the importance of this man and establishing an early friendship.

SKRAPINOV
Thank you, Colonel.

NOVOGROD
(raising his glass)
Let us toast to the success of the coup.

They all raise their glasses.

GROUP TOAST
Na zdorov'e!

The men and Mrs. Skrapinov drink their vodkas.

INT. SOPHIE'S HOUSE - NIGHT

The reception is breaking up. Eve, wearing her coat, searches for Chance in the crowd. She sees him, taps him on the shoulder from behind.

EVE
Chauncey, where have you been? I was afraid you got bored and left, or that you were with some mysterious woman.

CHANCE
No. I was with a man. We went upstairs.

EVE
Upstairs? Chauncey, you're always involved in some sort of discussion ...

                    CHANCE
          He was very ill, I stayed with him
          for a while.

                    EVE
          It must be the punch, and it is
          stuffy in here -- I feel it a
          little myself. You're an angel, my
          dear - thank God there are still
          men like you around to give aid
          and comfort.

Eve and Chance leave the reception.

INT. WHITE HOUSE - OVAL OFFICE - NIGHT

The President sits behind his desk in a bathrobe, his hair mussed. Standing before him are GROVER HONEYCUTT, the Director of the F.B.I., and CLIFFORD BALDWIN, C.I.A. Chief. Kaufman stands to one side. All are red-eyed, tired, and frustrated.

                    HONEYCUTT
          I never gave such a directive, Mr.
          President.

                    BALDWIN
          Nor I, sir - it would be out of
          the question.

                    PRESIDENT
          Gentlemen, I didn't call you here
          at such an hour to make
          accusations, I just want to
          explore the possibilities. Now, I
          have three questions; Is the man a
          foreign agent? Or, have we
          suddenly found that our methods of
          gathering data are grossly
          inefficient? Or, thirdly, have the
          man's files been destroyed? Now,
          I'd like some answers.

                    BALDWIN
          Gardiner is not a foreign agent,
          there are now sixteen countries
          investigating the man. We can rule
          that out.

```
                    PRESIDENT
          Very well ... Can we rule out
          inefficiency ...?

There is silence in the room. A couple of looks, but silence.

                    PRESIDENT (CONT'D)
          I see. What about question three?
          Is it possible to erase all traces
          of a man?

                    HONEYCUTT
          Highly unlikely, sir ... In fact,
          the boys around the Bureau feel
          that the only person capable of
          pulling it off would be an ex
          F.B.I. man.

                    BALDWIN
             (a look to Honeycutt)
          I don't think that's entirely
          true, Grover.

                    PRESIDENT
             (to Baldwin)
          And what do the boys around
          Intelligence think?

                    BALDWIN
          Well, Mr. President ... They don't
          quite know what to think.

                    PRESIDENT
             (rising)
          Gentlemen, needless to say, there
          is going to be a full
          Congressional investigation of
          your respective operations.
             (goes to door)
          Good night.
```

The President leaves the Oval Office.

INT. RAND MANSION - THIRD FLOOR HALLWAY - NIGHT

Eve and Chance walk down the hallway.

                    EVE
                (holding his hand)
            I feel so close to you, so safe
            with you, Chauncey ...
                (stops at her bedroom door)
            ... And Benjamin understands that,
            dearest ... He understands and
            accepts my feelings for you ...

                    CHANCE
            Yes, Eve. Ben is very wise.

                    EVE
                (opens her door)
            ... Come in, Chauncey - please
            come in ...

                    CHANCE
            Thank you.

Chance enters, Eve closes the door behind them.

INT. EVE'S ROOM - NIGHT

Eve turns on a soft lamp, Chance goes directly to her TV, turns it on.

                    EVE
            I can sense that you've been
            through a lot, Chauncey. But one
            day, when you feel like it, you'll
            tell me all about your life ...
                (Chance watches an old movie)
            ... But, even if you tell me
            nothing, even if it's too painful
            for you to reveal your past ...

As she talks, Chance watches a love scene on TV. The hero gives his lady a passionate kiss and embrace. The scene seems to 'sink into' Chance's mind. He abruptly turns, takes Eve into his arms and kisses her full on the mouth. Just as abruptly, he turns away and changes channels on TV.

                    EVE (CONT'D)
                (breathless)
            Oh, Chauncey ... I do love you so
            much!

She takes Chance in her arms, kisses him wildly. They fall
to her bed in an embrace. As she holds him, kisses him, runs
her hands over his body, Chance watches television, neither
resists nor responds to Eve's caresses. Suddenly she stops,
lets her head fall on Chance's chest.

>   EVE (CONT'D)
> ... You don't want me, Chauncey ...
> You don't feel anything for me ...
> Nothing at all ...

Chance sits up on the bed, then, feeling her sadness, gently
strokes her hair as he looks at TV.

>   EVE (CONT'D)
> I just don't excite you at all ...
> I don't know what you want ... I
> don't know what you like ...

>   CHANCE
> I like to watch.

>   EVE
>   (not understanding)
> To watch ...? To watch me ...?

>   CHANCE
> Yes. I like to watch.

>   EVE
>   (uncertain)
> ... Is that all you want ...?
>   (a hesitation)
> ... To watch me ...?

>   CHANCE
> Yes. It's very good, Eve.

>   EVE
> ... But I've never done ...
>   (another hesitation)
> ... You mean ...? When ... When ...
> When I do it? ... When I touch myself ...?

Eve slowly gets up from the bed, nervously paces the bedroom
as Chance watches TV. She makes a decision, moves to Chance,
kisses him.

                    EVE (CONT'D)
                (getting aroused)
            Oh, Chauncey ...

She steps back, slips off her dress. She does not undress any further, instead, leans close to Chance.

                    EVE (CONT'D)
            One of those little things you
            don't know about me yet, darling -
            I'm a little shy.

She smiles, gets in bed and pulls the covers over herself. Chance divides his attention between Eve and the TV, watching both with an equal detachment. Eve begins to respond to her own touch, finds a heretofore undiscovered pleasure with her own body. Chance changes the channel as she reaches orgasm. As Eve's body trembles, Chance yawns, gets up from the bed.

                    CHANCE
                (going to door)
            Good night, Eve.

A low purr is heard from Eve as Chance leaves.

INT. RAND'S HOSPITAL ROOM - MORNING

Allenby, Constance and Teresa are readying a transfusion for Rand. There is a feeling of urgency as they work. Rand, very weak, strains to speak to Allenby.

                    RAND
            No more, Robert ... No more
            needles ...

                    ALLENBY
                (sits on the side of the bed)
            It's not good, Ben - I'm sure you
            can feel it.

                    RAND
            I know, Robert ... But, strangely
            enough, I don't feel too bad about
            now ... I feel all right ... I guess
            it's easier ... knowing Chauncey is
            here ... to take care of things ...

Teresa is about to swab Rand's arm with alcohol but he
pulls away.

>   RAND (CONT'D)
>   No, I don't want any of that ...
>   Please ... please, just get me Mr.
>   Gardiner, Teresa - please ... he'll
>   head it up ...

Teresa looks to Allenby, he nods to her. Teresa puts the
cotton down, leaves the room.

EXT. RAND MANSION - PATIO - MORNING

A light snow is failing. Eve is in a fur coat, holds a
steaming cup of coffee. Chance stands next to her, an umbrella
in one hand. He holds his other arm out, catching the
snowflakes as they fall.

>   EVE
>   ... And I feel so free now,
>   Chauncey. Until I met you, I never
>   felt acknowledged by a man ...
>   (Chance gazes out at the
>   falling snow)
>   ... I always had the feeling that
>   I was just a vessel for a man,
>   someone that he could take hold
>   of, pierce, and pollute. I was
>   merely an aspect of somebody's
>   lovemaking. Do you know what I mean?

Chance turns to her, says nothing, presses the cold snowflakes
to his face.

>   EVE (CONT'D)
>   (presses close to him)
>   Dearest, you uncoil my wants;
>   desire flows within me, and when
>   you watch me my passion dissolves
>   it. You set me free. I reveal
>   myself to myself and I am drenched
>   and purged.

>   CHANCE
>   That's very interesting, Eve.

Teresa appears in the doorway.

                    TERESA
          Mr. Gardiner. Mr. Rand would like
          to see you.

                    CHANCE
          Yes. I would like to see Ben.

Chance gives Eve a warm smile, then follows Teresa into
the house.

INT. RAND'S HOSPITAL ROOM - MORNING

Allenby, with nothing more he can do to prolong Rand's life,
sits on the bed close to him, grips his hand tightly. Teresa
shows Chance into the room and Allenby motions to the nurses
to leave. As they do, Chance, once again breathing the oxygen
with a smile, goes to Rand's bedside.

                    RAND
               (slowly)
          ... Chauncey ... Chauncey ...

                    CHANCE
          Yes, Ben - are you going to die
          now?

Allenby winces.

                    RAND
               (a weak smile)
          ... I'm about to surrender the
          Horn of Plenty for the Horn of
          Gabriel, my boy ...

                    CHANCE
          Oh, I see.

                    RAND
               (reaches out to him)
          Let me feel the strength in your
          hand, Chauncey ... Let me feel your
          strength ...
               (holds Chance's hand)
          Yes, that's good ... I hope,
          Chauncey - I hope that you'll stay
          with Eve ... Take care of her,
          watch over her, she's a delicate
          flower, Chauncey ...

                    CHANCE
              (smiling)
        A flower ...

                    RAND
        She cares for you and she needs
        your help, Chauncey ... there's
        much to be looked after ...

                    CHANCE
        Yes. I would like to do that.

                    RAND
        ... I've worked very hard and
        enjoyed my life ... I've known
        success ... and I've felt love ...
        My associates, Chauncey - I've
        talked with them about you ...
        They're eager to meet you ... very
        eager to meet you ... I'm very fond
        of you, Chauncey ... And I
        understand Eve ... Tell her that ...
        tell her I'm madly in love with
        her ...

Rand slumps down, dead. Allenby checks his pulse, turns to
Chance.

                    ALLENBY
        ... He's gone, Chauncey.

                    CHANCE
        Yes, Robert. I have seen it
        before. It happens to old people.

                    ALLENBY
              (covers Rand's face)
        Yes, I suppose that's true.

Chance reaches out, uncovers Rand's face, gently touches the
man's forehead, feels the coldness. Allenby eyes him as Chance
stays with Rand for a moment, then replaces the sheet.

                    CHANCE
              (turns to Allenby)
        Will you be leaving now, Robert?

                    ALLENBY
          In a day or two, yes.

                    CHANCE
          Eve is going to stay. The house
          will not be closed.

                    ALLENBY
             (a moment, a look)
          ... You've become quite a close
          friend of Eve's - haven't you
          Mr...
             (a beat)
          ... Chance ...?

                    CHANCE
          Yes. I love Eve very much.

                    ALLENBY
          I see ...
             (another beat)
          ... And you are really a gardener,
          aren't you?

                    CHANCE
             (brightens)
          Yes, Robert - I am.
             (a smile at Allenby)
          I'll go tell Eve about Ben now,
          Robert.

Chance leaves the bedroom. Allenby watches him go, then sits back in a chair, his head spinning.

EXT. RAND MANSION - DAY

A cloudy, cold day, patches of snow are on the ground. The Rand servants are lined up in front of the mansion, listen to funeral services for Rand on a pair of loudspeakers. PAN AROUND, reveal the services being held on a hill overlooking the mansion. Fifty mourners are gathered around the Rand family mausoleum. Chance stands with Eve and Allenby. The President of the United States stands before a microphone.

                    PRESIDENT
          ... Millions of people across the
          world have heard of the passing of

> Benjamin Rand; but, unfortunately, only relatively few will feel the pain and sadness at such a loss. To most, Benjamin Rand was a legend; to those of us gathered here today, Benjamin was a beloved friend. My personal association with Benjamin dates back many years, and my memories of our friendship will stay with me forever.

As the President speaks, Chance turns and walks away. Eve and Allenby watch as he goes into the trees surrounding the area.

> PRESIDENT (CONT'D)
> I initially came in contact with the Rand name in 1943. I was a young lieutenant in the Air Corps, a navigator flying missions over Europe. That plane that I learned to know so well was manufactured by the Rand Aeronautics Corporation.
> (a beat)
> Benjamin Rand was an industrial giant, known to be powerful and uncompromising, and yet, on a personal level, we have all felt his warmth and humor ...
> (a beat)
> ... I would like to share with you a few quotes, and a few feelings from our dear friend.
> (holds up paper, reads)
> ... 'I do not regret having political differences with men that I respect; I do regret, however, that our philosophies kept us apart.'
> ... 'I have no use for those on welfare, no patience whatsoever ... But, if I am to be honest with myself, I must admit that they have no use for me, either.'
> ... 'I was born into a position of

extreme wealth, I have spent many sleepless nights thinking about extreme poverty - I do not know the feelings of being poor, and that is not to know the feelings of the majority of people in this world. For a man in my position, that is inexcusable.'
'Life is a state of mind.'
... 'When I was a boy, I was told that the Lord fashioned us from his own image. That's when I decided to manufacture mirrors.'

INT. LARGE AUDITORIUM - DAY

Ah auditorium with row upon row of empty seats. Huddled together at one end of the hall are six important businessmen, speaking in hushed tones. JAMES DUDLEY, a powerful industrialist, speaks.

          DUDLEY
But what do we know of the man? Nothing! We have no inkling of his past!

SEWELL NELSON, a corporation chairman, joins in.

          NELSON
Correct, and that is an asset. A man's past can cripple him, his background turns into a swamp and invites scrutiny.

Another executive, PETER CALDWELL, agrees.

          CALDWELL
To this time, he hasn't said anything that could be used against him.

CHARLIE BOB BENNET, a Texas oil millionaire;

          BENNET
Well, I'm certainly open to the thought - it would be sheer lunacy to support the President for another term.

                    NELSON
          No one will go along with that ...
          Look at the facts, gentlemen, the
          response from his appearance on
          'This Evening' was overwhelming;
          he has excited and awakened the
          people of this country at a time
          of despair.

LYMAN MURRAY, a banker;

                    MURRAY
          He's personable, elusive, yet
          seemingly honest. He's riding a
          crest of popularity that builds
          with every statement. As far as
          his thinking goes, he appears to
          be one of us. I firmly believe,
          gentlemen, that he is our only
          chance - Mr. Chauncey Gardiner!

EXT. WOODS - DAY

Chance, his umbrella under his arm, walks through the woods.

EXT. RAND'S FUNERAL - DAY

The services are over. Eve, Allenby talk with the President and the First Lady.

                    EVE
          It was very moving, Bobby - thank
          you so much ...

                    PRESIDENT
          We're all going to miss him, Eve ...
               (glances around)
          ... Where's Mr. Gardiner?

                    ALLENBY
          ... He walked off ...

                    EVE
          Chauncey is so sensitive ... He was
          overcome with grief ...

                    PRESIDENT
          I can certainly understand that ...

>   FIRST LADY
>   Of course ... I'm so sorry for you,
>   Eve ...
>
>   EVE
>   Thank you, Nancy.
>
>   FIRST LADY
>   I'll call you soon.

The President and First Lady head toward their limousine.

EXT. WOODS - DAY

Chance walks deeper into the woods, absorbed in the greenery. He stops by a tree, brushes some snow from a branch, moves on.

EXT. RAND'S FUNERAL - DAY

The majority of mourners have left. Eve and Allenby walk slowly to the RAND 1 limousine, look around for Chance.

>   EVE
>   ... Do you think we should look
>   for him?
>
>   ALLENBY
>   I don't think so, he should be
>   along soon ...
>
>   EVE
>   I wish he were here ...

Eve keeps looking as they walk to the limousine.

EXT. WOODS - DAY

Chance happens on a tree with a cracked limb, hanging to the ground. He stops, inspects the break, runs his fingers along the split in the bark. He looks to the ground, notices that an end of the limb has fallen on a seedling, bending it double. Chance pulls the limb away, then kneels beside the seedling. He removes an expensive pair of suede gloves, and, with gentle fingers, brushes the dirt and snow away from the seedling. Chance glances up to the remaining limbs of the larger tree which could fall and threaten the emerging tree. He unfolds his umbrella, places it over the seedling in a way to give it protection, yet to still allow it to receive light from the winter sun. Chance stands, puts his gloves back on and continues his walk, disappearing into a remote section of the woods.

EXT. RAND'S FUNERAL - DAY

Jeffrey stands holding the door for Eve and Allenby, all the other cars have gone. Eve is worried, gets into the car.

EXT. WOODS - DAY

Chance walks through the woods, his pace faster than before.

EXT. RAND'S FUNERAL - DAY

The limousine still waits for Chance.

INT. LIMOUSINE - DAY

Eve is deeply concerned for Chance.

>				EVE
> We have to find him, Robert - he could be lost, something may have happened, we can't leave him!
>
>				ALLENBY
> You really care for him, don't you, Eve?
>
>				EVE
> I do - we do - both of us, Ben and I feel so much for Chauncey ...
>
>				ALLENBY
> I think we'd better go look for him.
>   (he taps on the glass partition)
> David!

David starts up the limousine.

EXT. WOODS - DAY

Chance walks with determination through the woods.

INT. LIMOUSINE - DAY

Allenby and Eve search for Chance as David drives along a narrow road through the woods. Jeffrey, sitting in front, suddenly calls out.

                    JEFFREY
              Look!

About 100 yards ahead of them, Chance crosses the road,
continues on down a hill.

                    EVE
              There he is! Chauncey!

David stops the limousine at the point where Chance crossed.
Eve hurries out of the car.

EXT. SIDE OF ROAD - DAY

Chance is about twenty yards down the side of a hill. Eve
calls to him.

                    EVE
              Chauncey! Chauncey!

                    CHANCE
                (stops, looks up)
              Hello, Eve.

Eve runs, half falls as she goes down the hill.

                    EVE
              Oh, Chauncey ...!

She gets to him, holds him tightly.

                    EVE (CONT'D)
              Oh, Chauncey, darling ... Where
              have you been? We thought we'd
              lost you - we've been looking all
              over!

                    CHANCE
              Yes. I've been looking for you,
              too, Eve.

She hugs him one more time, then she leads him back up the
hill to the waiting limousine. Allenby gets out of the car,
greets Chance with a handshake and an arm around the shoulder.
Then the three get into the limousine.

                                                  FADE OUT.

              THE END

Notes

1. Films directed by Hal Ashby on which Haskell Wexler acted as cinematographer: *Bound for Glory* (1976, for which Wexler won his second Oscar for cinematography); *Coming Home* (1978); *Second-Hand Hearts* (1981); *Lookin' to Get Out* (1982). Ashby-edited films directed by Norman Jewison that Wexler shot: *In the Heat of the Night* (1967); *The Thomas Crown Affair* (1968).
2. Haskell Wexler, "Commentary," *In the Heat of the Night* (1967), DVD, directed by Norman Jewison, MGM, 2001.
3. Nick Dawson, *Being Hal Ashby: Life of a Hollywood Rebel* (Lexington: University Press of Kentucky, 2009), 144–5.
4. The editing process of *Lookin' to Get Out* was fraught with difficulties, with Ashby hiring and firing more than one editor, and Ashby and Jones had a falling out over the film. A rediscovered version of the film, edited by Ashby, was released as *Lookin' to Get Out*, Extended Version in 2009.
5. Dawson, *Being Hal Ashby*, 171.
6. Ibid., 176.
7. Ibid., 182.
8. In a fascinating, ferociously worded letter-to-the editor of *Vanity Fair* dated May 6, 2008, Nancy Dowd defends the final script as being mostly her work in response to a piece by Peter Biskind the magazine had run entitled "The Vietnam Oscars" in February of 2008: https://www.vanityfair.com/magazine/2008/06/letters200806.
9. For a fuller discussion of how Jones worked to incorporate the on-set improvisational work of the cast of *Coming Home*, see Aaron Hunter, *Authoring Hal Ashby: The Myth of the New Hollywood Auteur.* (New York: Bloomsbury Academic, 2016), 148–50.
10. Jones's Oscar, awarded at the fifty-first Academy Awards ceremony on April 9, 1979, came several months after he was hired by Ashby to redraft the *Being There* script.

3

Robert C. Jones: January 1979

Introduction

After reading Jones's first draft, Ashby said, "I knew I was into the film then. I'd always felt strongly about it being a film, but now I had my blueprint, my structure there. Then I sat down with Robert for three or four weeks and worked really hard on it, eight or nine hours a day.[1] We never worked with Jerzy on the script; when we sent it to him, he loved it."[2] I quote this again because it raises three significant points that are worth considering, particularly for burgeoning and practicing screenwriters. First is how it highlights a third stage of revision, after Kosinski's several efforts and Jones's first solo effort. Second is the amount of time and work that Ashby and Jones extended to constructing a draft of the script they deemed ready for production. Third is Ashby's insistence that these two drafts were written without Kosinski's help. While this latter may seem less significant over all to the process of writing a script, it highlights the way a writer's work can be regarded or disregarded within Hollywood's still highly regimented and overlapping industrial model and guild system.

Ashby was not a writer. In his entire career as a director, his only, shared, writing credit was for his final film, *8 Million Ways to Die* (PSO International/TriStar 1986). Like most Hollywood directors, though, he had consulted on several of the scripts he filmed, perhaps most extensively on *Shampoo* when he encamped with cowriters Warren Beatty and Robert Towne in the Beverly Wilshire hotel for ten days of intensive rewrites.[3] As a filmmaker with roots in editing, Ashby had a keen sense of pacing and narrative flow—he often spoke about "finding the film" in the editing—and many of the changes between Jones's two drafts center on increasing the flow and tightening the narrative pace, while still maintaining the very deliberate otherworldliness of the novel. The result is a script that in many ways mirrors Jones's first draft and might appear to benefit from only minor revisions. Those revisions, though, endow the finished film with much of its power. Comparing the first two drafts in this book provides insight into a major script overhaul; comparing the second two reveals how vital the fine-tuning process can be.

Such changes can be obvious, such as the aforementioned instances of cutting a full day from the opening scene, or having Eve leave Rand's funeral on her own to search for Chance. Or they can be quite minor. For example, when Chance exits the Old Man's house, the viewer becomes aware for the first time that the neighborhood around the house is dilapidated—likely a result of the Old Man's having ensconced himself in reclusive withdrawal from the world, while the world, on the other hand, moved on without him. One of Chance's first encounters on leaving the house is with a street gang who threatens him with a knife and gives him a message for somebody named Raphael. The scene (which is strikingly dated in its portrayal of urban, African-American youth) is played for laughs, which are heightened by the sense of danger Chance faces. Both Chance and the gang members mistake each other's identity, which also increases the absurdity of the dialogue. This dialogue is virtually the same in both drafts, but the second draft reworks it so that Chance's deadpan delivery becomes more comedic even as the danger of the situation becomes more apparent. For example, here's the second half of the exchange from Jones's first draft:

```
                    ABBAZ
          Bullshit. Who sent you here, boy?
          Did that chickenshit asshole
          Raphael send you here, boy?

                    CHANCE
          No. Thomas Franklin told me that I had to
          leave the Old Man's
          house, he's dead now, you know ...

                    ABBAZ
          Dead, my ass! Now get this,
          honkie - you go tell Raphael that
          I ain't takin' no jive from no
          Western Union messenger! You tell
          that asshole, if he got somethin'
          to tell me to get his ass here
          himself!
                (edges closer to Chance)
          You got that, boy?

Chance smiles at Abbaz and reaches into his pocket.

                    CHANCE
          Yes. I understand.
                (he takes out his remote
                 control TV changer)
          If I see Raphael I will tell him.

Chance points the changer at Abbaz and clicks it three
times, tries to change the picture. Abbaz immediately pulls
out a switchblade, whips the blade open.
```

>   ABBAZ
>   (holds knife at Chance)
> Now, move, honkie! Before I cut your
> white ass!

Chance, disappointed that the changer did not work, returns it to his pocket.

>   CHANCE
> Yes. Of course.
>   (as he leaves)
> Good day.⁴

The comedy here comes from Chance as a fish out of water in the rundown neighborhood, the mistaken identities, and Chance's fumbling for the remote control. Here is how the same scene plays out in the second draft. Notice how slight the changes are but how they heighten the scene's absurdity:

>   ABBAZ
> Bullshit. Who sent you here, boy?
> Did that chickenshit asshole
> Raphael send you here, boy?
>
>   CHANCE
> No. Thomas Franklin told me that
> I had to leave the Old Man's
> house, he's dead now, you know ...
>
>   ABBAZ
> Dead, my ass! Now get this,
> honkie – you go tell Raphael that
> I ain't takin' no jive from no
> Western Union messenger! You tell
> that asshole, if he got somethin'
> to tell me to get his ass down
> here himself!
>   (edges closer to Chance)
> You got that boy?

During this, as Abbaz becomes more hostile, Chance reaches into his pocket, takes out his remote control TV changer. He points the changer at Abbaz and clicks it three times, tries to change the picture. Abbaz immediately pulls out a switchblade knife, holds it at Chance.

```
                    ABBAZ
          Now, move, honkie! Before I cut
          your white ass.

     Chance, disappointed that the changer did not work,
     returns it to his pocket.

                    CHANCE
          Yes. I understand. If I see
          Raphael, I will tell him.
               (as he leaves)
          Good day.
```

Fundamentally, it is the same scene, but the second draft moves a line of Chance's dialogue—"I understand. If I see Raphael, I will tell him"—to the end of the scene, where it becomes almost a non sequitur after the silliness of the remote-control gag. The effect is that Chance's first response to Abbaz's intensified hostility is not to answer, but to attempt to "turn off" Abbaz with his remote control. Much of the scene's effectiveness in the film is down to Sellers's performance (as well as Ravenell Keller III's as Abbaz), but rewriting Chance's response as a silent click of the remote control both intensifies the character's fear—he desperately wants this encounter to be over—and increases the humor. Furthermore, having Chance end the encounter with his promise to tell Rapheal, *after* Abbaz's threat to cut him, also intensifies the humor. These small changes work to create more sympathy for Chance and his plight, to get the audience on his side.

The encounter with Abbaz and his gang does not appear in any of Kosinski's drafts because Kosinski did not write it. Nor do any of Chance's other encounters on first leaving the house: mistaking an old black woman for Louise and asking her for lunch, or informing a DC police officer that a tree on the sidewalk is sick and needs attending to. These scenes were entirely devised by Jones. In Kosinski's first two drafts (still set in Manhattan), when Chance leaves the house he is in an elegant neighborhood and he immediately comes across the electronic goods store in front of which he is hit by Eve Rand's limousine. In his third draft, he responds to Ashby and Mike Haller's directive to set the film in a DC ghetto with one line: "Once a grand house in a neighbourhood rich and fashionable in the twenties, it is now surrounded by similar houses that have long been divided into apartments where now many poor, predominately black or Hispanic families live in poverty."[5] He then comes across the electronic goods store, and there is no mention, let alone description, of any encounters Chance has before meeting Eve. By his own admission, redrafting *Being There* was a chore for Kosinski, and it occupied valuable time that he would have preferred to spend on writing his next novel, *Passion Play* (1979). Of the redrafting experience, he claimed, "I was competent, but I was not inspired,"[6] and he would later state that Ashby and Sellers "understood the story better than I did."[7]

In the autumn of 1978, in addition to writing *Passion Play*, Kosinski was travelling extensively while also working on several other projects. It was at this time that Ashby brought Jones on board. Throughout much of that winter, Kosinski seems to have been happy with Jones's work on the script. Jones's name was added to production documents as the co-screenwriter. As late as April of 1979, Kosinski accepted the credit "Screenplay by Jerzy Kosinski and Robert C. Jones."[8] Having read the script, he did however argue that he should get an additional credit, "Inspired by the Novel by Jerzy Konsinski," rather than the traditional "Based on the novel by." According to a memo from Andrew Molasky at Lorimar to Marge White at WGA, this change "more accurately reflects the basis or inspiration for the film."[9] Kosinski soon changed his mind, however, and in a telex from May 13—after filming had wrapped—he writes: "Have read final script and hereby protest tentative credit on 'Being There' and consider credit should be 'Screen Play by Jerzy Kosinski' 'Inspired by the Novel by Jerzy Kosinski.'"[10] Kosinski took his case to the WGA who found in his favor, and Jones's name was removed from the credits.[11]

In addition to Ashby's and Jones's claims that Jones's scripts were the basis of production, Peter Sellers also publicly argued in Jones's favor.[12] According to Kosinski's biographer, James Park Sloan, Sellers took Jones's side because he was angry at Kosinski for disclosing that Sellers had had a face lift in preparation for the role, and Sloan accepts Kosinski's claims to have written the majority of the script, including the unscripted walking-on-water ending (see Appendix).[13] Such disputes are not uncommon in Hollywood, which is rife with stories of writers, directors, producers, and others vying for writing credit. There can be no dispute, however, that Jones's two drafts are substantially different from anything Kosinski had written. While they maintain (one might even argue, restore) the backbone of Kosinski's novel, and are very much "inspired by" Kosinski's work, as the original credits make plain, there are too many differences at too late a date to think that they were Kosinski's. He had described himself as uninspired and was busy with several other projects throughout the autumn and early winter of 1979, when the very inspired changes were made. Furthermore, Kosinski's three drafts open virtually identically, end virtually identically, and all include the ornate literary description and direction that Jones's drafts would discard. Jones's drafts are more succinct, more visual, funnier, and, simply put, more cinematic. On the other hand, one would be hard pressed to argue that Jones contributed original material of 33 percent or more as WGA rules require. Thus, regardless of which script Kosinski submitted to the WGA, it is possible they would have found in his favor. By the letter, if not the spirit, of the law, Kosinski was the primary writer of the script; but the film we have today could not have come into existence without Bob Jones's extensive creative labor in converting an overwrought, overlong, and overly literary screenplay into a work of cinematic art.

In the script that follows, I have maintained the credits as they are printed on the original January 1979 draft of the script.

From the novel by Jerzy Kosinski

BEING THERE

Screenplay by

Jerzy Kosinski and Robert C. Jones

January 10, 1979

FADE IN:

1. INT. CHANCE'S ROOM - DAWN

   A large-screen color TV dominates a room sparsely decorated with expensive furniture of the twenties. There are no books, magazines, newspapers to be seen. A man, CHANCE, is in bed, sleeping. His eyes slowly open, and, with no change of expression, he sits up and turns on the TV with a remote control. He reaches for a pocketwatch on the bedside table, and, as he looks at it, the watch chimes. He gets out of bed, crosses to the closet, his eyes never straying from the TV. Chance puts on a bathrobe and leaves the room.

2. INT. POTTING ROOM - DAWN

   The room is filled with the tools of a gardener. Chance enters and turns on a 1940's black and white TV that sits on a shelf. A wheel with colored gels spins in front of the set, giving an early form of color television. He waters a few of the plants in the potting room as he watches TV.

3. INT. GARAGE - DAWN

   Chance, with a dust rag and feather duster, cleans off a 1935 limousine, in perfect condition.

4. INT. CHANCE'S ROOM - DAWN

   Chance takes off his robe, hangs it in the closet, changes channels on the TV, then goes into the bathroom.

5. EXT. GARDEN - MORNING

   A light snow is falling in a garden between a three-story brick townhouse and a one-story rear building, guarded on either side by a high brick wall. The door to the rear building opens, Chance peeks out, then goes back inside. A moment passes and Chance reappears, this time with an umbrella. Smartly attired in suit and tie, Chance, with an eye on the garden, crosses to the townhouse.

6. INT. TOWN HOUSE - REAR ENTRANCE/HALLWAY - MORNING

   Chance enters, hangs his umbrella on a door knob, then crosses through the hall. As he goes, we reveal that the furniture in the house is covered with sheets.

7.   INT. TOWN HOUSE - DINING ROOM - MORNING

A large table, covered with a sheet except for two place-settings. A TV is on the table. Chance comes into the room, sits and turns on the television. He watches the screen for a moment, then turns, as if expecting someone. No one appears, so he turns back to the TV. After a time, footsteps are heard and Chance smiles. LOUISE, an elderly Black maid, hurries into the room, visibly distraught.

>   CHANCE
>   Good morning, Louise.
>
>   LOUISE
>   (out of breath)
>   He's dead, Chance! The Old Man's
>   dead!
>
>   CHANCE
>   (flatly, turns back to TV)
>   ... I see.
>
>   LOUISE
>   Must of happened durin' the night,
>   I don't know ... Lord, he wasn't
>   breathin' and as cold as a fish. I
>   touched him, just to see, and you
>   believe me, Chance - that's doin'
>   more than I get paid to do ... Then
>   I just cover him up, pulled the
>   sheet over his head ...
>
>   CHANCE
>   (nodding)
>   Yes. I've seen that done.
>
>   LOUISE
>   ... Then I get the hell out of that
>   room and call the doctor and I
>   think I woke him probably, he
>   wasn't any too alert. He just
>   said, 'Yeah, he's been expectin'
>   it and said he'd send somebody
>   over ...' Lord, what a mornin'!
>
>   CHANCE
>   (watches news, flashes of
>   season's first snowfall)

                    ... Yes, Louise, it's snowing in
                    the garden today. Have you looked outside and seen
                    the snow? It's very white.

A beat of silence from Louise, then anger.

                              LOUISE
                    Gobbledegook! Dammit, Boy! Is that
                    all you got to say? More
                    gobbledegook?
                         (Chance smiles, is silent)
                    That Old Man's layin' up there
                    dead as hell and it just don't
                    make any difference to you!

Louise takes a long look at Chance, then softens, sits next to him.

                              LOUISE (CONT'D)
                    Oh, Lord, Chance - I don't know
                    what I was expectin' from you ...
                    I'm sorry for yellin' like I did
                    ... No sir, I just don't know what
                    I was expectin' ...
                         (Chance doesn't react,
                          watches TV)
                    ... I 'spose I'd better gather up
                    some breakfast for you ...

                              CHANCE
                         (a turn to her)
                    Yes, I'm very hungry.

                              LOUISE
                         (rises, looks upstairs)
                    Well, no more stewin' those prunes
                    every mornin', that's somethin', I
                    guess ...
                         (she starts out, stops by
                          the door)
                    ... What are you goin' to do now,
                    Chance?

                              CHANCE
                         (gazing at TV)
                    I'm going to work in the garden.

Louise gives Chance another look, then turns to leave.

                              LOUISE
                         (as she goes)
                    ... I'll get you some eggs.

     Chance nods in approval, then changes the channel on the TV.

8.   INT. TOWN HOUSE - SERVANT'S STAIRWAY - MORNING

     An enclosed stairway. Chance enters, proceeds up the stairs.

9.   INT. TOWN HOUSE - UPSTAIRS HALLWAY - MORNING

     Chance comes out of the doorway adjoining the main stair-case.
     He moves off down the hall.

10. INT. TOWN HOUSE - OLD MAN'S ROOM - MORNING

     The furniture in this room is not covered with sheets -
     but the OLD MAN is. There is a knock at the door, then Chance
     enters the room. He stands by the bed for a moment, then
     reaches down and pulls the sheet back from the Old Man's face.
     He touches the man's forehead, briefly, then replaces the
     sheet. Chance moves to the TV and turns it on. He sits in an
     easy chair next to the Old Man's bed and watches a movie from
     the early forties. Chance puts an arm out, rests it on the Old
     Man's covered body. He becomes absorbed in a scene in which
     a gentleman tips his hat to a lady. The scene seems to have
     'sunk into' his mind.

11. EXT. GARDEN - MORNING

     It has stopped snowing. Chance, wearing a hat, and a gardening
     apron over his suit, putters in the garden. Louise, dressed
     warmly, comes out of the main house. Chance sees her, tips his
     hat exactly like the man he saw on television.

                              LOUISE
                    ... Well, ain't you the gentleman
                    this morning ...
                         (a pause)
                    ... I'm gonna go now, Chance ...

                              CHANCE
                         (resumes working)
                    Yes.

                    LOUISE
          You're gonna need somebody, some
          one's gotta be around for you ...
                (he keeps working)
          ... You oughta find yourself a
          lady, Chance ...
                (she smiles slightly, with
                caring)
          ... But I guess it oughta be an old
          lady, 'cause you ain't gonna do a
          young one any good, not with that
          little thing of yours ...
                (she reaches out, puts a
                hand on his shoulder)
          ... You're always gonna be a little
          boy ain't you?
                (he smiles, keeps working)
          ... Goodbye, Chance ...

Louise hugs and kisses Chance, then turns to go.

                    CHANCE
                (as she goes)
          Goodbye, Louise.

Louise waves as she enters the townhouse. Chance tips his hat once again as she disappears.

12.   INT. TOWN HOUSE - FRONT HALLWAY - MORNING

Louise enters the hallway, picks up a couple of suitcases waiting by the door. She stops as she sees TWO Men carrying a stretcher down the main staircase. A THIRD MAN, a mortician, follows behind.

                    LOUISE
          ... He used to be a big man ...
          'Spose he wasted away to about
          nothin' ...
                (a beat - then she talks
                to the body of the Old Man)
          I guess I'll be goin' off to find
          me some folks, Old Man ... I'm not
          batty enough to stay around this
          neighborhood any longer ...

The stretcher bearers move to the front door. Louise steps in front of them.

                    LOUISE
          Wait up! I'm goin' out that door first.

     Louise takes one more look at the covered body, then opens the
     front door, leaves.

13. EXT. GARDEN - DAY

     Chance's pocketwatch chimes as he looks at it. He removes his
     gardener's apron as he walks toward the townhouse.

14. INT. TOWNHOUSE DINING ROOM.

     Chance enters and sits at his place. He turns on the TV,
     and watches for a moment, then turns, looks for Louise.
     She does not appear so he resumes watching TV. He changes
     channels, views a wildly exciting game show. At a peak in the
     excitement, he again switches channels to news coverage of the
     President of the Unite States greeting foreign dignitaries at
     the White House. CLOSE SHOTS on television reveal that the
     President uses a two-handed handshake when meeting his guests.
     Chance grips one hand with the other, the scene on TV seeming
     to have 'sunk into' his mind.

15. INT. TOWNHOUSE - FRONT HALLWAY - DAY

     A key is heard in the lock. The door opens and THOMAS FRANKLIN
     and SALLY HAYES enter. Franklin, an attorney, is in his
     late thirties, carries a large briefcase. Hayes is younger,
     attractive, also an attorney. She totes a briefcase, has the
     look of a modern woman.

                    FRANKLIN
               (as they enter)
          He and my father used to ride
          together back in the thirties ...
          Fox hunting ... Before I was
          born ...

                    HAYES
               (looking around)
          Will you give me a tour?

                    FRANKLIN
          Gladly ...
               (he smiles)
          ... The safe is in Mr. Jennings's
          bedroom, that'll be stop number one.

Franklin puts a hand on Hayes' shoulder as they go toward the stairway. Suddenly, they stop, listen to the off-stage TV.

16. INT. TOWNHOUSE DINING ROOM - DAY

Chance still watches TV as Franklin and Hayes appear in the doorway. They are surprised to see Chance.

>   FRANKLIN
> ... Why ... Hello, we thought we
> heard something ...
>   (moves to Chance, hand
>   outstretched)
> ... I'm Thomas Franklin.

Chance remains seated, takes Franklin's hand warmly in both of his like the President did on TV.

>   CHANCE
> Hello, Thomas ... I'm Chance, the
> gardener.

>   FRANKLIN
>   (a beat)
> ... The gardener?
>   (thinks it's a joke, laughs)
> ... Yes, of course ... Mr. Chance,
> this is Ms. Hayes.

Hayes moves to shake Chance's hand.

>   HAYES
> Mr. Chance, I'm very pleased to
> meet you.

>   CHANCE
>   (doesn't rise, again
>   shakes with both hands)
> Yes.

Chance turns back to the TV. Hayes and Franklin exchange looks, there is an uneasy pause.

>   FRANKLIN
> We're with Franklin, Jennings and
> Roberts, the law firm handling the
> estate.

                    CHANCE
               (a smile, totally at ease)
          Yes, Thomas - I understand.

                    FRANKLIN
          ... Are you waiting for someone? An
          appointment?

                    CHANCE
          I'm waiting for my lunch.

                    FRANKLIN
          Your lunch? You have a luncheon
          appointment here?

                    CHANCE
          Louise will bring my lunch.

                    FRANKLIN
          Louise? ... The maid? ...
               (a look to Hayes)
          But she should have left earlier
          today ...

                    CHANCE
               (smiles at Hayes)
          I see ...

                    FRANKLIN
               (a beat)
          All kidding aside, Mr. Chance, may
          I ask just what you are doing
          here?

                    CHANCE
          I live here.

     Franklin stares at Chance as Hayes unzips her briefcase.

17. EXT. GARDEN - AFTERNOON

     Chance talks to Franklin as Hayes quickly checks through some
     paperwork.

                    CHANCE
          The Old Man himself used to visit
          my garden. He would read and rest
          here.

FRANKLIN
Come now, the deceased ...
    (catches himself)
Mr. Jennings was bedridden for at least the last thirty-five years, since he fractured his spine.

CHANCE
Yes, Thomas. Then he stopped visiting my garden.
    (points to a small area)
I planted a lot of tulips right there. I like to watch them grow.

HAYES
    (looking up from papers)
There is no mention of a gardener. In fact, according to our inventories, there hasn't been a man employed here since 1933 ... except for a Mr. Joe Saracini, a brick mason, who did some repairs to a wall. He was here for two-and-a-half days in 1952.

CHANCE
Yes, I remember Joe. He was very fat and had short hair and showed me pictures from a funny little book.

HAYES
... Some pictures?

CHANCE
Yes. Of men and women.

HAYES
... Oh.

FRANKLIN
Just how long have you been living here, Mr. Chance?

CHANCE
Ever since I can remember, since I was a child. I have always worked in the garden.

                        HAYES
          ...Then you really are a gardener?

                        CHANCE
          Yes.
                (again points off)
          ... My roses ...

                        FRANKLIN
          ... We will need some proof of your
          having resided here, Mr. Chance.

                        CHANCE
          You have me, I am here. What more
          proof do you need?
                (he starts toward rear
                 building, points off)
          That's where Joe fixed the wall.

                        FRANKLIN
                (starts after Chance)
          Are you related to the deceased,
          Mr. Chance?

                        CHANCE
          No. I don't think so.
                (looks back to garden)
          In the springtime, you will be
          able to see my flowers.

     Chance goes into the garage. A perplexed Franklin and Hayes
     follow.

18. INT. GARAGE - AFTERNOON

     Chance enters, Franklin and Hayes close behind.

                        FRANKLIN
                (looking at limo)
          That's a nice car. Do you drive
          it, Mr. Chance?

                        CHANCE
          I've never been in an automobile.

                        HAYES
          You've never been in a car?

                    CHANCE
               Oh, no. I've never been allowed
               outside of the house.

19.   INT. CHANCE'S ROOM - AFTERNOON

       Chance turns on the TV as Hayes and Franklin inspect the room.

                    CHANCE
               I used to listen to the radio,
               then the Old Man started giving me
               television sets, this one
               has a remote control ... I like to
               watch ...
                    (motions to bed)
               You see? This is my bed ...
                    (to closet)
               ... This is my closet ...
                    (to bathroom)
               ... This is my bathroom ...

                    HAYES (goes to closet)
               You have a very handsome wardrobe,
               Mr. Chance.

                    CHANCE
               Yes. I am allowed to go to the
               attic and use the Old Man's
               clothes. They all fit me very
               well.

                    HAYES
               It is amazing how these clothes
               have come back into style.

                    FRANKLIN
               Could you show us something with
               your address? A driver's license,
               a checkbook? Anything to show that
               you were employed here?

                    CHANCE
               I don't have any of those
               things.

                    HAYES
               How about a birth certificate?

                    CHANCE
Oh, no.

                    FRANKLIN
What are your plans now, Mr. Chance?

                    CHANCE
My plans are to work in my garden.

                    HAYES
How much money did Mr. Jennings pay you for your work?

                    CHANCE
Pay me? ... Why nothing. I've never needed money.

                    FRANKLIN
Mr. Chance, I would like to know what sort of claim you are planning to make against the deceased's estate.

                    CHANCE
          (does not understand)
I'm fine, Thomas. The garden is a healthy one. There is no need for a claim.

                    FRANKLIN
I see. Would you be willing to sign a paper to that effect?

                    CHANCE
No, Thomas. I don't know how to sign.

                    FRANKLIN
Come now, Mr. Chance.

                    CHANCE
          (smiles)
I have no claim, Thomas.

                    FRANKLIN
But you won't sign, correct?

CHANCE
Yes, correct, thank you.

FRANKLIN
Very well, Mr. Chance. I have no alternative but to inform you that this house is now closed. If indeed, you have resided here, you have no legal right to remain. You will have to move out.

CHANCE
Move out? I don't understand, Thomas.

FRANKLIN
I think you do, Mr. Chance. However, I will reiterate. This house is closed and you must leave -- by, let's say - noon tomorrow.
    (he gives Chance his
    business card)
Call me if you change your mind about signing.
    (turns to Hayes)
C'mon, Sally - let's grab a bite ...

HAYES
    (stops by the door)
What about medical records? Could you give us the name of your doctor? Or your dentist?

CHANCE
I have no need for a doctor or dentist. I have never been ill.

HAYES
    (a smile to Chance)
I see ... Well, good day, Mr. Chance.

CHANCE
    (returns smile)
Good day, Sally.

Chance watches as they leave, then puts Franklin's card on a desk without ever looking at it and turns to stare at television.

20. INT. TOWNHOUSE - ATTIC - AFTERNOON

    A large attic filled with the Old Man's possessions of the past. Chance enters, turns on an old black-and-white TV with a magnifying lens attached to the front. As it plays, he selects a fine leather suitcase from several, takes a hand-made suit from a long rack.

21. INT. CHANCE'S ROOM - AFTERNOON

    The TV is on as Chance packs his belongings. He tries to fit in his umbrella, but it is too long for the suitcase.

22. EXT. GARDEN - AFTERNOON

    Chance, very nicely dressed, with his suitcase and umbrella, stands in the middle of the garden looking around.

23. INT. TOWNHOUSE - FRONT HALLWAY - AFTERNOON

    Chance is reluctant to open the front door. After some hesitation, he gathers up his courage, opens it and steps outside, closing the door behind him.

24. EXT. FRONT OF TOWNHOUSE - WASHINGTON, D.C. - AFTERNOON

    Chance stops short on the steps; the front of the townhouse is run down and the yard filled with trash. He tries to return to the safety of inside, but the door is locked. Chance stays on the steps for a moment, ponders which way to go. Making a decision, he steps to the sidewalk and walks down the street to reveal a decaying ghetto. Windows are shattered or boarded up, walls are smeared with grafitti [*sic*]. Chance passes a group of black people huddled together in threadbare stuffed furniture on the sidewalk, a fire burning between them for warmth. Chance nods politely to the people; they stare back, no sign of friendship in their faces.

25. EXT. GHETTO STREET - WASHINGTON, D.C. - AFTERNOON

    Chance walks along a ghetto sidewalk. He notices something, moves across the street toward a gang of eight to ten hardcore ghetto youths.

26.   EXT. GHETTO STREET - WASHINGTON, D.C. - AFTERNOON

Chance approaches the gang.

> CHANCE
> (friendly)
> ... Excuse me, would you please tell me where I could find a garden to work in?

They turn to him as one, silent. After a moment, LOLO, one of the gang, speaks.

> LOLO
> What you growin', man?

> CHANCE
> There is much to be done during the winter, I must start the seeds for the spring, I must work the soil ...

The leader of the gang, ABBAZ, moves forward and interrupts.

> ABBAZ
> Bullshit. Who sent you here, boy? Did that chickenshit asshole Raphael send you here, boy?

> CHANCE
> No. Thomas Franklin told me that I had to leave the Old Man's house, he's dead now, you know ...

> ABBAZ
> Dead, my ass! Now get this, honkie - you go tell Raphael that I ain't takin' no jive from no Western Union messenger! You tell that asshole, if he got somethin' to tell me to get his ass down here himself!
> (edges closer to Chance)
> You got that boy?

During this, as Abbaz becomes more hostile, Chance reaches into his pocket, takes out his remote control TV changer. He points the changer at Abbaz and clicks it three times, tries to change the picture. ABBAZ immediately pulls out a switchblade knife, holds it at Chance.

>   ABBAZ
>   Now, move, honkie! Before I cut
>   your white ass.

Chance, disappointed that the changer did not work, returns it to his pocket.

>   CHANCE
>   Yes. I understand. If I see
>   Raphael, I will tell him.
>   (as he leaves)
>   Good day.

Abbaz, Lolo and the gang watch him go, then begin to buzz with excitement: "Who the fuck died?" "Why'd he pull that changer on us, man?" "The Old Man died, must be Papa Joe!" "He's some weird honkie, man!"

27. EXT. PORNO AREA - WASHINGTON, D.C. - AFTERNOON

A street lined with adult book stores, X-rated movies and strip joints. An elderly Black Woman approaches carrying a
bag of groceries. Chance steps in front of the woman, stops her.

>   CHANCE
>   I'm very hungry now. Would you
>   please bring my lunch?

The woman looks up to Chance, becomes very frightened. She turns and half-runs into a sleazy bar for safety. Chance watches after her for a moment, then continues along.

28. EXT. PARK - WASHINGTON, D.C. - AFTERNOON

Chance stands looking through a chain-link fence watching some teenage boys playing basketball. He bangs on the fence, calls to them.

>   CHANCE
>   I have seen your game! I have
>   watched Elvin Hayes play it many
>   times! They call him 'Big E!'

The boys ignore him, Chance walks away.

29. EXT. - WASHINGTON, D.C. - LATE AFTERNOON

   Chance seems stumped on which way to walk. He looks one way, then the other, turns and looks behind him and sees a large statue of Benito Juarez pointing. Chance smiles and goes off in the direction that Benito points.

30. EXT. WASHINGTON, D.C. - LATE AFTERNOON

   Chance walks down the center meridian of a divided street. He seems oblivious to the automobiles passing on either side. In the background can be seen the Capitol Building.

31. EXT. REAR OF THE WHITE HOUSE - DUSK

   Chance is across the street from the White House, inspecting the branches of a potted tree. He moves to a POLICEMAN standing nearby.

                    CHANCE
         Excuse me ...
              (points to tree)
         ... That tree is very sick. It
         should be cared for.

   The Policeman looks at the tree, then at Chance, figures a man dressed that well must be important.

                    POLICEMAN
         Yes sir. I'll report it right
         away.

                    CHANCE
         Yes. That would be a good thing to
         do. Good day.

                    POLICEMAN
         Good day.

   The Policeman takes out his walkie-talkie as Chance leaves.

32. EXT. BUSINESS DISTRICT - EVENING

   A fashionable area. Expensive shops, well-kept streets and sidewalks. Chance stands by the display window of a TV store, looks in at a dozen or so color TVs, all turned on, playing various channels. A video camera points outward and is focused on the sidewalk to allow passersby to see themselves live on TV. Chance is intrigued by his own image. He poses, then steps back off the curb, frowns as his likeness disappears from the frame. Standing between two parked cars, Chance takes out his remote control, clicks it at the store. Four or five other sets in the window change channels, but he does not reappear on the giant screen. As he does this, the car to his left, a large, American-made limousine, backs up. The limo bumps Chance, pins him against the car to his right. Chance cries out in pain, drops his suitcase, his umbrella, his changer, and bangs his hand on the trunk of the limo. The chauffeur, DAVID, and the liveryman, JEFFREY, immediately jump from the car, run back to Chance.

>   DAVID
>   I'm very sorry, sir ... I ...

David and Jeffrey reach out to help, but Chance is wedged solidly between the two cars.

>   CHANCE
>   (in pain)
>   ... I can't move ... My leg ...

>   DAVID
>   (rushes back to limo)
>   ... My Lord ...

>   JEFFREY
>   This is terrible, sir - I hope
>   you're not badly injured ...

>   CHANCE
>   No. I'm not badly injured. But my
>   leg is very sore.

David pulls the car forward, freeing Chance. A few bystanders begin to gather as Jeffrey helps Chance to the sidewalk.

>   JEFFREY
>   Can you walk? It's not broken, is
>   it?

>   CHANCE
>   (leans against limo, holds leg)
>   I hope not.

                    DAVID
                (returning)
            Perhaps I should call an
            ambulance.

            A BYSTANDER interrupts.

                    BYSTANDER
            Somebody ought to call the police!

                    CHANCE
                (looks over, smiles)
            There's no need for police, it's
            just my leg.

During this, the rear door of the limo opens and EVE RAND
steps out. Eve is in her mid-thirties, and is rich. She is not
pleased with this inconvenience

                    JEFFREY
            Let's have a look, do you mind?

                    CHANCE
            Of course. I would like to look.

Chance bends, raises his trouser leg. A red-bluish swollen
bruise is forming on his calf. Eve moves closer, looks at the
bruise.

                    EVE
                (to Chance)
            ... Won't you let us do something
            for you? Your leg should be
            examined, we could take you to a
            hospital.

                    CHANCE
                (smiles at Eve)
            There's no need for a hospital.

                    EVE
            Why, there certainly is. You must
            see a doctor, I insist on it.
            Please, let us take you.

Eve turns to get back in the limo. David goes with her to hold
the door.

                    DAVID
          I'm terribly sorry, Mrs. Rand, I
          never saw the man.

                    EVE
          Oh, I don't think it was anyone's
          fault, David.

                    DAVID
          Thank you, ma'am.

Jeffrey holds the door open but Chance is hesitant about getting in the car.

                    CHANCE
          I've never ridden in an
          automobile.

                    JEFFREY
               (a beat)
          I assure you, sir, David is a very
          careful driver.

                    CHANCE
               (looks at the car, then
                decides)
          ... Yes. You can take me.

                    JEFFREY
               (as Chance gets in)
          Very good.

Jeffrey closes the door, goes back to pick up Chance's suitcase and umbrella but does not notice the remote control. As Jeffrey puts Chance's bag into the trunk, we see the personalized license plate "Rand 1."

33.   INT. LIMOUSINE MOVING THROUGH TOWN - EVENING

Chance and Eve are settled in the back seat. As they talk, Chance is experiencing his first ride in a car.

                    EVE
          I hope you're comfortable.

                    CHANCE
          Yes, I am.

                    EVE
          These situations can be so trying
          - everybody seems to make such a
          to-do over a simple little
          accident ...
                (eyes Chance)
          ... the insurance, police, the news
          and all ... Is your leg feeling any
          better?

                    CHANCE
          No, it isn't.

                    EVE
          I see.

Chance looks out the window at passing cars.

                    CHANCE
          It looks very much like television
          but you can see further.

                    EVE
                (not hearing him)
          Say - if you came to our house, we
          could take care of you there.

                    CHANCE
          Your house?

                    EVE
          Yes. My husband has been very ill.
          His doctor and nurses are staying
          with us. Those hospitals can be so
          impersonal - why, it might be
          hours before you are treated ...

                    CHANCE
          I agree.

                    EVE
          Fine, it will save a lot of
          unnecessary fuss and it will be so
          much more pleasant for you ...
                (leans forward)

>   David, we'll just go on home.
>   Jeffrey, would you call and let
>   them know?
>
>   JEFFREY
>   Yes ma'am.

Jeffrey closes the glass between them, then dials the limo telephone. There is a moment of silence. Eve, a bit uncomfortable, presses a button. The limo's bar moves out, revealing a row of decanters and glasses.

>   EVE
>   Would you care for a drink?
>
>   CHANCE
>   Yes. Thank you. I am very thirsty.

As Eve pours cognac into a monogrammed crystal glass, Chance notices the limo's TV set.

>   CHANCE
>   I would like to watch television.
>
>   EVE
>   (a bit surprised)
>   Oh? Certainly ...

She hands Chance the cognac, turns on the TV.

>   EVE
>   May I ask your name?

Chance takes a sip of the cognac, is not accustomed to alcohol, coughs.

>   CHANCE
>   (with a slight cough)
>   My name is Chance.
>
>   EVE
>   Pardon me, was that Mr. Chance?
>
>   CHANCE
>   No, I'm a gardener.

                    EVE
          Oh ... Mr. Gardiner ... Mr. Chauncey
          Gardiner ... You're not related to
          Basil and Perdita Gardiner are you?

                    CHANCE
          No ... I'm not related to Basil
          and Perdita.

                    EVE
          Oh. Well, they're just a wonderful
          couple, we've been friends for
          years. We visit their island quite
          often.

Chance suddenly starts going through his pockets, searching.

                    EVE
          Did you lose something?

                    CHANCE
          Yes. I lost my remote control.

                    EVE
          Oh ... Well, I'm very sorry ...

Another pause, Chance reaches out, changes channels on TV.

34.   EXT. HIGHWAY - WOODED AREA - NIGHT

The limo approaches, then turns into the entranceway of the Rand Estate. Two guards stand on either side of the open gate, salute as the car passes through.

35.   INT. LIMOUSINE - NIGHT

As Eve speaks, Chance is glued to the TV, switches channels to the news.

                    EVE
          Is there anything special you like
          to watch?

                    CHANCE
          I like to watch. This is fine.

                        EVE
                I know it's very important to stay
                informed of all the latest events,
                but I find there is so much to
                assimilate that it can become
                quite muddling at times ...

   Chance nods, changes the channel, watches a Mighty
   Mouse cartoon. Eve takes it for a small joke and smiles
   patronizingly.

36.   EXT. RAND MANSION - NIGHT

   At least three uniformed people, two valets, WILSON and
   PERKINS, and LEWIS, the Doorman, are waiting at the front of
   the Rand Mansion as the limousine arrives. There is a general
   hubbub as the three of them, along with Jeffrey, help Chance
   into a wheelchair.

37.   INT. RAND MANSION - FRONT HALLWAY - NIGHT

   As the group comes through the front doors, Wilson is
   wheeling Chance. A uniformed woman, GRETA, is waiting to take
   Eve's coat.

                        EVE
                   (to Wilson)
                You take Mr. Gardiner to the third
                floor guest suite.

                        EVE
                   (to Chance)
                I'll see you after Dr. Allenby has
                a look at your leg.

                        CHANCE
                Yes, I think he should examine my
                leg.

   Eve heads off partially revealing a remarkable and large place to
   live in as Wilson wheels Chance into the elevator.

38.   INT. ELEVATOR - NIGHT

   As the door closes on them, Chance looks to Wilson.

                    CHANCE
          ... I've never been in one of
          these.

Wilson thinks that Chance is talking about the wheelchair.

                    WILSON
          It's one of Mr. Rand's. Since he's
          been ill ...

                    CHANCE
              (looks around elevator)
          Does it have a television?

                    WILSON
              (laughs)
          No - but Mr. Rand does have one
          with an electric motor, that way
          he can get around by himself.

                    CHANCE
          I see.

Chance again checks out the elevator.

                    CHANCE
          How long do we stay in here?

                    WILSON
          How long? I don't know, see what
          the doctor says ...

The elevator stops on the third floor.

39.   INT. RAND MANSION - PALM COURT - NIGHT

Eve is talking to ROBERT ALLENBY. He is in his late fifties and has been Benjamin Rand's doctor for years.

                    EVE
          I pray that I did the right thing,
          Robert. I didn't want to take the
          risk of any publicity, especially
          with Benjamin being so ill.

                    ALLENBY
          I'm sure you did, Eve. But let's
          just hope he's not one of those
          opportunists that try and make a
          fortune out of every little
          bruise.

                    EVE
          Well, I'm sure we could make a
          settlement if we had to, but I'd
          rather not - find out what you
          can, I'm going to change.

                    ALLENBY
               (as she goes)
          Ben's been asking about you ...

                    EVE
               (over her shoulder)
          I'll see him soon.

Allenby watches after her for a beat, then turns, goes off in
the other direction.

40.   INT. GUEST SUITE - NIGHT

An enormous bedroom, filled with 18th Century antique
furniture. Allenby dabs Chance's ass with a piece of cotton
soaked in alcohol, prior to an injection. Chance stands with
his pants to the floor, looks to the television which is not
turned on.

                    ALLENBY
          This will ease the pain and
          swelling, Mr. Gardiner.

                    CHANCE
          I understand. I've seen it done
          before.

                    ALLENBY
          Now, you'll barely feel this. It
          won't hurt at all.

Allenby administers the injection, Chance reacts from
the pain.

                    CHANCE
          You were wrong, it did hurt.

                    ALLENBY
               (a chuckle)
          But not for long ...

As Allenby puts a band-aid [sic] on Chance's ass, Chance spots a remote control for the TV on the bedside table. He reaches out, picks it up.

                    ALLENBY
          It's good that there was no
          apparent damage to the bone.

                    CHANCE
          Yes. I think so, too.

                    ALLENBY
          There could be minor hemorrhaging,
          which really isn't too serious at
          the time, but can cause secondary
          problems if not looked after.

                    CHANCE
               (turns on TV)
          I see.

                    ALLENBY
               (a look to the TV, then to
               Chance)
          You can pull your trousers up,
          now.

                    CHANCE
          Oh, fine.

                    ALLENBY
          Just to take the proper
          precautions, Mr. Gardiner, I'd
          recommend we take you downstairs
          and X-Ray your leg.

There is no reaction from Chance, Allenby takes a long look at him.

                    ALLENBY
          ... By the way, Mr. Gardiner, I
          would like to ask you something
          straight out.

                    CHANCE
               (doesn't understand)
          ... Straight out?

                    ALLENBY
          Yes. Are you planning on making
          any sort of claim against the
          Rand's?

                    CHANCE
               (after a beat)
          Claim ...? ... Oh, claim, that's
          what Thomas asked me.

                    ALLENBY
          Thomas? Who's Thomas?

                    CHANCE
          Thomas Franklin, an attorney.

                    ALLENBY
          An attorney?

                    CHANCE
               (turns to TV)
          Yes.

                    ALLENBY
               (suddenly very cold)
          Then you wish to handle this
          matter through your attorneys?

                    CHANCE
          There's no need for a claim, the
          garden is a healthy one.

                    ALLENBY
               (gives Chance a look)
          Oh, I see ...
               (laughs)
          ... Well, then ... You caught me off
          guard, I must admit ...

                    CHANCE
                (changes channels, sits on
                bed)
            Thank you.

                    ALLENBY
            Good, keep your weight off that
            leg, Mr. Gardiner. In fact, it
            would be best if you could stay
            here for a day or two, if that
            would be possible. I can promise
            you the finest in care.

                    CHANCE
            Yes, I could stay here. Does this
            house have a garden?

                    ALLENBY
            ... Why, yes - many

Allenby picks up his bag, heads for the door.

                    ALLENBY
            I'll send Wilson up to take you
            for X-Rays, Mr. Gardiner. Feel
            free to use the telephone, and
            please let me know if you have any
            discomfort.

                    CHANCE
                (clicking changer)
            Yes, I will.

Allenby gives him a look, then leaves. Chance watches an old movie of a man lighting a cigar. The man enjoys the cigar, blows out smoke. The scene seems to 'sink into' Chance's mind.

41.   INT. EVE'S BEDROOM/SITTING ROOM - NIGHT

Allenby enters to reveal Eve standing in front of large double windows that are wide open. She is wearing different clothes, different hair.

                    ALLENBY
            Good God, Eve - you'll freeze.

                    EVE
          I wanted some fresh air. How is
          Mr. Gardiner?

                    ALLENBY
          A rather large contusion, but
          there isn't any ...

                    EVE
               (interrupts)
          That's not what I meant, Robert.

                    ALLENBY
               (a beat)
          Okay ... Well - he seemed to be a
          most reasonable man, I don't think
          he'll cause any trouble.

                    EVE
          Thank God for that.

                    ALLENBY
          I'd like to keep an eye on him,
          though - I suggested that he stay
          here for a couple of days.

                    EVE
          Stay here? Is that necessary?

                    ALLENBY
          Not necessary, but preferable.
          Don't worry, Eve - he might be a
          breath of fresh air ...

                    EVE
               (a beat)
          ... Yes, he is different ... He's
          very intense, and internal, don't
          you think?

                    ALLENBY
          Perhaps ... Actually, I found him
          to have quite a sense of humor.

                    EVE
          Good. It might be pleasant for a
          couple of days. ...

Eve is silent for a moment, looks out to the darkness.

>   EVE
>   I guess I should go see Ben now.
>   (turns)
>   I'll see you at dinner.
>   Eve leaves the room.

42. INT. RAND'S CONVERTED BEDROOM - NIGHT

Eve enters through heavy glass doors. BENJAMIN RAND, wearing a silk bathrobe, lies on a king-sized bed to one side of the room. Rand perks up as he sees Eve crossing to him. He is in his sixties, maintains an inner strength and dignity despite the sapping effects of his illness.

>   RAND
>   (with weakness)
>   ... Eve ...

Eve kisses him, holds his hand.

>   EVE
>   (with conviction)
>   Oh, Ben - I do miss you when I'm
>   out ... How are you feeling?

>   RAND
>   Tired ... And I'm getting tired of
>   being tired. Other than that, I'm
>   doing very well.

>   EVE
>   I'm so glad ... No headaches?

>   RAND
>   No, it's been a good day - better
>   than yours, from what I've been
>   told.

>   EVE
>   You heard?

>   RAND
>   I may be a shut-in, but I do not
>   lack for news. I'm sorry you had
>   to go through all that.

                    EVE
          Oh, it wasn't all that bad
          darling. We were fortunate that
          Mr. Gardiner turned out to be so
          reasonable.

                    RAND
          Reasonable? Good, I'd like to meet
          a reasonable man. Why don't you
          ask this Gardiner to join us for
          dinner?

                    EVE
          For dinner? Are you well enough
          for that?

                    RAND
               (smiles)
          Hah! ... Tell me the truth, Eve -
          if I wait until I feel better,
          will I ever meet the man?
               (Eve is silent)
          Constance!

CONSTANCE, in a nurse's uniform, appears in a side
doorway.

                    RAND
          Constance! I want new blood
          tonight, I'm getting up for
          dinner.

                    CONTANCE
          But, Mr. Rand ...

                    RAND
          Don't argue, tell Robert I want
          new blood!
               (turns to Eve)
          ... Ask him to dinner.

Rand pulls Eve's hand close, kisses it.

                    EVE
               (after a beat)
          ... I ran into Senator Jansen at
          lunch today and he all but ignored

me ... And it's starting to happen
a lot lately ... since you've been
sick.

              RAND
Dammit, there's no excuse for
that. I'll call him tomorrow.

              EVE
Thank you, darling.

43.   INT. RAND MANSION - FIRST FLOOR HALLWAY - NIGHT

The elevator door opens to reveal Wilson with Chance in the
wheelchair.

              CHANCE
        (as Wilson wheels him out)
... That is a very small room.

              WILSON
        (laughs)
Yes sir, I guess that's true -
smallest room in the house.

              CHANCE
        (glancing around)
Yes. It seems to be.

Wilson takes this as another joke, chuckles as he wheels
Chance toward Rand's hospital room.

44.   INT. RAND'S HOSPITAL ROOM - NIGHT

A glass-enclosed room, next to Rand's bedroom, filled with
the very latest in hospital emergency equipment. CONSTANCE
and another nurse, TERESA, stand by as Rand is being given a
transfusion. Rand lifts his head as Wilson wheels Chance into
the room.

              RAND
Welcome to Rand Memorial Hospital,
Mr. Gardiner.

              CHANCE
        (looks around room)
... I see.

Wilson pushes Chance to the X-Ray machine, where BILLINGS, a Black technician helps him onto the table.

                CHANCE
           (inhales deeply)
I feel very good in here.

                RAND
That's the oxygen! When I first got sick I had it all glassed in so I could have a little extra oxygen pumped in, keeps my spirits up.

Chance is now flat on his back as Billings lines up the X-Ray camera.

                CHANCE
You must be very sick.

                RAND
Aplastic anemia, Mr. Gardiner - aplastic anemia. Failure of the bone marrow to produce red blood cells ... Not a damn thing they can do about it. Oh, they can make me comfortable, prolong my life with steroid therapy and transfusions ... But what makes my blood boil, what little I have left, that is, Mr. Gardiner - is that it's generally a young person's disease ... Here I am, getting on in years and about to die of a young person's disease ...

                CHANCE
           (smiles at Rand)
I've never seen anything like this on television.

                BILLINGS
Please, hold still, Mr. Gardiner.

                CONSTANCE
You too, Mr. Rand, you must stay quiet.

                    RAND
          (lays his head back)
     ... You will join us for dinner,
     won't you, Mr. Gardiner?

                    CHANCE
     Yes. I am very hungry.

                    RAND
     ... So am I, my boy - so am I.

Chance stares at Billings, reacts to him being black.

                    CHANCE
     Do you know Raphael?

                    BILLINGS
     No sir, I don't believe I do.

                    CHANCE
     Oh. I have a message for him.

                    BILLINGS
     Yes, sir.

                    CHANCE
     A black man gave me the message.

                    BILLINGS
     Well, I still don't believe I know
     the man, Mr. Gardiner. Now, please
     hold still.

45.   INT. RAND DINING ROOM - NIGHT

The dining room is immense, a 75-foot ceiling, huge fireplaces. Allenby, Eve, Rand and Chance (both in wheelchairs) sit around the table. THURMAND, a waiter, and MARIANNE, a waitress, enter carrying trays of food. Eve turns to Chance.

                    EVE
     I do hope your injury won't
     prevent you from attending to
     business, Mr. Gardiner?

CHANCE
No. It won't do that.

EVE
... Would you like us to notify anyone for you?

CHANCE
No. The Old Man died and Louise left.

EVE
Oh. I'm very sorry. Well, if you have a need for any of our facilities, please don't hesitate to ask.

RAND
Do you need a secretary?

CHANCE
No, thank you. My house has been closed.

RAND
Oh, you mean to say that your business was shut down.

CHANCE
Yes. Shut down and locked by the attorneys.

RAND
What'd I tell you? ... I know exactly what you mean. Today the businessman is at the mercy of kid-lawyers from the SEC. All they want to do is regulate our natural growth!

ALLENBY
It's happening to everyone, I'm afraid. The way things are going they'll probably legislate the Medical Profession, as we know it, right out of existence.

CHANCE
Yes. Right out of existence.

RAND
And it's a damn shame - it's all happening too fast ...
    (sighs)
What are your plans now, Mr. Gardiner? Or may I call you Chauncey?

CHANCE
Yes. Chauncey is fine.

RAND
And I'm Ben.

ALLENBY
    (smiles to Chance)
Robert.

EVE
    (also smiles)
... Eve.

RAND
So tell me, Chauncey, just what are your plans?

CHANCE
I would like to work in your garden.

EVE
    (laughs)
Oh, I know exactly what you mean. I sometimes enjoy puttering around myself, such a pleasant way to forget one's troubles.

RAND
I never had a feel for it myself ... But, Eve - why don't you show Chauncey our gardens tomorrow ...

                    (to Chance)
          They're quite lovely.

                    EVE
          Well, it'll have to wait until I
          get back from Boston ...
          Unfortunately, my morning will be
          taken up by another one of those
          charity events.

                    CHANCE
          I am a very good gardener.

                    RAND
          Isn't that what a businessman is?
          A gardener? A person that makes
          flinty soil productive with the
          labor of his own hands, who waters
          it with sweat from his own brow,
          and who creates a place of value
          for his family and community? Yes,
          indeed, Chauncey, a productive
          businessman is a laborer in his
          own vineyard.

                    CHANCE
          I know exactly what you mean, Ben.
          The garden that I left was such a
          place. But I don't have that any
          more ...
               (points to ceiling)
          ... All that's left for me now is
          the room upstairs.

                    RAND
          Now, wait a minute, Chauncey – you
          have your health ... for God's sake
          don't give up on yourself! You
          have to fight! You can't let those
          bastards keep you down! I don't
          want to hear any more from you
          about the 'Room Upstairs.' That's
          where I'm going soon.

There is a long pause. Chance looks up, then smiles at Rand.

                    CHANCE
           It's a very pleasant room, Ben.

                    RAND
               (laughs)
           Yes, I'm sure it is. That's what
           they say, anyway.

Another period of silence. The servants bustle around the room as Allenby studies Chance.

46.   INT. RAND'S POOL ROOM - NIGHT

Allenby is shooting pool. Rand is offering Chance a cigar from a humidor.

                    RAND
           Have one of these, Chauncey -
           they're Cuban.

                    CHANCE
           Thank you, Ben.

Chance examines the cigar, does not see Rand clip the end of his own.

                    RAND
           It's one thing Robert can't keep
           me from. I've enjoyed a cigar as
           long as I can remember.

Rand turns the cigar clipper to Chance. As Chance tries to figure out the clipper, the flame from an ornate lighter catches his eye and Chance watches intently as Rand lights his own cigar.

                    RAND
           ... You know, Chauncey, there are
           thousands of American businessmen,
           large and small, that share your
           plight. I've been concerned with
           the situation for some time now.
               (hands lighter to Chance)
           ... I'd like to offer the decent
           'gardeners' of the community a
           helping hand. They've been

>   harrassed [*sic*] long enough by
>   inflation, excessive taxation,
>   unions, all sorts of indecencies ...

Allenby watches Chance as he first tries to light the lighter, then tries to light the unclipped cigar.

>   RAND (cont'd)
>   After all, they are our strongest
>   defense against the pollutants
>   that threaten our basic freedoms
>   and the well-being of our middle
>   class. So I've been thinking about
>   beginning a financial assistance
>   fund ... Tell me, Chauncey, would
>   you have any thoughts on such a
>   program?
>
>   CHANCE
>   (puffing, trying to light cigar)
>   No, Ben.
>
>   RAND
>   (a smile)
>   Reluctant to speak, eh, Chauncey?
>   Well, I can understand that. When
>   a man loses everything, anger has
>   a tendency to block out reason for
>   a time. Just give it some thought,
>   work with the idea, I'm sure
>   you'll have plenty to say in a few
>   days.

Chance puts the unlit cigar in the ashtray, smiles at a most curious Allenby.

47.   INT. MANSION - ELEVATOR - NIGHT

Wilson stands behind Chance in the wheelchair. Chance glances slowly around the elevator. Suddenly, Wilson breaks out into laughter.

>   WILSON
>   ... Sorry, sir ... I thought you
>   were going to come out with

                    another one of your jests about
                    the elevator ... Excuse me, sir ...
                    The elevator stops, the door
                    opens.

48.   INT. MANSION - THIRD FLOOR HALLWAY - NIGHT

        Wilson wheels Chance out of the elevator.

                              CHANCE
                    ... Hmmm ... Elevator.

                              WILSON
                         (laughs again)
                    ... Yes sir - elevator!

        Wilson stops laughing as he notices Eve coming toward
        them.

                              EVE
                    Chauncey, I wanted to tell you how
                    dreadful I feel about your leg,
                    but how delighted I am that you
                    are staying with us.

                              CHANCE
                    Thank you, Eve - I like this house
                    very much.

                              EVE
                    ... And Ben is just mad about you -
                    you've lifted his spirits so -
                    it's just ... Well, it's just a
                    real pleasure, your being here ...

                              CHANCE
                    Ben is very ill, Eve - I've seen
                    that before.

                              EVE
                    Yes ... I know Chauncey.

                              CHANCE
                    I like Ben very much ... He re-
                    minds me of the Old Man ...

                         EVE
              He does ...?

                        CHANCE
              Yes. Are you going to leave and
              close the house when he dies?

Eve is not prepared for such a question.

                         EVE
              ... Why ... No, I don't think so ...

                        CHANCE
              That's good.

Chance smiles at Eve and there is a moment of silence before Eve moves away.

                         EVE
              ... Good night, Chauncey.

                        CHANCE
              Good night, Eve.

Wilson wheels Chance toward the guest room.

49.   EXT. FRONT OF RAND MANSION - MORNING

Chance comes out of the front door, walking with a limp for his first view of the Rand grounds. The attendant, Lewis, hurries to Chance.

                        LEWIS
              Did you want a car, sir?

                        CHANCE
              Yes. I would like a car.

                        LEWIS
              Yes, sir.

Lewis goes to his post, picks up a phone. As Chance looks at the surroundings, Allenby and Wilson, with Chance's wheelchair, come out of the house.

                       ALLENBY
              Chauncey, there you are. What are
              you doing on that leg?

                    CHANCE
          It's fine today, Robert.

                    ALLENBY
          Shame on you, Chauncey - you
          should let me be the judge of
          that. Please, sit in the chair.

Wilson pushes a wheelchair to Chance, he sits.

                    ALLENBY
               (checks leg)
          I swear, Chauncey, between you and
          Benjamin, I've got my hands
          full ...
               (examines Chance's calf)
          ... Say, that is coming along, the
          swelling has gone down
          considerably ...

A limousine pulls up to the front of the mansion, waits for Chance.

                    ALLENBY
               (continues examining)
          ... Benjamin has been hounding me
          to allow him to address the annual
          convention of his Financial
          Institute today, but obviously,
          the strain would be impossible ...
          How about here, Chauncey, any
          soreness?

                    CHANCE
          Hardly any, Robert.

Lewis, the attendant, interrupts.

                    LEWIS
          Your limousine, sir.

                    CHANCE
          Oh, thank you.

                    ALLENBY
          ... Are you going somewhere?

                    CHANCE
          No, Robert.

                    ALLENBY
            (a beat)
    ... Oh ... Anyway, the President
    offered to sit in for Ben at the
    convention, quite a nice gesture.
    He's due here soon, I believe.

                    CHANCE
    Yes, Robert. I know about the
    President.

                    ALLENBY
            (mildly surprised)
    ... Oh? You've heard?

                    CHANCE
    Yes. Ben called me. He wants me to
    meet the President.

                    ALLENBY
    He does, does he?

                    CHANCE
    Yes, Ben asked me to be in his
    room at ten o'clock.

                    ALLENBY
    Why, that's terrific, Chauncey.

                    CHANCE
    How do I know when it's ten
    o'clock?

A long reaction from Allenby, then he looks at his watch.

                    ALLENBY
    ... It's five of, you'd best get on
    in there.

                    CHANCE
    Thank you, Robert. Wilson begins
    to push Chance.

                    CHANCE
    I would like to walk today.

                    ALLENBY
          Hell yes - walk. You're meeting
          the President, aren't you?

                    CHANCE
              (gets out of chair)
          Yes. I like to watch him on
          television.

Allenby, a bit puzzled, watches as Wilson opens the front door for Chance.

50.   INT. RAND'S ROOM - MORNING

Rand is in an easy chair, dressed for his meeting with the President. The two nurses are nearby. Rand smiles as Chance is shown into the room by Wilson.

                    RAND
          Chauncey, up and around this
          morning, are you?

                    CHANCE
          Yes, Ben. I like to walk.

                    RAND
          Well, that's good news, my boy.

                    CHANCE
          You're looking much better today,
          Ben.

                    RAND
          Hah! It's all makeup, Chauncey ...
          I asked nurse Teresa to fix me up,
          I didn't want the President to
          think I was going to die during
          our talk.

                    CHANCE
          I understand.

                    RAND
          No one likes a dying man, my boy -
          because few know what death is.
          All we know is the terror of it.

                    But you're an exception, Chauncey
                    - that's what I admire in you,
                    your marvelous balance. You don't
                    stagger back and forth between
                    fear and hope - you're a truly
                    peaceful man.

                              CHANCE
                    Thank you, Ben.
                         (looks at Rand closely)
                    ... Nurse Teresa did a very good
                    job, Ben.

          The nurses turn, look at Chance.

51.   INT. RAND MANSION - THIRD FLOOR HALLWAY - MORNING

          Allenby gets off the elevator, stands and thinks for a
          moment, then heads off down the hallway in the direction of
          Chance's room.

52.   EXT. FRONT RAND MANSION - MORNING

          Perkins is at the head of eight servants lined up on the front
          steps. Two black PLYMOUTH SEDANS pull up and EIGHT MEN in grey
          business suits get out. One of them, WOLTZ, goes directly to
          Perkins.

                              WOLTZ
                    Good morning, Perkins.

                              PERKINS
                    Good morning, Mr. Woltz, nice to
                    see you again.

                              WOLTZ
                    Thank you. How have you been?

                              PERKINS
                    Fine, thank you.
                         (hands Woltz paper)
                    We have an additional guest with
                    us today, Mr. Chauncey Gardiner.

                        WOLTZ
                    (reads list)
                I see ...
                    (turns to other men)
                Okay, let's go to work.

The eight servants pair up with the eight men in suits and go into the house.

53.   INT. RAND'S ROOM - MORNING

Chance watches television as Rand speaks.

                        RAND
                Yes, when I was younger I had
                thoughts about public office ...
                But I found, Chauncey -- that I
                was able to contribute more as a
                private citizen ... Of course, my
                wealth provided me with
                considerable influence, but I've
                tried, believe me, not to misuse
                that power ... It's extremely
                important, Chauncey, that you
                don't allow yourself to become
                blinded to the needs of the
                country even when the temptations
                are strong. I've been labeled a
                'kingmaker' by many, but I have
                tried to stay open to the voices
                of the people ... I have tried to
                remain honest to myself ...

                        CHANCE
                    (changing channels)
                ... I see, Ben.

54.   INT. RAND MANSION - A HALLWAY - MORNING

One of the servants accompanies Secret Service Agent RIFF as he knocks on each door, checks inside, then moves on.

55.   EXT. FRONT RAND MANSION - MORNING

Lewis picks up his phone and dials as he sees the President's motorcade come through the far gate.

                        LEWIS
                    (into phone)
                The President is arriving now,
                Mrs. Aubrey.

56.   INT. RAND MANSION - MRS. AUBREY'S OFFICE - MORNING

       MRS. AUBREY is Rand's executive secretary, but her office is
       the Nerve Center of Rand Enterprises.

                        MRS. AUBREY
                    (on phone)
                Very good, Lewis, thank you.

       Mrs. Aubrey clicks off, pushes another button.

57.   INT. RAND'S ROOM - MORNING

       Rand smiles at Chance as the phone buzzes.

                        RAND
                He's here.
                    (into phone)
                Yes, Mrs. Aubrey?
                    (listens)
                Fine. Show the President to the
                library, we'll be along in a few
                minutes.

       Rand hangs up the phone, turns to Chance with a twinkle in
       his eyes.

                        RAND
                It's an old habit that goes along
                with power -- keep them waiting ...

       Teresa brings Rand's wheelchair to him.

                        RAND
                    (stands, very week)
                Not now, Teresa. I'm seeing the
                President on my own two feet.

                        TERESA
                But, Mr. Rand ...

                    RAND
               (puts an arm around Chance
               for support)
          Shall we go, Chauncey?

                    CHANCE
          Yes, Ben. That's a good idea.

Rand walks slowly, clings to the limping Chance tightly as they leave the room.

58. EXT. HALLWAY - MORNING

The President and his entourage are seen on their way to the library as Rand and Chance enter and stop in front of Mrs. Aubrey's office.

                    RAND
          Mrs. Aubrey, have you received the
          papers on the Caracas agreement?

                    MRS. AUBREY
          Yes, sir. They're ready for you to
          sign.

                    RAND
          Excellent.
               (as they move away)
          A good woman, Mrs. Aubrey.

                    CHANCE
          I agree, Ben.

They shuffle off down the hallway and are met immediately by Woltz and another agent, Barker. Both carry small metal detectors.

                    WOLTZ
          Good morning, Mr. Rand.

                    RAND
          Woltz ...
               (nods toward Chance)
          This is Mr. Gardiner.

                         WOLTZ
                    (indicates detector)
               Just a formality, Mr. Gardiner.

     Barker passes the detector over Rand as Woltz checks Chance.

                         RAND
               Good thing we're not in our
               wheelchairs, you boys would have a
               devil of a time.

                         CHANCE
                    (as Woltz finishes)
               Thank you very much.

59.   INT. RAND LIBRARY - MORNING

       A somewhat nervous PRESIDENT waits for Rand and Chance. When
       they enter, he goes to Rand with both hands out- stretched.

                         PRESIDENT
               Ben!

                         RAND
               ... Mr. President, how good to see
               you.

                         PRESIDENT
               It's so good to see you too, Ben,
               you look terrific!

                         RAND
                    (with a look to Chance)
               Thank you, Mr. President. Let me
               tell you, your visit has raised my
               spirits ...

                         PRESIDENT
               Well, I've missed you, my friend.
                    (guides Rand to chair)
               Here, sit down, get off your feet.

       As Rand sinks into the chair, Chance approaches the President
       with both hands outstretched.

                    CHANCE
          Good morning, Mr. President.

                    PRESIDENT
               (smiling)
          ... Hello.

                    RAND
          Oh, Mr. President, I'd like you to
          meet my dear friend, Mr. Chauncey
          Gardiner.

Chance and the President exchange a two-handed handshake. The President reacts.

                    CHANCE
          You look much smaller on
          television, Mr. President.

                    PRESIDENT
               (a beat)
          ... Oh, really ...

                    RAND
               (smiling)
          You will find that Chauncey does
          not bandy words, Mr. President.

The President gives Chance a look, then laughs.

                    PRESIDENT
          Well, Mr. Gardiner, that's just
          fine with me - I'm a man that
          appreciates a frank discussion ...
          Be seated, please, Mr. Gardiner ...

                    CHANCE
               (sitting)
          Yes, I will.

                    PRESIDENT
               (also sits)
          Now, Ben, did you happen to get a
          chance to go over ...

Chance reacts to the mention of his name, interrupts.

>   CHANCE
>   Yes?
>
> There is a beat as the President look at Chance quizzically, then he continues.
>
>   PRESIDENT
>   ... I just wonder if you had gone
>   over my speech, Ben.
>
>   RAND
>   Yes, I did.
>
>   PRESIDENT
>   ... Well?
>
>   RAND
>   Overall - pretty good. But,
>   Mr. President, I think it's very
>   dangerous to resort to temporary
>   measures at this stage of the
>   game.
>
>   PRESIDENT
>   Well, Ben ... I ...
>
>   RAND
>   I sympathize with you and, I know
>   how difficult it is to be
>   straightforward, but I'm telling
>   you right now, Bobby - your
>   position on this is going to cause
>   more dissension than you want or
>   might even be able to stand.

60. INT. CHANCE'S ROOM - MORNING

Allenby is searching through Chance's clothes looking for something. There is a knock at the door, Allenby pulls back from the closet as Riff opens the door, looks inside.

>   ALLENBY
>   Oh ... Hello.

                    RIFF
                (entering)
            Good morning. I'm Riff, Secret
            Service.

                    ALLENBY
            ... Yes. Of course.

Allenby spreads his arms as Riff passes the metal detector over him.

61.   INT. LIBRARY - MORNING

The President paces, is worried about what Rand is telling him. Chance smiles through it all.

                    RAND
            ...There is no longer any margin
            for inflation, it has gone as far
            as it can. You've reached your
            limits on taxation, dependence on
            foreign energy is at a point of
            crisis, and, from where I see it,
            Mr. President, the so-called Free
            Enterprise System could be at the
            breaking point.

                    PRESIDENT
            You don't think I should take that
            chance, huh?

                    RAND
            Absolutely not.

Chance has reacted to his name, but doesn't know what to say. The President sits, turns, to Chance.

                    PRESIDENT
            Do you agree with Ben,
            Mr. Gardiner? Or do you think we can
            stimulate growth through temporary
            incentives?

                    CHANCE
                (a beat)
            As long as the roots are not
            severed, all is well and all will
            be well in the garden.

                    PRESIDENT
               (a pause)
     ... In the garden?

                    CHANCE
     That is correct. In a garden,
     growth has its season. There is
     spring and summer, but there is
     also fall and winter. And then
     spring and summer again ...

                    PRESIDENT
               (staring at Chance)
     ... Spring and summer ...
               (confused)
     Yes, I see ... Fall and winter.
               (smiles at Chance)
     Yes, indeed.

                    RAND
               (interrupts)
     I think what my most insightful
     friend is building up to, Mr.
     President, is that we welcome the
     inevitable seasons of nature, yet
     we are upset by the seasons of our
     economy.

                    CHANCE
     Yes. That is correct. There will
     be growth in the spring.

                    PRESIDENT
               (pleased)
     ... Well, Mr. Gardiner, I must
     admit, that is one of the most
     refreshing and optimistic
     statements I've heard in a very,
     very long time.
               (he rises)
     ... I envy your good, solid sense,
     Mr. Gardiner - that is precisely
     what we lack on Capitol Hill.
               (glances at watch)
     I must be going.
               (holds out hand to Chance)
     ... This visit has been most
     enlightening ...

Chance rises and shakes the President's hand.

>   CHANCE
>   Yes. It has.
>
>   PRESIDENT
>   ... You will honor me and my family
>   with a visit, won't you?
>
>   CHANCE
>   Yes. I will.
>
>   PRESIDENT
>   Wonderful, we'll all look forward
>   to seeing you.
>   (turns to Rand)
>   Is Eve around? I'd like to say
>   hello.
>
>   RAND
>   No, she flew up to Boston for some
>   charity event. She'll be sorry to
>   have missed you.
>
>   PRESIDENT
>   I'm sorry, too. Well, Nancy wanted
>   me to send along her best to the
>   two of you - and, Ben, I want to
>   thank you for your time and
>   thoughts.
>
>   RAND
>   Nonsense, Mr. President - I thank
>   you for coming to spend time with
>   a dying man.
>
>   PRESIDENT
>   Now, Ben, I won't have any of
>   that. Why don't you listen to your
>   good friend Chauncey - this is a
>   time to think of life!

The President claps Rand's hand.

>   RAND
>   You're right, Mr. President - I
>   don't like feeling sorry for
>   myself.

                    PRESIDENT
          Take care of yourself, Ben.

                    RAND
          You too, Bobby.

                    PRESIDENT
               (as he turns to go, a
               smile to Chance)
          ... Chauncey ...

                    CHANCE
          ... Bobby ...

The President leaves the library and Chance turns to Rand.

                    RAND
               (as the door closes)
          He's a decent fellow, the
          President, isn't he?

                    CHANCE
          I'm glad he came, Ben. It was nice
          talking to the President.

62.   INT. RAND MANSION - HALLWAY - MORNING

The President and his entourage are moving along toward the front door. One aide, KAUFMAN, walks next to the President.

                    PRESIDENT
          Kaufman, I'm going to need
          information on Mr. Chauncey
          Gardiner's background.

                    KAUFMAN
               (makes note of name)
          Gardiner, yes, sir.

                    PRESIDENT
          And I'd like it some time today.

                    KAUFMAN
          No problem, Chief.

63.   INT. RAND MANSION - TAPESTRY ROOM - MORNING

Rand has an arm around Chance as the two of them walk. Behind them, Wilson and Perkins push empty wheelchairs.

>   RAND
>   (very weak)
>   ... You know, Chauncey, there's
>   something about you... You don't
>   play games with words to protect
>   yourself. You're direct ...
>   (they walk a few more feet
>   in silence)
>   You know what I was talking to you
>   about last night?
>
>   CHANCE
>   (blankly)
>   No, Ben.
>
>   RAND
>   Oh, sure you do, the financial
>   assistance program for the
>   businessman.
>   (another beat)
>   Well, I think you might be just
>   the man to take charge of such an
>   undertaking. I'd like you to meet
>   with the other members of the
>   Board so you can discuss the
>   matter at greater length with
>   them.
>
>   CHANCE
>   I understand.
>
>   RAND
>   And, please, Chauncey - don't rush
>   your decision. I know you're not a
>   man to act on the spur of the
>   moment.
>
>   CHANCE
>   Thank you, Ben.

>   RAND
>   And now, Chauncey, I'm afraid you
>   must excuse me - I'm very tired ...

Rand sits down in his wheelchair and Perkins starts off
with him.

>   CHANCE
>   (as they go)
>   I'm sorry that you are so sick,
>   Ben.

Chance watches after them for a moment, then his interest is
taken by one of the large tapestries.

64.   EXT. RAND MANSION - MAIN GARDEN - DAY

Chance and Eve walk through the garden. At one end, is a huge
Victorian greenhouse, with smaller greenhouses next to it. Off
to one side, stands an attractive stone house. Five young men
work in one area, shoveling mulch.

>   EVE
>   There are over sixty thousand
>   tulip bulbs planted here. It's
>   quite a sight when they're
>   blooming. Of course, the roses are
>   beautiful, too. We have, I think,
>   around twenty thousand bushes.
>   (gestures to men working)
>   ... We plant something different
>   every year in that area ... But I
>   haven't decided what I would like
>   this spring. What do you think,
>   Chauncey?
>
>   CHANCE
>   I don't know.
>
>   EVE
>   Well, give it some thought.
>   (indicates stone house)
>   That's the gardener's house over
>   there.

Chance looks off to the two story [sic] stone house.

65.   INT. A GREENHOUSE - DAY

   Chance and Eve are in the middle of a huge potting
   green- house where hundreds of young plants are tended
   by four workers.

                    CHANCE
            I like to watch the young plants
            grow.

                    EVE
            It is wonderful, isn't it?

                    CHANCE
            Young plants do much better if a
            person helps them.

   Eve looks at Chance as he inspects some of the flowers.
   She has decided to make a move.

                    EVE
            ... Ben tells me the President was
            very taken with you this morning.

   Chance doesn't know what to say, continues inspecting
   the flowers.

66.   INT. VICTORIAN GREENHOUSE - DAY

   Chance and Eve move through a large and an extra
   lush green-house until they reach a long room filled
   with cacti.

                    EVE
              (as they move)
            ... Chauncey ... Last night you
            mentioned an old man, that died.
            Was a relative? Or an intimate
            friend?

                    CHANCE
              (looking at greenhouse)
            He was a very wealthy man, he looked after me
            since I was young.

                    EVE
          Oh, I see ... Your mentor.

                    CHANCE
               (quizzically)
          ... Mentor ...?

Eve takes his uncertainty as a reluctance to discuss the Old Man.

                    EVE
          Forgive me, Chauncey - I don't
          mean to pry. You must have been
          very close to him.

                    CHANCE
          Yes. I was.

                    EVE
          I'm sorry ...
               (getting more to the
                point)
          ... And what about Louise? You
          mentioned that she had gone. Were
          you close to her also?

                    CHANCE
          Yes. I liked Louise very much. She
          was his maid.

                    EVE
               (relieved)
          Oh, his maid! ... Stupid me, I
          thought perhaps she was someone
          that you may have been
          romantically involved with, or
          maybe your sister.

                    CHANCE
          Oh no. She brought me my meals.

                    EVE
               (pleased)
          Of course.

Eve edges slightly closer to Chance. Chance edges slightly closer to the cacti, is fascinated by it.

67.   INT. RAND'S ROOM - DAY

Rand is in bed, looking bad. Eve, Chance and Allenby are seated around him, the two nurses stand to one side. They all watch the President's address to the Financial Institute on TV.

>   PRESIDENT'S VOICE
>   ... I know that many of you believe
>   that we are on the brink of the
>   worst financial crisis in this
>   nation's history. And there are
>   some of you who would like to see
>   us put mandatory freezes on prices
>   and wages, and then call it a
>   temporary measure. Well, that's
>   exactly what I was going to do
>   until this moment. But I have
>   decided there are no temporary
>   stop gaps. So I am going to re-
>   think my position and find another
>   solution. And, you'll be very
>   pleased to know that your founder
>   and chairman-of-the-board,
>   Mr. Benjamin Turnbull Rand, agrees
>   with me on this ...
>   (beat)
>   ... for once.

There is applause and laughter from the audience.

>   PRESIDENT'S VOICE (Cont'd)
>   (after applause)
>   Chauncey Gardiner, Mr. Rand's
>   close friend and advisor, was at
>   our meeting this morning. I found
>   Mr. Gardiner to have a feeling for
>   this country that we need more
>   of. He likened us to a garden ...
>   ... To quote Mr. Gardiner, a most
>   intuitive man, 'As long as the
>   roots of industry remain firmly
>   planted in the national soil, the
>   economic prospects are undoubtedly
>   sunny.'

```
         Rand starts coughing, breathing heavily. Allenby and the nurses
         rush to his bedside. Allenby shoots a quick look to Eve and
         Chance.

                             ALLENBY
                       (motioning toward door)
                    I think you should leave.

         Eve and an interested Chance leave the room as Allenby
         administers aid to Rand.

                             PRESIDENT'S VOICE (Cont'd)
                       Gentlemen, let us not fear the
                       inevitable chill and storms of
                       autumn and winter, instead, let us
                       anticipate the rapid growth of
                       springtime, let us await the
                       rewards of summer. As in a garden
                       of the earth, let us learn to
                       accept and appreciate the times
                       when the trees are bare as well as
                       the times when we pick the fruit.


    68.  INT. RAND MANSION - HALLWAY - DAY

         Eve and Chance stand in silence near the palm court. Eve's
         eyes are swollen, red, she has been crying. She turns to
         Chance, reaches out, touches his hand.

                             EVE
                       (hesitates)
                    ... I'm ...
                       (pause)
                    ... I'm very grateful that you're
                    here, Chauncey ...
                       (pause)
                    ... With us ...

                             CHANCE
                    So am I, Eve.

         Allenby comes out of Rand's room, his mood is serious.

                             ALLENBY
                    ... This has been an exhausting day
                    for Ben ... He's resting
```

>   comfortably now. There's no cause
>   for alarm ...

Mrs. Aubrey approaches.

>   MRS. AUBREY
>   Mr. Gardiner, I have a telephone
>   call for you, Sidney Courtney.
>
>   CHANCE
>   ... Telephone call?
>
>   MRS. AUBREY
>   Yes, Sidney Courtney, the
>   Financial Editor of the
>   Washington Post.

Chance does not react.

>   MRS. AUBREY
>   (after a moment)
>   Would you care to take it, sir?
>
>   CHANCE
>   Yes.

Chance still does not move. Eve mistakes this for concern for herself.

>   EVE
>   I'll be all right, Chauncey - you
>   go ahead with Mrs. Aubrey ...
>
>   CHANCE
>   Yes, Eve. You'll be all right.

Chance follows Mrs. Aubrey. Eve watches Chance go, then turns to Allenby.

>   EVE
>   ... He's such a sensitive man, so considerate ...

69.   INT. MRS. AUBREY'S OFFICE - DAY

Three television sets are on. Mrs. Aubrey hands a phone to Chance, he looks at it, uncertain.

                    CHANCE
               (after a moment, into
               phone)
          ... Hello.

70. INT. WASHINGTON POST - COURTNEY'S OFFICE - DAY

     SID COURTNEY, a man in his fifties, wears a rumpled wool jacket, smokes a pipe.

                    COURTNEY
          Hello, Mr. Gardiner. I'm sorry to
          disturb you, but I watched the
          President's speech at the
          Financial Institute today, and I
          wondered if you have any comments
          on the meeting that took place
          between Mr. Rand, the President
          and yourself.

71. INTERCUT - MRS. AUBREY'S OFFICE/COURTNEY'S OFFICE - DAY

                    CHANCE
          The President is a nice person. I
          enjoyed it very much.

                    COURTNEY
          Good, sir. And so, it seems, did
          the President - but we would like
          to have some facts; such as, uh ...
          What exactly is the relationship
          between yourself and that of the
          First American Financial Corporation?

                    CHANCE
          I think you should ask Mr. Rand that.

                    COURTNEY
          Of course. But since he is ill I'm
          taking the liberty of asking you.

                    CHANCE
               (watching three TV sets)
          Yes, that is correct. I think you
          should ask Mr. Rand that.

Courtney doesn't understand but continues his questioning.

> COURTNEY
> I see. Then one more quick
> question, Mr. Gardiner.

Chance hangs up the phone, watches the TVs. Courtney listens to the dial tone, then puts the receiver down.

> COURTNEY
> (to himself)
> No wonder he's so close to Rand ...

72. INT. MRS. AUBREY'S OFFICE - DAY

Mrs. Aubrey puts a call on hold, speaks to Chance who is still intrigued by the three televisions.

> MRS. AUBREY
> Mr. Gardiner, I have the producer
> of the 'Gary Burns Show' on the
> line.

> CHANCE
> Yes, I have watched that on
> television.

> MRS. AUBREY
> Of course. They would like you to
> appear on the show tonight. The
> Vice-President was scheduled, but
> he had to cancel, and they asked
> if you would be interested.

> CHANCE
> Yes. I would like to be on
> television.

> MRS. AUBREY
> Fine.

Chance turns back to the televisions. Mrs. Aubrey talks to the producer.

                        MRS. AUBREY
                    (into phone)
                Hello, Mr. Hull ... Mr. Gardiner
                has agreed to do the show ... Yes,
                I'll tell him. The show will be
                taped and then shown at ten
                o'clock, but he's to be there at seven.

73.   INT. EVE'S BEDROOM - EVENING

       Eve is on the phone while being attended to by a MANICURIST
       and a HAIRDRESSER. Eve talks to Sophie as if they weren't
       there as one wig is taken off, another is put on.

                        EVE
                    (into phone)
                ... Are you kidding? Of course,
                I'll bring him, I promise - but
                I'll get Ben to suggest it ...
                Hands off, Sophie - this one's
                mine ... No, I haven't done that,
                but give me time ... Yes, be sure
                and watch the 'Burns' Show to -
                night, you'll see what I mean ...
                Ben? Oh, he's okay - he's got his
                ups and downs ...

74.   INT. CHANCE'S ROOM - EVENING

       Chance wears a velvet bathrobe, watches TV. Wilson and Perkins
       lay out a suit, shirt, tie, etc. There is a KNOCK at the door.

                        PERKINS
                Excuse me, sir.

       Perkins answers the door, it is Eve.

                        EVE
                    (entering)
                Chauncey, I wanted to wish you
                well. I know you'll be just
                smashing.

                        CHANCE
                    (rising)
                Thank you, Eve.

                    EVE
          And Benjamin sends along his best
          wishes.

                    CHANCE
          How is Ben feeling?

                    EVE
          He's tired, Chauncey - but he's
          going to watch you tonight. We'll
          both be watching.

                    CHANCE
          That's good. I like to watch, too.

                    EVE
          I know you do - you and your
          television ...
               (a pause)
          ... Good luck, Chauncey.

Eve impulsively steps forward, kisses Chance on the cheek.
Chance smiles at her. Eve returns the smile, then leaves the
room. Chance sits back down, watches TV as Wilson and Perkins
attend to his clothes with a whiskbroom.

75.   INT. WASHINGTON POST - RESEARCH ROOM - NIGHT

A woman, KINNEY, sits behind a stack of paperwork. She has
a downcast expression as Sidney Courtney, followed by three
staffers, enters the room.

                    COURTNEY
               (to Staffers)
          ... Gardiner is laconic, matter-
          of-fact. The scuttlebutt is that
          he's a strong candidate for one of
          the seats on the Board of First
          American.
               (to Kinney)
          ... Kinney, what did you come up
          with on his background?

                    KINNEY
               (after pause)
          ... Nothing.

                    COURTNEY
          ... Skip the levity, Kinney - what
          have you got?

                    KINNEY
              (another pause)
          ... I realize this sounds banal -
          but there is no information of any
          sort on Gardiner. We have no
          material on him - zilch ...

The room is quiet.

76.   INT. TV STATION - CORRIDOR - NIGHT

Chance is intrigued by the surroundings as MORTON HULL guides
him through the corridor.

                    HULL
          Of course, Mr. Gardiner, your
          position in the financial
          community carries a lot of weight,
          but what caught Gary's attention
          was your down-to-earth
          philosophy.

                    CHANCE
          I see.

They walk a while through the corridor.

                    HULL
              (making conversation)
          Do you realize that more people
          will be watching you tonight than
          all those who have seen theater
          plays in the last forty years?

                    CHANCE
          Yes. It's a very good show.

Hull takes Chance into the makeup room.

77.   EXT. AIRPORT - NIGHT

AIR FORCE 1 taxies on the ground.

78. INT. AIR FORCE 1 - NIGHT

The President sits on a couch in one of the compartments on the jet. With him are six of his STAFF, Kaufman included.

>PRESIDENT
>What do you mean, no background? That's impossible, he's a very well known [sic] man!

>KAUFMAN
>Yes, sir - we are aware of all that, but still, we haven't been able to ...

>PRESIDENT
>   (interrupts)
>He's an advisor and close personal friend of Rand's! For Christ sakes, they have volumes of data on Benjamin!

>KAUFMAN
>Yes, Mr. President, I plan on contacting Mr. Rand as soon as ...

>PRESIDENT
>   (again interrupts)
>I do not want Benjamin Rand disturbed! You have other ways of gathering information than to trouble a dying man. Use whatever agencies are necessary to put together a detailed history of Chauncey Gardiner, if you run into problems, alert Honeycutt.
>   (he stands)
>Have it in my office at seven in the morning.
>   (he starts for door)
>I've got to take a leak.

>KAUFMAN
>Right, chief.

As the President goes to the Men's Room, two of the aides reach for telephones.

79. INT. TV STATION - CORRIDOR/MAKEUP ROOM - NIGHT

A PAGE comes through the corridor carrying a glass of water. He turns into the makeup room to reveal Hull sitting next to Chance in front of the mirror. The makeup man, COLSON, works on Chance as he watches the guest preceding him on a TV monitor that is reflected in the mirror.

                PAGE
         (gives Chance water)
    I thought you might need this
    about now, Mr. Gardiner. It gets
    real hot under these lights.

                CHANCE
    Thank you. I am very thirsty.

The Page leans against the door jamb, smiles if anyone looks at him.

                HULL
         (briefing Chance)
    Now, if Gary wants to interrupt
    you, or ask you a question, he'll
    raise his left forefinger to his
    left eyebrow.

                CHANCE
         (to Colson)
    Nurse Teresa did Ben's makeup.

                COLSON
         (laughs)
    Oh? Did she do a good job?

                CHANCE
    Yes, very good.

On the TV, GARY BURNS finishes with his guest and the band goes into a hot instrumental number.

                COLSON
         (a last-minute dab)
    Okay, Mr. Gardiner, looks like
    you're up.

Hull leads Chance out of the makeup room. Colson sits and watches the TV monitor. The Page, his back to Colson, carefully picks up Chance's water glass so as not to smear the fingerprints, then leaves the room. On the TV monitor, the band plays, the audience applauds as Burns introduces Chance.

80. INT. RAND LIMOUSINE - NIGHT

Chance watches himself on TV as he is driven back to the mansion.

>   BURNS (on TV)
> I always find it surprising, Mr.
> Gardiner, to find men like
> yourself, who work so intimately
> with the President, yet manage to
> remain relatively unknown.
>
>   CHANCE (on TV)
> Yes. That is surprising.
>
>   BURNS (on TV)
> ... Well, your anonymity will be a
> thing of the past from now on.
>
>   CHANCE (on TV)
>   (doesn't understand)
> I hope so.
>
>   BURNS (on TV)
>   (a beat)
> Yes ... of course. Well, I assume,
> since the President quoted you,
> that you agree with his view of
> the economy.
>
>   CHANCE (on TV)
> Which view?

Applause and laughter from the TV audience.

81. INT. ALLENBY'S ROOM - NIGHT

Allenby watches, concerned as to which way it will go.

>   BURNS (on TV)
>   (a beat)
>   Well, the President compared the
>   economy of this country to a
>   garden, and stated that after a
>   period of decline a time of growth
>   would naturally follow.
>
>   CHANCE (on TV)
>   Yes, I know the garden very well.
>   I have worked in it all my life.
>   It is a good garden and a healthy
>   one;

82. INT. RAND'S ROOM - NIGHT

Rand is in bed. Eve sits in a chair next to the bed, squeezes Rand's hand in the excitement as they both watch Chance on television. Teresa and Constance watch in the Background.

>   CHANCE (on TV - cont'd)
>   its trees are healthy and so are
>   its shrubs and flowers, as long as
>   they are trimmed and watered in
>   the right seasons. The garden
>   needs a lot of care. I do agree
>   with the President; everything
>   will grow strong, and there is
>   plenty of room in it for new trees
>   and new flowers of all kinds.

The TV audience applauds Chance and Constance quietly leaves the room.

83. INT. WHITE HOUSE - PRESIDENT'S BEDROOM - NIGHT

The President and First Lady are in bed together watching the show.

>   BURNS (on TV)
>   So you're saying, Mr. Gardiner, if
>   the Stock Market collapses, and
>   unemployment keeps increasing,
>   that this is just another season,
>   so to speak, in the garden?

The First Lady cuddles up to the President.

84. INT. RAND LIMOUSINE - NIGHT

Chance continues to watch himself.

> CHANCE (on TV)
> Yes. In a garden, things grow -
> but first some things must wither;
> some trees lose their leaves
> before they grow new leaves ...

85. INT. THOMAS FRANKLIN'S BEDROOM - NIGHT

Franklin, the attorney that evicted Chance, comes out of the bathroom brushing his teeth. His wife, JOHANNA, is in the bed absorbed in the show. Franklin sits on the end of the bed.

> CHANCE (on TV - cont'd)
> ... And if you give your garden a
> lot of love, and if you work very
> hard and have a lot of patience,
> in the proper season you will see
> it grow to be very beautiful ...

More applause from the TV. Franklin leans closer to the set.

> FRANKLIN
> (puzzled)
> It's that gardener!

> JOHANNA
> Yes, Chauncey Gardiner.

> FRANKLIN
> No! He's a real gardener!

> JOHANNA
> (laughs)
> He does talk like on, but I think
> he's brilliant.

> BURNS (on TV)
> Well, that's very interesting, Mr.
> Gardiner, <u>but</u>, what about the bad
> seasons?

86.   INT. CHANCE'S ROOM - NIGHT

Constance is in Chance's closet searching through his clothing. Finding nothing, she checks the labels on his suits, copies them in a notepad.

> BURNS (Cont'd)
> (on TV)
> Such as prolonged droughts that have wiped out crops, disastrous winters, hurricanes? Doesn't a country need to have someone in charge that can see it through such crises? Don't we need a leader capable of guiding us through the bad seasons as well as the good?

> CHANCE
> (on TV)
> Yes. We need a very good gardener.

Constance continues her work in the closet.

87.   INT. PRESIDENT'S BEDROROM - NIGHT

The President and First Lady are very attentive.

> BURNS
> (on TV)
> I realize this might be a difficult question for you, Mr. Gardiner - but there are a lot of us around the country that would like to hear your thoughts on the matter.

> CHANCE
> (on TV)
> I understand.

> BURNS
> (on TV)
> Do you feel that we have a 'very good gardener' in office at this time, Mr. Gardiner?

                        PRESIDENT
            ... That bastard ...

                        CHANCE
                    (on TV)
            Oh, yes. It is possible for one
            side of the garden to be flooded,
            and the other side to be dry ...
            Some plants do well in the sun,
            and others grow better in the cool
            of the shade.

The First Lady moves closer to the President.

88.   INT. HOTEL LOBBY - NIGHT

A group of ELDERLY BLACK PEOPLE sit in the lobby, watching the show on an old black-and-white TV

                        CHANCE (on TV - cont'd)
            ... It is the gardener's
            responsibility to take water from
            the flooded area and run it to the
            area that is dry. It is also the
            gardener's responsibility not to
            plant a sun-loving flower in the
            shade of a high wall ...

During the preceding speech, Louise, the maid from the Old Man's house, chatters.

                        LOUISE
            Gobbledegook! All the time he
            talked gobbledegook! An' it's for
            sure a White man's world in
            America, hell, I raised that boy
            since he was the size of a pissant
            an' I'll say right now he never
            learned to read an' write - no
            sir! Had no brains at all, was
            stuffed with rice puddin' between
            the ears! Short-changed by the
            Lord and dumb as a jackass an'
            look at him now! Yes, sir - all
            you gotta be is white in America
            an' you get whatever you want!

                    Just listen to that boy -
                    gobbledegook!

There is a chorus of "Amens" as she finishes.

89. INT. RAND LIMOUSINE - NIGHT

Chance watches himself.

                    CHANCE (on TV - cont'd)
                    ... It is the responsibility of the
                    gardener to adjust to the bad
                    seasons as well as enjoy the good
                    ones.

Chance changes channels to a Game Show.

90. INT. PRESIDENT'S BEDROOM - NIGHT

The President and First Lady still watch Chance.

                    CHANCE (on TV - cont'd)
                    If the gardener does his job,
                    everything will be fine.

                    PRESIDENT
                    Oh, Jesus ...

Audience applause is heard on TV.

                    BURNS (on TV)
                    Before we take a break ... What
                    sort of gardener would you be?

                    CHANCE (on TV)
                         (with confidence)
                    I am a very serious gardener.

                    BURNS (on TV)
                    I'm sure you are, Mr. Gardiner.
                         (looks at camera)
                    We'll be right back.

As a commercial comes on, the President rolls over in bed. The First Lady reaches out, puts a comforting hand on his shoulder.

91.   INT. RAND'S ROOM - NIGHT

The commercial is on TV.

                    RAND
          He's a remarkable man,
          remarkable ...
                (to Eve)
          You're fond of him too, aren't
          you, Eve?

                    EVE
                (a beat)
          ... Yes, I am, Ben.

                    RAND
          That's good ... that's good.

Rand looks up as Constance comes back into the room.

                    RAND
          Constance! Where have you been?
          You missed the whole show -
          Chauncey was wonderful.

92.   INT. FRANKLIN'S BEDROOM - NIGHT

Franklin shuts off the commercial on TV, is talking on the phone.

                    FRANKLIN
          Okay, Sally, I'll see you in
          twenty minutes.

Franklin hangs up the phone, scurries around getting dressed. His wife, Johanna, sits grimly in bed.

                    FRANKLIN
                (notices her look)
          I won't be long, I've just got to
          talk to her about this Gardiner ...

                    JOHANNA
                (turns over in bed)
          Good night.

                    FRANKLIN
          Look, Johanna ...

                    JOHANNA
              (cuts him off)
          I said <u>good</u> <u>night</u>!

Franklin gives up, hurries from the room.

93. EXT. RAND MANSION - NIGHT

Some of the household staff are lined up applauding Chance as he steps from the limousine. Perkins and Wilson come forward.

                    WILSON
          Bravo, sir! You were outstanding.
          Outstanding!

                    PERKINS
          May I take your coat, Mr.
          Gardiner?

                    CHANCE
          Yes. Thank you, Perkins.

Perkins nods, takes Chance's overcoat, allows everyone to enter the house. Once alone, Perkins quickly searches through the coatpockets, finds nothing.

94. INT. PRESIDENT'S BEDROOM - NIGHT

The First Lady is snuggled up close to the President, caresses his body. After a moment, it becomes clear to her that he is not up to the occasion.

                    FIRST LADY
          ... Darling ... What's wrong?

                    PRESIDENT
          ... I can't ... I just can't right
          now ... I'm sorry, dearest ... I
          just can't ...

The First Lady looks at him for a beat, then turns, lies on her back and stares at the ceiling.

95. INT. RAND'S HOSPITAL ROOM - NIGHT

Rand is in his wheelchair, stripped to the waist. Eve stands nearby. Chance breathes deeply, enjoys the oxygen. Allenby and the nurses prepare four separate injections for Rand, which Allenby administers to him during the scene.

>   RAND
>   (with some effort)
>   Senator Rowley's widow is hosting
>   a reception tomorrow night
>   honoring the Soviet Ambassador and
>   I think it's rather obvious that
>   Robert won't allow me to attend.
>   So, Chauncey, you would be doing
>   me a great favor if you would
>   escort Eve, and go in my place.
>
>   CHANCE
>   Yes. I would like to escort Eve.
>
>   RAND
>   Good. Together, the two of you
>   should create quite a stir - I can
>   already hear the gossip.
>
>   EVE
>   ... Ben, really ...
>
>   RAND
>   ... You possess a great gift,
>   Chauncey, of being natural. And
>   that, my boy, is a rare talent -
>   tonight on television, you were
>   strong and brave and didn't
>   moralize. I hope the entire
>   country was watching - the entire
>   country.

Allenby gives Rand the last injection.

96. INT. COCKTAIL LOUNGE - NIGHT

An 'in' meeting place for the upper-middle Washington, D.C. crowd. Thomas Franklin and Sally Hayes sit at a table, drinks in front of them.

> FRANKLIN
> ... It didn't make any sense to me at all. I didn't know what the hell he was talking about ...
>
> SALLY
> It wasn't meant for us, Tom - he was talking to the masses. He was very clever, keeping it at a third grade level - that's what they understand ...
>
> FRANKLIN
> Yeah? Well, I don't understand why he was in Jennings' house? What was up his sleeve when he pulled that stunt with us? What was he doing? And why?
>
> SALLY
> Who knows ...? Maybe the government had something to do with it.
>
> FRANKLIN
> You know, Sally - he made a fool out of me, ... and you know what that means, don't you? ... It means that any political future I had is right down the toilet!

The CAMERA begins to slowly move away from the table, the sound of Franklin's voice continues.

> FRANKLIN (cont'd)
> ... Jesus, the thought of spending the rest of my life as an attorney, that is really a downer ... And, Christ, Sally, I almost forgot - Johanna is starting to think some - thing's going on between ...

Franklin's voice fades into the background hubbub. The voice of Kinney, the research assistant from the <u>Washington Post</u> is heard as the camera settles on a table occupied by Sidney Courtney and his staff.

                    KINNEY
          ... Sid, be reasonable - I've been
          everywhere, there's no place left
          to check!

                    COURTNEY
          Try again.

                    KINNEY
          Sure, try again - where? There's
          nothing, it's like Gardiner never
          existed!

                    COURTNEY
          Try again.

                    KINNEY
          It's useless!

                    COURTNEY
               (coldly)
          I said - try again.

Kinney stands, shoves her paperwork across the table.

                    KINNEY
          Up yours, Sid. You try again, I
          quit!

Kinney takes her drink with her as she leaves the lounge.

97.   INT. RAND MANSION - THIRD FLOOR HALLWAY - NIGHT

The elevator door opens revealing Eve and Chance inside.

                    EVE
               (as they come out)
          I'll bet you don't have a tuxedo
          with you, do you?

                    CHANCE
          No, thank you.

                    EVE
          ... Well, we can fix up one of
          Ben's for you tomorrow. Sophie
          insists on Black Tie.

                         CHANCE
                I see.

They walk in silence for a moment. Eve stops, then Chance.

                         EVE
                    (softly)
                 ... I have very few friends,
                 Chauncey ... And Benjamin's friends
                 are all quite a bit older ...

Eve gives Chance a long look, then kisses him on the lips. She steps back, smiles.

                         EVE
                 ... Good night, Chauncey.

                         CHANCE
                Good night, Eve.

Eve goes into her bedroom, closes the door. Chance heads for his room as though nothing had happened.

98.   INT. WHITE HOUSE - OVAL OFFICE ANTE ROOM - MORNING

Kaufman and the five other Aides nervously await the President's arrival. The door opens, the President briskly enters.

                         PRESIDENT
                Good morning, gentlemen.

                         AIDES
                    (as one)
                Good morning, sir.

The President leads the way into the Oval Office.

99.   INT. OVAL OFFICE - MORNING

As the President goes to his desk, Kaufman hands him a folder. The President sits, reads it quickly, it is very brief.

                         PRESIDENT
                    (to Kaufman)
                This is not what I requested.

                         KAUFMAN
                No, sir.

PRESIDENT
This information goes back a day and a half! I want the standard file, you know that.

KAUFMAN
Right, Chief.

PRESIDENT
So ...? Where the hell is it?

KAUFMAN
We ...uh, have been unable to come up with any information before Mr. Gardiner appeared at the Rand's ... and, uh ...

PRESIDENT
What the hell are you talking about, Kaufman?

KAUFMAN
Well, we do have some data from the Bureau, but it isn't pertinent.

PRESIDENT
I'd like to hear that data Kaufman.

KAUFMAN
Yes, sir.

Kaufman takes a clipboard from the man at his right.

KAUFMAN
(reading)
... Suits hand-made by a tailor in Chicago in 1928. The tailor went out of business in 1933, then took his own life.
... His shoes were hand-made in 1936. The cobbler has long since been dead. Underwear, all of the finest cloth, factory destroyed by fire in 1948. The man carries no identification; no wallet, no

>   driver's license, no credit cards.
>   ... He carries one item along with
>   him, a fine Swiss Patek-Phillipe
>   watch, made in 1887, but there is
>   no record of where or when it was
>   purchased.
>   ... Computers have analyzed
>   Gardiner's vocal characteristics;
>   it is impossible to determine his
>   ethnic back-ground, they feel his
>   accent may be northeastern, but
>   they will not commit to that.
>   ... Fingerprint check proved
>   negative, no identification
>   possible.
>   (a pause)
>   ... That's it, Mr. President.

The President stares at Kaufman for a beat, then speaks into his intercom.

>   PRESIDENT
>   Miss Davis - I'd like my eggs
>   poached this morning, please.

100.   INT. CHANCE'S ROOM - MORNING

Chance is in bed, a tray on his lap, eating breakfast. A pile of the morning's newspapers lie at the foot of the bed, untouched. The TV is playing, Chance watches as he eats. There is a knock at the door.

>   CHANCE
>   (without turning from TV)
>   Come in!

Eve enters, wearing a robe over her nightgown.

>   EVE
>   Chauncey! Have you seen the
>   papers?

>   CHANCE
>   No, Eve. I don't read the papers.

                    EVE
               (moving to bed)
          Well, it seems you've been
          described as one of the architects
          of the President's speech. And
          your own comments from the
          television show are quoted side by
          side with the President's.

                    CHANCE
          I like the President. He is a very
          nice man.

                    EVE
               (sits on bed)
          I know ...
               (a moment)
          ... So are you, Chauncey ...
               (another moment, Chance
                watches TV)
          ... Do you mind my being here, like
          this?

                    CHANCE
               (a bite of toast)
          No, Eve. I like you to be here.

Eve smiles, moves a little closer to Chance.

                    EVE
          ... You know, Chauncey ... I want us
          to be ...
               (with difficulty)
          I want us ... You and I to
          become ... close ... I want us to
          become very close, you know ...?

                    CHANCE
          Yes, Eve. I know that.

Eve suddenly begins to cry, sobbing quietly at first, then losing control, the tears flowing freely. To comfort her, Chance puts his arm around her shoulder, nearly tipping his breakfast tray. Eve responds to his touch, draws closer, holds Chance tightly. Chance does his best to avoid slipping his breakfast, keep an eye on the TV, and to comfort Eve. She begins to caress Chance, running her hand over his body. She kisses him, his eyes, his neck, his lips, his ears. Chance does not return the lovemaking, and Eve eventually catches hold of herself, stops. She lies quietly beside Chance for a time, regains her demeanor, then speaks.

> EVE
> ... I'm grateful to you, Chauncey ... I would have opened to you with a touch, and you know that ...
> (Chance, confused, turns to her)

> EVE (cont'd)
> ... But you're so strong - I can trust myself with you ...

> CHANCE
> Yes, Eve. I'm very glad that you didn't open.

> EVE
> I know you are, Chauncey ... And I appreciate why you've decided to wait ... until ... until ...

There is a long moment, then Eve rises, straightens her robe and moves toward the door.

> EVE
> (stopping by door)
> ... I do love you, Chauncey.

Eve leaves. Chance eats his once-warm scrambled eggs and watches "Mr. Roger's Neighborhood" on TV.

101. INT. RAND MANSION - ALLENBY'S ROOM - DAY

Allenby is at his desk, searching through the Washington, D.C. telephone book. He finds a number, dials.

> ALLENBY
> (into phone)
> Mr. Thomas Franklin, please.
> (a wait)
> Is Thomas Franklin in?
> (a beat)
> Yes, this is Dr. Robert Allenby,

would you please tell Mr. Franklin
that I would like to talk to him?
It concerns Chauncey Gardiner.

102. INT. RAND'S ROOM - DUSK

Rand is in bed, very still, deep in thought. Teresa and
Constance work in the background.

103. EXT. SOPHIE'S - NIGHT

Chance wears Ben's tuxedo and Eve is done to the teeth as they
emerge from the limousine and are met by the press: a couple
of reporters, 5 photographers and a mini-cam crew from a local
TV station.

                    REPORTER #1
Mr. Gardiner, what did you think
of the Posts' editorial on the
President's speech?

                    CHANCE
    (smiling for photogs)
I didn't read it.

                    REPORTER #2
But sir - you must have at least
glanced at it.

                    CHANCE
No. I did not glance at it.

                    REPORTER #3
Mr. Gardiner, the <u>New York Times</u>
spoke of your 'Peculiar brand of
optimism,' what was your reaction
to that?

                    CHANCE
    (continues to pose for
     pictures)
I did not read that either.

                    REPORTER #3
Well, how do you feel about that
phrase, 'Peculiar brand of
optimism?'

                    CHANCE
          I do not know what it means.

                    REPORTER #2
          Sorry to persist, sir, but it
          would be of great interest to me
          to know what newspapers you do
          read.

                    CHANCE
          I do not read any newspapers.
          I watch TV.

There is a moment of silence as the reporters digest this. The TV Reporter smiles, questions Chance.

                    TV REPORTER
          ... Do you mean, Mr. Gardiner, that
          you find television's coverage of
          the news superior to that of the
          news-papers?

                    CHANCE
               (flatly)
          I like to watch TV.

                    TV REPORTER
          Thank you, Mr. Gardiner.

                    CHANCE
               (thinks the interview is over)
          You're welcome.

Chance turns and goes toward the house, Eve follows. The TV Reporter turns to the TV camera.

                    TV REPORTER
          Well, that is probably the most
          honest admission to come from a
          public figure in years. Few men in
          public life have the courage not
          to read newspapers. None, that
          this reporter has met, have the
          guts to admit it.

104. INT. SOPHIE'S - EVENING

Chance and Eve move through the hallway toward the Living Room.

                    EVE
          I've never seen anyone handle the
          press the way you do, Chauncey -
          you're so cool and detached.

                  CHANCE
          Thank you, Eve.

They move on to reveal the Black Tie Reception in progress, crowded with Ambassadors and other such dignitaries. SOPHIE ROWLEY, the hostess, comes rushing toward to greet them.

105. INT. WASHINGTON, D.C. COCKTAIL LOUNGE - NIGHT

The same lounge as before. Sidney Courtney sits at the same table as earlier, only this time with the editor of the <u>Washington Post</u>, LYMAN STUART. Courtney puffs on his pipe as he speaks.

                  COURTNEY
          ... It's strictly rumor at this
          stage, Lyman - just something in
          the wind ...

                  STUART
          Something rather big in the wind,
          I'd say. So whose files were
          destroyed? The CIA's or the FBI's?

                  COURTNEY
          I don't know. But we should start
          nosing around, see if we can talk
          to some people ...

The CAMERA begins to slowly MOVE AWAY from their table.

                  STUART
          What is it about his past they are
          trying to cover up?

>   (his volume fades)
>   ... A criminal record? A membership
>   in a subversive organization?
>   Homosexual, perhaps?

The SOUND of Stuart's voice dissolves into Thomas Franklin's as the CAMERA SETTLES on Dr. Allenby and Franklin sitting at a table nearby.

>   FRANKLIN
>   ... And he told us that he had been
>   living there since he was a child,
>   working as a gardener. He showed
>   us a room in the garage, where he
>   said he stayed, and I ... Well, I
>   didn't really believe him, of
>   course - but why the act? He must
>   have been involved on some major
>   financial level with the
>   deceased ...
>   (catches himself)
>   Mr. Jennings, but our firm has no
>   record of any such transactions.
>
>   ALLENBY
>   Hmmm. You say he showed you his
>   garden?
>
>   FRANKLIN
>   Well, he said it was his, he
>   walked us through it.
>
>   ALLENBY
>   I see.
>   (leans close to Franklin)
>   Mr. Franklin, I must ask you and
>   Miss Hayes to keep this incident
>   with Mr. Gardiner to yourselves.
>   There's no telling what he was
>   involved in, and the matter may be
>   extremely confidential. So please,
>   not a word.
>
>   FRANKLIN
>   Of course, Doctor, I understand.

                    ALLENBY
          Fine. Thank you, Mr. Franklin.

                    FRANKLIN
          Certainly, glad to be of help.
          Allenby rises, leaves the bar.

106. INT. SOPHIE'S - NIGHT

Sophie pulls Eve and Chance to AMBASSADOR SKRAPINOV and
his WIFE. As they arrive, Eve steps in front of Sophie
and makes the introduction.

                    EVE
          Mr. Chauncey Gardiner, let me
          introduce you to the guest of
          honor, His Excellency Vladimar
          Skrapinov, Ambassador of the
          Soviet Union.

Chance warmly shakes Skrapinov's hand with both of
his own.

                    CHANCE
               (stumbles over name)
          Hello ... His ... His ...

                    SKRAPINOV
          Delighted, Mr. Gardiner ...
               (a nod to Eve)
          Mrs. Rand, delighted.

                    SOPHIE
          And this is Mrs. Skrapinov.

Chance smiles at Mrs. Skrapinov as The Ambassador puts
am arm around him.

                    SKRAPINOV
               (to Chance and Eve)
          You must sit with us, my friends,
          we have much to discuss.

                    CHANCE
          I agree.

                    SOPHIE
               (tugs at Eve)
          Come, Eve, let's let the men talk.
               (to Chance and Skrapinov)
          Would you two excuse us for a moment?

                    SKRAPINOV
          Regretfully - we shall yield the
          pleasure of your company to
          others.

                    CHANCE
          Yes, Eve. I shall yield, too.

                    EVE
          Fine. You two have a nice chat.

Skrapinov leads his wife and Chance to their table as Eve and
Sophie move through the crowd.

                    EVE
               (with self-importance)
          You see? Didn't I tell you?

                    SOPHIE
          Oh, I'm so glad you brought him,
          it makes everything perfect.
               (looks back at Chance)
          He's very, very sexy - don't let
          me alone with him for too long ...

A smiling Senator Jensen comes out of the crowd.

                    SENATOR JENSEN
          Mrs. Rand! How good to see you!

                    EVE
          Well, Senator Jensen.

                    SENATOR JENSEN
          I certainly would like to meet
          Mr. Gardiner.

                    EVE
          I'm sure you would.

Eve turns away, Sophie follows.

As they are met by the Senator, we CUT.

107. INT. SOPHIE'S - NIGHT

Chance is seated between Ambassador Skrapinov and his wife at their table.

                    SKRAPINOV
        (moves chair close to Chance)
Considering the gravity of your economic situation, Mr. Gardiner, shouldn't we, the diplomats, and you, the businessmen - get together more often to exchange our thoughts? What does a Russian know about business? On the other hand, what does an American know about diplomacy? So why not a coming together? An interchange of opinion? We may find, my friend, that we are not so far from each other, not so far!

                    CHANCE
        (an engaging smile)
We are not so far ...
        (motions at nearness of their chairs)
... our chairs almost touch.

                    SKRAPINOV
        (laughs)
Bravo! Bravo! Our chairs are indeed almost touching! And we want to remain seated on them, correct? We don't want them snatched from under us, am I right? Because if one goes, the other goes, and then - boom! Boom! And Boom, Boom! And we are both down before our time, you see? And neither of us wants that, do you agree?

                    CHANCE
I certainly do.

                    SKRAPINOV
Yes. Tell me, Mr. Gardiner - do you by any chance enjoy Krylov's

                    fables? I ask this because there
                    is something ... there is something
                    Krylovian about you.

                              CHANCE
                    Do you think so? Do you think so?

                              SKRAPINOV
                    So you know Krylov!

Skrapinov pauses, then leans close to Chance, speaks softly in
Russian. Chance, having never heard this language, raises his
eyebrows and laughs. Mrs. Skrapinov remains impassive.

                              SKRAPINOV
                         (amazed)
                    So you know your Krylov in
                    Russian, do you? Mr. Gardiner, I
                    must confess I had suspected as
                    much all along.

                              CHANCE
                         (beat)
                    Would you tell me your name again,
                    please?

                              SKRAPINOV
                         (slaps Chance on the back)
                    Ho! Ho! A dash of American humor!
                    Vladimar Skrapinov!

                              CHANCE
                    Yes. I like that name very much.

                              SKRAPINOV
                    And yours, sir - Chauncey
                    Gardiner!
                         (in Russian)
                    How poetic! Chauncey, a name of
                    uncertain meaning! And Gardiner, a
                    bit of French, a suggestion of a
                    stroll through the flowers! A
                    beautiful name, my friend!

108. INT. WHITE HOUSE - PRESIDENT'S BEDROOM - NIGHT

A light from the adjoining bathroom filters into the darkened bedroom. The President and the First Lady are in bed. They each lie on their backs, a distance apart and are silent.

> FIRST LADY
> (after some time)
> ... Maybe you should talk to somebody, darling.

> PRESIDENT
> No, that won't do any good.

> FIRST LADY
> (another pause)
> ... Is it me? Is there something I've done?

> PRESIDENT
> Oh, no, sweetheart - it's not you ...

> FIRST LADY
> (another pause)
> It's your damn job. It never happened when you were a senator ...

> PRESIDENT
> It's not that, I just ...

The inter-White House phone buzzes, the President reaches for it.

> PRESIDENT
> (into phone)
> Yeah, Kaufman - what is it?

> KAUFMAN'S VOICE
> (over phone)
> Chief, we have a break in the case. Our man at the Washington Post says they are working on a story that either the CIA or the FBI destroyed Gardiner's files before anyone could get to them.

                    PRESIDENT
              What? Why?

                    KAUFMAN'S VOICE
                      (over phone)
              I can't say at this time - neither
              agency will admit to a thing.

                    PRESIDENT
                      (getting out of bed)
              Okay, get Honeycutt and Baldwin
              over here, I'll be right down.

The President hangs up the phone as the First Lady stares at the ceiling.

109. INT. SOPHIE'S - NIGHT

Eve and Chance are talking. AMBASSADOR GAUFRIDI of France edges toward them.

                    EVE
              Chauncey, you had Ambassador
              Skrapinov eating out of your hand,
              and you never told me you spoke
              Russian. That's incredible!

Gaufridi joins in.

                    GAUFRIDI
              It's extremely useful to speak
              Russian these days. Are you
              proficient in other languages, Mr.
              Gardiner?

                    EVE
              Mr. Gardiner is a modest man,
              Ambassador Gaufridi. He doesn't
              advertise his accomplishments, his
              knowledge is for himself.

Chance smiles, then turns away to select an hors d'oeuvre, where he is approached by RONALD STIEGLER, a publisher.

                    STIEGLER
              Mr. Gardiner, I'm Ronald Stiegler,
              of <u>Harvard Books</u>.

CHANCE
(a two-handed handshake)
Hello, Ronald.

STIEGLER
Mr. Gardiner, my editors and I have been wondering if you'd consider writing a book for us? Something on your political philosophy. What do you say?

CHANCE
I can't write.

STIEGLER
(smiles)
Of course, who can nowadays? I have trouble writing a post card to my children! Look, we could give you a six figure advance, provide you with the very best ghostwriters, research assistants, proof readers ...

CHANCE
I can't read.

STIEGLER
Of course not! No one has the time to read! One glances at things, watches television ...

CHANCE
Yes. I like to watch.

STIEGLER
Sure you do! No one reads!
... Listen, book publishing isn't exactly a bed of roses these days ...

CHANCE
(mild interest)
What sort of bed is it?

110. INT. SOPHIE'S - NIGHT

KARPATOV, an aide, sits next to Skrapinov and his wife.

> SKRAPINOV
> I want to know everything about his relationship with Rand. And find out the <u>real</u> reason the President has singled him out.
> (Karpatov takes notes)
> And I want this quote included in the TASS coverage ... "Chauncey Gardiner, in an intimate discussion with Ambassador Skrapinov, noted that 'unless the leaders of the opposing political systems move the chairs on which they sit closer to each other, all of their seats will be pulled from under them by rapid social and political changes.'"

Karpatov writes out the quote.

111. INT. SOPHIE'S - NIGHT

Eve is with SENATOR SLIPSHOD, MRS. SLIPSHOD, and DENNIS WATSON of the State Department.

> SENATOR
> I heard that he speaks eight languages, and on top of everything else, holds a degree in medicine as well as law. Isn't that true, Eve?

> EVE
> Well, I really don't know, Senator, but it wouldn't surprise me.

> MRS. SLIPSHOD
> He's very attractive.

> EVE
> Isn't he?

DENNIS
Yes ... Very.

112. INT. RAND'S ROOM - NIGHT

Allenby enters the room quietly and stands in the shadows watching Rand sitting up in bed with a large loose-leaf type book on his lap. He has a dictaphone mike in one hand, with the other, he moves his finger down a page and stops.

RAND
(into mike)
Sell all 750,000 shares of C.C.T.

His finger continues down the page, does the same to two more pages before stopping again.

RAND
(into mike)
... Let's see - just sell a million shares of Inland Oil.
(takes a beat)
Oh, and Mrs. Aubrey, have 30,000 shares of Standard transferred into your name. That's for you.

ALLENBY
(steps out of shadows)
... Ben.

RAND
(looks up)
Robert ... I was just cleaning up some loose ends - getting rid of some of the dead wood so Eve won't have to put up with it ...

ALLENBY
(a beat)
... Ben, I want to talk to you about Chauncey.

RAND
(smiles)
Oh, yes - Chauncey - you know, Robert - there's something about him that I trust - he makes me

                    feel good. Since he's been around,
                    the thought of dying has been much
                    easier for me.

Allenby is silent and thoughtful.

113.   INT. SOPHIE'S HOUSE - NIGHT

Dennis Watson is a homosexual and is coming on strong to
Chance.

                              DENNIS
                    ... You're fascinating,
                    Mr. Gardiner - I've never met anyone
                    like you in Washington before.

                              CHANCE
                    Yes, I've been here all my life.

                              DENNIS
                    Really? Well, where have you been
                    all my life?
                         (Chance smiles)
                    Tell me, Mr. Gardiner, have you
                    ever had sex with a man?

                              CHANCE
                       (a beat)
                    No. I don't think so.

                              DENNIS
                    We could go upstairs right now.

                              CHANCE
                    Do they have a TV upstairs?

                              DENNIS
                    A TV? I'm sure they do.

                              CHANCE
                    I like to watch.

                              DENNIS
                    You like to waaaaaatch? Well - you
                    wait right here, I'll go get
                    Warren.

Dennis hurries off. Eve appears, moves to Chance.

                    EVE
            Let's get out of here, Chauncey -
            Let's go home ...

Eve takes Chance by the arm and they move off.

114. INT. WHITE HOUSE - OVAL OFFICE - NIGHT

The President sits behind his desk in a bathrobe, his hair mussed. Standing before him are GROVER HONEYCUTT, the Director of the FBI, and CLIFFORD BALDWIN, CIA Chief. Kaufman stands to one side. All are red-eyed, tired, and frustrated.

                    HONEYCUTT
            I never gave such a directive,
            Mr. President.

                    BALDWIN
            Nor I, sir - it would be out of
            the question.

                    PRESIDENT
            Gentlemen, I didn't call you here
            at such an hour to make
            accusations, I just want to
            explore the possibilities. Now, I
            have three questions: Is the man a
            foreign agent? Or, have we
            suddenly found that our methods of
            gathering data are grossly
            inefficient? Or, thirdly, have the
            man's files been destroyed?
            Now, I'd like some answers.

                    BALDWIN
            Gardiner is not a foreign agent,
            there are now sixteen countries
            investigating the man. We can rule
            that out.

                    PRESIDENT
            Very well ... Can we rule out
            inefficiency?

There is silence in the room. A couple of looks, but silence.

                    PRESIDENT
          I see. What about question three?
          Is it possible to erase all traces
          of a man?

                    HONEYCUTT
          Highly unlikely, sir ... In fact,
          the boys around the Bureau feel
          that the only person capable of
          pulling it off would be an ex-
          F.B.I. man.

                    BALDWIN
               (a look to Honeycutt)
          I don't think that's entirely
          true, Grover.

                    PRESIDENT
               (to Baldwin)
          And what do the boys around
          Intelligence think?

                    BALDWIN
          Well, Mr. President ... They don't
          know quite what to think.

More silence, more looks.

115. INT. RAND LIMOUSINE - NIGHT

Chance watches TV. Eve sits beside him, her hand on his thigh.

                    EVE
          I feel so close to you, so safe
          with you, Chauncey ... and Benjamin
          understands that, dearest ... He
          understands and accepts my
          feelings for you ...

                    CHANCE
          Yes. Ben is very wise.

Eve moves her hand up higher on Chance's thigh, there is no
reaction.

116. INT. RAND MANSION - 3rd FLOOR HALLWAY - NIGHT

Eve and Chance stand close together in the hallway.

> EVE
> ... It's difficult to say good
> night to you, Chauncey - it's very
> hard for me to leave you.

> CHANCE
> It's very hard for me, too, Eve.

> EVE
> ... Oh.

Flustered at the thought, Eve turns and leaves. Chance watches her go, then moves off to his room.

117. INT. CHANCE'S ROOM - NIGHT

Chance is propped up in bed, watches an old movie on television. The hero gives his lady a passionate kiss and embrace. The scene seems to 'sink into' Chance's mind. Suddenly, Eve, robe over her nightgown, comes into the room.

> EVE
> Oh, Chauncey - I just couldn't
> stand it any longer.

She goes to the bed, takes Chance in her arms, starts to kiss him, when he abruptly takes Eve into his arms and kisses her full on the mouth. Once done, Chance's attention returns to the television while Eve is in a frenzy of passion. She holds him, kisses him, runs her hands over his body. Chance neither resists nor responds, he just watches television. Suddenly Eve stops, lets her head fall on Chance's chest.

> EVE
> ... You don't want me, Chauncey ...
> You don't feel anything for me ...
> Nothing at all ...

Chance, feeling her sadness, gently strokes her hair as he looks at TV.

                         EVE
               ... I just don't excite you ...
               I don't know what you want .. I don't
               know what you like ...

                         CHANCE
               I like to watch.

                         EVE
                    (not understanding)
               To watch ...? To watch me ...?

                         CHANCE
               Yes. I like to watch.

                         EVE
                    (uncertain)
               ... Is that all you want ...?
                    (a hesitation)
               ... To watch me ...?

                         CHANCE
               Yes. It's very good, Eve.

                         EVE
               ... But I've never done ...
                    (another hesitation)
               ... You mean ...? When ... When ...
               When I do it? ... When I touch
               myself ...?

Eve slowly gets up from the bed, nervously paces the bedroom
as Chance watches TV. She makes a decision, moves to Chance,
kisses him.

                         EVE
                    (getting aroused)
               Oh, Chauncey ... I do love you so
               much.

She steps back, slips off her robe. She does not undress any
further, instead, leans close to Chance.

                         EVE
               One of those little things you
               don't know about me yet, darling -
               I'm a little shy.

She smiles, drops to the floor. Chance divides his attention between Eve and the TV, watching both with an equal detachment. Eve becomes more and more involved with herself, finding immense pleasure with her own body. Chance changes the channel with the remote control. Eve reaches orgasm, her body shaking violently, then a delicate tremor. Then she is still. Chance turns off the TV with the remote, turns over in bed.

      CHANCE
    Good night, Eve.

A low purr is heard from Eve.

118. INT. RAND'S ROOM - MORNING

There is a feeling of urgency as Allenby and the nurses attend to Rand.

      ALLENBY
     (to nurses)
   Get set up for a transfusion right
   away.

      RAND
     (very weakly)
   ... No more, Robert - no more
   needles ...

      ALLENBY
   It's not good, Ben - I'm sure you
   can feel it.

      RAND
   I know, Robert ... I know ...

119. INT. RAND MANSION - PATIO - MORNING

A light snow is falling. Eve is in a fur coat, holds a steaming cup of coffee. Chance stands near her next to the railing. He reaches out, catches snowflakes as they fall.

      EVE
   ... And I feel so free now,
   Chauncey. I never felt so
   acknowledged by a man ... Until I
   met you, I always had the feeling
   that I was just a vessel for a

> man, something that he could take
> hold of, pierce, and pollute. I
> was merely an aspect of somebody's
> lovemaking. Do you know what I
> mean?

Chance turns to her, says nothing, presses the cold snow-flakes to his face.

> EVE
> You uncoil my wants; desire flows
> within me, and when you watch me
> my passion dissolves it. You set
> me free. I reveal myself to myself
> and I am drenched and purged.

Teresa appears in the doorway.

> TERESA
> Mr. Gardiner. Mr. Rand would like
> to see you.

> CHANCE
> Yes. I would like to see Ben.

Chance gives Eve a warm smile, then follows Teresa into the house.

120. INT. RAND'S ROOM - MORNING

Allenby, with nothing more he can do to prolong Rand's life, stands close to him, grips his hand tightly. Teresa shows Chance into the room and Allenby motions to the nurses to leave. Chance, with a smile, goes to Rand's bedside.

> RAND
> (slowly)
> ... Chauncey ... Chauncey ...

> CHANCE
> Yes, Ben - are you going to die
> now?

Allenby winces.

                    RAND
               (a weak smile)
          ... I'm about to surrender the Horn
          of Plenty for the Horn of Gabriel,
          my boy ...

                    CHANCE
          I see.

                    RAND
               (reaches out to him)
          Let me feel the strength in your
          hand, Chauncey ... Let me feel your strength ...
               (holds Chance's hand)
          Yes, that's good ... I hope,
          Chauncey - I hope that you'll stay
          with Eve ... Take care of her,
          watch over her, she's a delicate
          flower, Chauncey ...

                    CHANCE
               (smiling)
          A flower ...

                    RAND
          She cares for you and she needs
          your help, Chauncey ... there's
          much to be looked after ...

                    CHANCE
          Yes. I would like to do that.

                    RAND
          ... My associates, Chauncey - I've
          talked with them about you ...
          They're eager to meet with you ...
          very eager ...
               (trails off)
          ... Tell Eve ...

Rand slumps down, dead. Allenby checks his pulse, turns to Chance.

                    ALLENBY
          ... He's gone, Chauncey.

>   CHANCE
> Yes, Robert. I have seen it
> before. It happens to old people.
>
>   ALLENBY
>   (covers Rand's face)
> Yes, I suppose that's true.

Chance reaches out, uncovers Rand's face, gently touches the man's forehead, feels the coldness. Allenby eyes him as Chance stays with Rand for a moment, then replaces the sheet.

>   CHANCE
>   (turns to Allenby)
> Will you be leaving now, Robert?
>
>   ALLENBY
> In a day or two, yes.
>
>   CHANCE
> Eve is going to stay. The house
> will not be closed.
>
>   ALLENBY
>   (a moment, a look)
> ... You've become quite a close
> friend of Eve's - haven't you ...
>   (a beat)
> ... Chance ...?
>
>   CHANCE
> Yes. I love Eve very much.
>
>   ALLENBY
> I see ...
>   (another beat)
> ... And you really are a gardener,
> aren't you?
>
>   CHANCE
>   (brightens)
> Yes, Robert - I am.
>   (a smile at Allenby)
> I'll got tell Eve about Ben now,
> Robert.

Chance leaves the bedroom. Allenby watches him go, then sits back in a chair, his head spinning.

121. EXT. RAND ESTATE - DAY

Rand's funeral services are being held on a hill overlooking the mansion. Six distinguished-looking men stand near Rand's casket, which is placed on a concrete block. They are the PALLBEARERS. The Rand mausoleum is fifty yards further up the hill, while the MOURNERS, all close friends and associates of Rand's, stand fifty yards down the hill from the pallbearers. Chance stands with Eve and Allenby. The President of the United States is before the microphone, which feeds loudspeakers for the Rand servants lined up in front of the mansion.

> PRESIDENT
> ... I know that Ben said keep it small and quiet... No eulogies, no fanfares ... And I don't want to go against Ben's wishes. But I thought it would be good, while our close friends carry Ben to his last resting place, to read from his quotes, which I'm sure will have special meaning to all of us who are gathered here today.

With this, the Pallbearers pick up the casket and begin the chore of taking it to the mausoleum. It is hard work.

> PRESIDENT
> (reading quotes)
> ... 'I have no use for those on welfare, no patience whatsoever ... But if I am to be honest with myself, I must admit that they have no use for me, either.'
>
> ... 'I do not regret having political differences with men that I respect; I do regret, however, that our philosophies kept us apart.'

>   ... 'I was born into a position of
>   extreme wealth, but I have spent
>   many sleepless nights thinking
>   about extreme poverty.'

As the President speaks, Chance turns and walks away. Eve and Allenby watch as he goes toward the trees surrounding the area.

>   PRESIDENT
>   (continues reading)
>   ... 'When I was a boy, I was told
>   that the Lord fashioned us from
>   his own image. That's when I
>   decided to manufacture mirrors.'
>
>   ... 'Life is a state of mind.'

The Pallbearers are enroute, they are all breathing heavily. JAMES DUDLEY, a powerful industrialist, speaks.

>   DUDLEY
>   Yes, I agree, Maxwell would be an
>   excellent man for the job - but
>   he's boring, he would never take
>   an election.

SEWELL NELSON, a corporation Chairman, speaks.

>   NELSON
>   Correct, the people of this
>   country need to be awakened.

PETER CALDWELL, another executive:

>   CALDWELL
>   What about Lawson? He's
>   charismatic, exciting...
>
>   DUDLEY
>   A bit too exciting, I'm afraid ...
>   Once they start bringing things up
>   about his background.

WEBB, Railroad money:

>   WEBB
>   Well, gentlemen. Time is running
>   out, we must come to a decision.

122. EXT. WOODS - DAY

Chance, his umbrella under his arm, walks through the woods. He stops by a tree, brushes some snow from a branch, moves on.

123. EXT. RAND ESTATE - DAY

The President is still reading Rand's quotes.

> PRESIDENT
> (reading)
> 'The world parts with Rand, and Rand parts with the world: A fair trade, don't you agree? Security, tranquility, a well-deserved rest: All the aims I have pursued will soon be realized.'

Eve is concerned about Chance, she turns to Allenby.

> EVE
> (quietly)
> I've got to find Chauncey.

She leaves the funeral, heads toward the trees.

> PRESIDENT
> (reading)
> ... 'I do not know the feelings of being poor, and that is not to know the feelings of the majority of people in this world. For a man in my position, that is inexcusable.

The Pallbearers near the mausoleum, they are struggling.

> DUDLEY
> But what do we know of the man? Nothing! We have no inkling of his past!

> NELSON
> Correct, and that is an asset. A man's past can cripple him, his background turns into a swamp and invites scrutiny.

                            CALDWELL
                  ... Up to this time, he hasn't said
                  anything that could be used
                  against him.

                            NELSON
                  The response from his appearance
                  on the 'Burns Show' was
                  overwhelming; mail and telephone
                  response was the highest they ever
                  had, and it was ninety-five
                  percent pro!

CHARLIE BOB BENNET, a Texas oil millionaire;

                            BENNET
                  Well, I'm certainly open to the
                  thought - it would be sheer lunacy
                  to support the President for
                  another term.

LYMAN MURRAY, a banker;

                            MURRAY
                  Exactly. That is why I agree with
                  Ben's final wishes, and I firmly
                  believe, gentlemen, if we want to
                  retain the Presidency, that our
                  one and only chance is Chauncey
                  Gardiner!

124. EXT. WOODS - DAY

Chance happens on a tree with a cracked limb, hanging to the
ground. He stops, inspects the break, runs his fingers along
the split of the bark. He looks to the ground, notices that an
end of the limb has fallen on a seedling, bending it double.
Chance pulls the limb away, then kneels beside the seedling.
He removes an expensive pair of suede gloves, and, with gentle
fingers, brushes the dirt and snow away from the seedling.
Chance glances up to the remaining limbs of the larger tree
which could fall and threaten the emerging tree. He unfolds
his umbrella, places it over the seedling in a way to give
it protection, yet still allow it to receive light from the
winter sun. Chance stands, and is putting his gloves on when
Eve appears, running towards him.

                    EVE
               (breathless)
          Chauncey! Chauncey!

                    CHANCE
               (looks)
          Hello, Eve.

                    EVE
               (holds him)
          Oh, Chauncey, darling. Where were
          you? I've been looking for you. I
          was scared.

                    CHANCE
          Yes. I've been looking for you
          too, Eve.

She hugs him one more time, then leads him back from
whence she came. The President can still be heard
reading quotes.

                    PRESIDENT'S VOICE
               (in the distance)
          I've lived a lot, trembled a lot,
          was surrounded by little men who
          forgot that we enter naked and
          exit naked and that no accountant
          can audit life in our favor.

                                        The End

Notes

1. Jones does not recall them putting in that many hours. Robert C. Jones, "some Ashby questions, finally," email, September 27, 2010.
2. Jordan R. Young and Mike Bruns, *Hal Ashby Interviews*, ed. Nick Dawson (Jackson: University Press of Mississippi, 2010), 100.
3. Nick Dawson, *Being Hal Ashby: Life of a Hollywood Rebel* (Lexington: University Press of Kentucky, 2009), 153; and Peter Biskind, *Star: The Life and Wild Times of Warren Beatty* (London: Simon & Schuster, 2010), 185.
4. Incidentally, Sellers's continued failed efforts to relay Abbaz's speech to Rand's doctors later in the film—he and the crew keep cracking up—make up the extended blooper reel that plays over the end credits.
5. Jerzy Kosinski, *Being There* (unproduced screenplay), July 1978, 21.
6. Louise Sweeney, "Jerzy Kosinski and the Nine Million Dollar Glass of Water," *Christian Science Monitor*, March 27, 1979.
7. Glenys Roberts, "Being There, Here, and Everywhere," *London Times*, July 12, 1980, 8.
8. Notice of credits, April 20, 1979, Box 3, Folder 24, Hal Ashby Papers, Margaret Herrick Library, Los Angeles.
9. Letter from Andrew Molasky to Marge White, April 16, 1979, Box 3, Folder 24, Hal Ashby Papers, Margaret Herrick Library, Los Angeles.
10. Jerzy Kosinski, telex, May 13, 1979, Box 3, Folder 24, Hal Ashby Papers, Margaret Herrick Library, Los Angeles.
11. According to Ashby biographer Nick Dawson, Jones believes that Kosinski submitted one of Jones's drafts to the WGA as part of the arbitration process, which is the reason the WGA found in Kosinski's favor. Dawson, *Being Hal Ashby*, 222.
12. Ed Sikov, *Mr Strangelove: A Biography of Peter Sellers* (London: Sidgwick & Jackson, 2002), 372.
13. James Park Sloan, *Jerzy Kosinski: A Biography* (New York: Plume, 1997), 358.

Appendix: Getting a Guy to Walk on Water

A reader of these screenplays who is familiar with the film and its famous ending will immediately notice a huge discrepancy: none of the scripts features Chance walking on water at the end. This is because, according to most accounts, the walking-on-water ending was never part of the production script. Rather, it was conceived on set near the end of principal photography. While competing stories of how the ending was devised and whose idea it was have been told many times, the story is worth reconsidering briefly as an example of the impact that production can have on the scripting process. For, while the screenplay is often thought of as a blueprint—in other words, a prescribed set of directions meant to be followed closely—it is worth remembering Steven Price's description of the screenplay as a "modular text":

> Significant sections are retained from multiple previous iterations, including, very frequently, from quite early stages in development. A screenplay of this kind has quite literally been assembled by taking some pages from one iteration, more from a second, still others from a third, and so on, and placing them together in a provisional sequence.[1]

Practically speaking, what Price describes here is the color-coded studio script in which rewrites and revised pages are simply added to the original draft.[2] However, he is just as well describing the palimpsestuous nature of screenplay revision. While none of Kosinski's pages show up directly in any of Jones's drafts, many of Kosinski's descriptions and actions and much of his dialogue do appear in Jones, creating, in effect, a modular text. The ending then, conceived during production and shot almost spontaneously, while never scripted remains a component of the script's modularity.

For screenwriters, a vital lesson here is that even when a script is locked and ready for production—or production is fully underway—it can still be subject to the vagaries of on-set decision making by producers, directors, or actors (in the case of improvisation). A famous instance of this is the film *Chinatown* (Paramount 1974). Robert Towne wrote an intricate, imaginative script and producer Robert Evans put together a cast and crew of some of 1970s Hollywood's brightest talents, including Jack Nicholson and Faye Dunaway, in the leads and John Huston in a scene-stealing performance as Noah Cross. There was also director Roman Polanski, cinematographer John Alonzo, production designer Richard Sylbert, composer Jerry Goldsmith, and editor Sam O'Steen. Together they made one of the preeminent films of the New Hollywood era, arguably one of the greatest Hollywood films of any era. But Towne and Polanski fought vociferously over the ending. Towne's version of the script ended with Evelyn Mulwray (Dunaway) killing her father, Cross, and saving her daughter from his vicious clutches—in short, a happy ending. Polanski considered this ending a betrayal to the viewer, to the film's tone, and to the overall meaning of the script, and he insisted on a reversal—Cross, the villain would win, and Evelyn would lose her life and daughter. Polanski won the fight, and he and Towne had a dreadful falling out, with Towne eventually being barred from the set.[3] Towne, who went on to win the Golden Globe and Academy Award for Best Screenplay, has since declared the filmed ending to be stronger. In 1997, Gove Press published *Robert Towne:* Chinatown *and* The Last Detail, with full copies of two of Towne's classic New Hollywood scripts. The *Chinatown* screenplay as published includes Polanski's ending.

In the case of *Being There*, there was little in the way of a fight over the ending; rather, the contention lies over who devised it. Most sources contend that Ashby conceived of the ending himself near the close of principal photography. He was exceedingly pleased with the performances of his cast, in particular Sellers and Melvyn Douglas as Benjamin Rand, and he had come to believe he "could have them walking on water by the end," and so that is what he had Chance do. Ashby recounted this version of the story himself on several occasions and it is the version put forth by Ashby biographer Nick Dawson and Sellers biographer Ed Sikov.[4] According to Dawson, a final touch was added by Sellers in a moment of last-minute improvisation:

> When the scene was shot, Sellers left his umbrella by the tree for the first two takes but for the third took it with him as he walked out across the water. In a moment of inspiration, he stopped, dipped the umbrella into the water, and then started walking once again.[5]

In a sense, one could describe the ending of *Being There* itself as a distilled modular text: Chance, a creation of Jerzy Kosinski, leaves the funeral of Benjamin Rand, an ending scripted by Bob Jones, walks across the water, as devised by Hal Ashby, and, in a moment of improvisational acting by Peter Sellers, dips his umbrella into the pond.

This version of events seems likely. In addition to Ashby and Sellers, Melvyn Douglas describes it as such in his autobiography.[6] In an email exchange with Bob Jones in 2010, I asked him about the change in ending. He writes, "They were on location, I was in L.A. so I was not involved. If I was, I would have argued for the one written, much more organic to the film. Walking on water is great and cinematic, but it pulled me out of the story."[7] Jones's recollection asserts that the decision to shoot the walking-on-water scene was clearly made during production (on location, in North Carolina). (His distinction between "organic" and "cinematic" is fascinating in this case, as both endings could be described as cinematic and organic, depending on whether one is talking about narrative, character, or tone. Critics remain split on the effectiveness of the filmed ending). Finally, it is necessary to point out that before Ashby decided to shoot the walking-on-water sequence, he had filmed Jones's ending—Eve leaving the funeral on her own to look for Chance, finding him, and telling him she has been looking for him. This version is available as an extra on the Warner Bros. issued Blu Ray of 2009, as well as on the 2017 edition from the Criterion Collection. If the walking-on-water sequence had been previously scripted, it is unlikely that Ashby and the production would have taken the time to film an already-discarded ending.

Kosinski, however, claimed that he wrote the ending, inspired by a line in his original novel. As described by Sloan,

> Another problem was the ending, which originally had a very flat encounter between Chauncey and EE (author's note: EE is how Eve is referred to in the novel), while the audience missed the voiceover of the president discussing Chauncey for vice president. Now, ingeniously, Kosinski reached back to page six of the novel, in which Chance "floated into the world, buoyed up by a force he did not see." Out of that brief passage, he invented the stunning final scene, in which Chance walks into the woods and out onto the lake, thrusting his umbrella deep into the water, but himself being "buoyed up"—walking on water with a multiply suggestive "lightness."[8]

Kosinski made the same claim himself in an interview with Roger Copeland in 1980.[9] However, in Sloan's case, his reporting of events mistakes different drafts of the script and also confuses the real-world time line. For example, in none of the versions featuring Rand's funeral does the president suggest Chance for vice president. The president being a party to the discussions about Chance's future only occurs in Kosinski's 1971 draft at the concluding meeting of Rand's shady business associates (in Kosinski's later two drafts, the man running the meeting is, first, the head of the Republican Party and, second, unnamed). Rather, it is the pallbearers discussing Chance's future, while the president, in voiceover, reads from Rand's diary. Furthermore, Sloan describes these revisions as having taken place in the autumn of 1978, with "the script in seemingly good order by December 20."[10] That date falls just a few days after the December 16 date of Jones's first draft, in which the president's speech is delivered in one block of dialogue, entirely on camera.

Speaking of dates, while preparing this book, I made one of those inadvertent discoveries that sometimes pleasantly surprise researchers. I came across a draft of *Being There* among the Kosinski collection at the Spertus Institute in Chicago. This is a photocopy of the script dated January 10, 1979—in other words, the script crafted by Jones in consultation with Ashby, which was used for shooting. The script includes several handwritten notes that provide some intriguing insight into the final scene's authorship. First, handwritten across the front page of the script is the date December 20, 1979, which is the date of the film's premiere, in New York City (Figure 1). This copy of the script, otherwise identical to Jones's second draft, as produced in Chapter 3, has a cover page that credits only Kosinski as screenwriter (Figure 2). The rest of the script is unmarked upon until the closing scene, where the meeting between Chance and Eve in the woods is crossed out in pencil and blue pen, and retyped, with several notes written between the lines that change the scripted ending to the walking-on-water ending (Figure 3). Finally, the script ends with an inserted page on which a scripted end for the walking-on-water scene is typed (Figure 4). Both the handwritten corrections and the typed ending include specific reference to the line from the novel quoted above—"Chance floated into the world"—and even references the page number.

It would be impossible to tell exactly when these revisions were made, or even who made them. The presence of the script among Kosinski's papers and the removal of Jones's

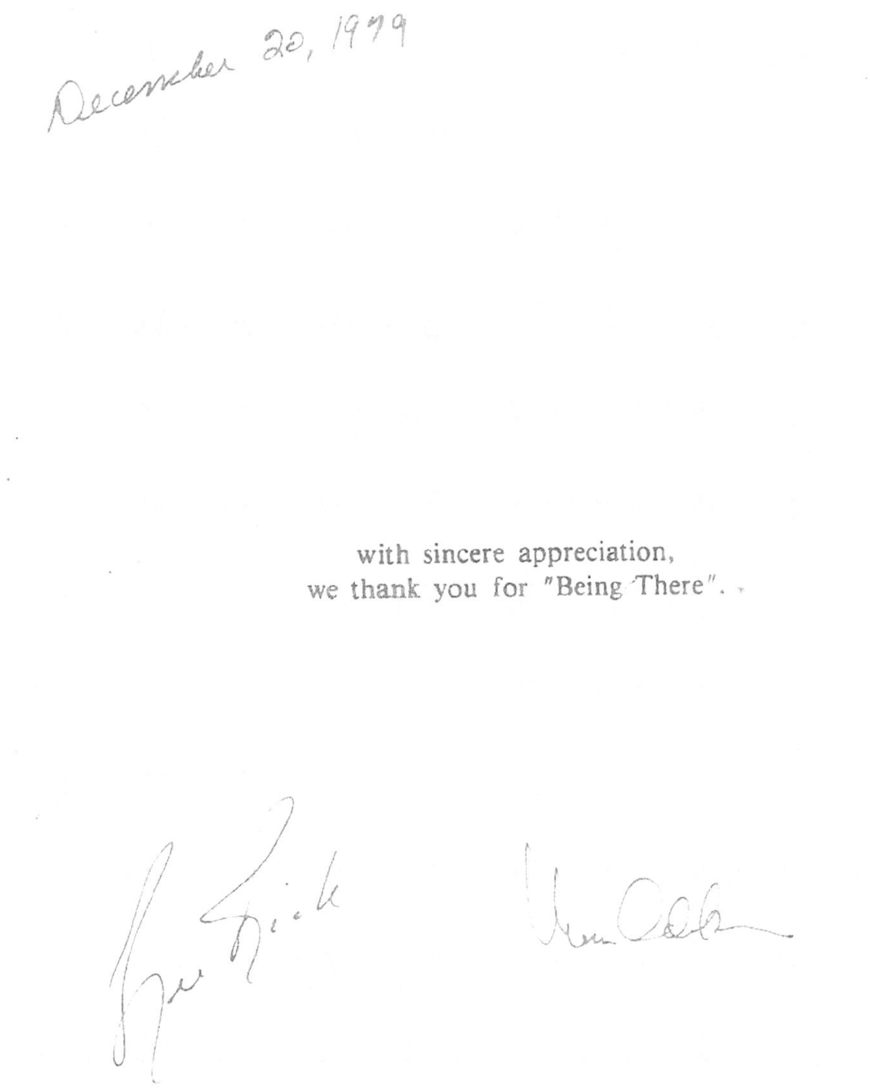

December 20, 1979

with sincere appreciation,
we thank you for "Being There".

Figure 1 Cover page of *Being There* script in Jerzy Kosinski archives. Courtesy of Spertus Institute for Jewish Learning and Leadership.

name from the title page, however, seems to indicate the copy belongs to Kosinski. The date on the cover page being the exact date of the film's initial release in New York could be an odd coincidence, but leads one to wonder whether Kosinski had seen the premiere in New York then added the changes to the ending based on what he saw. The writing style leans toward Kosinski, with detailed descriptions such as Chance's "expensive pair of suede gloves" or the way the water of the pond barely wets his "trousers."

A final, intriguing piece of evidence comes in the form of an as-produced script housed among Ashby's papers in the Herrick library. Such scripts are common instruments of Hollywood studios. Usually transcribed by a production assistant, they are meant to produce a script of the final film, after photography and editing. These scripts are then

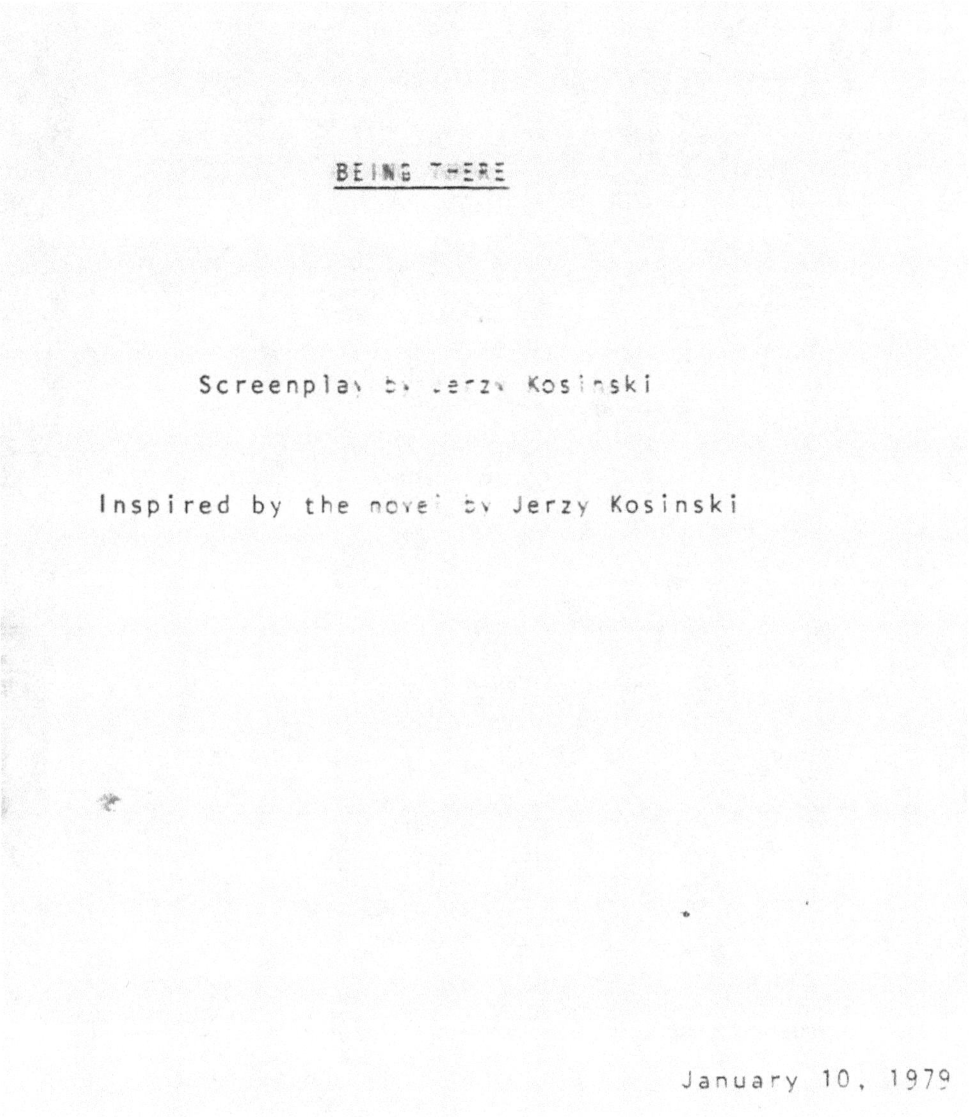

BEING THERE

Screenplay by Jerzy Kosinski

Inspired by the novel by Jerzy Kosinski

January 10, 1979

Figure 2 Title page of *Being There* script in Jerzy Kosinski archives. Courtesy of Spertus Institute for Jewish Learning and Leadership.

used for a variety of purposes including in negotiating TV broadcasting and in preparing overdubs or subtitles for foreign distribution. The script in the Herrick is undated, but closely resembles the January 1979 draft. Where it differs is in small instances likely inspired by on-set decisions or improvisation. For example, after the president has quoted Chance in his speech, Chance receives a call at Rand's mansion from Syd Courtney at the *Washington Post*. In Jones's script, while Chance, never having used a phone, is somewhat flustered, he nevertheless puts the phone properly to his ear and says "hello" (401). In the film, however, there is a bit of business where he first puts it to his ear and, not hearing anything on the other end, says to Mrs. Aubrey, "He's not there." She takes the phone from him, checks that

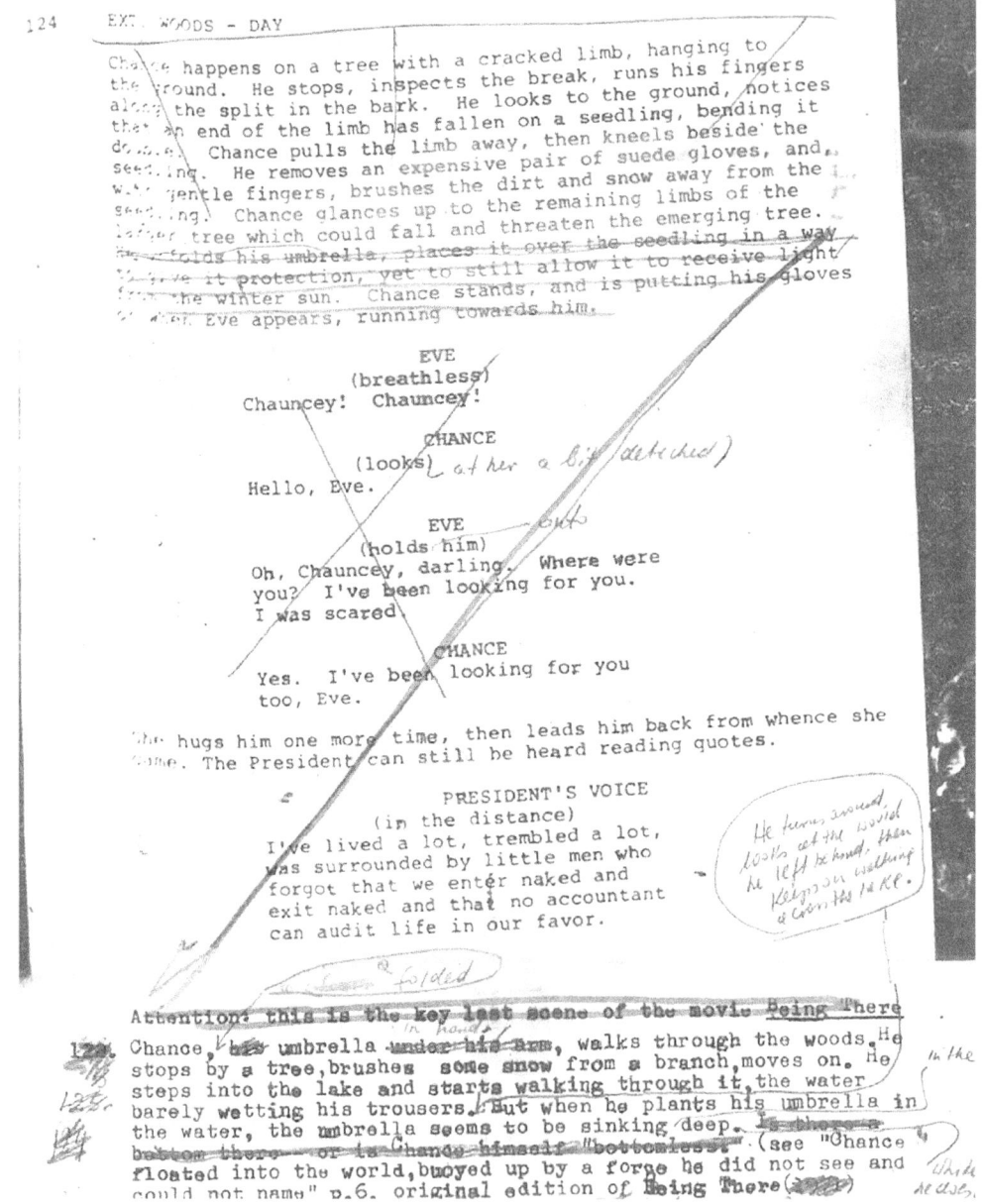

Figure 3 Notes and rewrites for final scene, *Being There* script in Jerzy Kosinski archives. Courtesy of Spertus Institute for Jewish Learning and Leadership.

Courtney still is there, and hands the phone back to Chance and the phone call proceeds as initially scripted. A small humorous beat, it is easy to see how Ashby or Sellers could have come up with it during filming. The as-produced script includes the film version with the "he's not there" line and Mrs. Aubrey's response.

For the ending, this script also includes the walking-on-water scene. Here is how it is written:

124 EXT. WOODS - DAY

Chance happens on a tree with a cracked limb, hanging to the ground. He stops, inspects the break, runs his fingers along the split in the bark. He looks to the ground, notices that an end of the limb has fallen on a seedling, bending it double. Chance pulls the limb away, then kneels beside the seedling. He removes an expensive pair of suede gloves, and, with gentle fingers, brushes the dirt and snow away from the seedling. Chance glances up to the remaining limbs of the larger tree which could fall and threaten the emerging tree.

Chance, a rolled umbrella in hand, walks through the woods. He stops by a tree, brushes some snow from a branch, moves on. He steps into the lake and starts walking through it, the water barely wetting his trousers. He turns around looks at the world he left behind, then keeps on walking across the lake. But when he plants his umbrella in the water beside him, the umbrella seems to be sinking in the deep, while he does not. (See "Chance floated into the world, buoyed up by a force he did not see and could not name" p.6, original edition of the novel Being There.

The End

Figure 4 Retyped final scene, *Being There* script in Jerzy Kosinski archives. Courtesy of Spertus Institute for Jewish Learning and Leadership.

EXT. WOODS—DAY

Chance gets up from fixing the little tree and walks over to a nearby lake, the Rand Mansion visible in the background.

> PRESIDENT'S VOICE
> I've lived alot, trembled alot,
> was surrounded by little men
> who forgot that we enter naked
> and exit naked and that no
> accountant can audit life in
> our favor.

```
There is a dead tree sticking up in the middle of the small
lake. Chance walks into the lake, walking on the water.
Halfway across the lake, he realizes that his feet are staying
on top of water. He sinks his umbrella into the water and it
goes down to the handle, where he is holding it. He looks
around a moment, confused, then continues to the tree, where
he examines the branches.

                    PRESIDENT'S VOICE
                       (reading)
                 Life is a state of mind.
```

It seems odd that, except for obvious changes that occurred on set, while so much of the as-produced script resembles the January 1979 draft, this key scene—a scene that everybody involved knew was special—would be vastly different from a supposedly previously scripted version. It seems highly unlikely that the rewritten version presented in Kosinski's copy of the script was ever used for actual production. Why Kosinski would take the time to rewrite his copy of a Jones-drafted script based on the film's actual ending is anybody's guess.

Perhaps, though, what matters is not whose idea the ending was. While it seems most likely that Ashby, Jones, and Sellers's version of events is closest to the truth, more important is that the scripting process and film production that did occur afforded a group of imaginative practitioners the opportunity to create the film *Being There*. For scriptwriters, it is a lesson in the ways that collaborative writing and revision can at once both muddy the waters of individual credit and also result in a work of stunning originality that any one individual in the process is unlikely to have conceived on their own.

Notes

1. Steven Price, *A History of the Screenplay* (London: Palgrave Macmillan, 2013), 236.
2. While there are variations in color-coding across television and film studios and production companies, the WGA recommends: white (first draft); blue (second); pink (third); yellow (fourth); green (fifth); after which follow several more colors recommended for later drafts.
3. Peter Biskind, *Easy Riders, Raging Bulls* (New York: Touchstone, 1998), 166, 188.
4. Nick Dawson, *Being Hal Ashby: Life of a Hollywood Rebel* (Lexington: University Press of Kentucky, 2009), 212–13; Ed Sikov, *Mr Strangelove: A Biography of Peter Sellers* (London: Sidgwick & Jackson), 364; Jordon R. Young and Mike Bruns, *Hal Ashby Interviews*, ed. Nick Dawson (Jackson: University Press of Mississippi, 2010), 100.
5. Dawson, *Being Hal Ashby*, 213.
6. Melvyn Douglas and Tom Arthur, *See You at the Movies: The Autobiography of Melvyn Douglas* (Lanham, MD: University Press of America, 1986), 227–8.

7 Robert C. Jones, "some Ashby questions, finally," email, September 27, 2010.
8 James Park Sloan, *Jerzy Kosinski: A Biography* (New York: Plume, 1997), 352.
9 Jerzy Kosinski, "An Interview with Jerzy Kosinski," interview by Roger Copeland, *New York Art Journal*, 21 (1980), 10–12.
10 Sloan, *Jerzy Kosinski*, 352.

Bibliography

Ashby, Hal. "Hal Ashby: Satisfaction in *Being There*." Interview by Jordan R. Young and Mike Bruns (1980). *Hal Ashby: Interviews*. Edited by Nick Dawson. Jackson: UP Mississippi, 2010, 99–105.

Beach, Christopher. *The Films of Hal Ashby*. Detroit: Wayne State UP, 2009.

Biskind, Peter. *Star: The Life and Wild Times of Warren Beatty*. London: Simon & Schuster, 2010.

Boozer, Jack, ed. *Authorship in Film Adaptation*. Austin: U Texas P, 2008.

Bordwell, David, Janet Staiger, and Kristin Thompson. *The Classical Hollywood Cinema: Film Style & Mode of Production to 1960*. London: Routledge, 2002.

Braunsberg, Andrew. Memo to Hal Ashby. July 31, 1978. Box 1, Folder 6, Hal Ashby Papers, Margaret Herrick Library, Los Angeles.

Carrol, Noël. "Defining the Moving Image." In *Philosophy of Film and Motion Pictures*. Edited by Noël Carrol and Jinhee Choi. Malden, MA: Blackwell, 2006, 113–34.

Carrol, Noël. *The Philosophy of Motion Pictures*. London: Blackwell, 2008.

Chapman, James, and Nicholas J. Cull. *Projecting Empire: Imperialism and Popular Cinema*. London: I.B. Tauris, 2009.

Dasko, Henry. "Kosinski's Afterlife." *The Polish Review*, 49, no. 1 (2004), 687–710.

Dawson, Nick. *Being Hal Ashby: Life of a Hollywood Rebel*. Lexington: UP Kentucky, 2009.

Dawson, Nick. *Hal Ashby: Interviews*. Jackson: UP Mississippi, 2010.

Douglas, Melvyn, and Tom Arthur. *See You at the Movies: The Autobiography of Melvyn Douglas*. Lanham, MD: UP of America, 1986.

Dowd, Nancy. Letter to the editor. *Vanity Fair*, May 6, 2008. https://www.vanityfair.com/magazine/2008/06/letters200806.

Epps Jr., Jack. *Screenwriting Is Rewriting: The Art and Craft of Professional Revision*. New York: Bloomsbury Academic, 2016.

Field, Syd. *The Screenwriter's Workbook*, revised edition. New York: Delta, 2006.

Grant, Catherine. "The Haunting of *The Headless Woman*." *tecmerin multimedia*, no. 2, July 2019, https://tecmerin.uc3m.es/en/journal-2-1/.

Gruner, Oliver. "Hippie Superannuated Leprechaun: Waldo Salt, Screenwriting, and the Hollywood Renaissance." *Historical Journal of Film, Radio and Television*, 39, no. 2 (2019), 251–70.

Hemingway, Ernest. "The Art of Fiction No. 21." Interview by George Plimpton. *The Paris Review*, 18, Spring 1958. https://www.theparisreview.org/interviews/4825/ernest-hemingway-the-art-of-fiction-no-21-ernest-hemingway.

Hunter, Aaron. *Authoring Hal Ashby: The Myth of the New Hollywood Auteur*. New York: Bloomsbury Academic, 2016.

Jones, Robert C. *Being There* (unproduced screenplay), December 1978. Box 2, Folder 11, Hal Ashby Papers, Margaret Herrick Library, Los Angeles.

Jones, Robert C. *Being There* (screenplay), January 1979. Box 2, Folder 12, Hal Ashby Papers, Margaret Herrick Library, Los Angeles.

Jones, Robert C. Personal interview. Los Angeles, January 28, 2009.

Jones, Robert C. "Some Ashby questions, finally." Email. September 27, 2010.

Kosinski, Jerzy. *Being There*. London: Black Swan, [1970] 1983.

Kosinski, Jerzy. *Being There* (unproduced screenplay), August 1971. Box 1, Folder 2, Hal Ashby Papers, Margaret Herrick Library, Los Angeles.

Kosinski, Jerzy. *Being There* (unproduced screenplay), January 1978. Box 1, Folder 5, Hal Ashby Papers, Margaret Herrick Library, Los Angeles.

Kosinski, Jerzy. *Being There* (unproduced screenplay), July 1979. Box 1, Folder 6, Hal Ashby Papers, Margaret Herrick Library, Los Angeles.

Kosinski, Jerzy. "An Interview with Jerzy Kosinski." Interview by Roger Copeland. *New York Art Journal*, 21 (1980), 10–12.

Kosinski, Jerzy. Telex. May 13, 1979, Box 3, Folder 24, Hal Ashby Papers, Margaret Herrick Library, Los Angeles.

Lazar, Mary. "Jerzy Kosinski's Being There, Novel and Film: Changes Not by Chance." *College Literature*, 31, no. 2 (2004), 99–116.

Lewis, Roger. *The Life and Death of Peter Sellers*. London: Century-Random House, 1994.

Molasky, Andrew. Letter to Marge White. April 16, 1979, Box 3, Folder 24, Hal Ashby Papers, Margaret Herrick Library, Los Angeles.

Murphy, J. J. *Me and You and Memento and Fargo*. New York: Continuum, 2007.

Nannicelli, Ted. "The Ontology and Literary Status of the Screenplay: The Case of 'Scriptfic.'" *Journal of Literary Theory*, 7, no. 1–2 (2013), 135–53.

Nannicelli, Ted. "Why Can't Screenplays Be Artworks?" *Journal of Aesthetics and Art Criticism*, 69, no. 4 (Fall 2011), 405–14.

Notice of credits. Box 3, Folder 24, Hal Ashby Papers, Margaret Herrick Library, Los Angeles, April 20, 1979.

Price, Steven. *A History of the Screenplay*. London: Palgrave Macmillan, 2013.

Roberts, Glenys. "Being There, Here, and Everywhere." *London Times*, July 12, 1980.

Sikov, Ed. *Mr Strangelove: A Biography of Peter Sellers*. London: Sidgwick & Jackson, 2002.

Sloan, James Park. *Jerzy Kosinski: A Biography*. New York: Plume, 1997.

Snyder, Blake. *Save the Cat: The Last Book on Screenwriting You'll Ever Need*. Studio City: Michael Wiese Productions, 2005.

Staiger, Janet. "Blueprints for Feature Films: Hollywood's Continuity Scripts." In *The American Film Industry*. Edited by Tino Balio (Madison: U Wisconsin P, 1985), 173–95.

Sweeney, Louise. "Jerzy Kosinski and the Nine Million Dollar Glass of Water." *Christian Science Monitor*, March 27, 1979.

Towne, Robert, and Warren Beatty. *Shampoo* (undated screenplay). Box 60, Folder 660, Hal Ashby Papers, Margaret Herrick Library, Los Angeles.

Towne, Robert, and Warren Beatty. *Shampoo* (screenplay), April 1974. Box 60, Folder 664, Hal Ashby Papers, Margaret Herrick Library, Los Angeles.

Wexler, Haskell. "Commentary," *In the Heat of the Night* (1967). DVD. Directed by Norman Jewison. MGM, 2001.

Writers Guild of America. *Screen Credits Manual*. November 2018. https://www.wga.org/uploadedfiles/credits/manuals/screenscredits_manual18.pdf.

Yale University School of Drama. Bulletin, 68, number 12, 1972.

Index

Ashby, Hal 2-4, 24, 33, 183, 333, 454-6, 458, 460
   Being There script 3, 7, 15-16, 20-3, 29, 37-8, 184, 336-7, 455
   relationship with Peter Sellers 2, 3
Attaway, Ruth 22

Beatty, Warren 24, 183, 333
Being There 1, 14
   screenwriting dispute 336-7
   film 2, 23
   novel 1-2, 184
   screenplay 2-3, 4, 6, 8, 15, 24, 30, 336
Boozer, Jack 12, 13
Braunsberg, Andrew 3, 21, 29, 33, 181 n. 1

Carrol, Noël 5, 12
collaborative revision xi, 14, 23, 38
Coming Home 2, 3, 184, 332 n. 9

Douglas, Melvyn 2, 454
Dowd, Nancy 3, 184, 332 n. 8
Dysart, Richard 2

Eilenberg, Larry xi, 2
Epps, Jr., Jack 13, 14, 29

Field, Syd 7-8, 10
Fonda, Jane 184

Haller, Mike 34 n. 13, 183, 336
Hellman, Jerome 184

Jewison, Norman 183
Jones, Robert C. 6-7, 14-15, 23-7, 29, 32-3, 37-8, 185-7, 333-4, 336-7, 453-5, 457, 460
   career as editor 3, 16, 183
   career as screenwriter 3, 22, 184

Keller III, Ravenell 336
Kosinski, Jerzy 1-4, 6-7, 14, 16, 32-3, 33 n. 6, 333, 453-4, 460
   as literary star 2, 3
   at Yale 2, 33 n. 6
   Being There script 3, 15, 16, 19-22, 24-6, 29-31, 37-8, 184, 186-7, 336-7, 455-6

Last Detail, The 3, 24, 183, 454
Lorimar Pictures 2-3, 183, 337

MacLaine, Shirley 2
Murphy, J.J. 7, 8

Nannicelli, Ted 5, 12-13

Price, Steven 9-11, 13, 16, 36 n. 47, 453

Salt, Waldo 3, 184
screenwriting
   history 9-11
   cinematic vs. literary 3, 4, 7-8, 19, 28
Sellers, Peter 2-3, 21-2, 184, 185, 336-37, 452 n. 4, 454, 458, 460
Shampoo 3, 24, 183, 333
Sloan, James Park 337, 455
Snyder, Blake 7-8, 35 n. 25
Staiger, Janet 9-11

Towne, Robert 5, 183, 333, 453-4

United Artists 2, 3, 183, 184

Warden, Jack 2, 25, 183
Wexler, Haskell 183, 332 n. 1

www.ingramcontent.com/pod-product-compliance
Lightning Source LLC
Chambersburg PA
CBHW080532300426
44111CB00017B/2684